RESISTING MCCARTHYISM

RESISTING MCCARTHYISM

*To Sign or Not to Sign
California's Loyalty Oath*

Bob Blauner

STANFORD UNIVERSITY PRESS
Stanford, California

Stanford University Press
Stanford, California

Printed in the United States of America on acid-free, archival-quality paper

Library of Congress Cataloging-in-Publication Data

Blauner, Bob.
  Resisting McCarthyism : to sign or not to sign California's loyalty oath / Bob
Blauner.
      p. cm.
  Includes bibliographical references and index.
  ISBN 978-0-8047-5922-9 (cloth : alk. paper)
  1. University of California (1868–1952)—History. 2. Loyalty oaths—California—
History—20th century. 3. Academic freedom—California—History—20th
century. 4. Anti-communist movements—California—History—20th century.
5. United States—Politics and government-1945–1953. 6. United States—Politics
and government-1953–1961. 7. McCarthy, Joseph, 1908–1957. I. Title.
  LD736.5.B55 2009
  378.1'21309794—dc22   2008041872

Designed by Bruce Lundquist
Typeset by Classic Typography in 10.5/15 Adobe Garamond

CONTENTS

President Sproul with Clarence Dykstra. UCLA's provost's early death was hastened by the stress of defending his faculty from charges of subversion. (Courtesy Bancroft Library)

The two leading antagonists in the Loyalty Oath drama, President Sproul (far right) and Regent Neylan (second from left) are shown with Regent Donald McLaughlin, who would help resolve the crisis (far left), as Berkeley scientist Edward MacMillan receives an award. (Courtesy Bancroft Library)

On March 6, 1950, Berkeley's Greek Theater was filled to capacity as the student body rallied on behalf of the nonsigners. (Courtesy Bancroft Library)

The much smaller mass meeting one month later was addressed (from left to right) by student leader—and not-so-secret Communist Party member—Leslie Fishman; an unidentified professor; Arthur Brodeur of Scandinavian Languages and a former party member; and chemist Joel Hildebrand, the faculty's leading anticommunist. (Courtesy Bancroft Library)

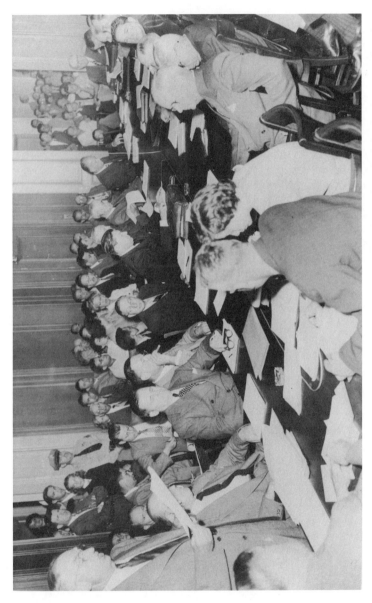

At the August 25, 1950, meeting of the Board of Regents, President Sproul (standing, far left) pleads to save the jobs of the faculty's nonsigners. But John Francis Neylan (seated at the head of the table) won a close vote for their dismissal, despite the opposition of Earl Warren (third from left in bottom row). (Courtesy Bancroft Library)

The two members of Sproul's Advisory Committee, Joel Hildebrand (top) and Benjamin Lehman (bottom), were close friends and two of the most influential leaders of the Academic Senate. (Courtesy of Bancroft Library)

The four most important resisters. Clockwise from top left, Joe Tussman, who first sounded the alarm; Ernst Kantorowicz, whose fiery oratory framed the crisis as a battle between totalitarianism and freedom; Edward Tolman, the beloved leader of Berkeley's nonsigners; and John Caughey, his counterpart at UCLA. (Courtesy of Bancroft Library and, for Kantorowicz, the Leo Baeck Institute)

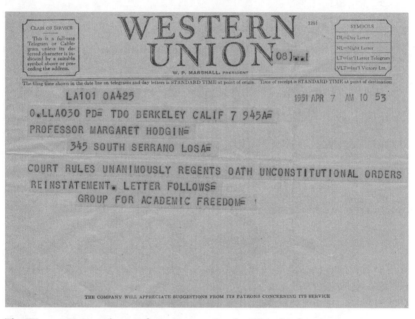

The Western Union telegram from attorney Stanley Weigel informing nonsigner Margaret Hodgen of the Group for Academic Freedom's victory in the courts. (Courtesy Bancroft Library)

PREFACE

There will be no witch hunts at Yale, because there will be no witches. We do not intend to hire communists.

—Charles Seymour, president of Yale University, 1950[1]

O F THE SIXTY-NINE PROFESSORS FIRED FOR political reasons during the period that we now call the McCarthy Era, almost half were dismissed by the Board of Regents of the University of the California (UC). These thirty-one were terminated in August 1950 for refusing to sign a noncommunist loyalty oath. Taking place during the years between 1949 and 1952, the oath crisis, according to Clark Kerr, was "the greatest single controversy between a university faculty and its board of trustees in American history."[2] For Alexander Meiklejohn, the nation's leading civil libertarian, it was "the most important issue ever faced by an American university."[3] To put a human face on these generalizations: the stress and suffering of the conflict brought on four deaths from heart attacks, one debilitating stroke, and several nervous breakdowns.

Today the witch hunts that followed in the wake of the beginning of the Cold War are associated in the public mind with one political figure. Yet the activities of Wisconsin senator Joseph McCarthy were only a small part of a complex of actions, measures, and policies aimed at uncovering and rooting out all manifestations of "subversion" in America. These included investigations and hearings conducted by national and state committees on "un-American activities," the dismissals of people considered too radical or liberal by labor unions and universities, and an overall climate of fear, which made individuals and in-stitutions hesitant to do anything that might be considered controversial. However, within government bodies and at colleges and universities, no anti-communist vehicle was more widespread than the loyalty oath.

By 1954 there were only five states that did not require them for their em-ployees. This meant that almost every professor in a state university had to swear that he or she was not a member of the Communist Party or any other subversive organization. And almost everywhere, faculties set aside their reser-vations and acquiesced, often quite meekly, by attesting to their loyalty. The University of California was the only major university where a faculty mounted a spirited, sustained, and ultimately successful resistance to such a requirement.

Émigrés from Germany and Italy were prominent among the resisters, es-pecially at Berkeley. Several of them had left their native countries in protest against loyalty oaths imposed by Hitler and Mussolini. These refugees often remarked on the similarities between what they had experienced in Europe and what was happening in the United States. To nonsigners such as the me-dieval historian Ernst Kantorowicz and the theoretical physicist Gian-Carlo Wick, as well as to many of their American-born colleagues, the Regents' Special Oath was a harbinger of a totalitarian police state. America, in their view, was on the road to fascism.

The irony is that their own actions, their own courage, belied such an analysis. For as historian Ellen Schrecker has pointed out, the resistance to the Loyalty Oath at the University of California proved that the political repres-sion of the early Cold War period was not total.[4] Though it created a climate of fear that stifled free expression, the anticommunist hysteria did not elimi-nate civil society, with its space, restricted as it may have been, for political protest.

Inspired by the resistance at Berkeley and UCLA, teachers at other colleges and universities donated money to help pay the salaries of the nonsigners, sent them letters of encouragement, and protested to the Board of Regents. Above all they mobilized the groups to which they belonged, so that by the end of 1950 virtually every professional association in the nation, including the pow-erful Modern Language Association, was urging its members not to accept po-sitions at the University of California. It was an unprecedented manifestation of solidarity, all the more remarkable given the entrenched individualistic atti-tudes of university professors.

The thirty-one who were fired at UC included some of the university's most eminent professors. Almost fifty others resigned in protest, including the psychoanalyst Erik Erikson, the physicist Wolfgang Panofsky, and many of Berkeley's most promising young scientists. And the boycott against the university was so successful that these losses could not be made up by new hiring. A veritable honor roll of American scholars and scientists would turn down offers from Berkeley and UCLA, citing the Loyalty Oath and its abrogation of tenure as their reason. In the early 1950s it was by no means certain that the University of California would regain its stature as one of the world's great universities.

OTHER CONSEQUENCES OF THE OATH CRISIS

The Loyalty Oath would have many ripple effects. The first grassroots environmental movement in the Bay Area was organized in 1961 by women whose husbands had been active in the controversy ten years earlier. For years San Francisco Bay, Northern California's scenic and ecological treasure, had been shrinking, as commercial and residential developments intruded on its shorelines. A "Save the Bay" group stopped the city of Berkeley from doubling the area that had been filled in and inspired similar projects in other communities.[5]

The Loyalty Oath was also a forerunner of the student movements of the 1960s. The 1964 Free Speech Movement (FSM) can be seen as an attempt to complete the unfinished business from the oath years; it began as a protest against the restrictions on student political activity. Clark Kerr has argued that the FSM broke out at Berkeley, rather than at Harvard or Columbia, because the oath had radicalized what had been a relatively conservative faculty, creating an anti-administration mentality that predisposed it to join with the rebellious students in a united front.[6] The epilogue to this book explores the connections between the two crises.

Just as the rebellion of 1964–1965 became the model for student movements at predominantly white campuses across the country (and indeed throughout the world), the FSM cemented the idea of Berkeley as the site of political resistance in the cultural imagination. But that association began fifteen years earlier in the fight against the oath.[7]

WITH ITS MOTTO *FIAT LUX*, the University of California cultivated an enlightened liberal image. In 1949 this was reflected in its president, the lib-

eral Republican Robert Gordon Sproul, as well as in its faculty, whose deliberative body, the Academic Senate, exerted an unusual degree of autonomy
and, especially at Berkeley, a remarkable control over the governance of the
university. But the Loyalty Oath controversy revealed that much of this
vaunted liberalism was a veneer. For when critical issues came into play, the
faculty's prestige and power would mean little. The legal authority over the
truly important matters, for example the hiring, promotion, and dismissal of
professors, resided in the Board of Regents. And there was no state university
in the nation with as many of its trustees sitting on the boards of big business
enterprises.[8] One of them was John Francis Neylan, so fervent an anticommunist that he would become a supporter of Senator McCarthy. All in all, the
regents were a predominantly conservative body.

The anticommunist impulse expressed in the 1949 oath did not come out
of the blue. The University of California had a long history of anticommunism, a tradition going back to the 1917 Bolshevik Revolution. An early pro-
ponent was David Prescott Barrows, a professor of political science at Berkeley
who was also a military man. In the two years before he became president of
the University of California in 1919, Barrows had been the chief intelligence
officer for the American forces in Siberia attempting to overthrow the young
Soviet regime and a leader of the ultra-Right American Legion, and had locked
horns with the Socialist Party over the question of whether to recognize Lenin's
government. In 1934, when he was the regional commander of the National
Guard, his soldiers protected scab waterfront workers from Harry Bridges's
longshoremen during San Francisco's General Strike.

That 1934 strike created so much fear in the university administration that
Robert Gordon Sproul and his provosts at Berkeley and UCLA set up intelligence networks to keep tabs on student activists.[9] And to ensure there would
be no Red professors, Sproul asked his friend Joel Hildebrand to write a new
regulation. University Regulation 5, which became official policy, stipulated
that to have academic freedom there must be no communists on the faculty. It
stated that their ideological and organizational imperatives made them incapable of the free pursuit of truth in teaching and research.[10]

That argument was echoed in 1940 when the Board of Regents established
its own policy barring communists from the university. Neylan was the chief
advocate, although he did not vote then to fire Kenneth May, a teaching assis-

tant in mathematics at Berkeley and a leader of the Communist Party in Oakland. May's firing was the first time a member of the university's teaching staff had been dismissed for political reasons since 1874.[11] 1940 was a time when anticommunist feelings were high because of Stalin's pact with Hitler and the Red Army's invasion of Finland, and that may be why neither the policy nor the dismissal were opposed by the faculty. However it is telling that no similar policy was introduced to ban fascists from teaching.[12]

During the oath crisis Neylan and Hildebrand would be the loudest voices for barring Red professors. More liberal faculty members such as psychologist Edward Tolman, the leader of Berkeley's nonsigners, had a different conception of the relation between academic freedom and anticommunism. They subscribed to the position of the American Association of University Professors (AAUP), which held that the academic community should be inclusive enough to encompass people of all political persuasions. For the AAUP, the only grounds for barring a professor from the faculty were clearly demonstrated bias, incompetence, or "moral turpitude,"[13] and not, as Hildebrand and Neylan were arguing, membership in the Communist Party per se.

DURING THE FIRST YEAR of the conflict several dramatic events exacerbated the anticommunist hysteria in America, most notably the fall of Nationalist China; the trial and conviction of Alger Hiss, as well as other highly publicized espionage cases; and the emergence of McCarthy as the nation's leading Red hunter. As a result, support for the AAUP position weakened. In early 1950 a mail ballot of Academic Senate members at both Berkeley and UCLA produced overwhelming majorities in favor of excluding communists from their ranks. The vote made UC the first major university whose faculty banned party members from teaching.

There was also a steady attrition in the number of nonsigners, as more and more resisters bit the bullet and complied with the requirement—in most cases out of fear of losing their livelihood. Deciding to sign could cause great anguish. Dr. Norman Reider, a faculty member at the university's medical school who would later become head of the San Francisco Psychoanalytic Institute, informed Tolman in 1950 about the loss of self-esteem he had noticed among people who had signed. Because their rationalizations were inadequate, the Loyalty Oath had done "incalculable damage to the minds and souls of these people."[14] And George Stewart, a Berkeley English professor conducting interviews for a book on the oath, found many of his colleagues unable to sleep, too distracted to carry out their research, and in general quite demoralized.

In 1950, when the crisis was still unresolved, Stewart published *The Year of the Oath*, a work that viewed the resistance of the nonsigners in a favorable light. Appearing at a critical moment during the conflict, the book affected the debate between the regents and the faculty. It is discussed in Chapter 12.

The most thorough and influential account of the crisis was published in 1967. When David Gardner wrote *The California Oath Controversy* as a doctoral dissertation in Education at Berkeley, he was already an assistant chancellor on the Santa Barbara campus, and the book reflects his administrative bias.[15] For the future university president, the nonsigners' refusal to compromise made them as responsible as the most reactionary regents for the prolongation of the crisis. Thus the Loyalty Oath was "a vain and futile episode" in the history of the university.[16]

Despite this bias and the lack of drama in his colorless account, *The California Oath Controversy* is a valuable book that has been indispensable for the writing of *Resisting McCarthyism*.

Except for informal discussions, there was no way for the faculty to dispute Gardner's melancholy thesis on the Loyalty Oath for more than three decades. And then in 1999 the university organized a symposium to mark the oath's fiftieth anniversary.

The event was significant because the oath had cast a shadow on the university's image of enlightened liberalism. While the Free Speech Movement of the 1960s had been heralded as a critical turning point—and even celebrated with the dedication of a student cafe named for it—the institution had chosen to suppress how ignobly it had succumbed to the hysteria of the McCarthy Era.

With Gardner in the audience, a series of speakers, including Berkeley chancellor Robert Berdahl and several who had fought the oath fifty years earlier, took issue with the former president's view. Ellen Schrecker gave the keynote address that opened the two-day event, and it was then that she suggested that the resistance at Berkeley and UCLA had tested the limits of repression in the postwar period.

GOALS OF THE PRESENT STUDY

Resisting McCarthyism examines the nonsigners' fight as part of the critical resistance that was beginning to develop against the excesses of anticommunism. The question arises: Did their willingness to sacrifice their careers play a role, if only a minor one, in contributing to the movement that would eventually turn back McCarthyism? Or were the actions of Tolman and his followers futile and even counterproductive, as Gardner believes?

This study places the struggle between those who pushed for academic freedom and those whose priority was anticommunism in a broad historical context. It suggests that the Loyalty Oath was a continuation of previous institutional policies and was foreshadowed in the earlier actions of administrators, regents, and faculty members.

Another central concern has been to provide a fuller treatment of UCLA's role in the crisis, for previous accounts have focused predominantly on Berkeley. UCLA's importance goes beyond the fact that it was the only branch of the university that came close to Berkeley in size and academic quality. For the professional anticommunists, the problem of subversion at the university was centered at UCLA. Its faculty members appeared more frequently than did Berkeley professors in the State Senate Fact-Finding (Tenney) Committee's reports on un-American activities. And because of its history of student radicalism in the 1930s and 1940s, UCLA was labeled "The Little Red School on the Hill."

In contrast to earlier accounts, *Resisting McCarthyism* highlights the role of students in the controversy. At both Berkeley and UCLA, the graduate student teaching and research assistants were the most radical segment of the faculty. Resisting the oath in much higher proportions than their mentors, many more of them were fired. Focusing on its own situation, the faculty did not do a good job of defending its student assistants. To monitor the activities and the outlooks of undergraduates, the book relies on articles and editorials in the university's two major student newspapers, the *Daily Californian* and the *Daily Bruin*. Strongly anti-oath, they encouraged student involvement in the controversy and criticized the faculty's penchant to compromise and abandon its principles.

A final goal is to depict the people involved in the oath crisis as complex human beings. Brief bios are included to help readers understand why the actors behaved as they did. Above all the book portrays the crisis as a human drama, not unlike a Greek tragedy in which the actions of its protagonists had consequences that returned to haunt both the individuals involved and the University of California as an institution.

The only account of the Loyalty Oath that does justice to it as a human drama is *The Searching Light* by Martha Dodd. Dodd, the daughter of America's ambassador to Germany during the 1930s, was a member of the Communist Party who spied for the Soviet Union before giving that up to become a novelist.[17] Even though, like a good espionage agent, she changed names, places, and events to mask the identities of her subjects, it is clear that the novel was a portrayal of Berkeley's oath crisis.[18] But in *Resisting McCarthyism*, I hide no identities, spare no reputations, and have had the benefit of research materials that were not available to Ms. Dodd when she published her anti-McCarthy novel in 1955.

CHAPTER I

MCCARTHYISM AND THE CRISIS OF LIBERALISM

It was un-American to mention unpleasant facts about the social order. . . . it was un-American to plead for international understanding.

—Robert MacIver.[1]

The miasma of thought control that is now spreading over the country is the greatest menace to the United States since Hitler.

—Robert Maynard Hutchins.[2]

To SIGN OR NOT TO SIGN, THAT WAS THE question faculty members at the University of California (UC) asked in 1949 and 1950. It was a period of ever-increasing hysteria, when loyalty oaths that required government employees to swear that they were not communists or subversives were the rage. Workers at every level, from top directors to lowly custodians, had to submit to these political tests. But professors at state universities were a favorite target, for they bore the responsibility of educating America's youth, who were considered vulnerable to indoctrination. And even though loyalty oaths would be required of employees in virtually every state, California's requirement was special.

For only in the Golden State were university teachers singled out as a suspect group, and only at the University of California did a faculty vigorously resist. Before those who refused to comply finally won in the state Supreme Court, thirty-one of the "nonsigners," as they were called, had been dismissed by UC's Board of Regents, accounting for almost half of all the professors fired in the United States for political reasons during the McCarthy Era.[3]

In California and in the nation at large, university faculties viewed these contentious matters through the lens of one principal idea, that of academic freedom. Academic freedom is the value most cherished by America's professoriat, but as historians of the concept have pointed out, the idea is inherently vague, and neither college presidents nor teachers always agree on its definition.[4] During the McCarthy Era the meaning of academic freedom was bitterly contested, as the question of whether members of the Communist Party and their supporters were fit to teach became a burning issue.

ACADEMIC FREEDOM

Erich Fromm distinguished between two classes of freedom. In his view there are freedoms *from* threats and dangers, and freedoms *to* pursue goals and lines of action.[5]

"Freedom from" was initially the more important notion. The idea of academic freedom emerged in late 19th- and early 20th-century America as college faculties vied for the autonomy to conduct their affairs without being dictated to by outside interests. They were trying to fend off political interference by state governors and university boards of directors, who often would fire controversial professors. The principle of academic tenure, which means that a teacher who has undergone a probation period cannot be dismissed except for cause, for example, "moral turpitude," was institutionalized in large part to protect this notion of academic freedom. In post–World War II America, those who viewed it as freedom from outside interference tended to support vigorous action against communist and "subversive" professors, arguing that compliance with loyalty oaths and similar policies would safeguard the autonomy of their institution.[6]

From the viewpoint of "freedom to," academic freedom was seen as the freedom to teach, to explore ideas, to write, and to conduct research in pursuit of "the truth," wherever that pursuit might lead. Here the idea is that no conclusion or result should be considered beyond the pale on *a priori* grounds. Those who held this concept typically concluded that loyalty oaths were a violation of academic freedom. This was the position of the most important organization of college faculty, the American Association of University Professors (AAUP).

In December 1915, the year in which the AAUP was established, the new organization proposed procedural safeguards for tenured professors facing dismissal. With America's entry into the war "a mob fanaticism" swept the country, and more college teachers were fired or disciplined for being insufficiently patriotic than the short-staffed AAUP was able to protect. And yet, though academic freedom tends to be one of the first casualties of war, as was apparent in 1918, this did not happen in World War II. Only during the postwar conflict with Soviet communism would it come under significant attack again.[7]

During the Cold War the AAUP was an influential association whose pronouncements on academic freedom were considered authoritative. But its position was also controversial, and during the McCarthy period it was not as widely subscribed to among college presidents and professors as the other, more restrictive, notion of academic freedom.

McCarthyism and the various loyalty oaths the era spawned posed grave challenges to the academic world. University professors, devoted to scholarship and "the life of the mind," have a special competence in, and concern for, ideas. They study ideas, write about ideas, and help determine which ideas become the leading ideas of the day, as well as how these ideas are viewed by other citizens. As the number of "free-floating" public intellectuals declined in 20th-century America, college professors became the core of America's intellectual class, the equivalent of Europe's traditional *intelligentsia*.

Of all the ideas that dominated the concerns of intellectuals, both in Europe and the United States, none have been more important than those concerned with freedom of thought and freedom of expression. So the overarching question for academic men and women in postwar America became, Do loyalty oaths violate basic American freedoms? Or are their potential infringements on core liberties of little consequence compared to the larger threats of the Cold War and domestic subversion?

To answer this it is necessary to look at the changes that American liberalism underwent in the second half of the 1940s. During the first few months of 1945, Franklin Roosevelt's New Deal coalition was held together by the force of the president's charismatic leadership, as well as the need for unity to win the war. But when FDR died in April and the war ended some months later, a schism began to develop among America's liberals.

The historian Alonzo Hamby has called the wartime coalition "Popular Front liberalism" because its goal was the defeat of fascism, and in order to achieve that, the United States allied itself with the Soviet Union at the same time that domestic liberals worked together with communists and "fellow travelers."[8] But Roosevelt's death and the end of the war strained Popular Frontism. The new president, Harry Truman, was not as committed as his predecessor to negotiating with the USSR; his instinct was to rely on tough talk and military might. Also, Truman lacked the personality and leadership skills to maintain the unity of the New Deal coalition he had inherited.

The end of the war was even more fateful. As long as the Red Army was helping to save the country from Hitler, the Soviet leader could be viewed as a benevolent "Uncle Joe" and not as a ruthless dictator. But when Germany and Japan surrendered, the police state nature of the USSR, highlighted during the purges of the 1930s, returned to the forefront of the nation's consciousness.

Long before the 1951 publication of Hannah Arendt's *The Origins of Totalitarianism*,[9] the concept was being used to characterize the Soviet Union and to equate its political and social structures with those of Nazi Germany. For the historian Abbott Gleason, "Totalitarianism was the great mobilizing and unifying concept of the Cold War." The discourse over it was instrumental in shifting America's view of the Soviet Union from an anti-fascist ally to a threatening enemy.[10]

Early in 1946 Florida senator Claude Pepper, a prototypical Popular Fronter, spoke out against what he saw as the "sinister forces" who were bent on supplanting "antifascism with anticommunism."[11] This trend became unstoppable during 1946 and 1947 after Winston Churchill's "Iron Curtain" speech helped Truman convince the American public that the blame for the emerging Cold War rested with the Soviet Union. At home anticommunism received a boost from revelations that communists in the United States (as well as in England and Canada) had spied for the Soviet Union. An old debate would be renewed among liberals over whether the Communist Party was a legitimate political vehicle, the far-Left wing of American liberalism, or instead a conspiratorial organization loyal to a foreign power and thus a tool of the Soviet Union. For

Harry Truman the answer was clear. He considered domestic communists disloyal to their country.[12]

Two events in March 1947 accelerated the split in the liberal movement. For months Truman had worried about Greece, where communist guerrillas seemed on the brink of victory, as well as about the weakness of Turkey, an ally strategic to keeping Middle Eastern oil flowing to the West. To deal with these contingencies, he announced his "Truman Doctrine," a program of lavish economic and military aid intended to keep both nations out of the Soviet orbit. Ten days later he issued Executive Order 9835, which instituted a loyalty security program aimed at weeding out subversives in the federal government. Thus it was a Democratic president who originated the system of loyalty checks that would characterize an entire era.

The opposition to these programs was led by Henry Wallace. Having become editor of the *New Republic,* Wallace had a ready-made forum with which to attack the administration's foreign policy, as well as to defend the civil liberties of communists and other Leftists.

Popular Front liberals believed that Wallace, rather than Truman, belonged in the White House. He had been FDR's vice-president until 1944, when he was replaced on the ticket by Truman, largely due to the influence of Edwin Pauley, an oilman who was also one of the most Right-wing members of the University of California's Board of Regents. Wallace had been Truman's Secretary of Commerce, but he was dismissed in 1946 after calling for negotiations with the Soviet Union.

In 1947 Wallace and his followers formed the Progressive Citizens' Alliance (PCA), while those liberals who saw communism as a greater threat than fascism established the Americans for Democratic Action (ADA). With its first chairman, Minnesota senator Hubert Humphrey, the ADA included leading intellectuals such as Arthur Schlesinger Jr., who advocated a theory of the "vital center," opposed to totalitarianisms of the Left and the Right.[13]

As the issue of communism at home and abroad intensified, a schism had developed in the old New Deal coalition. The dominant group, represented by the ADA, were *anti*-communist liberals; the smaller but still significant group, followers of the old Popular Front strategy, were *non*-communist liberals. In 1948 the PCA became the basis for Wallace's Progressive Party, which after a very promising campaign lost most of its backing because communists and fellow travelers were so prominent among its supporters. After the third party's decisive defeat in the November 1948 elections—narrowly won by Truman against Republican Thomas Dewey—those who remained committed to a "third force" in American politics would call themselves "progressives." Earlier the term had been another word for liberals.[14]

Despite these divisions, liberals were the most sizable political group in post–World War II America. It was still a time when leaders such as President Truman, Illinois governor Adlai Stevenson, and most Democratic senators were proud to call themselves liberals. The term was not yet a pejorative, even though the attack on liberals as people whose patriotism was suspect had begun. Indeed, Truman adopted his relatively hardline approach to the Soviet Union to forestall Republican charges that he was "soft on communism."

The anticommunist hysteria posed a challenge to liberalism, in part because it was liberals such as Truman who bore the major responsibility for its postwar flowering. In establishing a security program for federal employees, Truman legitimated the loyalty oath as the method of choice for fighting internal subversion. To enforce this policy, Attorney General Tom Clark made public in November 1947 a list of ninety-three "subversive organizations." Based on the files of FBI director J. Edgar Hoover, the notorious "Attorney-General's List" would become a critical instrument of what would eventually be called McCarthyism.[15]

Set into motion by liberals, the anticommunism of the late 1940s was soon hijacked by the Far Right and would become associated in the public mind with the archconservative federal and state Un-American Activities committees, and above all with the person of Joseph McCarthy, especially after the Wisconsin senator electrified the nation in February 1950 with his claim that more than two hundred "card-carrying" communists were still employed in the State Department.

But McCarthyism did not pose problems for most conservatives. Their political outlook was in sync with the emerging *zeitgeist*. It was the liberals who were in a difficult situation.

In an irony of history, liberals had created a political dynamic that would threaten the very values associated with their philosophical tradition. They were faced with a dilemma. Would they remain true to the principles of classical liberalism that were advanced in John Milton's *Areopagetica* and John Stuart Mill's

On Liberty? That would mean defending the idea that no social group, not even a despised minority such as communists, should be denied rights enjoyed by other citizens. If they did adhere to classical liberalism—and this was the position of the American Association of University Professors—they could expect to be labeled unpatriotic, disloyal, and subversive. The pressure to conform to an anticommunist orthodoxy strained the ideology of liberalism, revealing faultlines in its worldview.

The most prominent representative of classical liberalism in the academic community was Robert Maynard Hutchins, the chancellor of the University of Chicago. Hutchins's stature and charisma insulated him from allegations that he was unpatriotic, but those who would resist the Loyalty Oath at the University of California would not be as fortunate.

The classical liberals were viewed as "soft idealists" by the more establishment-oriented liberals. The latter were the "realists" who strove to enlist liberalism in the service of anticommunism. This is what Truman and Hubert Humphrey did. The Minnesota senator would introduce legislation to make membership in the Communist Party a crime.

Another leader of the Americans for Democratic Action, the historian Arthur Schlesinger Jr., supported Truman's loyalty program, defended the firing of communist teachers, and favored the prosecution of Communist Party leaders under the Smith Act. He agreed with Humphrey that the Communist Party was "a political cancer in our society." Adlai Stevenson went even further. For the Illinois governor, communism was "worse than cancer, tuberculosis, and heart disease combined."[16] But Stevenson also vetoed loyalty oath legislation in his state on two occasions.[17] He was a liberal who tried to find middle ground between a reflexive anticommunism and a strict civil liberties position. The most thoughtful liberals found ways, according to Irving Howe, to oppose "both Communism and McCarthyism."[18]

THE FACULTY

The University of California, as I have suggested, was a conservative institution, despite its facade of enlightened liberalism. But there were contradictions in its governing structure. Its Academic Senate, a legislative body that included all regular faculty members, had more autonomy than almost all of its counterparts across the nation. Berkeley's Senate was proud of a long history of standing up to the administration. During the oath crisis, its belief that it wielded the authority, indeed the final say, over decisions that it considered its jurisdiction, the hiring and firing of its colleagues, would be sorely tested.

The faculty fancied itself *primus inter pares* in its relations with the other two centers of university authority, the administration, led by President Sproul, and the Board of Regents. Indeed, many professors looked down on the president as well as the regents because they were not scholars, scientists, or intellectuals. The faculty also took pride in the way it governed itself. The Academic Senate conducted its business through a network of committees led by the most respected members of the faculty. And at its monthly meetings, which were open to all tenure-track professors, decisions were made through careful deliberation, appeals to reason, and majority votes.

In normal times these procedures worked well, but the years of the oath crisis would prove that the Senate's deliberative decision making put it at a disadvantage. The body it found itself contending with, the Board of Regents, was not constrained by the niceties of democracy. The regents made their big decisions in executive sessions closed to the public, and as a small group, they could be dominated by a powerful leader. Even more important was the fact that it was the regents and not the faculty whose constitutional and legal authority was paramount.

And yet there were ways in which the faculty was as undemocratic as its adversary. First, it was virtually all male. During the years of the oath the proportion of the professoriat at the University of California that was female was between 1 and 2 percent.

The scarcity of women professors was the result of a system of institutional sexism that infused the culture of graduate study. Until as late as the 1970s the prevailing belief was that a female graduate student could not be serious in her aspirations. If she were single, she would get married and then drop out. And if she were married, then she'd have children, with the same result. This was the rationale for denying women research and teaching assistantships and, if they were tenacious enough to finish, for failing to sponsor them for teaching positions.

Since most male students and professors believed that her place was in the home, a woman was reluctant to speak up in a graduate seminar. And when she did, she was often put down.[19]

Second, the faculty was elitist in structure and outlook. The Academic Senate only included those of the rank of assistant professor and higher. Excluded were instructors and lecturers, as well as the teaching assistants who bore the main responsibility of face-to-face contact with undergraduates. These teaching assistants, along with their compatriots who worked as research assistants and course readers, had to join with the low-level instructors in separate organizations such as the Non–Academic Senate Employees and the Graduate Students Association. Their status was a marginal one, between students and professors, and that helps explain why they would resist the oath more vigorously than their faculty mentors.

THE REGENTS

During the first three decades of the 20th century, the formative years for the University of California, the Board of Regents had been dominated by members of the Progressive Movement, who saw building a great university as a way to express their ideals of public service.[20] But many of them, including John Francis Neylan, the most powerful member during the oath crisis, moved to the Far Right during the 1930s, in reaction to the perceived anti-business and autocratic tendencies of the New Deal.

In theory, the regents represented the people of California. But in actuality the board's twenty-four members were a most unrepresentative body. Although eight of the sixteen appointed members were attorneys, with only one exception they represented businesses such as the Bank of America or San Francisco's big shipowners. Other regents included an oil and gas tycoon and the head of one of California's largest agrobusinesses. Agriculture was also overrepresented among the eight regents who held ex officio positions. The rules that designated these seats had not been changed since they were established to reflect the demographic realities of California in 1868.

The result, as Berkeley English professor George Stewart put it, was a board that was "an expensive gentleman's club," without one "person of broad intellectual stature."[21]

Not only that, in 1949 the regents were all white men of Western European descent. There were no women on the board, although there had been in the past.[22] Jews, however, had always been included; Isaac Friedlander was one of the original eight regents, and Jacob Reinstein joined the board in 1895.[23] And during the oath crisis there were three Jewish regents.[24] But despite this, the men who dominated the regents' decision making were Gentiles who bonded together in the Bohemian and Pacific Union Clubs, fraternities from which Jews and other minorities (including women) were excluded.[25]

In contrast, the faculties of Berkeley and UCLA had more Jewish professors than most leading American universities at the time, including a critical mass of refugees from Nazism and fascism who would be particularly outspoken against the oath. That is why Kevin Starr argued that anti-Semitism was a sub-text in the mid-century conflict, underlying the attitudes of the Right-wing regents toward a faculty that included a significant number of rebellious Jews.[26]

The Board of Regents had a sizeable liberal minority, including two of its most important members, President Sproul and Governor Earl Warren. Extremely well-liked, Sproul had considerable influence over the regents and the faculty, even though the administration's constitutional authority was not as great as that of the trustees or the Academic Senate.

UC's president was also active in the Republican Party, in which he was considered a potential candidate for senator, governor, or even the vice-presidency. In Republican politics, Sproul allied himself with Governor Earl Warren, who was the leader of the party's liberal wing. The Right-wing faction was controlled by the Knowland family.

Joseph Knowland, who had become rich as the publisher of the ultra-conservative *Oakland Tribune,* had also established a political empire. In 1949 his equally Right-wing son, William, was representing California in the U.S. Senate, having replaced the former Progressive Hiram Johnson in 1945. John Francis Neylan was squarely in the Knowland camp. Therefore the split within the Board of Regents between its extreme anticommunist faction led by Neylan and its moderately liberal minority that included Warren and Sproul reflected cleavages within Republican Party politics. But geography was also at work. Although San Francisco–based Neylan was an exception, regents from Northern California would be more likely to side with the faculty during the conflict than would those from the Los Angeles area.[27]

Although Earl Warren was more liberal than Neylan and the Knowlands, he was a pragmatic politician who carried out conservative policies when it suited his purpose. As the next chapter details, as attorney general of Alameda

County during the 1930s he provided Sproul with intelligence on Cal's Left-wing students. In 1940, as California's attorney general, he forced Governor Culbert Olson to withdraw his nomination of the highly esteemed Max Radin to the state Supreme Court on the grounds that the Berkeley law professor was too radical. And two years later Warren ordered the state's Japanese-American citizens to be rounded up and incarcerated in detention camps.

However, the Warren action that proved most fateful was his 1944 appointment of Neylan to another sixteen-year term on the Board of Regents. By 1950 he was regretting that decision. It had become clear that had Neylan not been on the board, the Loyalty Oath crisis would have been resolved in its early stages.

The governor opposed the oath from the outset, but during the first year of the controversy he neither attended board meetings nor spoke out publicly. His real power lay in his mandate to appoint new regents when vacancies occurred. And with one exception he appointed liberals, so that by late 1950 the politics of the Board of Regents would be transformed.[28]

THINKING ABOUT MCCARTHYISM

The McCarthy Era was only one of the many waves of political repression that have plagued American society. Civil liberties were subject to even more systematic attacks during the "Red Scare" that followed World War I. But the mid-century repression surpassed those 1919–1920 events in the breadth of its targets and the variety of its forms—loyalty oaths, investigations by Un-American Activities committees, accusations in the press. And the post–World War II reaction lasted much longer, an entire decade from 1946 to 1956.

The Red Scares of 1920 and 1950 were created out of the same ingredient, fear. When fifteen thousand foreign-born "radicals" were rounded up during the "Palmer Raids" of 1919, the result was a citizenry anxious about enemies lurking within. Americans became hesitant of exercising their right to dissent, just as they did thirty years later when the actions of HUAC and demagogues such as McCarthy produced a climate of fear again.

These waves of repression reflect a phenomenon deeply embedded in the dynamics of American politics. According to Richard Hofstadter, the core of "the paranoid style" is "the positing of the existence of a vast, insidious, preternaturally effective international conspiratorial network designed to perpetuate acts of the most fiendish character." In the mind of the political paranoid, "What is at stake is always a conflict between absolute good and absolute evil." Thus there is no interest in compromise, for the enemy is conceived as "totally evil and totally unappeasable," and must be "totally eliminated."[29]

Hofstadter, along with Daniel Bell, S. M. Lipset, and others, argued that McCarthyism was a "populist" uprising with a social base of white workers and the lower middle class. It signaled a new status politics rather than the old class politics based on economic interests. In this view, identifying with a demagogic leader attacking communists provided relief for "status anxieties" and psychological insecurities. McCarthyism ushered in a "New American Right," unlike traditional conservatism, which reflected the economic and political interests of the elites.[30]

The late Michael Rogin attacked this thesis in *The Intellectuals and McCarthy.* Through an analysis of voting data, he undermined the argument that McCarthy's support came from the same parts of the Midwest that had provided the social and political bases of earlier Populist movements. The political scientist suggested that McCarthy's backing, rather than coming from the alienated "masses," was derived instead from traditional conservative elites, namely the leadership of the Republican Party in the farmbelt states.[31]

A conclusive answer to the cause of McCarthyism is beyond the scope of this study. But the evidence from the years of the oath at the University of California does not support the interpretation that it was a phenomenon of a New American Right. The lower middle classes and the industrial workers in the state may have been staunchly anticommunist, but they had little impact on what happened at the university. In the broadest sense the Loyalty Oath was a product of the overall anticommunist hysteria. But it was also the outcome of the actions of three major figures. The first, Jack Tenney, was a state senator in Sacramento and California's leading Red hunter. The second was University president Robert Gordon Sproul, and the third was regent John Francis Neylan. All three were part of California's power structure. And each was a Republican, so the present case study does lend support to the Rogin thesis that McCarthyism was a product of the political maneuverings of the Republican Party leadership.

PART I

ANTICOMMUNISM AND ACADEMIC FREEDOM BETWEEN TWO WARS

CHAPTER 2

A MOST CONTRADICTORY HISTORY

The hue and cry against communism has become the
leitmotiv of modern America.

—John Caughey, UCLA nonsigners' leader.[1]

"LET THERE BE LIGHT" ARE THE WORDS
inscribed on the seal of the University of California. A
noble sentiment, and as a motto for the institution, not wholly misleading.
For the university has a history of welcoming people who were previously denied the light of learning. But the dark side of university history, a tradition of
anticommunism and anti-labor practices, is less well known.

Underlying the institution's inclusiveness was the mandate it had been
granted by the legislature in the early years of the 20th century. A monopoly
over public education on the graduate level in one of the nation's largest states
meant that it was able to expand its student enrollment almost indefinitely,
both on the original Berkeley campus and at an increasing number of new
branches.

From the time of its origins as the College of California, the institution
was more open to the residents of its state than were the public universities of

the East. Both the state and the university pioneered the idea that every high school graduate was entitled to higher education, and to make this possible, Benjamin Ide Wheeler, UC's first great president, supported a junior college movement.[2]

California's democratic vision came closest to being realized in the area of gender equality. In 1900, when most Ivy League universities were all male, and institutions such as Stanford and Michigan had quotas limiting females to 25 percent of their student bodies, almost half of Berkeley's undergraduates (46 percent) were women.[3] Of course, the campus was still dominated by men and by male assumptions. Women undergraduates were steered into such "female fields" as English, education, and home economics, and few went on to graduate school. But this situation began to improve in the 1930s, as a new president, Robert Gordon Sproul, went out of his way to assure women that their educational experience would be equal to that of men.[4]

The faculty would remain overwhelmingly male until late in the 20th century. The pioneering Jessica Peixotto began teaching economics in 1899 and later became Berkeley's first woman full professor. She taught the university's first course in socialism, a cause that she espoused. And Peixotto was Jewish.[5]

In 1919 one of her students, Barbara Nachtrieb Armstrong, became the first woman member of the faculty at a major law school. Two other of Peixotto's students, Emily Huntington and Margaret Hodgen, would, like Armstrong, become major figures in the resistance to the oath.

By 1930 twenty-seven tenure-track professors at Berkeley were female, an unusually high number for the time among major universities.[6] And yet there were only six tenured women professors on a faculty of about five hundred throughout most of the 1930s.[7]

Perhaps the most underappreciated aspect of the University of California's inclusiveness was an absence of the tradition of anti-Semitism that infected institutions such as Harvard, Yale, and Princeton. Although the democratic ethos of the frontier and the Gold Rush era was compatible with powerful prejudices against both indigenous Mexicans and Asian immigrants, it was relatively open-minded with respect to Jews. It helped that San Francisco's Jewish population was never as large as New York's or Chicago's, and that the critical mass that arrived in the 19th century came from Germany, rather than Eastern forces came to power, if only briefly, in parts of Germany, Austria, and Hungary. Fearing that Leon Trotsky's dream of world revolution had arrived, the ruling classes of the Western world responded by repressing these new governments by armed force. In America there was no possibility of revolution, but a general strike closed down Seattle for five days in 1919, and bombings by anarchists and radicals in other cities evoked strong anticommunist feelings. A low point of the Red Scare, which convulsed the nation for more than a year, was the Palmer Raids. A. Mitchell Palmer was Woodrow Wilson's attorney general, and it was he who ordered the roundup that led to the deportation of thousands of noncitizens suspected of having communist ties.

David Barrows approved of the crackdown on the American Left and did all he could to aid it. As California commander of the new American Legion, he made ultrapatriotism and anticommunism its priorities. Then in 1919, in a debate with Berkeley's Socialist Party on the question of whether the United States should recognize the new Soviet regime, he stated that the Bolsheviks were such a danger to civilization that they all should be killed. In refusing a second debate, he accused the socialists of being "Bolsheviks in sheep's clothing" because of their willingness to recognize Lenin's government.[13]

Barrows became president of the university as a result of a series of events known as "the Faculty Revolution." The popular but autocratic Benjamin Wheeler was already in ill health when war broke out in Europe in 1914. A friend of Kaiser Wilhelm, he became an "ardent neutralist" and blamed England for the Great War. Whether Wheeler was pro-German remains a matter of dispute to this day, but the perception that he was forced him to resign in 1919.[14] By 1918, anti-German hysteria was so pervasive that the teaching of the language was dropped from America's high schools. Although a campaign to eliminate German from the curriculum at Berkeley did not succeed, three professors were fired on dubious charges of disloyalty, and all candidates for degrees were required to sign pledges attesting to their Americanism.[15]

To replace Wheeler an interim committee was established. When it proved ineffective, the Academic Senate, which for years had been content to let the regents and the president run the university, rose up and instituted a series of reforms that were accepted by the still Progressive Board of Regents. Professors could now vote on their department chairs, and could decide on what courses would be offered, which students to admit, and who would serve on

Academic Senate committees. From 1920 on, Berkeley's faculty Senate would have more control over the governance of the university than almost all of its counterparts in the nation.[16]

David Barrows did not participate in the Faculty Revolution; its assertiveness offended his conservative sensibilities. And after he became president in 1919, he bristled under the new limitations to his authority. But he was not as authoritarian as the faculty feared he might be, given his military background. He would serve for only four years, and although he did improve what had been abysmally low salary levels, his leadership style came into conflict with the Academic Senate. Today he is considered to have been a poor administrator; one observer noted that he was more interested in putting on his army uniform and marching in parades than in tackling the budget.[17]

THE SOUTHERN BRANCH

Another criticism of Barrow's presidency is that he fought against the university's expansion in Southern California. In 1919, the year in which he became president, UC took over the facility of Los Angeles State Normal School, a teachers' college in downtown L.A. But even with a new name—"the Southern Branch" of the university—it was stigmatized because of its lowly origins. The faculty and the students of the University of Southern California, in the running during the 1920s for the honor of being rated the area's most prestigious institution, liked to refer to the Southern Branch as a girls' school and as a mere junior college, even though its academic standards were already higher than USC's.[18]

From the outset the Southern Branch's faculty members compared themselves with Berkeley. Hungry to be recognized as a worthy institution, they wanted to be considered equal to the northern campus. But they received little support from Barrows, nor from the Board of Regents, which was dominated by Northern Californians.[19] And in the period after the Southern Branch became known as UCLA in 1927, Jim Corley, the university's influential representative to the legislature in Sacramento, did everything he could to block its progress.

To its faculty and administration, the very name "Southern Branch" symbolized a stepchild status. But even after the resented appellation was dropped, a pervasive bitterness persisted, as future president Clark Kerr discovered on a visit to the campus in 1932.[20] Indeed, the belief that the northern campus monopolized the resources and the name of the university, as well as the prestige that accompanied that name, was so strong that in the early 1930s, Provost Ernest C. Moore and others at UCLA talked openly of seceding from the University of California.[21]

And the southerners' case had merit. For in 1929 UCLA had begun to acquire a core of distinguished faculty, due to Moore's eye for talent and his aggressive recruiting.

1929 was also the year when UCLA moved from downtown Los Angeles to its present campus in the Westwood district. But since it was also the year of the stock market crash that ushered in the Great Depression, money was lacking for construction. On that same 1932 visit Kerr found that only four buildings had been completed. Most of the site's four hundred acres were still forestland.[22]

OF ALL THE ANTICOMMUNISTS in the history of the university, UCLA Provost Ernest Carroll Moore was the most extreme. A Progressive in his youth, he had worked as a social worker at Chicago's Hull House with Jane Addams. During the upsurge of reform early in the 20th century he served on California's Board of Charities and Corrections. Before becoming president of the L.A. State Normal School in 1917 he taught at Berkeley, Yale, and Harvard, and spent four years as Los Angeles's superintendent of schools. Moore would shepherd the Normal School's evolution to the Southern Branch and then to a full-fledged university.

In 1926 Provost Moore dissolved the Liberal Club because its students were too radical for his taste. Suspending one of them for "communistic tendencies" shortly after, he warned that the "University of California cannot allow the Third International of Moscow to establish a cell of agitation on the grounds of the university."[23] UCLA political scientist Dean McHenry believed that the provost would have liked to reach out to students, but "just didn't know how." It didn't help that he was "a severe man (who) never smiled."[24] So it was Moore's personality, as well as his politics, that accounted for his difficulties with student activists.

PRESIDENT SPROUL AND REGENT NEYLAN

After six years of unexceptional presidents, Robert Gordon Sproul assumed the leadership of the university in 1929. The fact that he had fought for the interests of the Southern Branch during his tenure as university comptroller and vice-president was a big factor in his selection. For as it became clear that Southern California would surpass the north in population, the regents finally recognized the southland's potential. And Sproul, an astute politician, would go out of his way not to slight UCLA. A sports fan who never missed a Cal football game, he would spend half his time on UCLA's sidelines when the Golden Bears were playing the Bruins.[25]

At thirty-eight Sproul was younger than most university presidents. His origins were also much more modest, as he was born into a lower-middle-class family and raised in a working-class section of San Francisco. Spending virtually his entire life at the university from which he had graduated in 1913, he had worked his way up the ladder, having started out as an assistant cashier.

The regents' selection raised doubts among the faculty. Wheeler, Barrows, and his predecessor William Campbell all had Ph.D.s, but Sproul had no formal education beyond his undergraduate years, when he had studied business and engineering. Thus many professors viewed him as too business-oriented, too much of a "Rotarian," to understand the academic mind.[26] And indeed the gregarious Sproul was an organization man. As president he served on the boards of more than a hundred civic groups, including the Republican Party and the Sierra Club, in which he was especially active.

The president-elect took these concerns seriously. Before taking office he spent six months consulting with university heads on the East Coast about the demands of his new job. This helped, as did a friendship with John Francis Neylan, who had been appointed to the Board of Regents a year earlier in 1928. The new regent took the new president under his wing, and over drinks and lunch at his posh Pacific Union Club, he dispensed advice on how to run the university.

In 1929 Neylan was still a Progressive reformer. Born in New York City in 1885, six years before Sproul, he came from a wealthy family and attended an exclusive prep school and college. A youthful idealist when he went to work for the *San Francisco Call*, his mission was to expose the corruption that was rife among city officials. When he succeeded in this, the Progressive Governor Hiram Johnson made him the first director of California's Board of Control. Neylan did straighten out the state's finances, but in doing so he sent so many bigwigs to prison on graft charges that the governor joked that his young protégé was "running the state by putting all of its officials in jail."[27]

The ambitious young man then went to law school. As an attorney his clients would include A. P. Giannini, the head of the Bank of America; Safeway Stores; and the nation's leading presslord, William Randolph Hearst. Neylan also won a pardon for Anita Whitney, a social worker who was unjustly convicted in 1916 on the charge of participating in a bomb plot hatched by the Industrial Workers of the World. Neylan was the only lawyer willing to represent her, and even though he thought that the IWW was "a terrible outfit," his ties to mainstream labor were so strong that some industrialists thought he was a Bolshevik.[28]

During the 1920s Neylan was the most powerful figure in California's Progressive Movement, and what he accomplished then still affects people's lives. Although the San Francisco–Oakland Bay Bridge would not be built until the mid-1930s, its planning began a decade earlier. The Southern Pacific, which ran the ferries, wanted to own the new bridge. Neylan, who like other Progressives devoted much energy to fighting the railroads, made sure that the Bay Bridge and the others that followed would be publicly owned. He also won public ownership for San Francisco's railway and bus system, as well as for the region's water supplies. But he was unable to municipalize the other utilities, and that is why Bay Area citizens today pay their gas and electric bills to Pacific Gas and Electric.[29]

By the end of the 1920s, Neylan, who had become rich through investments in oil and gas, was the single most powerful politician in California. For a period he was Hearst's number one advisor, and he counted many of America's most influential people as friends. His personal presence and charm enabled him to dominate people and situations such as regents' meetings. English professor Benjamin Lehman described him as a "an enormous man, very handsome, very Irish, (and) very persuasive."[30]

In his oral history Neylan boasted of his role in the election of Franklin Delano Roosevelt. To secure FDR's nomination in 1932, California's votes were needed, and it was Neylan who responded to boss James Farley's request to get

Hearst and his newspapers behind the effort. In return, the isolationist press-lord exacted a promise from Roosevelt to stay out of foreign entanglements, which of course he didn't keep.

Like his mentor Hiram Johnson and other Progressives, Neylan voted for Roosevelt in 1932. But early in the new administration, many in the movement broke with the Democrats. Those who were pro-business didn't like FDR's policies encouraging the organization of workers into unions. They also believed that the president's "alphabet soup" of new agencies was too radical an instrument to fight the economic crisis. And worst of all, Roosevelt was usurping the power that belonged to other branches of the government; the anti-FDR Progressives believed he would establish a dictatorship.

THE GENERAL STRIKE

The Great Depression encouraged a plethora of social movements. Even before FDR became president, there was a march of World War I veterans who demanded a bonus they had been promised. Although Hoover refused to meet with them, "the Bonus Army" helped bring the plight of the poor to public consciousness. The Communist Party helped organize demonstrations of the unemployed that called for jobs and economic relief. The party also mobilized people to stop evictions of those who couldn't pay their rents. And there was a new activism on the nation's campuses, where keeping America out of war was the students' favorite cause. But no movement had more impact than a San Francisco strike in 1934.

Until that year corruption was rife on the nation's waterfronts, for it was customary for longshore workers to bribe their bosses to get a day's work. But on May 9, 1934, a rank-and-file group of San Francisco stevedores led by an Australian-born radical went on strike against this practice. Lined up against Harry Bridges and his supporters was the combined might of Northern California's business classes and the police forces of the entire region. But the strikers were still able to shut down the waterfront. In response, the shipowners hired "scab" workers—including members of Cal Berkeley's football team—to unload the ships lined up along the Embarcadero. The strikers then set up barricades, and in pitched battles with the strikebreakers, two of their number were killed by the police. That prompted Bridges to call a "general strike." As a result, workers in other industries in San Francisco and Oakland left their jobs in support.

During the 1933–34 academic year, political science professor David Barrows was lecturing at the University of Berlin. But he cut short his classes in order to return to California to run for governor in the 1934 Republican primary. Barrows never did enter the race because he was also the head of the National Guard for the entire Western region. Instead of pursuing his personal ambitions, the general put patriotism first, and proceeded to suppress the General Strike.

For Barrows, Harry Bridges and his followers were part of a larger communist conspiracy. As he would write in his memoirs twenty years later, the 1934 strike was the "prelude for a Communist overthrow of the government," for the Reds behind Bridges were intending to seize all public buildings, paralyze lines of communication, and stop all public services, as well as the movement of goods and people. But here the general was distorting history, for Bridges took pains to allow the transport of vital necessities such as food and milk during the General Strike.[31]

While former president Barrows was responsible for the *military* crackdown, another University of California leader would play the crucial *political* role in ending the uprising.

As a former journalist, John Francis Neylan retained close ties with the press. So as soon as the General Strike began, he called a meeting of Bay Area publishers and got them to agree to cover it in such a way that that public support for the workers evaporated.[32] The regent then called a meeting of the shipowners and chastised them for their long neglect of the workers' legitimate grievances. And he bullied them into accepting government mediation, which led to an acceptable settlement.[33]

The San Francisco General Strike was only one of many labor conflicts that racked the nation in 1934. But lasting two months, it was the longest and the most widespread. The labor unrest of the mid-1930s awakened America's working class and led to a new labor federation, the progressive Congress of Industrial Organizations, which would unionize unorganized workers in mass production industries such as steel, automobile manufacturing, and rubber.

These militant movements frightened many of America's college administrators, who took action against student radicals in response. Nowhere was the impact as profound as it was at the University of California, where the after-shocks from the 1934 General Strike would reverberate for decades.

On July 23, 1934, less than a week after the strike had been broken, Sproul and Berkeley provost Monroe Deutsch, with the encouragement of Sproul's fishing buddy Earl Warren, then the district attorney of Berkeley and Oak-land's Alameda County, began gathering secret intelligence on Left-wing students. A network of informers was organized that included the sheriffs and district attorneys of several counties, the police chiefs of four cities, and the commanders of three American Legion posts, as well as the head of California's National Guard, Major General Barrows.[34]

Deutsch and Sproul made it clear that there was no place for radicals on the Berkeley campus. The provost would call students into his office, ask them about their political affiliations, and, after being given noncommittal answers, spring on the unsuspecting victims the facts of their organizational ties in an effort to intimidate them from future activity.[35]

But if Deutsch was Sproul's point man for dealing with student radicals, it was Joel Hildebrand who made sure that the faculty would be free of subversive influence.[36] Hildebrand was as popular with his colleagues as he was with his chemistry students; many had wanted him named president instead of Sproul. Having taught at Berkeley since 1913, he had participated in the Faculty Revolution and was equally devoted to the Academic Senate and the administration, which he had served in important positions.

It was the General Strike that spurred Hildebrand to draft University Regulation 5. At a Senate meeting on August 27, 1934, Sproul read the statement as an announcement of "Free Speech," and it was accepted without dissent.[37]

Although the document was called "academic freedom," its purpose was to establish the principle of a contradiction between that value and membership in the Communist Party. Because Hildebrand believed that communists adhered slavishly to a rigid dogma, he felt that they lacked the objectivity to teach and to do research, and should therefore be barred from the university.

Assuming a posture of sweet reason, the Hildebrand-Sproul declaration stated that radicals on the Left and reactionaries on the Right each threatened the university. Based on the unquestioned assumption that objective truth exists—unaffected by social structures, economic interests, or historical change—the document warned in somber terms of the dangers to the university from those who lack scientific objectivity and would use the classroom to convert. After asserting the institution's prerogative to eliminate such professors, the president told the Academic Senate that "The University of California is the creature of the State and its loyalty to the State will never waver. It will not aid nor will it condone actions contrary to the laws of the State."[38]

As Michael Otten emphasizes, Regulation 5 restricted students as much or more as it did the faculty. They could no longer invite anyone who might be suspected of having communist ties to speak on campus.[39]

President Sproul elaborated on the philosophy underlying Regulation 5 in an article published two years later in the influential educational journal *School and Society*. University professors, he argued, "can never be quite as free in speech and action as many other men for they cannot enjoy the license of speaking without investigation." And in an oblique reference to radical students and invited speakers, he emphasized that it was the duty of college presidents "to silence those engaged in spreading the poison gas of class warfare." For society, in his view, cannot long tolerate those "who give aid and comfort to enemies seeking its destruction."[40]

IF ERNEST MOORE WAS SO THREATENED by the relatively few radical students during the conservative 1920s, he would become almost unhinged in response to the movements of the 1930s. UCLA's provost saw student radicalism as part and parcel of the coming communist revolution. And two 1934 events convinced him that the long-feared revolution was at hand. The first was the strike in San Francisco, the second was the likelihood that an avowed socialist would be elected governor of California.

In May 1934, during the early stages of the waterfront strike, Provost Moore told President Sproul that the goal of student radicals was to destroy the university by making the public believe that Berkeley and UCLA were training young people to overthrow the government. They had calculated that good citizens would then refuse to pay taxes to support the institution, with the result that the university would be destroyed. "*The class war is on*," he wrote his boss, and we should "*make battle plans*" to defeat it.[41] And when the conflict escalated into the General Strike, he wrote that "The Revolution . . . ought to be put down definitely, for a general strike is civil war—a form of defiance which does not belong in a civilized society."[42]

The big strike was followed by another radical *cause celebre,* Upton Sinclair's quest to become governor. The socialist writer's campaign was part of a broader movement known as EPIC (for End Poverty in California). For Moore, the possibility that a socialist would be elected, which seemed likely in mid-summer 1934, was the last straw. Feeling that the situation was desperate, he refused to allow UCLA's student-run open forum to sponsor a debate between the election candidates.[43] He was concerned that one of the forum's leaders was UCLA's most prominent radical, Celeste Strack. The undergraduate had already achieved fame as a woman's intercollegiate debating champion; years later she would become an official of the Communist Party in California.

In 1934 Strack was a leader of the National Student League, a group close to the Communist Party, and a thorn in Moore's side. Once on observing her talking to a group of students, he had ordered her to stop her harangue, stating, "You cannot hold a communist meeting here, Miss Strack." He had then called her into his office and warned her against causing the kind of trouble at UCLA that she recently had caused at USC.[44]

When classes resumed for the fall semester, Provost Moore decided that "a radical housecleaning" was needed to forestall revolution at UCLA. To carry out this plan he decided to go after the student forum. Except for Strack, the panel's leaders were liberals, including the student body president, who simply wanted the freedom to debate all issues without restriction.

But Moore, who had already vetoed a debate on communism between Berkeley and UCLA students, ordered them to cease agitating for their forum. When they refused, he suspended five leaders, charging that they were destroying the university by turning it into "a hotbed of communism."[45]

Moore's impolitic move ignited the campus, bringing about a student strike for the reinstatement of the suspended five. To quash a growing movement, the provost approved the formation of a committee of 150 students, predominantly athletes, "to purge the campus of student radicals."[46] But it was to no avail, for the reactions to his actions, according to historian Robert Cohen, led to the single most successful free speech fight at a university during the 1930s. Moore's actions were so indefensible that he became an embarrassment to the university. Forced to fly south to investigate, President Sproul lifted the suspensions of the four liberals among the group. He had wanted to exonerate all five, but Moore insisted that Strack remain punished. The campus Red would be reinstated later, because there was no evidence she had broken any university rules.

It is not clear whether Sproul forced Moore's 1936 resignation, but instead of naming a new provost, the president moved to Los Angeles for several months so that he could devote his full attention to the problems of the Westwood campus.[47]

THE 1934 GENERAL STRIKE radicalized many of Berkeley's students also. A long-standing concern of these activists had been the plight of migrant workers. Decades before Cesar Chavez and his United Farm Workers, agricultural laborers had gone on strike in the Central Valley, and college students had rallied to their support. The Board of Regents included rich farmers, as well as other representatives of institutions such as the Bank of America, which financed agro-business. They had encouraged hiring undergraduates as strikebreakers in labor conflicts, which led the National Student League to publish a "shame list" of Berkeley students who had worked as scabs.

The big strike cast a long shadow. A question in the final exam for the 1936 course in the Reserve Officers' Training Corps program asked how students would deploy the ROTC and the National Guard to put down future labor insurrections. Once exposed, the exams were changed, and radicals redoubled their efforts to make military training voluntary rather than compulsory. It would be years before they succeeded, but they did win a major victory when they forced local businesses that hired students to pay a minimum wage of 40 cents an hour, considerably higher than the prevailing standard.[48]

Robert Gordon Sproul never hesitated to crack down on radical students. He disciplined the editors of the student newspaper for supporting striking migrant workers, as well as other causes he felt were beyond its jurisdiction. And yet the Hearst press began calling for his ouster in the late 1930s. Sproul was blamed for the sizeable communist presence at Berkeley and UCLA, and because he favored a free speech policy, he was seen as too lenient in handling student radicals.[49]

Since Neylan was still writing editorials for California's Hearst papers, and remained one of the publisher's main advisors, one has to assume that the

Right-wing regent was troubled by the president's "liberalism." This may have been the beginning of the rift between the two men, a falling out that would prove critical during the Loyalty Oath crisis.[50]

Two of Berkeley's most dedicated student activists were Kenneth May and Gordon Griffiths. Close friends from high school, they entered Cal together in 1932 and were radicalized two years later by the General Strike. In their senior year they each joined the American Student Union.[51]

Ken's father was a Berkeley political science professor. Samuel May took pride in his son's accomplishments as a brilliant math student, a highly ranked tennis star, and a varsity soccer player.[52] But when Ken became more and more public about his politics, his conservative father, worried about his own reputation as much as his son's future, disowned him.

Gordon Griffiths also had a father problem. Farnham Griffiths was a lawyer who served on the Board of Regents and whose clients included San Francisco's biggest shipowners. This put father and son on the opposite sides of the barricades in 1934. Even more troubling to Gordon was the fact that his dad, a major figure in the Bohemian Club, justified the group's exclusion of Jews as members.[53]

When Ken May invited him to become a member of the Communist Party, he was enthusiastic, since he was convinced that communism was "the only solution to the crisis of capitalism," a system "that rested on imperialism and led to war."[54] But unlike his pal, the shy, introverted Griffiths did not have the courage to openly defy his father. There was no way that he could become a radical activist while living at home. But Farnham unwittingly provided the solution to his son's dilemma when he offered to pay for his postgraduate study at Oxford.

In England Gordon marched on behalf of the unemployed, fell in love with his "date" for the event, and then married. Mary Jeffery was a communist, but she quit the British party when Stalin signed his nonaggression pact with Hitler in 1939. She could not go along with the idea that imperialist Britain was as much an enemy of progressive humanity as Nazi Germany and

Fascist Italy. Gordon, on the other hand, felt that Stalin and the world communist movement must know what they were doing.

When they returned to America in 1939, it would be May who would solve the dilemma that Mary had created. Gordon wanted to be a party member, but his wife, fearing that she might be deported to England—much like the government was trying to send Harry Bridges back to Australia—didn't want him involved. So Ken proposed that Gordon could be the conduit between the party and a secret cell of Berkeley professors who met regularly as a group purportedly devoted to the discussion of current affairs. Griffiths would bring them Marxist literature and collect dues and occasional pamphlets that they produced to educate the Berkeley faculty on the issues of the day.[55]

Although the membership of this professional party unit would fluctuate, it consisted of three Berkeley faculty members when Griffiths began his assignment. One was Arthur Brodeur, a scholar of Scandinavian languages in the English Department. The second was the most conspicuous Left-wing professor at Berkeley, Haakon Chevalier, an assistant professor of French. Chevalier had been transformed from a radical bohemian intellectual into a committed communist by the Left's number one cause during the late 1930s, the Spanish Civil War. The fight against fascism in Spain would also mobilize the cell's third member. Recruited by Chevalier, he was J. Robert Oppenheimer, the nation's leading theoretical physicist.

Griffiths makes it clear that none of the members actually held party cards and that Oppenheimer made donations to the cause rather than pay dues as the others did. So it is possible that the physicist may have been ideologically committed to communism without having been an actual party member. This is the conclusion that Oppenheimer's biographers, Kai Bird and Martin Sherwin, came to in their *American Prometheus*.[56]

DURING THE MID-1930S the Communist International announced a major change in strategy. All Communist Parties were ordered to stop fighting socialists and other Leftists, a policy that had led to disaster in pre-Hitler Germany. Instead they would join with them in coalitions to stop fascism. In France this "Popular Front" strategy led to the election of the socialist Leon Blum as prime minister in 1936. But nowhere was it as successful as in Spain, where that year a Republican government based on a coalition of socialists, communists, anarchists, and Basque and Catalan separatists was elected.

Almost immediately, the military, led by General Francisco Franco, the head of the Nationalist Party who was supported by monarchists and other Right-wing elements, rose up in revolt. Money and weapons poured in from Hitler and Mussolini, but the democratic nations of the West, including the United States, refused to help the Spanish Republic.

Instead, aid came from an unprecedented outpouring of anti-fascist solidarity.[57] By 1937 communists and other Leftists, some of whom had been pacifists, were putting on uniforms and learning to shoot rifles and machine guns, as they prepared to fight for the beleaguered Republic. These regiments of the International Brigade played a big part in the defense of Madrid and Barcelona, and many of its soldiers would lose their lives in Spain before the Republican armies surrendered in 1939. Franco's fascist dictatorship would last for thirty-six years.

The defense of the Spanish Republic would be seen as the most noble cause in the history of the international Left, inspiring a generation of radicals with its romance of proletarian solidarity. The conflict also polarized politically conscious Americans. In Berkeley it rekindled the martial spirit of an old soldier, the same Major General Barrows who had put down San Francisco's General Strike. Barrows considered resigning his university position and moving his wife and family to Spain, because he wanted to add his "own small efforts to the struggle to overcome the Communist Conspiracy which was rife in that country."[58] He would remain in Berkeley, but his willingness to come to the aid of a fascist regime because the government it was fighting included communists speaks volumes to his political priorities.

Oppenheimer, on the other hand, raised money to support the Republican cause. At one point he used a blackboard at Berkeley's Radiation Laboratory to invite staff members to a Spanish War Relief benefit. Even though Ernest Lawrence, the Rad Lab's director, was a good friend, he erased the invitation in disgust. Like Oppenheimer, Lawrence was another of physics' "boy geniuses"; in 1939 he would become the first Berkeley professor to win a Nobel prize. But he believed that scientists shouldn't get involved in politics.[59]

Oppenheimer had a prodigious intellect and an insatiable appetite for knowledge. Becoming interested in Marxism, he was said to have read all three volumes of *Das Kapital* in German during a three-day train ride. Then came the *Complete Works of Lenin,* followed by a realization that it was necessary to act and not just read about the world's problems. When Chevalier learned of this, he set up the "study group" that was the cover for the professional unit of the Communist Party.

The group had two purposes: first, to raise the members' understanding of Marxism, and second, to raise the political consciousness of Berkeley's faculty. Oppenheimer was the educational leader, for his knowledge of Marxism dwarfed even party leaders such as Steve Nelson, who was amazed at how much he had read.

But "Oppie," as he was called, also led the work related to the "mass organizations" the unit was oriented to, the teachers' union on campus (which he and Chevalier had helped organize), and the faculty itself. On at least two occasions the group discussed an issue in order to arrive at a position they could present in a pamphlet. And each "Report to Our Colleagues" was drafted and edited by Oppenheimer. The first, circulated early in 1940, was a justification of the USSR's invasion of Finland. Later in the same year, the second of the reports that are still extant—there may have been more—castigated FDR as a "counterrevolutionary warmonger" and called for America to stay out of Europe's war. Signed "College Faculties Committee, Communist Party of California" the reports were printed on bond paper, an expense presumably financed by Oppenheimer, who had inherited a considerable fortune.[60]

THE FIRING OF KEN MAY AND A
NO RED PROFESSORS POLICY

During the time when Gordon Griffiths was studying in England, his friend Kenneth May made two trips to the Soviet Union. Continuing his rise within the party, by 1940 he had become its number one organizer in Oakland.

May went public about his politics in 1940, when anticommunist feelings were especially strong. The Soviet Union had signed its nonaggression treaty with Nazi Germany a year earlier, and the Red Army had also invaded its smaller, weaker neighbor, Finland.

Closer to home, the university was under attack as "a center of communist propaganda and general subversive activities." With comptroller Jim Corley warning that the legislature might withhold funds from its budget, the administration felt it had to crack down. The first victim was the American Student Union, which lost its status as a recognized campus organization.[61] The second would be Ken May.

In September 1940, May identified himself as a communist in two letters to the *Daily Californian*. In one he urged students "to resist those who are preparing the University for participation in World War II," and in a second explained that he had become a communist because the party had fought consistently for the interests of students.[62]

As a result, Samuel May disinherited his son. Then the Mathematics Department fired him from his teaching assistant job, charging that he was using the university "as a platform for propaganda," rather than devoting his energies to teaching.[63] At their October meeting the Board of Regents took up the matter.

According to Neylan, Sproul wanted to dismiss May without a hearing. The president was under pressure to demonstrate that he was tough on student radicals. But Neylan's anticommunism was not in doubt, so he stood up for May, asking why "the boy" was being given only thirty minutes to defend himself. But even so, Neylan reports that May still "demolished" the charges made against him, except for being a party member, which he freely admitted, and using his party affiliation on university letterhead.[64]

After May was officially fired, the board put into place a policy against hiring communists, arguing that the party "gives its first loyalty to a foreign political movement," and takes advantage of young people who are both idealist and immature. Thus "membership in the Communist Party is incompatible with membership in the faculty of a State University."[65]

Neylan cast one of the two votes against the new policy. His position didn't reflect any lack of commitment to the anticommunist cause. May in his view was the tip of the iceberg. There were many communists, not just among teaching assistants, but on the regular faculty as well. But the regent didn't think the new policy would have the result the board was looking for. And he liked to play the role of a maverick courageous enough to go against the crowd.

RECALLING THE LANGUAGE in Regulation 5 that the university was just as threatened by reactionaries of the Right, it is telling that no policy was put into place against fascists. For it was a time when the military and political successes of their regimes were threatening the West's most cherished values and its very existence. Of course Right-wing reactionaries were well represented on the Board of Regents and had allies within the administration.[66]

CHAPTER 3

FROM WORLD WAR
TO COLD WAR

Those who do not believe in the ideology of the United States shall not be allowed to stay in the United States.

—Attorney General Tom Clark[1]

T HE DEBATE DURING THE OATH CRISIS WOULD be framed by three precedents. One was the regents' 1940 policy against the employment of communists on the faculty. An earlier one was 1934's Regulation 5, which posited a contradiction between Red professors and academic freedom. The third benchmark was added in 1942. As a result of the patriotic fervor of wartime, the state assembly passed a bill requiring all employees to sign an oath of allegiance to the constitutions of California and the United States.[2]

Unlike Regulation 5 and the 1940 regents' policy, the Constitutional Oath, as it was called, did not target communists, nor did it mention subversion or even political parties. It was an oath to which few could object, and it would in time become routine. No one could have imagined how prominently it would figure seven years later when President Sproul recommended that the regents amend it to include a clause on subversive activities.

The outbreak of war, after Japan's attack on Pearl Harbor on December 7, 1941, transformed the university. Many male undergraduates, and even some young professors, were drafted. The student body would have become largely female, had it not been for the hundreds of soldiers sent to campus to prepare for overseas assignments. Military units, in full uniform, marched to their classes, "hip-hupping all the way," according to eyewitness Robert Nisbet.

In addition, every student was required to take a war-related course each semester. That could mean ROTC or physical education, but there was also an "America at War" class and others such as German History or American Nationalism. Nisbet, an assistant professor of social institutions before being drafted to fight in the Pacific, thought that Berkeley was much like the U.S. Military Academy at West Point.[3]

Once the country was at war, scientific research exploded on campus, especially work with military implications. As funds from the federal government poured into the university, the war would speed up another transformation. The University of California, in its first seventy-five years a teaching institution, would now be dominated by research.

The war unified a divided nation. Two unlikely bedfellows, David Barrows and Kenneth May, reflected this at Berkeley. Both the reactionary general and the young radical rallied to the defense of the nation.

Like the majority of the faculty, Barrows was at first against America's involvement in "Europe's war." Because England and France were imperialist powers with colonial empires, there had been little sympathy for them when the war began in 1939. In 1940, after the Battle of Britain and the Fall of France, this opposition softened, but support for intervention became widespread only after the Japanese bombings in December 1941.[4]

Barrows had his change of heart when France fell to the Nazis in May 1940. After Pearl Harbor, the old soldier offered his services to the secretary of war as a consultant and served as the West Coast director of military intelligence.

With the Soviet Union threatened by Hitler's armies, the Communist Party viewed the war as the critical battlefront against fascism. Ken May joined the Army and served with such distinction that his father was moved to reconcile with him.

For his pal Gordon Griffiths, the turning point was June 22, 1941, the day the Nazis invaded Soviet Russia. It was a relief to no longer have to justify the

Hitler-Stalin pact. But not for long, for during the early stages of the invasion, Germany moved almost effortlessly through Russian territory. Then as the Soviets dug in and heroically defended Leningrad and Stalingrad—as no other nation invaded by the Nazis had done—Gordon would see the Russian resistance as another sign of the superiority of the socialist system.[5]

By 1942 Griffiths had completed a Ph.D. in diplomatic and military history, focusing on Napoleon's Adriatic policy. Instead of arguing politics with his professors as he had at Oxford, he buckled down and earned a doctorate in three years. Then he worked as an electrician's helper at Oakland's Todd Shipyards, one of the many facilities that had been established to build and repair naval vessels for the war. While waiting to be drafted, he considered "going into the labor movement," as many of his comrades were doing. But instead of becoming an industrial worker or a soldier, he decided to do war-related work with the Board of Economic Warfare.[6]

In Washington, D.C., Griffiths joined a Communist Party branch of government employees that integrated the cafeteria at the Department of Commerce, which long had seated black workers at separate tables. They were not successful in desegregating the city's segregated swimming pools, but they did help African-American women get better jobs and promotions.[7]

The secret party group last met in the fall of 1942. Their conduit, Gordon Griffiths, was in Washington; Arthur Brodeur was in the army; and Robert Oppenheimer was spending more and more of his time attending meetings in the East and in New Mexico, involved in the top-secret Manhattan Project that would culminate in the atomic bombs unleashed on Hiroshima and Nagasaki. As a condition for this new employment, "Oppie" had to drop his contacts with communists. Though he moved to the right politically, he continued to see his old friend Haakon Chevalier on his trips to Berkeley, who was the only member of the now defunct cell still teaching at the university.

SPROUL AND NEYLAN: THE RIFT WIDENS

The war may have unified the nation, but it only aggravated the emerging rift between Neylan and Sproul. During the 1930s and early 1940s, when the regent was affiliating with extreme Right-wing groups, Sproul's free-speech policy at the university had troubled him. And then the Japanese-American question became a bone of contention between them.

Early in 1942 the military command of the Western region ordered that all Americans of Japanese descent be rounded up and sent to relocation camps. In California the order was carried out, without protest, by Attorney General Earl Warren. This pained his friend Sproul, who would be one of the few prominent Californians to speak out against the internment. The president had developed close relations with his Japanese-American faculty members, and he went out of his way to help them. As an example, he stored art professor Chiura Obata's furniture at his house during the war.[8]

The hysteria toward Japan and people of Japanese descent was so intense that only one daily paper in California spoke out against the internment, and that was UCLA's student paper, the *Daily Bruin*.[9] To Neylan, the attitude of Sproul, the *Bruin,* and others like the *Nation's* editor Carey McWilliams who believed that the Japanese-American population did not harbor spies was naïve "bleeding-heart" liberalism. Neylan, who like his boss Hearst and other isolationists had opposed American intervention in "Europe's War," had long believed that the key to the nation's defense lay in the Pacific basin, where Japan loomed as the big threat to U.S. security. And who were more likely to become a "fifth column" of spies and saboteurs for Japan than California's Isseis and Niseis?[10]

The regent could tolerate this difference, but another action of his friend's would be unforgivable. It took place during the spring of 1945, as the United States emerged from the decisive but deadly Battle of the Bulge, the war in Europe all but won. With the goal of positioning themselves for the postwar period, American and Russian troops were each trying to conquer as much territory as possible in Germany and Eastern Europe.

At this moment Soviet foreign minister V. M. Molotov was in San Francisco for the organizational meetings of the United Nations. Why not ask him to cross the Bay to receive an honorary degree at Berkeley's June graduation ceremonies? To Sproul this seemed like a good idea, but not to Neylan. "If it is a gesture of appeasement," the regent wrote his friend, "It is both unworthy of a great university and obviously futile."[11] Sproul thought better of the matter, but his intention to award the degree only confirmed Neylan's feeling that he was becoming "soft on communism."[12]

The president's action gave the regent more leverage over him, and the man who would suffer was Haakon Chevalier. The French teacher had languished for almost two decades in nontenured positions, despite an important book on Anatole France, translations of André Malraux, and a record of distinguished service as a translator at the founding meetings of the United Nations. Haakon's promotion to associate professor was long overdue, so in 1945 he received unanimous recommendations for tenure from the French Department, the Budget Committee, and Provost Monroe Deutsch.

Neylan knew about Oppenheimer's politics, the questions about his loyalty, and his friendship with Chevalier. So it seems likely that he took advantage of Sproul's vulnerability on the issue of subversion and persuaded him to veto the favorable promotion recommendation. The president wrote in his office diary that "I expressed my opinion that Chevalier will never be a great scholar, and it would be better if he went somewhere else."[13]

And the regent would prove more prescient than the president with respect to the future of American-Soviet relations. Some historians believe that the atomic bombings in August 1945 were aimed at Russia as much as Japan, although this remains a minority view.[14] But there can be little doubt that the American attitude toward Soviet Russia hardened after Truman replaced Roosevelt and the war ended.

Russia played its part, tightening its grip on the East European nations it had liberated and directing the international communist movement to replace the Popular Front strategy of the late 1930s with a hardline stance. An early manifestation of this change was an open letter from the French party leader Jacques Duclos to the American Communist Party. Acting for the Communist International, he attacked America's top Red Earl Browder for "Right-wing revisionism." Browder had called communism "20th Century Americanism," and it was his undogmatic policies that had made possible the alliances between communists and liberals during the 1930s and 1940s. Yet he had also coordinated a network of American communist spies whose classified information he transmitted to Russia![15]

Gordon Griffiths had appreciated the openness of Browder's leadership during the Popular Front era, and he was not happy about his ouster. The Soviet Union's aggressive posturing also disquieted him. In his view America was most to blame for Cold War tensions, but he couldn't deny the USSR's contributions to the problem. So Griffiths decided not to rejoin the Communist Party when he returned to the United States in 1946 to begin his teaching career at a small college (Farragut) in Idaho.[16]

ON MARCH 5 1946, Winston Churchill, Britain's wartime prime minister, came to America and delivered a speech that for decades would reverberate on the relations between the United States and the Soviet Union, and immediately influence American politics.

In Fulton, Missouri, Churchill told the world that an "Iron Curtain" had descended across Europe and that the communists had established "fifth columns" intent on subverting democratic governments. The speech provided ammunition to America's Right wing. That June the head of the Republican Party stated that the coming midterm elections "would offer a stark choice between Communism and Republicanism," for the top policymakers of the Democratic Party "were committed to the Soviet Union." That the Democrats were "soft on communism" became the GOP's battle cry. The party also attacked Truman and labor for the postwar inflation, which enabled it to capture the House and the Senate that year.[17]

Looking ahead to the 1948 elections, Truman moved sharply to the Right, hoping to defuse the "soft on communism" issue. On March 12, 1947, he announced his "Truman Doctrine": the United States would stop further communist expansion by providing arms and economic aid to endangered nations. The immediate threat was a communist-led guerrilla movement in Greece, which was on the way to winning a civil war.[18]

Moving swiftly on the domestic front, only nine days later the president issued Executive Order 9835 barring communists from federal employment. The head of the board set up to investigate employees suspected of being security risks was selected by J. Edgar Hoover, the director of the FBI and the nation's most fervent anticommunist. Within a year more than three thousand workers would be fired or would choose to resign, and in many cases the accused were never told what they had been charged with or who had questioned their loyalty.[19] Historian Alonzo Hamby called the workings of the board "Kafkaesque," its actions "capricious."[20]

THE 1947–48 TURNING POINT

In the year following Truman's March 1947 initiatives, a major change would take place in public opinion. Until the Truman Doctrine, Americans were skeptical of "internationalism," preferring to concentrate on domestic problems. A majority still believed that the country could coexist peacefully with the Soviet Union, and the Communist Party remained a legal (indeed legitimate) organization. Although it no longer had the prestige and numbers it had during the war, it was not yet seen as a subversive element, the tool of a foreign power, or a cancer in the body politic. True, ex-Reds such as Elizabeth Bentley and Whittaker Chambers had defected, but their claims that Communist Party members routinely spied for the Soviet Union had not been widely publicized.

Four events that took place in 1947 suggest the sea change rocking the nation at this time.

Early in the year Congress passed the Taft-Hartley Act. Much less favorable to organized labor than the Depression-era Wagner Act, the new legislation included a clause requiring union officials to swear that they weren't communists.[21] Although Truman vetoed Taft-Hartley, Congress passed it into law. In August, L.A. County's Board of Supervisors established a loyalty oath for all its employees.[22] Two months later the House Committee on Un-American Activities began investigating subversion in the film industry. Finally, in November, Attorney General Tom Clark published a list of ninety-three organizations he labeled subversive. It included a wide variety of communist front groups, many of which were long defunct, and would be an important tool in the arsenal of the witch hunters for years to come.

In February 1948 Cold War tensions were aggravated by a coup in Czechoslovakia that transformed a democratic government into a people's democracy firmly in the Soviet camp. Three months later relations between the United States and the USSR reached their lowest point when the Russians imposed a blockade on the western sectors of Berlin. Truman then ordered an airlift to bring food and supplies to the beleaguered metropolis. That summer a majority of Americans believed World War III was imminent.[23] Bomb shelters were refurbished and new ones were built. But how could such precautions stave off the unthinkable destruction of a war in which the Soviet Union would deploy the atomic bombs it had recently tested?

Although Truman had ushered it in, the anticommunist movement would be pushed most aggressively by Congress. The House Committee on Un-American Activities (HUAC) had been established in 1938 to investigate domestic subversion. Although its original mission encompassed native fascist organizations as well as communism, it concerned itself almost exclusively with Left-wing radicals. In 1947 its first important target would be the film industry.

HUAC's alleged purpose was to gather information on subversive activities in particular organizations and social worlds. But its hearings were actually rituals of degradation in which witnesses were exposed and shamed into naming their Left-wing associates. Those who "named names" were called "friendly witnesses." Most people refused to do this. Such "unfriendly witnesses" gained legal protection by invoking the Constitution's Fifth Amendment, with its safeguard against "self-incrimination."

The "Fifth Amendment communists" faced a problem. They could not discuss their own politics without being forced to answer questions about their associations and those of others. To the average American they were "hiding behind the Constitution."[24]

There were also Un-American Activities committees in the legislatures of many states, such as Jack Tenney's in California, and these "Little HUACS" as they were called were often more aggressive in hunting subversives than their parent body in the House of Representatives.

THE COLD WAR AND THE UNIVERSITIES

The transformation of America's universities from teaching to research institutions accelerated during the early Cold War period. With national security concerns prominent, the University of California received more than its share of government grants. A new type emerged in the academic world, the professor as entrepreneur and fundraiser. And higher enrollments, sparked by returning veterans on the GI Bill, meant that more faculty members were needed. In a booming post–World War II America, the salaries of professors rose sharply, especially for the new stars.[25] Like baseball players traded from team to team, big-name professors moved from Harvard to Berkeley to Columbia, augmenting their salaries and research budgets in the process.

In this same period, burgeoning anticommunism led to political repression on a number of the nation's campuses.

The first mass firing of a college faculty in the postwar era had occurred in 1946.[26] It received little publicity because few people knew of tiny Olivet College, a Christian school in central Michigan. The story began when a new president terminated a political science professor without a hearing or the filing of charges, and a few months later fired five others who had protested the original dismissal and had been active in the campus teachers' union. One hundred and forty students pledged that they would not return to school, and by the following fall Olivet had lost half its enrollment. Even more remarkably, eighteen of the school's thirty-five faculty members resigned in protest.[27]

The Olivet events took place before anticommunism had become institutionalized and mass hysteria would stifle dissent. Perhaps that's why there would not be such a demonstration of civic courage in higher education during the McCarthy era. But Olivet set the precedent of firing professors who were Leftist or otherwise noncomformist. Although there were a number of honorable exceptions, among whom Chicago's Robert Hutchins stands out, university presidents more often cooperated with repression than they protested threats to academic freedom.

The incident that most affected the University of California took place in the Pacific Northwest. The state of Washington, with a history of labor radicalism (for example a thriving Industrial Workers of the World movement early in the 20th century), had a "Little HUAC" that was especially sensitive to the threat of subversion. In 1948 this "Canwell Committee" claimed that the University of Washington housed 150 professors who were Communist Party members or sympathizers. That July eleven were called to testify. Several admitted past membership in the party and identified others as communists. Two months later a dean accused the six who had refused to cooperate with the committee of "present or past membership in the Communist Party," and recommended their dismissal. A trial was conducted by the faculty's Committee on Tenure and Academic Freedom that lasted several days and produced three thousand pages of testimony. They voted 8 to 3 to exonerate all of the accused.[28]

But Washington's president, Raymond Allen, recommended that three men (psychologist Ralph Grundlach, English professor Joseph Butterworth, and the philosopher Herbert Phillips) be terminated, and they were dismissed by the school's Board of Regents in January of 1949. None would hold an academic position again. Phillips, who would play a special role in the events that precipitated California's Loyalty Oath, became an unskilled laborer.[29]

A few days later the president of Oregon State refused to renew the contracts of two professors who had supported Progressive Party candidate Henry Wallace in 1948.[30] Linus Pauling, the school's most famous alumnus, came to their defense, rebuking the president and calling for their reinstatement.

But it was the Washington case that was most important for California. It established the precedent that a board of regents could fire faculty members for membership in the Communist Party, regardless of any specific wrongdoing.[31]

THE COMMUNISM ARGUMENT AT BERKELEY

Although the politics of Berkeley's faculty remained moderate to conservative in the period before the oath, its liberal minority included many respected professors. One was Edward Strong, a philosopher who had testified on behalf of Phillips when the latter's dismissal hearings were taking place. In Seattle he had argued that the Marxist philosopher was a serious scholar who should not be fired for his political beliefs or affiliations. Then in a speech to Berkeley Engineering majors, Strong charged that the dismissals, based on guilt by association, set a dangerous precedent. Phillips and his colleagues were accused of thinking "naughty thoughts," but dangerous thoughts like those of Socrates and Christ, he added, often turn out to be true.[32]

With a commitment to civil liberties and world peace, Strong was a charter member of the Union of Concerned Scientists.[33] The philosopher was no communist sympathizer, but he was a man of the Left who taught a philosophy of history course that gave serious attention to Marx, in addition to his specialty, Dewey and the American pragmatists.

Towering over his colleagues at six feet six inches, Ed Strong was a natural leader and also well rounded for an academic man. He wrote poetry, was an accomplished outdoorsman, and was so good with tools and machinery that during World War II he had taken leave from teaching to manage the technical operations at the Radiation Laboratory. The lab's director, Ernest Lawrence, had become rich after receiving the Nobel Prize, so he was able to loan Strong the money for a new home, which the philosopher built with his own hands.[34]

Strong was also a member of the Berkeley chapter of the American Association of University Professors. In 1947 the AAUP's Committee A on Academic Freedom had issued a statement that argued that communist professors should be dismissed only for specific acts, or professional unfitness, and not simply because they were communists.[35] The AAUP position would become another benchmark that would frame the debate over the Loyalty Oath, dividing the faculty for the next three years. And it would put Strong in direct conflict with Joel Hildebrand.

Hildebrand had written Regulation 5, the university's first anticommunist statement, in 1934. Fifteen years later he again became the point man in the fight against subversion. In the late winter of 1949, during the two months before the oath was proposed, the chemist embarked on an all out campaign against the AAUP and his liberal colleagues who supported the organization's position.

First he wrote the AAUP, hoping to dissuade it from censuring Washington and Oregon State for violating academic freedom. Failing in that effort, he turned his attention to the group's supporters at Berkeley, for it disturbed him that so many of his colleagues were justifying the right of party members to teach.

At this time Hildebrand was a leader of the Senate's Advisory Committee as well as Sproul's close friend. Thus he was the most important influence on the president in the period before the adoption of the oath.

Edward Strong defended the AAUP position in a series of letters exchanged with Hildebrand in which he argued that barring communists because they were communists was bad logic, a reliance on *a priori* reasoning. We can't assume, the philosopher wrote, that every individual member of the Communist Party "jeopardized and sacrificed his integrity of thought." To fire someone, proof is needed. "The worst tyranny of our times," Strong continued, "was that which condemned individual citizens in Germany of guilt by race and executed Jews because they were Jews."[36]

In his letters to colleagues, Hildebrand liked to quote Thomas Jefferson to underscore his commitment to "eternal hostility against every form of tyranny." Strong used his own words against him: "In our eternal hostility against every form of tyranny must we not be ever vigilant not to condemn communists because they are communists, but only as individuals, in what they have done or failed to do in an area of obligation?"[37]

Other faculty liberals offered similar arguments. English professor James Caldwell warned Hildebrand against using a political test to exclude a suspected communist from teaching. In his view, such exclusion, were it ever justified, should be on intellectual grounds. And Caldwell went even further, saying that "if we could find a Communist whose intellectual power, personal integrity, and stability would be clearly established, we should joyfully have him teach a course on Communism."[38]

Hildebrand countered Caldwell with the argument that the communist professor has already abandoned his intellectual freedom because "Communism itself is an intellectual tyranny which makes it impossible for a real university to function."[39] Two weeks later he argued with David Rynin of the Speech Department. Rynin's point was that nothing prevented communists from being accomplished scholars in fields that were untainted by political ideology, citing Sanskrit as an example. Since in Hildebrand's view Soviet communism's "stranglehold" on intellectual freedom was even more powerful than that of Nazi Germany, the party would find a way to impose its orthodoxy in Sanskrit also.

The economist Carl Landauer, who had served as a Social Democratic representative in the Reichstag before Hitler came to power, warned Hildebrand of another danger. If communists are banned by a political test, this would set a precedent for excluding others, as had happened to him and his socialist comrades in Germany.

Hildebrand packaged his ideas in a letter to the *Bulletin* of the AAUP, hoping to influence the debate on whether communists should be allowed to teach. After receiving no reply from the magazine, he sent a brief essay on the subject to *Harpers*. When it was also slow to respond, he published it in the *Pacific Spectator,* one of the West Coast's "little magazines."[40]

In the essay Hildebrand argued that the academic profession, in its vigorous defense of its own civil liberties against outside attacks, had failed to police its ranks of professors working under the control of the international communist movement. He faulted the AAUP for misguided priorities and bewailed the fact that many of his colleagues had accepted their false premises. In closing, he again invoked Jefferson's "eternal hostility against every form of tyranny over the mind of man," and emphasized that the communist movement surpassed "the Nazis in crushing academic freedom."[41]

There is no awareness in the brief four-page essay that anticommunism could present any dangers for the academic community. Similarly, Hildebrand's letters never acknowledged the possible merit of his colleagues' arguments. Apparently his mind was made up when he entered into discussions with the faculty liberals, so he was not open to learning from them. But the essay and the letters do show how seriously this "apolitical" chemistry professor took his role in the global struggle between democracy and communism in the early years of the Cold War.[42]

A week before the Board of Regents met on March 25, Hildebrand wrote Sproul about his informal survey of faculty opinion. He emphasized the support he had received, while minimizing the opposition from AAUP supporters. He also recommended that the president republish University Regulation 5, as well as the regents' policy barring communists, so that the liberals on the faculty would be clear in their minds that the AAUP's position contradicted that of the university.[43]

Most commentators have downplayed this influence, but not John Francis Neylan, who would later refer to the Loyalty Oath as the "Hildebrand-Sproul Oath."[44]

If Hildebrand didn't respect Berkeley liberals for their position on communists, he had even less respect for colleagues who didn't live up to his scientific ideals. In the period that he was lobbying AAUP members, he went all out to stop Erik Erikson—only a few years away from becoming the world's most famous psychoanalyst—from being awarded permanent status on the faculty.

The Danish-born Erikson had been analyzed by Freud's daughter Anna, a pioneer in the psychoanalysis of children. Prescient about Hitler's impending threat to Central Europe, he left Austria in 1933, and after five years during which he worked at Harvard and Yale, he accepted a clinical research position at Berkeley's Institute for Child Welfare. During his first decade in California, he wrote the essays that would form the core of his *Childhood and Society.*

As a lecturer in the Department of Psychology and a clinical researcher, Erikson lacked the security of academic tenure. So in 1949 two Berkeley psychologists, Donald MacKinnon and Edward Tolman, pushed for him to be appointed as a regular professor.

The idea was controversial. Even among psychoanalysts Erikson stood out for his humanism, a methodology and writing style that was as much artistic and literary as scientific and empirical. That is why the Budget Committee opposed the appointment, stating that Erikson lacked "scientific responsibility" and didn't support his conclusions with "adequate data."[45] Sproul called upon Hildebrand for an evaluation. Without attempting to conceal his contempt, the chemist disparaged Erikson by stating that his lack of scientific rigor reminded him of "the phrenologists of old" and of present-day astrology![46]

Sproul was ready to quash the appointment, but pressure from MacKinnon and above all from Tolman convinced him to reverse his decision. Tolman's support of Erikson showed that he had a broader notion of intellectual creativity than the narrowly focused Hildebrand. It also reflected the fact that, unlike many academic psychologists, he understood that Freud and the psychoanalytic tradition had made invaluable contributions to their discipline.[47]

There was no one like Joel Hildebrand on UCLA's faculty during the early Cold War period, no professor of comparable prestige who would make anticommunism his personal project. In the Southland, the militant leadership against radical subversion came from outside the university and not within it. UCLA's faculty would coalesce against what it saw as outside interference, and that's one of the most important reasons why it would be more united than Berkeley's during the years of the oath.

CHAPTER 4

UCLA AND THE ORIGINS OF THE LOYALTY OATH

Banner headlines in the local Hearst newspaper read, in describing UCLA: "Little Red Schoolhouse on the Hill."

—Kenneth Roose[1]

I understand Laski is a communist.

—Regent Sidney Ehrman[2]

T HAT IT WAS AT UCLA AND NOT BERKELEY where the 1949 incidents that precipitated the Loyalty Oath took place can only be understood by examining how the city of Los Angeles and the Westwood campus became sites for "Popular Front" politics in the 1930s.

The Comintern instituted its Popular Front strategy in 1935, and soon after, America's Communist Party began sponsoring new organizations intended to have a broader appeal than its earlier front groups. Several of them formed in Los Angeles during the war appealed to liberals and progressives, including some UCLA professors.

The first organization was the Hollywood Writers Mobilization, a 1943 gathering officially hosted by UCLA. Even though it had a Leftist tinge, the "Mobe," as it would be called, was endorsed by President Roosevelt and his Republican rival, Wendell Wilkie. Robert Gordon Sproul gave the opening address, and Thomas Mann was a speaker. The meeting also heard from such Hollywood eminences as Daryl Zanuck, Arch Oboler, Rex Stout, and Dore Schary, as well as two screenwriters who would be members of the blacklisted Hollywood Ten four years later: John Howard Lawson and Edward Dmytryk.

The purpose of the Hollywood Writers Mobilization was to enlist film industry personnel in the war effort. One of its founders was Kenneth Macgowan, who at the time was a Hollywood producer with the reputation of never having made a bad movie.

Macgowan, who would join UCLA's faculty in 1945, was a typical Popular Front liberal. Born in 1888, he had graduated from Harvard in the same class as Berkeley's English professor Benjamin Lehman. They became life-long friends, and each would form a department of theater arts on his campus. Macgowan began his career as a journalist and gained fame as one of the first critics to recognize the importance of Eugene O'Neill. The critic and the dramatist became friends, and O'Neill asked Magowan to reorganize his Provincetown Players. Macgowan then produced plays himself on Broadway and movies in Hollywood.

In the film capital he joined liberal groups in which communists were prominent, including the Hollywood Council for the Arts, Sciences, and Professions (ASP), as well as "the Mobe." The party tried to recruit him, inviting him to a Marxist study group, but the producer refused. In his economics class at Harvard he had learned all he needed to know about Karl Marx.[3]

After Clarence Dykstra became UCLA's provost in February 1945, one of his first acts was to organize a department of theater arts. He offered the job of building it to Macgowan, who then gave up a lavish income as one of Hollywood's best paid producers for the relatively measly salary of a college professor. His dream was to establish the most innovative department in the nation, one that would encompass not just traditional theater but also America's number one cultural product, the movies, and in time television and other new media.

TENNEY AND HIS COMMITTEE

Before approving Macgowan's appointment, Sproul asked Jack Tenney for information on him. The head of California's Little HUAC told the president that the Hollywood mogul was a fellow traveler, if not an outright communist, and should not be hired. But Dykstra fought for the man he wanted, and

Macgowan left Hollywood for UCLA. Sproul would deny that he cleared controversial appointments like Macgowan's with Tenney, but the latter's counsel has confirmed the 1945 incident.[4]

Like many professional anticommunists, Tenney had once been a Leftist, so his fervor to root out subversion was a personal expiation. He had first been elected an assemblyman, part of the "procommunist" wing of the Democratic Party. He was so radical that Martin Dies, chairman of the House Committee on Un-American Activities (HUAC), labeled him a subversive in the 1930s.[5] For Carey McWilliams, Tenney was "redder than a rose." During the Spanish Civil War he had introduced a resolution in the assembly to lift America's embargo on sending arms to the antifascist Republicans.[6]

Tenney was also a professional piano player who had composed the popular waltz "Mexicali Rose." During the 1930s he was the president of L.A.'s musicians' union as well. But in 1939 the communists in the union opposed his reelection bid.[7] The next year he sponsored legislation to keep the Communist Party off the ballot in California.[8]

Having moved up to the state Senate in 1942, Tenney became the chair of that body's Little HUAC. This gave him a second weapon in addition to holding public hearings on communist influence at the university: the annual publication of a report on subversive activities. Because the Tenney reports were considered authoritative, they helped ruin the careers of many Popular Front liberals. They were also filled with inaccuracies and exaggerations. McWilliams noted that he received a "Tenney listing" as a member of the executive committee of the American Peace Crusade when someone nominated him at a meeting he didn't even attend![9] Because this was his practice, Tenney made Macgowan, Tolman, and other liberals appear more Left-wing than they actually were.

In his crusade to expose communism at the University of California, Jim Corley was Tenney's ally. As comptroller and chief financial officer, Corley was a powerful figure. Each year he presented the university's budget to the state legislature, and this influence was magnified by his ability to make friends with members of both political parties.

An easy-going, gregarious Irishman, Corley was as Right-wing as John Francis Neylan. Tenney called upon Corley regularly for support, and he would provide the intelligence for the charges in his 1943 committee report that a "considerable number of professors" were fellow travelers or actual members of the Communist Party.[10] The next year the senator gave him galley proofs of his forthcoming report, and with the material in his briefcase, Corley flew to Los Angeles to stop UCLA's plan to publish a new magazine, the *Hollywood Quarterly*. But even though Tenney had identified many editorial board members as Reds, the university's sponsorship of the project went forward.[11]

The *Hollywood Quarterly* would be an influential film magazine, an avant-garde journal ahead of its time. To celebrate its October 1945 maiden issue, Clarence Dykstra, still in his first year as UCLA's provost, held a party at his house. Without his knowledge Tenney sent his operatives to the event, and they recorded the names of those present. The spies took special note of the film writer John Howard Lawson, one of the magazine's editors and the most open member of the Communist Party in Hollywood. But as Macgowan, another *Hollywood Quarterly* editor, has attested, Lawson was impeccably professional in his work on the magazine, never engaging in propaganda.[12]

DYKSTRA UNDER FIRE

Clarence Dykstra's good friend, the political scientist Dean McHenry, thought that the position of provost at UCLA was too small a job for someone of his stature.[13] A 1908 political science Ph.D. from the University of Chicago, he had served on the board of Los Angeles's Department of Water and Power and taught at UCLA during the 1920s. As a specialist in public administration, he carved out a distinguished career in municipal government. Dykstra successfully fought the patronage-based machines as the city manager of Cleveland and other metropolises and then became a national hero when his strong leadership saved Cincinnati from disaster during the great floods of 1937.

Having ameliorated what Lincoln Steffens had called "the shame of the cities," Dykstra moved into higher education. He was president of the University of Wisconsin until he became the nation's first director of Selective Service in 1940. After organizing the military draft, he spent the rest of World War II as the head of the National Defense Mediation Board.

By 1945, when Dykstra became provost, UCLA was already one of the nation's largest universities, with a student body of about 15,000, having shot up from only 2,500 at the time the Westwood campus opened in 1929. The period after World War II is still called the southern campus's "golden years," for that was when UCLA experienced its most rapid growth in facilities and in the quality of its faculty.[14]

Still, Dykstra's tenure was beset with frustrations. At Wisconsin he had made his own decisions, answering to no one but the trustees and the legislature. But the University of California was run by a president who wanted to manage everything himself. Dykstra continually had difficulty getting Sproul's approval for his actions.

And it was Dykstra, and not his boss, who came under fire for the alleged subversion at UCLA. From the moment he assumed office he was forced to defend himself. First he took the heat for the actions of radical students who had marched in support of striking workers from Warner Brothers: they had violated a regulation in identifying themselves as from UCLA on their picket signs. Soon afterward the popular Right-wing columnist Upton Close blamed him for the Mobilization, which took place two years before he was in Los Angeles. Close concluded his attack by calling for the removal of an educator "helping with the destruction of the Republic."[15]

Dykstra was a star witness when Tenney held hearings in January 1946. When the legislator zeroed in on Lawson and the *Hollywood Quarterly*, the provost held his ground with a spirited defense of academic freedom. Immediately he became the target of Southern California's Right-wing newspapers.

The third group on Tenney's radar screen was the Peoples Educational Center. According to McHenry, who helped organize it in 1943 and remained on its Board of Directors in 1946, the PEC's goal was "to bring trade unions into active participation in adult and continuing education." During its peak years from 1943 to 1945, a number of UCLA professors offered classes, or like McHenry, gave occasional lectures.[16]

Born in 1910, McHenry would spend most of his life with UCLA. He was the first student body president who hadn't come from the fraternity system. A liberal with socialist leanings, he wrote his Ph.D. thesis on the British Labor Party and was a friend of Harold Laski, one of its leaders, Only twenty-nine when he began teaching political science at UCLA, McHenry had traveled in the Soviet Union. The experience had disabused him of his youthful belief that the Bolshevik Revolution was the most exciting event of the 20th century.

A Popular Front liberal like Macgowan, McHenry looked like a subversive to Jack Tenney, who called him to testify in January 1946. By this time he knew the "secret communists" in the PEC leadership, but was too principled to reveal their names. Instead he challenged Tenney's assumption that communists controlled the school. His role on the board, he assured Tenney, was to counter communist influence by opposing the party members when they advocated something he didn't believe in.[17]

Looking back at his testimony more than twenty-five years later, McHenry felt that he had comported himself quite well. Indeed, Tenney told Dykstra afterwards that he considered McHenry "a fine young man." Nevertheless, the publicity hurt him. Many of his colleagues would always wonder how someone trained in political science could be "so naïve as to get associated with those people." And his Left-wing associations probably cost him the opportunity to become provost of a new branch of the university at Santa Barbara. McHenry's reputation as a fellow traveler would haunt him for years.[18]

After the 1946 hearings, the attacks on UCLA's faculty intensified. Dykstra defended himself by assuring the *Los Angeles Times* that Tenney had found no evidence of subversive actions and that his was a "loyal and devoted faculty."[19] But L.A.'s neighborhood weeklies, even more Right-wing than its major newspapers, continued to turn up the heat. A 1947 editorial in the *West Los Angeles Independent* with the title "Here Are Some Names, Dr. Sproul!" accused all the UCLA professors who had been called before the Tenney Committee of being communist sympathizers, whose presence on the faculty cast doubt on the president himself. The list included McHenry and other sponsors of the Peoples Education Center.[20]

The editorial noted with glee that it would be the provost's turn to appear before the committee the following week. After his testimony, another local paper, the *Santa Monican,* commented on how Dykstra was "known widely for his leftist leanings," as well as for his skill at parrying statements of his when they were quoted back at him. The provost's answers, according to the editor, "have the same hollow sound detailed these days in the mouths of the officially recognized agents of the Kremlin." And the writer concluded by asking whether UCLA's provost was the type of leader President Sproul "so warmly eulogizes."[21]

The problem for Dykstra was that he was a liberal in a conservative region, heading an institution that the Right-wing press referred to as "the little red schoolhouse on the hill."

UCLA'S STUDENT RADICALS

Dykstra also took the heat for the activities of UCLA's student radicals, another concern of the press. Like the City College of New York, UCLA was a magnet for the city's Jewish population, attracting so many students from the Fairfax district that historian Kevin Starr called it "CCNY with palm trees."[22]

In the spring of 1948, the *Los Angeles Times,* in that era as conservative as the Hearst papers, published an exposé of how UCLA had been chosen by the Communist Party as one of its most important educational targets. It was so earmarked because the completion of its expansion plan would make it the largest university in the West and the campus included a number of strategic sites for infiltration: an atomic medicine research facility and an avante-garde computer center.[23]

The *Times* claimed to have discovered the party's *modus operandi* for training student cadres. The plan had been initiated before the war when the most trusted Red undergraduates were "handpicked" from breeding grounds such as CCNY and other New York colleges. They were then sent to schools in the Midwest where they underwent more training. Finally, after the war the most ideologically committed organizers were sent to schools such as UCLA and Berkeley. They were key targets because of their size and prestige, as well as the fact that UC's student bodies had more autonomy than their counterparts at other universities. The *Times* revealed that UCLA's communists were planning to take over the student council and the campus paper, the *Daily Bruin.*

Even though there were only thirty "dyed-in-the-wool Communists" at UCLA, their power was multiplied by four hundred or so "fellow travellers, sympathizers, front organization members and misguided dupes." The Reds and their allies were organized into cells that met off campus, and that was where they planned their campaigns to win the student government election and to agitate against Universal Military Training and the Marshall Plan, and to overturn the policies of the campus Bureau of Occupations, which listed jobs for white students that were not available to blacks and other minorities.

And the *Times* noted how crafty UCLA's communists were in hiding their identity: the Young Communist League had recently transformed itself into the "Four Freedoms Club."[24]

Such articles about communist students at UCLA appeared frequently in both the local and the national press, while Berkeley rarely got this kind of treatment. In addition, most of the "subversive" professors that Jack Tenney exposed were teaching on the Westwood campus. So the question becomes whether UCLA was really the "hotbed of Communism" as Ernest Moore first labeled it, and as it continued to be portrayed in the late 1930s and 1940s, or was its "Redness" a matter of perception, a reflection of the conservative public opinion in the southland compared to the more liberal Bay Area?

Because Tenney was from Los Angeles he took a much closer look at the southern campus, and that's probably why its faculty figured so prominently in his reports. And while Northern California had at least one relatively liberal newspaper, the *San Francisco Chronicle,* all the major papers in the L.A. region were extremely conservative. The impact of the local press may be one reason why both the city and the county of Los Angeles required loyalty oaths for their employees, while San Francisco never did.[25] It also may explain why UCLA political science professor J.A.C. Grant, a middle-of-the-roader who considered himself "far right of center," could regularly be called a "commie," while this did not happen to an Academic Senate leader with similar politics at Berkeley such as Joel Hildebrand.[26]

In addition, although Hollywood was a radicalizing influence in the south-land, the Bay Area had experienced its General Strike, and its working class was more organized than L.A.'s. So the fact that UCLA and not Berkeley be-came the "little red schoolhouse" was probably due to the huge gap between its relatively liberal faculty and the conservative public opinion surrounding it, as well as to Jack Tenney's interest in his personal bailiwick.

THE LOYALTY OATH'S PRECIPITATING EVENTS

Three incidents took place in the first two months of 1949 that had an influ-ence on Robert Gordon Sproul's decision to recommend a loyalty oath to the regents. Only weeks earlier the political climate had been transformed by the Chinese Communist conquest of Chiang Kai-shek's Nationalist armies.

The triumph of the new Peoples' Republic of China was international communism's greatest victory since the 1917 Russian Revolution, and immediately the professional anticommunists began looking for the "traitors" in the State Department and the Foreign Service responsible. And yet for the Far Right, the "loss of China" would be a blessing in disguise. No other event in the postwar era so well confirmed its argument that domestic communists were a threat that had to be eradicated.

Tenney's response was to draft thirteen new laws to eliminate subversion in California. His Senate Constitutional Amendment 13 would have stripped the Academic Senate of its authority over faculty personnel decisions in the case of professors suspected of communist sympathies and delegated it instead to the state legislature.

The idea that action was needed to counter such a threat to the university might have made more sense ten or fifteen years earlier when Berkeley and UCLA had been strongholds of Left-wing student movements. But by the late 1940s, the communist presence was quite minimal among students, and close to nonexistent among the faculty. And yet in the Right-wing circles that included Tenney and Neylan, there was an unshakeable belief that a significant segment of the professoriat was indoctrinating its students in communism.

With proposals like Tenney's being considered not only for college faculties but also for the nation's high schools, Robert Hutchins stated that "the entire teaching profession is now intimidated." For America's most eminent college president, it was not a question of how many teachers had already been fired, but of "how many think they might be."[27]

In 1949 the University of California was far behind universities such as Harvard in its rules regulating who could appear on its campuses.[28] As McHenry recalls, there was a general belief that *nobody* considered controversial could speak to students. As late as 1952, Adlai Stevenson, the Democratic Party's candidate for president, had to campaign on the street corner across from the entrance to the Berkeley campus.[29]

These restrictions provided the backdrop to the two events at UCLA that helped bring about the Loyalty Oath. On February 14 a group of students tried to invite a truly controversial speaker, Herbert Phillips, the philosophy professor who had been recently fired from the University of Washington as an admitted communist. Milton Hahn, UCLA's conservative dean of students, tried to stop his appearance. But the next day Phillips gained the sponsorship of the Graduate Students Association, and Provost Dykstra approved him as a participant in a debate. The event was to be low-key, with a small attendance limited to graduate students, faculty, and staff. However UCLA's student body tried (unsuccessfully) to open it to the entire campus, so the controversy made headlines in the newspapers.[30]

To ensure that the gathering remained orderly and small, the campus police locked the doors of the meeting room before the debate. Phillips spoke first, arguing affirmatively to the question whether a member of the Communist Party could "be an objective teacher and an impartial researcher for truth." He was followed by a former Washington journalism professor, Merritt Benson,[31] who alleged that the fact that Phillips had been a party member for thirteen years was sufficient grounds to send him to prison. The latter's defense was that neither he nor the Communist Party favored the overthrow of the government by force and violence.

According to Dean McHenry, it was an excellent debate, with numerous issues discussed and both sides represented fairly. But the appearance of the now notorious Phillips infuriated several UC regents and got Dykstra into hot water.

The provost, according to his friend McHenry, was unusual in 1949 in believing that "the winds of freedom" should "blow through the university."[32] And in justifying the debate to Sproul and the regents, he exhibited a courage that was all too rare among educators at the time. "It is of high importance to raise the question," Dykstra wrote, "of *thought control* on our campus and (to) strike early, if it appears that such control is raising its ugly head."[33] The provost wanted to take a stand against the view that "vital issues, strongly held . . . cannot be discussed on a campus of the University of California." And in an idea that he would soon he disabused of, he added, "In my opinion the rule of the Regents does not prevent the discussion of controversial questions so long as both sides are presented, and the meeting is a bona fide meeting of recognized organizations."[34]

The third event also took place at UCLA and again concerned a speaker who was considered "too controversial." The socialist Harold Laski, one of the world's most respected political scientists and an influential leader of the British Labour Party, had been invited in January 1949 to give two talks on labor unions in April. Dykstra approved his appearance, which was cosponsored by UCLA's Political Science Department and Institute of Industrial Relations. Indeed, Laski's visit seemed like a routine matter, for he had spoken at UCLA in the past. In addition the labor leader had been Dykstra's house guest when he had visited the University of Wisconsin to lecture and the then President Dykstra had introduced him to the audience.

As the former head of a great university, Dykstra was accustomed to making such decisions himself. But in the UC system final authority on these matters rested with the president. And because the provost was already "gunshy" as a result of Phillips' appearance, he wanted to be doubly sure that Sproul would support his decision to bring Laski to UCLA.[35]

For almost a month Dykstra waited for Sproul's response. Arriving as a teletype to the director of the Institute of Industrial Relations, the president's reply stated that "Dr. Dykstra has full power to act." However ten days later, when the two met at Charter Day ceremonies, the president informed Dykstra that "the appearance of Laski . . . would not be pleasing to the Board of Regents because some have charged Laski with being ultra-left and the Regents have a very firm policy as to Communists and *alleged Communists*."[36]

So Dykstra cancelled the talks. Of everything he had done during his life of public service, this would be the act he most regretted.[37] And Harold Laski was "deeply offended."[38]

However the British statesman did speak in Los Angeles. His sponsors rented the biggest downtown arena and a huge crowd from the campus, the labor unions, and the community was able to hear him. Exhibiting the same civic courage as his friend Dykstra, McHenry presided over the meeting.

The Laski affair cost Dykstra sleepless nights, and almost his job. But, despite deeply resenting being "the man in the middle" without responsibility, he took the blame on his shoulders, making up a story about a lack of coordination between Laski's Los Angeles and Berkeley visits. This let Sproul and the regents off the hook.

But that didn't satisfy the regents who figured that UCLA's provost had to be a socialist himself, or even a communist, to have invited the British leader to his campus.[39] There was talk of dismissing him, but he was defended by Paul Hutchinson, on the board in his capacity as president of UCLA's Alumni

Association. Several regents urged that the provost be summoned to their next meeting to explain his actions. But that was seen as too humiliating, so the matter of reprimanding Dykstra, and reining him in, was left to President Sproul.

The cancellation of Laski's appearance was front-page news in the national press, for the Labour Party leader had arrived in the city with Winston Churchill. Invidious comparisons were made between UC and Columbia, where Laski spoke without incident on the campus where Dwight Eisenhower was now president. He also spoke at the University of North Carolina, where he was introduced by Senator Frank Graham, as well as at Harvard, the New School, and many other institutions.[40]

The Laski affair underscored the fearful and vacillating nature of President Sproul's leadership during the period when anticommunist hysteria was heating up. Given his history of intolerance for radical political expression, it's not surprising that he was unwilling to take a stand for intellectual freedom when it would have meant defying Neylan and his allies. Sproul's proclivity to compromise and equivocate would lead to one defeat after another for the university and his faculty. The way in which he dealt with Dykstra early in 1949 became his modus operandi in his relations with the faculty and the Board of Regents during the ensuing "year of the oath."[41]

Students of the Loyalty Oath differ on what was its most important precipitant, the events at UCLA or the threat of Jack Tenney's amendment. Most commentators favor the latter explanation, for the State Senator's ally Jim Corley told the press that he recommended a new oath to President Sproul as early as January 1949. His goal was "to save the State University from being wrecked by possible political influences," and to do so he reportedly made a deal with Tenney. The comptroller would get Sproul to propose a loyalty oath for his faculty, and in exchange the state senator would withdraw his pending legislation. And that is precisely what happened.[42]

But the events at UCLA were also critical. During the executive session of the board meeting at which the oath was adopted, Regent Sidney Ehrman inveighed against those who were bringing the doctrines of the Communist Party to the university and went so far as to state that "I understand [that] Laski is a communist."[43]

This explains why both Clark Kerr and a leader of UCLA's Academic Senate, J.A.C. Grant, argue that Dykstra and the events at UCLA were more important as the backdrop of the new requirement. According to Kerr, the purpose of the oath was to provide legal cover for the policy of barring Left-wing speakers from the university that Sproul had forced Dykstra to carry out at UCLA.[44]

But there is no need to choose between the two theories. Both the UCLA events and Tenney's legislation were essential precursors of the Loyalty Oath.

PART II

A FACULTY DIVIDED

CHAPTER 5

THE FACULTY RESISTS
SPROUL'S OATH

It is the duty of all governing boards and of all administrators
to protect the faculty from the demands of those who do not
appreciate the goals of scholarship.

—Robert MacIver[1]

I never really thought that the oath controversy had much
to do about the oath. I thought it had to do with Neylan's
vendetta against Sproul.

—Clark Kerr[2]

EVEN THOUGH IT WOULD BE THE MOST
fateful session in the history of the Board of Regents, only
eleven of the twenty-four regents came to the March 25, 1949, meeting in
Santa Barbara. And it was only at the tail end of the one-day gathering when
President Sproul introduced the oath almost as an afterthought. During the
two public sessions that morning and the first of the afternoon, there had been
no discussions of the Tenney bills, the use of facilities by communists and subversives, or the possibility of a new oath. These issues did come up in the executive session closed to the public and in the informal discussions during
breaks between meetings. Sproul must have calculated this in advance, for he
had his friend and advisor Jim Corley iron out a draft of the new requirement
during the lunch hour, working with the attorney for the regents.[3]

As the board's deliberations were drawing to a close, the president introduced an article of new business, seemingly "out of the blue." He asked for

"unanimous consent" on a motion to amend the state oath then required of faculty members.[4] Known as the Constitutional Oath, it had been a simple pledge to uphold the constitutions of the United States and California. Sproul proposed the addition of a clause stating that the oath taker does not believe in, nor is a member of, "any party or organization that believes in, advocates, or teaches, the overthrow of the United States government, by force or by any illegal or unconstitutional methods." Most of the debate that followed turned on whether the new "negative" disclosure of nonmembership should come before or after the old "positive" affirmation. That matter settled, California's Loyalty Oath was adopted unanimously.[5]

Sixteen years later, Regent Edwin Pauley, an oil and gas entrepreneur, said that he had supported the measure only to please Sproul. Having worked with communists on the postwar Reparations Commission, he thought the oath would be useless, for the Reds would sign anything. He warned against the new requirement, and in 1965 would boast that "I was the first person to ever oppose the Loyalty Oath."[6]

In another sign that Sproul had considered the matter in advance, he informed the board that the amended oath would be included in the contracts for the coming year. And in response to the concerns of several regents, he assured them that *the faculty would not seriously object to the new requirement.* The president's lack of foresight would cost him and the university dearly.

Some months later Neylan asked his former friend, "Why in the name of God didn't you talk this over with the faculty before you sprung it originally in March 1949?" And the president answered, "I didn't think they'd have the slightest objection."[7]

In the measure that was adopted on March 25, 1949, there was no mention of communism, communists, or the Communist Party. That addition would come three months later.

President Sproul's advocacy of an oath was a miscalculation, but it was also consistent with his belief system and past practices. Albeit a liberal Republican, he was deeply antagonistic to communism and to Left-wing radicals. It was he who had sponsored the intelligence networks on student activists after the 1934 General Strike.

Benjamin Lehman has the best analysis of why Sproul pushed for the Loyalty Oath. In 1949 he had been president for almost twenty years, and he had reached the point of "crowning the university with greatness." But his dream was threatened by Jack Tenney, whose committee was talking about holding up the university's budget if it did not deal with its communist problem. Normally a man of extraordinary insight and impeccable political instincts, he suffered a "momentary failure of insight." Because "his life work was threatened, he panicked."

"When (Jim) Corley said that he thought they could get the budget through in all this stir if they had the faculty sign the oath, (he might) have said, 'No, I don't think the faculty will stand for that; we have to devise other ways and means.' Or he might have consulted with Hildebrand, or with Stephen Pepper,[8] or even with me, and said, 'What do you think?' But he did it on his own and he did it at the end of the Regents' meeting, when they were finished, so that there was not time to discuss it."[9]

Had Sproul consulted with his faculty advisors there very likely would never have been a Loyalty Oath. And had Neylan been present when Sproul suggested amending the Constitutional Oath, his idea very likely would have been shot down. Had Neylan known that Sproul would propose an oath regarding communist professors, he would have cut short his vacation to attend the meeting. And had he been there, the outcome would have been different. In March 1949 Neylan did not favor oaths as tools to deal with subversion at the university. In fact, he didn't believe an oath was worth the paper it was written on.[10] He agreed with Pauley that a communist would not hesitate to sign it.

By 1949 the influential regent didn't have much use for Sproul, another reason he might have thrown his weight against the measure. That's why Clark Kerr asked, "What if Neylan had attended the Santa Barbara meeting of the Board of Regents in March 1949 and had stated then, as he did later in June, that he opposed the idea of the oath? Would Sproul have withdrawn it in the face of this opposition?"[11] Kerr doesn't answer the question, but the reader senses that it's clear he thought that would have ended the matter. And Neylan bluntly stated, "Had I been at the March meeting, there would have been no oath."[12]

HOW CHICAGO'S HUTCHINS MET
A SIMILAR CHALLENGE

During the spring of 1949, the chancellor of the University of Chicago, Robert M. Hutchins, faced a challenge almost identical to that of Sproul's. The Broyles Commission, the group in the Illinois State Senate that investigated Un-American activities, was the equivalent of the Tenney Committee. With several bills in the hopper for dealing with communist professors, it called Hutchins to the state capital to testify about the Reds on his faculty.

As defiant as Sproul was compliant, Chicago's chancellor asserted that there were no communists on his faculty. But more important was that the University of Chicago totally rejected the "Un-American doctrine of guilt by association." And Hutchins was proud of his professors who had joined "front organizations" on the attorney general's list. By combating fascism and racial discrimination they were being good citizens and not subversives.

As Hutchins addressed the Broyles Commission: "(The) danger to our institutions is not from the tiny minority who do not believe in them. It is from those who would mistakenly repress the free spirit upon which these institutions are built. The miasma of thought control that is now spreading over the country is the greatest menace to the United States since Hitler."[13]

Cross-examined by one of the nation's foremost professional anticommunists, Hutchins made a fool out of his inquisitor. In an exchange about faculty members who had retired, J. B. Matthews came across as an ignoramus because he didn't know what *professor emeritus* meant. And in defending the cancer researcher Maude Slye, who had belonged to more than a few organizations on the attorney general's list, Hutchins emphasized that the indoctrination Matthews was accusing her of was directed not at students—for she did not teach—but at the mice she experimented on in her laboratory.

Hutchins so demolished the Broyles inquisition that the State Senate voted to stop funding it. But as Carey McWilliams pointed out, credit for this victory against McCarthyism must also go to Chicago's trustees. Backing their chancellor to the hilt, they stated that "To be great, a university must adhere to principle. . . . It cannot shift with the winds of public opinion. . . . Today our tradition of freedom is under attack. There are those who are afraid of freedom. We do not share these fears."[14]

Why, when he was faced with an almost identical situation, did Sproul act so differently from Hutchins? Chicago's chancellor became an exemplar of the civic courage badly needed during the McCarthy Era, while California's president, in appeasing the Far Right, exacerbated the prevailing hysteria.

First, there is the matter of character. Hutchins was a fighter who reveled in going against public opinion. Sproul, on the other hand, was a compromiser who liked to find the middle ground that would avoid a battle. Those close to him recall that he almost never said no to people. Rather than confront someone with a negative response, he just didn't answer many of the requests that were sent to him.

And then there is their backgrounds. Hutchins had been a professor, so he could be confident that his strong stand would earn him respect from his faculty. Sproul's career had been wholly in administration. True, he was a relatively unbureaucratic president who relied on a personal style of leadership. But he sought advice only from a narrow segment of the faculty, those who shared his conservative to middle-of-the-road opinions.[15]

But to be fair to the president, the situation he faced was much more difficult. UC was a public institution, unlike the University of Chicago. The Broyles Commission that the chancellor stared down did threaten to end the university's tax-exempt status. But unlike California's legislature, it didn't control the purse strings. Chicago's budget came from its endowment and its support from some of the wealthiest people in the region. And Sproul was up against a Board of Regents that tilted in the direction of its conservative faction, whereas the trustees on Hutchins' board, who represented many of the titans of monopoly capitalism (the Rockefellers and corporations such as Inland Steel) were staunch liberals when it came to questions of academic freedom.

TUSSMAN MOBILIZES TOLMAN
TO FIGHT THE OATH

Joseph Tussman, an obscure young assistant professor, would play a critical role in mobilizing faculty resistance to the new requirement. Political activism ran in his family—his father had been a socialist—and Joe was also influenced by the "guilt" he carried for not having fought in Spain, unlike many of his peers.[16]

As an undergraduate at the University of Wisconsin, Tussman had been a student of Alexander Meiklejohn. The civil libertarian would become Joe's life-long intellectual and political inspiration, and it was because his mentor lived six months of the year in Berkeley that he had come to the university for a Ph.D. in philosophy.[17] After earning a Bronze Star for valor during World War II, Tussman completed that degree in 1947 with a dissertation on Hobbes, and begin teaching in the Speech Department the same year.[18]

In the spring of 1949, the young philosopher was working on his first book, the book he would have to finish were he to have a chance to be promoted to tenure. And although *Obligation and the Body Politic* eventually became a classic in political theory, it would appear only after its writer had long left Berkeley. Yet it made a difference to the unfolding of the Loyalty Oath controversy. While writing it Tussman was consumed with the relationship between citizens and their government, which gave him the sensitivity to do a "double-take" one day in April while reading a rather boring publication called the *Faculty Bulletin*.

For reasons that have never become clear, Sproul and his administration took a casual attitude toward the new oath in the period after it was approved in late March. Three weeks would pass before the appointment letters that contained it were printed, and they were not mailed out for several days afterward. In mid-April, Sproul's assistant was still ignorant of the oath's existence. When George Pettitt did learn about it, he and the regents' secretary Robert Underhill decided that they'd better notify the faculty. But they made the questionable decision of using the *Faculty Bulletin* to do this. Few read that bureaucratically written monthly, and the next issue wasn't scheduled to appear for several weeks.

When the notice in the *Bulletin* appeared in the second week of May, all it said was that an oath of allegiance was included in employment acceptance letters for the next academic year, and that paychecks would not be released until it was signed, notarized, and returned to the regents. There was nothing about the oath's content, no mention of communism or subversion, nothing to suggest that the new requirement was anything but routine.[19]

From Meiklejohn, who was a political activist as well as a scholar, Tussman had internalized an important lesson: defenders of civil liberties need to be vigilant at all times. So he actually read the *Faculty Bulletin,* and when he saw the harmless-looking notice about an oath, "alarm bells" went off in his head. Instead of assuming it was just another formality like others had, he decided to look into the matter.

The new oath had not yet been published, but it was available in the office of the secretary of the regents. As soon as Tussman read it, it became clear to him that "We were being asked to disavow political ideas and political associations. That seemed to me to be a fundamental violation of freedom of speech and academic freedom."[20]

He copied the text and took it to his friend, the blind political scientist Jacobus tenBroek. TenBroek, who also taught in the Speech Department, had already become known for his advocacy on behalf of disadvantaged groups. After talking it over, the two men agreed that the new requirement was "a terrible thing." They discussed it further at lunch that day, and that was when they decided to immediately consult Edward Tolman.[21]

At sixty-two, Tolman was one of the most respected members of Berkeley's faculty, as well as one of the nation's leading psychologists. A lifelong pacifist, he had opposed America's entry into World War I. When he expressed this position in a socialist magazine, Northwestern University decided not to rehire him, and so he came to Berkeley in 1918.[22]

Joe Tussman, who had lived with the Tolmans as a graduate student, characterized him as a man of "great integrity" and "unimpeachable character."[23] He was also modest, even shy, but he would speak out against injustice. During World War II he helped organize the first interracial group in the city of Berkeley devoted to fighting discrimination. Here the psychologist was carrying out a family tradition, for his grandparents had operated a station on the Underground Railroad in Rhode Island during the slavery era.

Neighbors and friends of Meiklejohn, Tolman and his wife were two of the Bay Area's most dedicated advocates of civil liberties. Since there was no other liberal of Tolman's stature on the faculty, Tussman and tenBroek knew that if they could convince Tolman to oppose the oath, his views would be taken seriously.

As the three hashed out the problem, the import of the requirement became apparent. There were academic freedom issues, including the professoriat's right to teach, write, and pursue the truth without being constrained by political pressures. But there was a more dire threat. The new requirement jeopardized the job security of every faculty member, from the most senior full professor to the most lowly new instructor.

In 1949 the university did not have a system of "continuous tenure" for its faculty. Associate professors and full professors had achieved tenure, but that status, with all it implied for their job security, had to be renewed with each year's contract. So Tolman, Tussman, and tenBroek concluded that conservative regents might be planning to use the oath to purge the faculty of its most liberal professors. If they refused to sign they could then be fired.[24]

In the weeks that followed, the three professors alerted colleagues likely to oppose the oath. It was Tolman who enlisted Jack Kent, the head of the Department of City and Regional Planning, who was also his son-in-law. He also notified Gordon Griffiths, who alerted Arthur Brodeur, his former Communist Party comrade. Tussman informed philosophy professors who had been his teachers: Ed Strong, George Adams, Stephen Pepper, and Jacob Loewenberg. Others found out about the oath by word of mouth.

AT UCLA IT WOULD TAKE LONGER for the import of the requirement to be understood. During April and May the campus community was still discussing what was called "L'Affaire Laski," so the *Daily Bruin* published front-page stories about the campaign for a more open speakers' policy. On May 24, the Graduate Students Association met to discuss the threat of Tenney's proposed legislation; that there was a much greater threat already in the books had not yet sunk in. And during the last week of May and the first week of June the *Bruin* published lengthy features on the Board of Regents without mentioning the new oath, even though the second article included a catalog of all the board's actions that had violated the rights of professors and students.[25]

May came and went, and the oath had yet not been made public. New faculty members read it when they opened their contract letters, and it was through running into one such professor that Kenneth Bock of Sociology and Social Institutions learned that something was afoot. "What is this loyalty oath that I'm supposed to sign?" Bock was asked.[26]

In the first week of June, the full text was finally published in the *San Francisco Chronicle*. Liberal professors, determined to fight the requirement, wondered why the administration had waited so long. Why had the oath become public at a time when people were preparing to leave Berkeley for the summer? Was the plan to undermine an effective protest by the Academic Senate? If so, the idea backfired. The faculty's belief that Sproul had not acted in good faith only increased its determination to resist.

The long delay would be an issue for months. Led by Philosophy's Strong, a delegation of liberal faculty members demanded an explanation as the administration tried to quell the storm. Neylan blamed Sproul's assistant Pettitt, whose "ineptitude and misjudgments . . . gave the Faculty the impression that the Board had indulged in sharp tactics by withholding information (until) the last minute."[27]

The Senate's last meeting of the semester was scheduled for June 7. But because the notice had been mailed out weeks earlier, the agenda items were minor procedural matters. And yet the attendance was unusually high. But because two hundred professors was still a minority of the Senate's membership, Tolman moved that a special meeting be held a week later to consider the new oath.[28]

In the period between the two Senate meetings, *1984* was published. Orwell's book is a parable of a regimented society in which "Big Brother" supervises the activities of every citizen. So it was fitting that on the day it appeared the FBI reported that many of America's most beloved celebrities were secret members of the Communist Party: the list included Helen Keller, Dorothy Parker, Danny Kaye, and Edward G. Robinson. Meanwhile, the party's top eleven leaders were being tried under the Smith Act on charges of conspiring to overthrow the U.S. government by force and violence. Where communists were in power, they were not doing much better; in Hungary Premier Laszlo Rajk had been arrested and would soon be executed.

To evoke the political climate, Berkeley English professor George Stewart compiled a list of the *San Francisco Chronicle* headlines on the morning of the June 14th meeting. The S.F. daily was a relatively liberal organ, the only major paper in California to oppose the oath. So the headlines that follow did not come from a Hearst paper noted for "yellow journalism" or militant anticommunism, which suggests how pervasive the Red Scare had already become.

Atom Inquiry

"Are You a Communist?"

Hiss Perjury Trial

Condon to Be Called in Coplon Trial[29]

U.N. Official Sotirov Denies He's Russ Agent

Business View of Red China

U.C. Loyalty Oath New Pledge Scheduled for Heated Debate in Academic Senate Today

U. Illinois Says Its Loyalty Oath Is 10 Years Old

Maryland Professors Must Sign by July 1

Phi Beta Kappa Opposed to Oath

Two Public Issues, Pro and Con, "Should Schools Let Communists Be Teachers?"

Supreme Court to Rule on L.A. Anti-Communist Law[30]

TOLMAN AND KANTOROWICZ SPEAK OUT

The four hundred professors who came to the Senate meeting didn't fill half of Wheeler Auditorium, but they still constituted more than half of the faculty. And although many came forward to speak, two men emerged that day as outspoken opponents of the Loyalty Oath. For Edward Tolman, who spoke first, the atmosphere might have been intimidating, for he was much more comfortable in small graduate seminars. He was not at his best in large lecture classes, as even his own daughters attested.[31]

While Tolman was presenting a resolution that affirmed the loyalty and patriotism of the faculty, raised questions about the oath's impact on academic freedom and tenure, and requested that it be deleted,[32] Gordon Griffiths sat in the back of the room. With a shy, retiring personality and the insecurities of an assistant professor without tenure, he lacked the confidence to speak up at Senate meetings. Looking back on that day, Griffiths recalled how astonished he was to see fellow historian Ernst Kantorowicz walk to the front of the auditorium. For until then Kantorowicz had not gotten involved in American politics.[33]

A Jewish émigré from Germany, Kantorowicz had fought for the Kaiser in World War I. Afterward he joined a Right-wing militia, the Frei Korps, and helped suppress a 1919 uprising of the ultra-Left Spartacists in Berlin. Then he went to Bavaria, where his unit overturned a Soviet-style commune in Munich. After getting a Ph.D. in political economy, he became a part of the circle around the romantic poet Stefan George. With the latter's encouragement, Kantorowicz, who liked to be called "Eka," wrote his first great book, a biography of the 12th-century emperor Frederick the Second.

Admired by Mussolini, Goering, and Hitler (who was said to have read it twice), *Frederick the Second* was viewed by many readers as an apology for fascism. So, as a German nationalist on the Far Right, Kantorowicz felt betrayed when his classes were interrupted by noisy Nazi students after Hitler came to power. Concerned about the new regime's crusade against homosexuality as well as its anti-Semitism, he applied for a leave of absence and instead of protesting these policies asked, "How can you do this to me, I who fought in the war and against the communists afterwards, I who am so fervent a patriot and such a supporter of our fatherland?"[34]

That was the beginning of a transformation as dramatic as that of John Francis Neylan's, but in the opposite political direction. In 1934 Kantorowicz refused to sign the oath of allegiance to the German state and to "its Supreme Leader, Adolf Hitler." But it was not until *Kristallnacht* in November 1938 that he gave up on Germany. Influential friends saved him from arrest and arranged his escape to England. And then in 1939, Provost Monroe Deutsch asked Sproul to hire Kantorowicz. He became a "smashing success," as his students loved "his sing-song way of talking, his romantic gestures, his elegant continental clothes, (and) his astonishing erudition in a dozen languages."[35]

The historian's formal grandeur was well-suited for Berkeley's largest lecture hall. According to Stewart, another eyewitness, Eka delivered his prepared statement "in a strange rhythmical incantation, high-pitched with fervor, his foreign accent now and then making his words scarcely intelligible."[36]

Establishing his authority as a historian who had studied loyalty oaths, Kantorowicz stated that they appear harmless at first, but then take on lives of their own and become extremely dangerous. "It is the harmless oath that hooks; it hooks *before* it has undergone those changes that will render it, bit by bit, less harmless. Mussolini Italy of 1931, Hitler Germany of 1933, are terrifying and warning examples for the harmless bit-by-bit procedure in connection with politically enforced oaths."

The "Regents' Oath," Eka continued, may seem harmless, but it could endanger the most basic human and academic values. And because it was imposed under duress, it was not even legal. The crude method of "Take the oath or leave your job" creates an "economic coercion . . . close to blackmail." To sign the oath, one must lie or become cynical. Its methodology of the oath, a "black or white," is the modus operandi of "modern and bygone dictatorships," which brand "non-conformists as un-Athenian, un-English, (or) un-German." "The fundamental issue" that is at stake, he concluded, is that of "professional and human dignity."[37]

Griffiths was bowled over by Eka's eloquence. The speech, he would later write, would prove to be a turning point in the discourse over the oath. Until Kantorowicz spoke, it would have been possible to dismiss the controversy as a local matter, a dispute between various parties at a California university. But by putting the oath in historical perspective, Eka framed it as something that involved universal questions of human freedom.[38]

A few months later, in letters to the Senate leader Frank Kidner and to Sproul, Kantorowicz explained why he felt so strongly about the Regents Oath. "I have twice volunteered to fight actively, with rifle and gun, the left-wing radicals in Germany . . . against the Spartacist Revolt in Berlin and the *Sovjet Republik* in Munich. These 'White' battalions helped lead to Hitler, although (that) was not my intent. *It is demanding too much of a historian to commit the same blunder twice.*"[39]

Despite Kantorowicz's eloquent plea, Tolman's resolution was too strong for Berkeley's Senate, which like most faculties preferred a carefully worded, politically moderate statement to a principled stand. In its place an amendment was passed that emphasized the Senate's willingness to work with the regents to modify the oath in a way acceptable to both parties.

The Senate's Advisory Committee was charged with conveying the faculty's position to Sproul. It included two powerful members of the faculty's "Old Guard," English professor Lehman and chemist Hildebrand. But Gardner, the historian of the oath controversy, believed that the ambiguous wording of the amended resolution would "aggravate relations among members of the faculty and between the Senate and the regents."[40]

After the substitute resolution passed, Tolman asked whether the university wanted to endorse the principle of guilt by association, on which the oath was based. "I cannot and will not sign (this) oath. . . . I hope, of course, that enough other members of the Senate will join with me in this protest to demonstrate to the Regents the seriousness with which we view the oath as a threat to academic freedom, and indeed as a threat to mere decency, and the honest use of the English language."[41]

This was the first expression of an intention to refuse to sign the Loyalty Oath, so June 14, 1949, was the beginning of the resistance by a still-unorganized group who would later be called "the nonsigners."

NEYLAN'S "BIGGEST MISTAKE"

During the period following the meeting the situation remained fluid, as the oath was not yet set in stone. Two sessions of the Board of Regents would reveal that a significant minority, perhaps even a majority, had serious doubts about the Loyalty Oath.

On June 14, Kantorowicz had referred to the new requirement as "the Regents' Oath." Indeed, three-and-a-half months would go by before the faculty and the public would learn that it been Sproul's idea. For the president had told reporters in early June that it had been recommended by the regents and that he had been "a mere draftsman" or "an assistant draftsman."

This made Neylan furious. And determined to confront Sproul at the earliest opportunity.[42]

When the Committee on Finance and Business Management met on June 24, Neylan mentioned the stories in the press, turned toward Sproul, and blurted out, "What do you mean by telling the newspapers that you were 'a mere draftsman?'"

Not knowing that his nemesis had the minutes of the March 25 meeting in front of him, the president responded that he had indeed been "a mere draftsman." "You were not, you were the author. Don't tell me what you were, because here are the minutes." And then Neylan told Sproul, "You're going to tell the newspapers the truth and you're going to tell the faculty the truth, that it was you and not the Regents who originated the oath."

At this point, according to Neylan, Sproul threw up his hands and "whined: 'My God, if you insist on that, you'll end my usefulness with the faculty.'"[43]

But Farnham Griffiths, Neylan's friend and personal attorney, talked him out of forcing the president to go public with an admission that the oath had been his idea. In his oral history Neylan said that this was "the biggest mistake I ever made in my political life."[44]

Then Griffiths and Neylan prepared a resolution for the next day's board meeting that stressed the university's policy of barring communists, but made no mention of the March 25 oath. In fact Neylan went to Los Angeles with the idea "that the oath was out the window," and his friend Farnham supported him in this. But Sproul was now wedded to the idea that an oath was essential.[45]

When the full board met on June 24 the tension was palpable. Neylan and Griffiths presented their resolution, and the discussion indicated that they had the votes to pass it. Had it come to a vote, the Loyalty Oath would have been rescinded, and years of crisis would have been averted.

But Sproul told the board that if it didn't keep the oath it would be "embarrassing" to him. "Do you mean to say they want an oath?" Neylan asked the president, referring to the faculty. And Sproul answered, "I've got an agreement with the faculty."[46]

Neylan couldn't believe his ears. In a tone that he would later call "insulting," he asked Sproul whether he had that agreement in writing. Sproul then mentioned a letter signed by Hildebrand and Lehman of his Advisory Committee.

"Have you got a copy of that letter?" Neylan pressed further, convinced that Sproul was bluffing. And to his surprise, the president pulled it from his coat pocket. Signed by Hildebrand, it authorized an amendment to the March 25th oath that for the first time made reference to membership in organizations advocating the overthrow of the government by force and violence.

The amendment was one of two resolutions that Hildebrand had prepared for Sproul. The first called for the elimination of the Loyalty Oath, a return to the Constitutional Oath, and a statement of acquiescence in the policy that communists were unacceptable. The second, to be invoked only if "the public relations of the university made it indispensable," stipulated an addition to the Constitutional Oath stating that "I am not under any oath, nor a party to any agreement, nor as a member of any party or organization am I under any commitment, that is in conflict with my obligation under this oath."[47]

After reading Hildebrand's letter, Neylan gave up and did not object to an addition to the oath specifying that professors must swear they were not members of the Communist Party.[48] Years later he would state that Sproul never sold him on the idea of the oath, that he went along strictly on the basis of that letter. And he added, "Here's where I'll never forgive Joel Hildebrand."[49]

Hildebrand in his role as Sproul's chief advisor had given "no hint that the issue was in active dispute," that an important segment of the faculty felt that it was not party membership per se, but "demonstrable professional unfitness" that should be the criterion for barring professors from teaching. His assurance that the revised oath would be "almost universally acceptable" was a serious misreading of the mood of the faculty at Berkeley and UCLA. This is why even conservative members of the Academic Senate would blame him for the failure to resolve the oath crisis in its early stages.[50]

Whether or not Hildebrand purposely misled the president and the regents out of his obsession with communism, a consensus soon emerged at Berkeley and UCLA that his leadership had exacerbated the crisis. For if the Advisory Committee had worked with the faculty in alerting Sproul, Neylan, and the rest of the regents to the growing opposition to the oath during the early summer of 1949, such a united front might have led to the return to the 1942 Constitutional Oath along with an affirmation of the policy of excluding Red professors.

The evening after the regents' meeting Hildebrand issued a press release that evoked the national political climate. "While many members of the faculty will feel sad that any oath is regarded as necessary," he stated, "they recognize that the present state of public opinion may make it seem expedient."[51]

Tolman disagreed and spent the same evening calling up other faculty resisters. Until then opposition to the oath had been increasing, but had been expressed only in speeches at the June 14 Senate meeting and in informal grousing at the Faculty Club.

When Tolman and his supporters met on June 27, they concluded that the revised oath was much worse than the one enacted on March 25 and that Hildebrand and Lehman had sold them "down the river."[52] This would be just the first of many disagreements between the nonsigners and the Advisory Committee, reflecting the philosophical differences between Tolman and his group and Hildebrand and Lehman.

As Gordon Griffiths noted with respect to Kantorowicz's June 14 speech, the dissidents had begun to frame the conflict in terms of such issues as total-itarianism and academic freedom. The approach of Hildebrand and Lehman was based on their sense of the welfare of the university and above all retaining Sproul as president. Even the sophisticated Lehman dismissed the civil liber-ties aspects of the oath crisis.[53]

At the end of June it was still not inevitable that there would be a crisis that would roil the university for years to come. That may be why UCLA's fac-ulty had not yet organized and the *Daily Bruin* only began publicizing the issue after the June 24 regents' meeting. But even that story did not discuss the oath and its implications at any length.[54] By this time the *Daily Californian* had begun publishing one or more front-page articles in every edition, as well as hard-hitting editorials. Instead of taking the regents' commitment to the "freedom of the human mind and spirit" at face value, a typical editorial de-cried how these virtues were now qualified at the university, for the board was now controlling the faculty's thoughts.[55]

The new requirement was not firmly established, and as long as the board's most powerful member was ambivalent, the situation remained fluid. At the June 30 meeting of the Finance Committee, Neylan stated that if he were on the faculty he would not sign the oath. There was still time for Sproul to re-verse himself, for the idea put forward by Farnham Griffiths at this meeting to drop the oath had enough votes to pass.[56]

But the president quashed Griffiths' motion, arguing that most of the re-gents who were not present, as well as the majority of the faculty, wanted an oath. "They want to put themselves on record," he explained.[57]

The president had now made the same error three times. First, by suggest-ing a new oath on March 25, and assuring the regents there would be little fac-ulty opposition. Then three months afterward, he compounded that mistake at the regents' meeting, and a week later with the Finance Committee, missing two more chances to get himself off the hook.

Even Gardner is unable to explain why Sproul "so insisted that the oath be kept." He suggests that the president was confident that only a handful would resist "to the point of not signing" and that they could be won over through persuasion.[58]

To accomplish this, Sproul sent personal letters to all faculty members in mid-July, reminding them of the regents' resolution. Enclosing a copy of the oath, he expressed the hope that the recipient would sign and notarize it by the October 1, 1949, deadline. Writing individual letters to the faculty was unusual, so Sproul must have believed that such a personal touch would persuade people on the fence to sign.[59]

According to George Stewart, "a considerable number" of professors did sign right away. Many complied out of sympathy with the regents' actions. Others did so because they wanted to get the matter out of the way and return to the research and writing they concentrate on during summers free from teaching. Many who had left Berkeley signed because they assumed that the Senate had approved the measure. And others signed because they felt that the Advisory Committee had approved the oath's new language that had been added by the regents on June 24.[60]

At the June 30 committee meeting the regents had agreed to separate the issue of signing from that of awarding contracts for the new academic year. They were not yet prepared to fire nonsigners: everyone was supposed to receive a contract. *But by late July only signers had received their contracts.* This was another error on the part of Sproul and the administration. For as Stewart put it, the faculty considered this "a breach of faith," and there was so much indignation over this "high-pressuring" that a divided faculty began to coalesce in opposition to the Loyalty Oath, including professors who had already signed.[61]

It was only at the end of August, when Lehman informed Sproul that hostility to the oath was widespread, that the president began to understand the degree of faculty opposition.

CHAPTER 6

NEW LEADERS: CAUGHEY, LEHMAN, AND THE NASE

Being a man is the continuing battle of one's life; and one
loses a bit of manhood with every stale compromise to the
authority of any power in which one does not believe.

—Norman Mailer[1]

THERE WAS A FORTUITOUS REASON WHY
UCLA responded so slowly to the oath. John Caughey
(pronounced "Coy"), the historian who would emerge as its most energetic resister, had left California in June to teach summer school in Colorado.

Born in 1902, Caughey grew up in Kansas and Nebraska before moving to
Berkeley, where he studied for a doctorate with Herbert Bolton. Like his mentor,
he was a historian of the American West and would write the first biography of
Hubert Howe Bancroft and a study of the impact of the Gold Rush on California. An authority on vigilantism and mob rule, he saw the anticommunist
hysteria as a reflection of that mentality.

Much like Berkeley's Edward Tolman, Caughey was mild-mannered, shy,
even retiring. As a scholar he was not as distinguished as the northern resistance leader, but he was his equal as a man of principle and a fighter. A life-

long idealist, the historian liked to refer to himself as a "champion of lost causes."[2] As early as 1930 he had advocated for California's farmworkers. In 1942 he spoke out against the internment of Japanese Americans. Active in the American Civil Liberties Union, he lobbied against the ACLU's policy of excluding communists, Nazis, Ku Kluxers, and other extremists as members.[3] His concern for the civil liberties of racists and fascists distinguished Caughey from the Popular Front liberals.

When the historian received Sproul's letter requesting him to sign the revised oath he was furious, and he spent the weekend working on his reply.[4] He began by praising the president for his "consistent and staunch support of academic freedom" and then added that given such a commitment, "neither the original or the revised wording of the oath" could have come from his initiative. He warned that unless the oath was overturned, it would discourage the free pursuit of truth and lead to conformity.

Caughey also told Sproul that "some idealist" would be so upset that he would refuse to sign, and thus "martyr himself." But he assured him that he did not harbor any such intention himself, the only one of his predictions that would prove untrue.[5]

Caughey also urged fellow historian Charles Mowat to call a meeting of the UCLA chapter of the American Association of University Professors. The two men were the AAUP's leaders, so it was because of them that it, and not the Academic Senate, led the fight during the early stages of UCLA's resistance.

When the chapter met in late July, it passed a resolution asking the Senate to approve a "memorial" to the regents that would replace the new requirement with the old Constitutional Oath. At the same time the Committee of Non-Academic Employees, a group of graduate student research assistants, teaching assistants, and course readers, was getting organized on the Westwood campus. It sent a newsletter to its membership calling for a meeting "to determine what action we can take to have the loyalty oath rescinded."

Graduate students who were employed as teaching or research assistants were required to sign the oath to keep their jobs, just as were their professors. So on August 4 philosophy professor Donald Piatt urged them not to sign before the Academic Senate met in the fall.[6] Piatt, as the faculty's liaison to the group, would become one of the most active—and radical—of UCLA's resisters. A

Popular Front liberal, his sponsorship of the American Youth for Democracy, the Communist Party's youth organization, as well as his affiliation with the Peoples Education Center, had made him a leading target of the Tenney committee.[7]

At Berkeley the Graduate Students Association (GSA) represented all students working for higher degrees. Those who were employed as teaching assistants, research assistants, and course readers could also join the Non–Academic Senate Employees Association (NASE). Throughout the controversy the NASE, which also included instructors, lecturers, and acting assistant professors, would be much more militant than their Academic Senate elders in fighting the Loyalty Oath.

The NASE had begun organizing earlier than its UCLA counterpart. On July 20 the group fashioned a petition to protest the requirement. Even with most members off campus for the summer, the four hundred signatures it had collected by the beginning of the fall semester represented more than half its constituency.[8]

The highlight of the NASE's meeting on September 15 was a dramatic speech by Leslie Fishman. Fishman, who would emerge as the group's leading spokesman, had joined the Communist Party in 1939, and because of his politics had been kept out of officer training school during the war. A staff sergeant when he had landed in Normandy shortly after D-Day,[9] five years later he was a lecturer in business administration and studying for an economics Ph.D. He was not public about his party affiliation, but his friends and fellow resisters were aware of the fact.[10]

Robert Colodny, however, was open about his communist sympathies. He had been severely injured while fighting in Spain with the Lincoln Brigade. As a leader of grad students in history, he was considered "a great orator" and the sparkplug of the resistance in his department.[11]

Another history grad student, Bill Doyle, was a fellow traveler, if not an outright party member. As the featured speaker at an NASE forum on September 15, he told the audience that the overwhelming majority of grad students opposed the oath, but many were too intimidated to speak out.[12]

Fishman, Colodny, and Doyle were only a few of the grad student leaders on the Far Left. Bob Martinson, head of the Socialist Youth League, was another important spokesman, as was John Bunzel.[13] At the time when there was not a single communist in the Academic Senate leadership and very few fellow travelers on the faculty, party members and sympathizers were prominent, even dominant, in the organizations of the grad students.

Still, this leadership was exclusively male, a reflection of the obstacles women faced in graduate school, as well as of an insensitivity of the NASE and the Left on gender issues.[14]

Although the students began their resistance a month later than the faculty, and in less dramatic fashion, they would soon be more aggressive in carrying on the fight. Their more radical leadership reflected the outlook of their constituency, which was more Left-leaning than the undergraduate student body.

DURING THE SUMMER OF 1949, while the faculty was on vacation, the Soviet Union exploded its first nuclear bomb. With China's Red Army capturing more and more territory from the Nationalists, the United States saw the handwriting on the wall and stopped all aid to Chiang Kai-shek. At home the anticommunist hysteria led to an especially ugly incident. At a Paul Robeson concert at Peekskill, New York, on September 4, the audience leaving the event was barraged with volleys of rocks, accompanied by anti-Semitic and anti-black taunts. Despite serious injuries to audience members, police stood by without arresting or restraining the rioters.

Two days later Sproul told his Advisory Committee that only 50 percent of Berkeley's professors had signed the oath, and an even smaller number, 40 percent, had complied at UCLA.[15]

By this time the president, realizing the seriousness of the faculty's opposition, was beginning to have doubts of his own. Meeting once more with Hildebrand and Lehman, they decided that there was still a chance to rescind the oath, or at least reword it so it would be acceptable to all parties.[16]

During the summer of 1949 UCLA's Academic Senate was not yet taking an active role in the controversy. At Berkeley the faculty leadership was firmly in the hands of Sproul's Advisory Committee. Both Hildebrand and his partner Lehman shared a cautious and deliberate style. Although moderation was not the best way to fight the oath, it's unlikely that the two could have acted differently. For years each had served in administrative positions, so their loyalties were with the president. They were also friends who worked well together.

With the faculty now more conscious of the seriousness of the crisis, a considerable majority, 650, attended the first Senate meeting of the new term on

September 10. Wheeler Auditorium that afternoon was "alive and vital, with the movement of men about it persuading, cajoling, and with a sense of tenseness and expectation," according to Ben Lehman.[17] Responding to questions from the faculty, Sproul promised that the regents' resolution was solely aimed at the Communist Party and "that no noncommunist faculty member who regards the regents' policy as unwise will be deemed to have severed his connection with the University."[18]

With only six "no" votes, the Senate passed a resolution aimed at ending the impasse. In place of the Regents' Special Oath, which specifically barred communists, it endorsed instead University Regulation 5 (drafted by Hildebrand in 1934) "which prohibits the employment of persons whose commitments or obligations to any organization, Communist or other, prejudices impartial scholarship and free pursuit of truth." By substituting it for the Loyalty Oath, the faculty was trying to change the emphasis from a "negative" test of loyalty to a "positive" affirmation of traditional academic values.[19]

The distinction between barring a professor for his or her membership in an organization as compared to "commitments prejudicial to scholarship" may seem academic. But during the first year of the oath crisis, the controversy often turned on semantic issues.

An amendment to include non–Academic Senate members in the motion was voted down. This set a precedent. From that point on the faculty would focus almost single-mindedly on itself and neglect the interests of the teaching and research assistants who worked for them.

LIVELY DEBATES IN THE *DAILY CAL*

From the beginning of the fall semester the *Daily Californian* covered the oath crisis with front-page stories as well as editorials that appeared virtually every day. The paper's staff was strongly anti-oath and much more liberal than the student government. Although most Cal students may have been politically apathetic in 1949, there was a substantial minority who were actively engaged in the issues of the day. They contributed guest editorials on the oath as well as on topics such as the Smith Act trials of the top communists and debated whether the civil liberties of Communist Party members should be protected.

In these "As I See It" editorials, as well as in letters to the editor, students responded to one another, producing a lively exchange. Like the *Daily Cal* itself, most of these contributors expressed a Left-liberal politics, but the paper also published views in support of the oath and the crackdown on communists.

During the same period the oath and related issues were debated at off-campus meetings. At the YMCA and YWCA, the same liberal professors who had tangled with Hildebrand earlier in the year—Strong, Caldwell, and Rynin—discussed the oath with interested students.

The Student Progressives, the group that had supported Henry Wallace in 1948, was especially active, holding open-air meetings at Sather Gate and other entrances to the campus. The Welfare Board, a liberal component of the otherwise conservative student government, set up tables at which passersby could sign petitions. The organization reported that at least one in four students stopped to sign; in time they would collect more than 2500 signatures, inspiring a similar project at UCLA. Not to be outdone, the graduate students affiliated with the NASE had now collected more than 500 signatures, representing two-thirds of their constituents.[20]

The fall semester also saw vigorous coverage of the crisis in the UCLA student paper, as the *Daily Bruin* had a new editorial staff. Editor-in-chief Jim Garst and managing editor Clancy Sigal were both Leftists who had supported Wallace. This was too much for the Publications Board, an organization that reflected the conservative student body. Although Garst and Sigal had been elected by the *Bruin*'s staff, the board disqualified them because they had engaged in "too much political activity" and thus were out of touch with the student majority. But the editors chosen to replace them refused to serve, and with the entire *Bruin* staff united behind them, the Leftist editors kept their jobs.[21] Sigal, a World War II veteran and a Communist Party member who would become a well-known novelist, then wrote a series of front-page articles on the oath. And in an editorial published just before the Academic Senate was scheduled to meet, he implored UCLA's faculty to act as forcefully as had Berkeley's a few days earlier.[22]

When the assembly met, they went farther than their northern counterparts, adding the point that commitments that could bar someone from teaching must be *demonstrable*. And as Sigal had suggested, they called for a return to the Constitutional Oath. Caughey, back from Colorado, gave an impassioned speech, replete with rhetorical splendor, that enumerated seven reasons why the oath was harmful.[23]

UCLA's faculty was now involved, but its September 22 resolution still came more than three months after Berkeley's Senate had acted. And while the resistance in the north was meeting to plan its strategy, UCLA nonsigners such as Caughey and David Saxon had no contact with one another, so they had no idea how many like-minded colleagues there were.

The regents met on September 23, the day when Truman informed the nation that the Soviet Union had become a nuclear power. Again Neylan tried to get Sproul to admit that he had advocated the oath. The faculty and the press were still referring to it as "the Regents' Oath," which continued to infuriate the regent. So he moved that the full record of the board's meetings be made public. But Sproul pleaded again that his relations with the faculty would be compromised, and he was able to keep the information from the faculty and the public.

The president was also successful in getting the release of the nonsigners' September salary checks: they had gone almost a month without pay. But he was not able to separate the oath from the 1949–1950 contracts. It was now *no oath, no job.*

LEHMAN'S "SICKENING EXPERIENCE"

By the end of September faculty dissatisfaction with Hildebrand had extended to the president's Advisory Committee. An overwhelming majority was opposed to the oath, yet their views were not represented on that influential panel. So philosophy professor William Dennes was named to replace Hildebrand on the committee. Dennes, a liberal who had been against the oath from the outset, was influenced in his politics by his experiences in Germany before Hitler came to power. The intelligentsia had not taken the Nazi leader seriously, dismissing him as "a clown."

Invoking Aristotle, who had warned against "dogmatic universalization," Dennes believed that criminality and guilt must be determined only by the careful examination of an individual case. From this standpoint he was appalled by a tendency among many Berkeley scientists to be "dead sure" that every member of the Communist Party was a criminal, unfit to teach. That someone like Hildebrand took this position shocked Dennes, for he was violating his commitment to the principle that the scientific method is based on evidence. Because one of his own friends had been a party member, he knew that it was possible for a communist to exhibit intellectual independence and integrity.[24]

With Hildebrand out, the leadership of the committee (and the faculty in general) was assumed by Lehman. The English professor was, in the words of his younger colleague Charles Muscatine, "larger than life." Living in the world of culture and the arts, Lehman thumbed his nose at the ideal of the specialist that had been gaining ground in the academic world. His first book was a novel, and he would write other works of fiction.[25]

Ben Lehman had come to Berkeley in 1920, even though his Harvard teachers had warned him against moving to the "intellectual desert" of California. His first wife had written films for Hollywood, and with his second marriage to Judith Anderson, one of the most famous actresses of the 20th century, his circle of friends was made up of leading people in the theater, including Katherine Cornell and Lawrence Olivier. Lehman was also close to Thomas Mann, Sherwood Anderson, John Muir, Ansel Adams, Charles Chaplin, and Paul Robeson.[26] Another friend was Robinson Jeffers; Lehman would edit a volume of his poetry.[27]

When the Advisory Committee met with representatives of the regents on September 29,[28] Lehman took every opportunity to let them know how strongly the faculty felt about the oath. With the October 1 deadline to sign only two days away, more professors were complying, but despite this the faculty was more opposed than ever to the requirement. The summer had given it time to examine the issue in depth, so members now viewed the oath more critically.

Lehman argued that control over appointments, promotions, and dismissals must remain with the Academic Senate. Hoping to convince the board that the oath violated Anglo-American traditions by imputing "guilt by association," Dennes invoked Aristotle. When the argument fell flat the philosopher realized that he was not in the same league as the other more worldly committee members, let alone the regents.[29]

The strongest position was taken by a member from UCLA, the philosopher Hugh Miller, who warned that professors on his campus were concerned that "a blanket political disqualification of service with regard to communism" could set a dangerous precedent. It might lead to "the disqualification of other minority groups," and even to "the destruction of the University."[30]

Neylan lost no time in rebutting this idea. "Communism is not a political party but a criminal conspiracy and . . . the disqualifying of a person for membership in the communist movement would (not) set a bad precedent any more than the dismissal of members of Murder, Inc."[31]

The regent also used the meeting to needle Sproul about his role in proposing the oath. And this time he had him trapped. For with so many Academic Senate leaders in on the secret, the faculty, as well as the general public, would soon be informed.

Learning about the oath's origins was disillusioning to Lehman, who felt that Sproul had lied to him.[32] But that didn't swing him to Neylan's side. In fact, being in the same room as the regent was tightening the rope around the president's neck was "one of the most sickening experiences" of his life.[33]

That night Neylan invited Lehman to lunch at his exclusive Pacific Union Club. When they met the next day in the club library, Lehman warned him that one can't just "foist things of this sort on a faculty of world renown." Neylan's reply: "Oh, you're right as rain."

"We began talking and he said suddenly, abruptly, 'You know Ernest Lawrence?'" The physicist lived three houses up the street from the English professor on Tamalpais Road, so they knew each other well. According to Lehman, Neylan then began building up Lawrence as his choice to replace Sproul as president.

And then he offered a deal. If the Senate condemned Sproul, he would prevail on the board to eliminate the oath.

Lehman had heard that Neylan wanted to oust Sproul, but he "couldn't believe that it was (so) carefully calculated," or that the regent's determination was so extreme to be almost manic. Sensing how irrational Neylan's obsession was, the other regents at the conference meeting didn't respond to his tirades.

That evening Lehman wrote the regent about how the oath had failed to trap any communists and yet it was requiring "hundreds of honorable and devoted Americans" to attest to their loyalty. Without mentioning the "deal" to oust Sproul, he praised Neylan for his earlier opposition to the oath and for agreeing to "see that the whole nonsense of the oath would be withdrawn."

As soon as he opened the letter, Neylan called him back. "Don't get me wrong, this is a tit for tat business, you know."[34]

THE LINES HARDEN

Ben Lehman had been an early signer, for he felt faculty opposition would carry more weight if it did not appear disloyal. Unlike Tussman, tenBroek, and Tolman, he didn't feel that the oath violated academic freedom or civil liberties. To much fanfare Hildebrand signed in early October, just days after Mao Tse Tung proclaimed a new Peoples' Republic of China. Soon another new communist state, the German Democratic Republic, sealed the division of that country into two nations, the Federal Republic of Germany having been established a month earlier.

Just before the October 10 Senate meeting, student groups mobilized to influence their professors. A liberal representative on the Executive Committee of the Associated Students, the top council of the students' organizational structure, offered a resolution reaffirming "faith in the principles of academic freedom" and support for the faculty's opposition to the oath. But with Ex Com influenced by its administration representatives, the mild statement passed by only one vote. The dean of students had a vote, as did an alumni member and a faculty member. The latter was paleobotanist Ralph Chaney, widely known as a spy for Neylan. In speaking against the resolution, he claimed it was sponsored by a group whose only interest was to promote discord.[35]

The organization of instructors and graduate assistants was not controlled by the administration, and it was much more radical than the Academic Senate. So NASE's resolution to abrogate both the oath and *the policy of excluding Reds from the faculty* passed with only one dissenting vote. A second measure urging the membership not to sign was approved unanimously.[36]

When four hundred professors assembled in Wheeler Hall on October 10, Lehman moved again that the faculty should demand that the regents rescind the oath. He also asked the faculty to express its agreement with the no Red teachers policy. But the Senate could not agree on these measures, and two substitute motions were introduced.

The first came from George Adams, an esteemed philosopher who had joined the faculty in 1908 and was a veteran of the Faculty Revolution. Directly contradicting Lehman, he spoke against dismissing professors because they were communists, and for such dismissal only if they failed to abide by impartial scholarship in the pursuit of truth.[37] The second new motion was authored by tenBroek, who was ushered to the podium by his friend Tussman. As Gordon Griffiths recalled, the speech professor set aside his Braille notes and gave a long elaborate presentation from memory.[38]

TenBroek's measure affirmed the faculty's right to govern itself, and though it was cloaked in lofty academic language, its blunt message was clear. The regents' role was to maintain the conditions necessary for the university to function and not to interfere in matters that belonged to the faculty: how the professoriat taught; did its research; and selected, promoted, or dismissed its peers.[39] He then returned to his seat, accompanied by loud sustained applause.[40]

Although the Senate adjourned without voting on either measure, the tenBroek resolution would eventually be fateful in polarizing the parties involved in the crisis.

A few weeks later on October 29, during a football game at Cal's Memorial Stadium, two fans in UCLA's rooting section hoisted a banner that read, "Bail, Not Jail, For The 11 Communists." The reference to the trial of the party's leadership upset campus police and the county sheriff's office, but despite strenuous efforts they were unable to find the perpetrators.[41]

On November 1, Sproul's speech to the American Bankers Association included the strongest language he'd ever used against communists teachers. Invoking Lenin's statement that "The school must become a weapon of the dictatorship of the proletariat," he called them "purblind fanatics" and asserted that "No man can be a member of this subversive organization without taking on the coloration of its leaders and sharing in their guilt." He ended by stating that "The struggle between Communism and Democracy is not a debate, it is a War."[42]

This provocative speech, coming at a time when negotiations between his Advisory Committee and the Academic Senate hung in a delicate balance, made the public, as well as many faculty members, doubt that Sproul had reversed his position on the oath. The talk met with so much criticism that at the next Senate meeting a defensive president had to repeat several times that his speech had nothing to do with the oath, which he had not mentioned to the bankers.[43]

The young historian Gordon Griffiths had been chosen to reintroduce the tenBroek resolution at that same meeting. There was no department at Berkeley whose members were more divided over the oath than History. Ernst Kantorowicz was the most militant anti-oath spokesman on the entire faculty, and he was supported by several younger colleagues, including Griffiths. But he was not supported by Raymond Sontag, one of Berkeley's most Right-wing professors.

An older man with considerable clout in department politics, Sontag warned Griffiths before the November meeting against "playing so public a role" and made it clear that speaking out should be left to his elders. The introverted assistant professor didn't respond, but he would not be intimidated by the implicit threat: "If you don't behave, you can forget about your future at Berkeley, for I and others will vote against promoting you to tenure."[44]

The ex-communist and regent's son flouted Sontag's advice on the very day (November 7, 1949) on which the Soviet Union was celebrating the 32nd anniversary of the Bolshevik Revolution. And for Hildebrand and Neylan, faculty liberals utilized "typical communist tactics" to get their way that day. For only at the end of an unusually long meeting, after more than a third of the four-hundred-plus professors in attendance had left to have dinner with their families, were the Adams and the tenBroek resolutions passed. The regents took these motions as a challenge, with the result that "a *sharp disagreement* between the faculty and the regents" was turned into "a *very real and bitter controversy*."[45]

The passage of these measures antagonized several middle-of-the-road regents and led to a pro-oath majority on the board. Equally upset were faculty moderates, the very people who had voted down the motions four weeks earlier and who had left the meeting confident that no important business would be taken up.[46]

The deadline for signing had been extended from October 1st to November 30, which gave more of the faculty the opportunity to comply. By November 18, Sproul could report that 84.5 percent of university personnel were now in compliance, including 75 percent of Academic Senate members.[47]

On November 30, 1949, Berkeley's nonsigners, along with a few friendly signers, formed a steering committee, with law professor Frank Newman as acting chair. The other seven members included the two former comrades Griffiths and Brodeur and the two friends tenBroek and Tussman, as well as

Tolman's son-in-law Jack Kent, Philip Griffin of journalism, and the philosopher Stephen Pepper. For the next month, the group would meet Friday evenings at the Faculty Club, with attendance anywhere from fifty to two hundred people. Although he was not on the new committee, Tolman was the "titular head" of the group, the man who spoke with the most authority as it met to decide on strategy and tactics for the period ahead.[48]

There was no such organization at UCLA, even though a Senate-authorized survey suggested that faculty opposition to the oath was at least as strong in the south. The poll was organized by a committee headed by Marion "Gus" Wenger, a liberal psychologist active in the local AAUP chapter. Wenger was an expert on psychological testing as well as the autonomic nervous system, and was also the chair of the Psychology Department.

By mid-November, when the results were tallied, 78 percent of UCLA's faculty had signed the oath. Wenger found that 11 percent of those who had signed had done so almost as soon as they received it in the mail. Forty-three percent had complied during the summer, and 38 percent during the fall. Seventy-four percent gave fear of losing their jobs as the reason for signing. Overall, 69 percent not only disapproved of the oath, they also disagreed with it vehemently. A solid majority of the signers were also unhappy with the requirement.

About two-thirds thought that the oath had had a detrimental effect on faculty morale and had hurt the university's reputation in academic circles. A similar majority feared that barring communists established a dangerous precedent; in time members of other groups might face exclusion. Only 12 percent believed that failure to sign should be cause for dismissal.

On the other hand, 37 percent believed that membership in the Communist Party was sufficient cause to disqualify a professor from teaching. Fifty-four percent disagreed with this position. But there was a strong consensus that professional competence should be the yardstick for judging fitness, and the majority believed that the Academic Senate, and not the regents or the president, should make these decisions. And yet 87 percent agreed with the regents' policy that if a faculty member was committed to "non-constitutional means" of transforming the government he or she should be dismissed. The apparent discrepancy can be explained by the fact that more than half of the faculty was not yet convinced that communists believed in force and violence.[49]

At the time Wenger was polling the faculty, his colleague in psychology, Franklin Fearing,[50] along with one of his graduate students, was conducting a survey of student opinion. The results showed that UCLA's students were much more conservative than their professors, for 41 percent of the 424 undergraduates polled were in favor of the oath. Only half opposed the requirement, in contrast to virtually all the faculty. Half of the students believed that their teachers were now more fearful of discussing controversial issues. They were split down the middle on whether communist teachers could be objective in the classroom. Thirty-six percent believed that nonsigners should be fired, three times the equivalent figure for their professors.[51]

IN DECEMBER 1949 the Davisson-Grant committee, officially known as the Academic Senate's Combined Conference Committee, became the most influential faculty group in the oath crisis. Malcolm Davisson was a Berkeley economist, a liberal who was trusted by both the nonsigners and the moderate faculty, and was as well liked as any professor on campus. He was trained in law, and because of this background it was believed that he would be able to stand up to Neylan.[52]

Political scientist J.A.C. (Cliff) Grant of UCLA was more conservative than Davisson, but he too was a respected faculty leader. The committee also included two leaders of the anti-oath struggle, John Caughey of UCLA and Robert Aaron Gordon of Berkeley, as well as two of Berkeley's most eminent scientists, Joel Hildebrand and the virologist Wendell Stanley.

But it was Davisson and Grant who ran the group. On December 13 Neylan took them to lunch in an attempt to break the ice and soften the opposition. He began by stressing that the oath was Sproul's brainchild and that the faculty (meaning Hildebrand and Lehman) had pushed it as vigorously as the regents had. But once the pleasantries were over, the three men settled in to what would be a four-hour meeting. Playing hardball, Neylan scoffed at the idea that there were no communists on the Berkeley faculty; he knew at least twenty![53]

Davisson and Grant replied that the system in place since 1940 was working well, for all those communists were nowhere to be seen and if they existed at all, their very quietness suggested that they were no real help to the party.

Neylan then revealed that as a member of an Atomic Energy Commission committee that reviewed security cases for the Radiation Laboratory he had information that he could not reveal, but would shock his guests. So the faculty, which had remained apathetic in the face of these threats, had better act. It was the Senate's responsibility to find these hidden Reds and then to dismiss them. Davisson and Grant had to do something about the Academic Senate also, for its leadership was a gang of "Leftist politicians who were followed by a bunch of dupes."[54]

The regent believed that UC Berkeley was the Communist Party's number one target because of its Rad Lab and its many scientists doing research in such top-secret areas as atomic energy. And that is why the communists on the faculty, as well as their supporters among "the dissident minority" leading the fight against the oath, were such a danger.[55]

With the expanded Conference Committee set to meet on January 4, Neylan ended the session by warning Davisson and Grant that there would be no meeting unless they could convince the faculty to prepare a plan to eliminate its communists. Throughout much of the session the regent had been acting like a trial lawyer, hammering away at the professors as if they were defendants guilty of a crime. He repeated his ideas over and over, and neither Davisson nor Grant could get anywhere with their own arguments. They left feeling very discouraged and without realizing that Neylan had been recording their words to use against them.[56] Or that the regent now considered Davisson "the number one enemy of the university," even worse than Sproul.[57]

REGENTS FIRE IRVING DAVID FOX

Neylan put his ideas into practice when Irving David Fox, a teaching assistant in physics, appeared at the next board meeting. Fox had been a member of communist front organizations in the late 1930s, and in 1942 he had attended some party meetings. But in 1943 he had broken with the Communist Party, deciding he didn't agree with its policies.

In September 1949 the House Un-American Activities Committee was investigating communist infiltration at the Radiation Laboratory, and Fox was called to the stand. He was a polite, even cooperative witness, except when it came to the question of the Communist Party. On the advice of his attorney he declined to answer questions about his party affiliations, as well as about those of people he had known.

For Neylan, Fox was living proof that there were communists on the Berkeley faculty. Except for his own party membership, the young physicist had been open about his radical past, and for Neylan that was enough to hang him. In an executive session with the young physicist out of the room, the regent moved his dismissal. Sproul wasn't sure it was a good idea, but he eventually voted against Fox. Only Edward Heller, the board's most liberal member, demurred. For him what mattered was that the young man was no longer a communist.[58]

Fox was dismissed by the regents on December 16, 1949. Whether or not the timing was intentional, the decision came as students and faculty were leaving Berkeley for an inter-semester break of almost a month. So it wasn't until January 11 that the NASE protested the decision. The group's steering committee reported that the TA had an exemplary record, having received positive recommendations from his chair, Raymond Birge. For the NASE the firing of Fox was a violation of due process. Because no charges had been filed against him it could only conclude that the regents' goal was to enforce "political orthodoxy."

A few weeks later, Bill Doyle, speaking for the NASE leadership, published an open letter to Sproul and the regents demanding Fox's reinstatement. Doyle also attacked the board's no communist policy and demanded that future criteria for evaluating graduate assistants should be teaching ability and academic proficiency.[59]

Because Irving David Fox had signed the oath, his case questioned how valuable that vehicle was in exposing and rooting out Reds. He was also the first member of the teaching staff fired since Kenneth May in 1940. But he wouldn't be the last.

CHAPTER 7

THE "SIGN OR GET OUT" ULTIMATUM

The Board of Regents, with its heart in Sacramento and its head in a bank vault, (is) methodically teaching our faculty to live on its knees.

—Clancy Sigal[1]

A S 1950 BEGAN, INTERNATIONAL EVENTS provided new ammunition for the zealots of anticommunism. The Soviet Union was now a nuclear power, and China, the most populous country in the world, was firmly in communist control. The Peoples' Republic of China gained a new legitimacy when the United Kingdom formally recognized it on January 6, with Israel and Finland soon following. But not the United States. Truman was under attack for permitting China to fall to the communists. It would become an axiom of Right-wing Republicans that we had "lost" China because of the treason of subversives in the Foreign Service and the State Department.

At UCLA the *Daily Bruin* became a target once again. Jim Garst had graduated, so Clancy Sigal was editor-in-chief when the winter term began. But not for long. This time the administration succeeded in removing the radical from his post. And even though the staff rallied behind him, the paper could not get the decision reversed. All it did was exact a promise that the matter would be decided by a vote of the student body. That did not bode well for re-instatement, given how conservative the students were.[2]

But Sigal got the last word in a farewell editorial. UCLA, he wrote, had succumbed to "the political lynchings which are sweeping the nation." His firing had been engineered by a "Board of Regents with its heart in Sacramento and its head in a bank vault, methodically teaching our faculty to live on its knees."[3]

On January 4 the Conference Committee met without Malcolm Davisson. The stress of having been the object of Neylan's tirades had brought about a breakdown in his health, so he became the first of the oath's many casualties. He was replaced by Robert Aaron Gordon, another economist.

Gordon was one of several Berkeley professors who were catapulted into leadership by the crisis. Born in 1908, he was a product of the Great Depression, and after working for the New Deal in the late 1930s, he became an expert on the business cycle and full employment. A liberal strongly opposed to communism, he had joined the Americans for Democratic Action in 1948. Outside the university Gordon worked to improve race relations, and was a leader of Berkeley's influential Consumer's Cooperative movement.[4] Called Aaron by his friends, Gordon had a striking presence. He was tall, he exuded gravitas, and he had the ability to sway an audience.

It was Aaron Gordon who had edited the draft of a report by Davisson and Grant after the former became ill. A survey of the issues raised by the oath crisis, along with proposals for its solution, it was intended as a basis of discussion for the upcoming conference meeting. But Gordon, who was much less politic than Davisson, also charged that the oath "had done violence to the conditions that nurture greatness in a university—the faculty's devotion to teaching and research, the faculty's pride in the University, and the University's reputation in the academic world—by creating suspicion where there had been trust, by causing disunity where there had been harmony, and by engendering doubt where there had been confidence—both within the University and between the institution and the country's scholarly societies."[5]

Such language incensed Neylan. For the remainder of the controversy he would point to Gordon's report, along with the tenBroek resolution, as repudiations by the faculty of agreements that had been worked out between the regents and the Advisory Committee on the policy that communists should be barred from the university. At the January 4 conference, Wendell Stanley, a Nobel Prize–winning Berkeley virologist, took issue with Neylan, arguing that the Advisory Committee "could not bind the Senate." And UCLA's Grant emphasized that the faculty simply would not approve the policy of dismissing someone for "Communist Party membership per se." Toward the end of the session, Gordon confronted Neylan again when he asserted that the problem wasn't the threat of communism, but the effects of the oath on the future of the university.[6]

Although it was never overtly stated, a shift was taking place in the nature of the conflict between the regents and the faculty. The controversy over a general noncommunist policy and a specific new oath was becoming a power struggle over the governance of the university. Were the regents merely trustees whose role was to ensure the smooth functioning of an institution run by the faculty and the administration? Or were they in control, with the authority to make policy?

ON JANUARY 24, 1950, Klaus Fuchs, a German-born physicist who had worked at Los Alamos on the nuclear bomb, walked into the War Office in London and confessed that he had provided the Soviet Union with atomic secrets. His would be the first of many espionage cases in early 1950 that would have an impact on the political climate in the United States and intensify the pressure on the resisters to sign the oath.

By far the most important of these was that of Alger Hiss. Hiss was a State Department employee who had been at Yalta in 1945 as an advisor to FDR. But though supported by the liberal establishment, he was arrested in 1949, and in the course of a long trial, accused by the ex-communist Whittaker Chambers of having provided him with secret documents. When the jury could not reach a unanimous verdict, the judge declared a mistrial.

When Hiss came to trial again, the government was able to convince a New York jury to convict him of perjury, even though America's intellectual class viewed Chambers as untrustworthy and most likely lying. After Hiss was sentenced to five years in prison, Secretary of State Dean Acheson continued to support his former employee, an action that would bring about calls for his ouster and even for his impeachment.[7]

The conviction of Hiss had a profound effect on events in California. During the first trial, Neylan had remained skeptical of, if not outright hostile to, the Loyalty Oath. But contemplating the verdict in the second trial, he decided that an oath could be useful. For if Red faculty members signed it, as he was certain the party had instructed them to, then that meant that it might provide the legal basis to convict and imprison. It was the Hiss verdict on January 25, 1950, Neylan reported four years later, that changed his mind about the oath.[8]

By late January, Neylan and Sproul each had made an about-face. Ten months after the president had proposed the measure, he was looking for ways to eliminate it. And Neylan, who had been an opponent, would soon become its chief advocate on the Board of Regents. Because the president had also reversed his position, the regent could draw upon his animus toward Sproul to thwart him. Make him pay for his mistakes and keep him "twisting in the wind."[9]

On January 31 the last remnants of Chiang Kai-shek's army surrendered. On the same day Truman announced that the United States would go forward to produce a hydrogen "super-bomb." On national television, still a new medium (with fewer than eight million Americans owning a set), Albert Einstein warned that "general annihilation beckons." The "radioactive poisoning of the atmosphere, and hence annihilation of any life on earth, has been brought within the range of possibilities."[10]

But no event would effect the university's oath crisis as much as the emergence of Joseph McCarthy. Although McCarthy did not burst into the spotlight until February 9, 1950, all the elements of the anticommunist crusade were in place long before then. Therefore, historians view the "McCarthy Era" as spanning the decade from 1946 to 1956. Speaking at Wheeling, West Virginia, the Wisconsin senator claimed that there were 205 card-carrying communists employed at the State Department. Even though he would keep revising this number downward, he immediately became the most militant voice promoting the national hysteria. The fact that his inaccurate statements were not investigated by the press, and that it would be months before any of his colleagues challenged him in the Senate, helps explain how such a little known politician could so readily assume the power to intimidate his critics and spread fear throughout the nation.

NEYLAN'S ULTIMATUM UNITES
BERKELEY'S FACULTY

The Wisconsin senator and the California regent shared a worldview that Richard Hofstadter called "the paranoid style," so it's not surprising that Neylan would become McCarthy's strongest supporter within the university community. And the latter's speeches strengthened the regent's position on the oath. When the board met in executive session on February 24, Neylan made it clear that he believed it was the regents, and not the faculty, who ran the university. Disagreeing with a compromise motion of Sproul's, he moved that if the oath was not signed by April 30, the nonsigner "will be deemed to have severed his connection with the University." By a vote of 12 to 6, the board accepted Neylan's bombshell, which became known as the "Sign or Get Out Ultimatum."

By this time two opposite theories had emerged about the future of the university. Agreeing only that UC was on the road to ruin, they differed as to why this was happening. Neylan and his supporters claimed that the nonsigners were a "dissident minority" within the faculty bent on ruling and ruining the university. A growing number of professors at Berkeley and UCLA—likely the majority by late February 1950—worried that it was the oath that was undermining UC's status as a leading academic institution.

The two positions were well expressed in the editorial commentary of San Francisco's two largest newspapers immediately after the regents' meeting.

On February 27 Neylan published a front-page editorial in the *Examiner*. The feature was unsigned, but the regent regularly wrote the opinion pieces on the oath for that paper, as well as for other Hearst dailies. Highlighting the text, which reflected Neylan's inimitable style, was the statement that "a minority group (and the problem is a minority within the minority) appears to favor a situation in which the faculty COULD NOT DISMISS A COMMUNIST UNTIL AFTER HE HAD STOLEN ATOMIC LABORATORIES AND TRANSFERRED THEM TO MOSCOW." The editorial continued in upper and lower case: "The recalcitrants should be required to accept or should be eliminated. They can be replaced in a short time by equally competent men."[11]

On the following day a *Chronicle* editorial accused the regents of threatening to ruin the university "by destroying the atmosphere of intellectual freedom on which it has thrived." With UC the only top ranking university in the nation with a loyalty oath, the control that the regents had imposed on the faculty "must be pleasant for the Kremlin to behold."[12]

But the *Chronicle* was a voice in the wilderness. The only other Bay Area paper opposing the oath was the low-circulation *San Francisco News,* part of the Scripps Howard chain. In the Sacramento and San Joaquin valleys, three McClatchy-owned papers in Sacramento, Fresno, and Modesto were also anti-oath. But the combined circulation of these five papers was dwarfed by the pro-oath Hearst dailies in San Francisco and the *Oakland Tribune.* And in Los Angeles, every major paper supported the oath, including the then conservative *Times.*[13]

If Neylan's goal was to escalate the conflict, he was successful. The ultimatum united the faculty. For the next two weeks not a day passed without meetings, as every segment of the faculty gathered to plot its strategy. Creative juices flowed, and all kinds of ideas were floated. Among the nonsigners there was also a measure of paranoia. Many were convinced that their phones were tapped, so they only spoke to their comrades face to face.

Everyone advocated that the Senate step up its pressure, for a decisive moment was at hand. Some wanted department chairs and deans to resign, so that the workings of the university would break down. Others requested that Sproul return their signed oaths, so that that they could tear them up in a dramatic public protest. Talk of lawsuits against the regents was heard, and a campaign to threaten mass resignations began.

Kantorowicz took the most radical position. In a letter to Strong, he wrote, "We can no longer dally. We have to answer alternatives with alternatives, deadlines with deadlines, and ultimata with ultimata. And we have to stop building treacherous 'golden bridges' which can only lead to defeat and disaster."

Eka asked the faculty to sign a declaration that if the regents did not revoke the oath at their March 31 meeting, they would "immediately and automatically discontinue to discharge our duties in offices and classrooms." And were anyone, even a teaching assistant, to be dismissed for not signing, the faculty would resign en masse.[14]

George Adams, the philosopher who had taught at Berkeley for forty years, said that he had never seen the faculty so united.[15] But this unity was not transformed into action, for as always, the faculty proved better at talking than acting.

At the point when militant action was needed, the anger of the professoriat dissipated, and hope was placed once again in negotiating committees.

On February 28 the Committee of Seven was formed with the mandate to represent the faculty in its negotiations to overturn the oath. Its chair was John Hicks, who for the next six weeks would be the faculty's most important leader. At sixty, Hicks was at the high point of his career, famous for important works of history, including *The Populist Revolt*.[16] As with Tolman, one of Hicks's grandparents was an abolitionist, and with his father a "strong protagonist of the Negro," he inherited a liberal tradition.

But the historian's conservative style would cause tensions in his relations with Tolman's group. Just a day before his appointment, he had met with the nonsigners. Feeling confident and strong in their numbers (150 resisters at this point), they had pledged to stand together and not sign the oath, no matter what threats came their way. Energized by the "Sign or Get Out" ultimatum, they were now more firm in their commitment to the AAUP position that "discrimination against members of the Communist Party, as such, constitutes an infraction of academic freedom." Hicks thought this was a mistake and that the nonsigners were "bent on insisting that the rest of the faculty, the overwhelming majority, must come over to its (minority) position, and that without compromise."[17]

And yet as the deadline neared, many nonsigners were breaking ranks. After much soul searching one unnamed professor went to the administration building on February 28 to get the unpleasant task over with. There he found "a bored secretary doubling as a notary public." He had expected his signing to be "solemn and dignified," but he was not even asked to hold up his right hand. The secretary threw his signed oath into a big pile and said that she would stamp it with the others as soon as she could get around to it. What to a professor was an issue of great seriousness, a moment of agonizing torment, was to the system that processed it just one more bureaucratic task.[18]

EIGHT THOUSAND STUDENTS RALLY
AT FIRST MASS MEETING

The organizations of graduate students continued to respond more assertively than their faculty mentors. Toward the end of February Jack Bunzel, the head of the Graduate Students Association, began calling for a dramatic gesture like a mass meeting of the student body. During this period more than seventy people (the most ever) attended an NASE steering committee meeting. According to Bill Doyle, the group felt that the time for diplomacy was past, for the regents had "declared war."[19] For days the two organizations kept up the pressure, until they were able to get the ever-cautious student government (Associated Students of the University of California, or ASUC) to agree to sponsor the event. On March 6, 1950, between eight and ten thousand people, of whom more than 90 percent were students, thronged into the Greek Theater.

In 1950 there were twenty thousand students at Berkeley. Although the *Daily Cal* and the NASE had taken strong stands against the oath, and as recently as February 19 the Student Progressives had sponsored a rally attended by 1500, the vast majority remained uninvolved. For Leon Litwack, then the leader of the Student Progressives and later a historian of the black experience, they were too concerned about their careers and too intimidated by the pre-rally hysteria.[20] Thus the enormous turnout surprised him and other student leaders.

The meeting was chaired by Danny Coelho, a conservative head of the ASUC. Coelho had resisted the event, and even after agreeing to it, had kept insisting that its purpose was only "informational." When he told the crowd that this was not a protest meeting, and that they were going to hear both sides of the controversy and then make up their minds, the response came immediately and in one voice: "We've made up our minds!"[21]

Since all the scheduled speakers were anti-oath, the "other side" referred to John Francis Neylan. The regent had been invited to give a major address, but he had to remain in Arizona to nurse "a badly neglected cold." Sick or not, Neylan was too savvy to subject himself to the abuse he would have received from a student audience. So a conservative member of the Executive Committee of the ASUC read his statement.

The regent began by protesting that he had had nothing to do with the oath, which had originated with the president and the faculty. And the crisis had come from the Academic Senate's reneging on agreements it had made. The students responded with hisses, catcalls, and derisive laughter. But then they fell silent when they heard the regent's conciliatory final words. If the faculty (scheduled to meet the next day) would adopt a resolution "in plain English" unequivocally endorsing the 1940 regents' policy of excluding communists from the university, the regents could "work out a compromise at their next meeting."[22]

The first speaker, Aaron Gordon, presented a history of the controversy that rebutted Neylan's claim that the faculty's bad faith had caused the crisis. Responding to the latter's point that almost 90 percent of university personnel had signed the oath, Gordon said that didn't gainsay the fact that on April 30 there would be 1600 employees subject to termination, including 200 Senate members from Berkeley and 150 from UCLA. The "Sign or Resign" edict, he continued, "violates the principles of academic freedom and tenure, the safeguards of the academic profession for centuries." If it were to be enforced, 200 faculty members would hand in their resignations and others would leave because they "cannot stand by and see their colleagues fired for no other reason than this." And the university would be investigated and censured by the American Association of University Professors.

Gordon was followed by Peter Odegaard, chair of the Political Science Department, who emphasized that while the 1942 Constitutional Oath remained an effective vehicle to bar communists, the Regents' Special Oath "interferes with intellectual integrity." "If California yields to transitory fear and hysteria, how can we expect weaker institutions to resist?" Finally, Wendell Stanley, who was playing an increasingly important role in the controversy, said that it was the regents who had closed the door to negotiation and that in all his years at Berkeley he had found no communists on the faculty.[23]

A week had passed since the regents' ultimatum without a response from UCLA. No mass meetings had been scheduled, nor had faculty leaders spoken out. But on March 7 the Senate's combined Steering and Policy Committee held a press conference. Dean Paul Dodd was the spokesman, but it was Ken Macgowan who had personally invited the group of reporters that included CBS's Chet Huntley. Dodd read a statement that had been endorsed by more than half the faculty and by every one of the campus's forty department heads, except those from Military Science, Engineering, and the Law School. The oath, Dodd charged, infringed on academic freedom, was an "entering wedge" for the regents to encroach on faculty prerogatives, and implied distrust and suspicion of the faculty. If not reversed, it would bring "irreparable damage" to the university, he concluded.[24]

Hal Watkins, who had replaced Sigal as the *Daily Bruin*'s editor, exulted that "Our faculty has burst out of its classrooms and has come out swinging against the loyalty oath."[25] But John Caughey, who attended the conference as a member of the policy committee, was not pleased. The historian had been lobbying for such an aggressive outreach to the press for months, so for him it was too little, too late. The moderate strategy of Senate leaders Dodd and Grant was over-cautious, and in his eyes almost as much of a problem as the regents' actions.[26]

When 750 professors crowded into Wheeler Hall on March 7, it was the largest attendance at a Senate meeting since the controversy began, if not in its history. The most important business came from Malcolm Davisson, who felt sufficiently recovered to participate. But while proposing two measures that the faculty would vote on through a mail ballot, the economist collapsed, unable to finish reading his motion.[27]

The first measure on the mail ballot was a vote on whether the 1942 Constitutional Oath, without the Regents' Special Oath, was a sufficient guarantee that professors were loyal Americans. The 1942 measure simply required swearing allegiance to the constitutions of the United States and the State of California; it did not mention subversive activities or Communist Party membership. The Regents' Special Oath was the Loyalty Oath of March 1949 as amended three months later; it required swearing that one was not a communist and did not belong to any group intent on overthrowing the government.

The second proposition was a vote on whether to accept the regents' policy that Communist Party members were unfit to teach. This was the very issue on which faculty liberals had tangled with Hildebrand early in 1949. It was fitting that the university's number one anticommunist wrote the argument in favor of this proposition, and that it was based on Hildebrand's thesis of the inherent contradiction between communist ideas and affiliations and a capacity for unbiased teaching and scholarship.[28]

Voting up or down on the AAUP position was the concession Davisson and his committee had made to Neylan after their January meeting. But in the view of one Berkeley professor, the regent had suckered the faculty into voting "on whether it was for or against Communism, (when) the faculty should have been voting on whether it was for or against academic freedom."[29]

Optimism reigned after the results of the balloting were announced two weeks later. With 90 percent of the faculty having returned their ballots, both the Northern Section and the Southern unit of the Academic Senate voted overwhelmingly against the Loyalty Oath.[30] And they decisively repudiated the AAUP position when they agreed with the proposition that "proved members of the Communist Party, by reason of such commitments to the party, are not acceptable as members of the faculty." Tolman and his non-signers, who supported the AAUP, were able to get only 203 votes from the 949 professors who cast their ballots in the north (21 percent).[31]

At UCLA there was even less support for the AAUP position, as only 17 percent voted against Proposition 2. At face value the result is puzzling, because only four months earlier Gus Wenger's survey had found an over-whelming majority of the faculty against excluding communists just be-cause they were communists. John Caughey provided part of the answer: many of his colleagues felt forced to reverse their position after Berkeley's Wendell Stanley appeared at their Senate meeting and urged them to vote yes, saying that this would give the regents just what they wanted and that it would not compromise the faculty's continued opposition to the larger principle.[32]

But something more dramatic is needed to explain how the proportion of UCLA professors in favor of barring Reds could more than double (from 37 to 82 percent) in such a short time. And that can only be the climate of fear sweeping the nation. For in this period the big news stories were those of communist espionage, with the Hiss trial joined by another sensational case almost weekly. And during the time when the faculty was marking its ballot, Joseph McCarthy was also making headlines exploiting the hysteria. The "where there's smoke there's fire" mentality may have operated on a subcon-scious level, but it contributed to the growing feeling that communists qua communists were undesirable as teachers and scholars.[33]

At Berkeley some of the credit for the stunning defeat of Tolman's group goes to Ralph Chaney, who mobilized many of the "yes" votes. Chaney was one of those scientists referred to by Dennes who believed that the Commu-nist Party was a criminal conspiracy. Almost fifty at the time, he had been a liberal in his youth, but now believed that you had to be "a little disloyal" to continue in that outlook.

The paleobotanist, who had distinguished himself with his discovery of a redwood species believed to have been extinct, was a member of the Senate's influential Committee on Privilege and Tenure. Shocked by the liberal positions taken by professors as they argued with the regents, he copied the most "damning" points, and in his own words, "did a Paul Revere," sounding the alarm to the conservative faculties of Agriculture, Engineering, and Medicine.[34]

Chaney also had a special relationship with Neylan, who sent him transcripts of closed sessions of the board. In return he informed the regent on the thinking of Berkeley's liberal professors. This was no secret: the scientist was frequently referred to as "Neylan's spy."[35]

The likelihood that the controversy could be resolved increased after the remarks of two Right-wing regents. Edward Dickson told the Associated Press that it was "highly gratifying" that the faculty was as determined as the board to bar communists. And Neylan called the vote "a bold and decisive settlement of the issue of civilization versus barbarism."[36] However the *Daily Californian* was not happy: from this time on its editors would accuse the faculty of selling out its principles.

The results made moderate professors jubilant, but greatly discouraged the militants. At UCLA, Senate leader Carl Epling lauded the outcome, but David Saxon, the young physicist who would later become president of the university, was "very disappointed" in the "compromise of academic freedom" involved.[37] As for Caughey, who almost single-handedly was trying to build an opposition movement among UCLA's faculty, the vote totally deflated him.[38] And at Berkeley, the faculty's repudiation of the AAUP position took "the heart out" of Joe Tussman's determination to keep up the fight.[39]

The young philosopher was also beginning to feel alienated from the nonsigners' community. In his view the resistance was made up of interlocking circles. The innermost radical circle consisted of men such as Griffiths, Brodeur, and Kent. They had adopted the Communist Party tactic of forming their own caucus, which would meet and plan strategy before every gathering of the larger nonsigners' group. Tussman felt this was unethical, and when he was invited to join them, he refused.[40]

THE FIRING OF IRVING FOX posed a dilemma for the Academic Senate. Its leadership worried that defending the right of an ex-communist to teach would jeopardize their own resisters. In fact only one faculty member spoke publicly on behalf of the physics TA, and that was the maverick political scientist Harold Winkler.[41]

To the NASE, the faculty Senate's failure to fight for Fox suggested that professors were concerned only with their own interests and not with those of their students. The response of the Academic Senate was that if the faculty resolved the oath crisis to its satisfaction, graduate students would benefit as much as their professors.

When the NASE met on March 10, 1950, it reaffirmed its opposition to the 1940 policy of barring communists from the faculty by a vote of 105 to 4. During the meeting two spies were discovered jotting down the names of those present. A commotion resulted, and as the two fled, one threatened to attack his accuser.

Even though one informer turned out to be an administrative analyst in the Office of the President, Sproul told John Hicks that he was shocked to learn of the incident, and that the two men had been there without his knowledge.[42]

NASE's counterpart at UCLA was also trying to promote more opposition to the oath. In a series of newsletters to its members, the non–Academic Senate employees group bewailed the weakness of its resistance compared to that of Berkeley's grad students. It also pushed for a campuswide mass meeting.[43]

On March 6, 1950, about half of Berkeley's student body had thronged to the Greek Theater. Nine days later the attendance on the Westwood campus (between two and three thousand) represented approximately one-fourth of UCLA's students. And yet it was an impressive showing, because no prominent speakers were featured, either from the faculty or the community. A letter from Regent Dickson in favor of the oath was read, as well as one in opposition from Thomas Mann.[44]

Dean McHenry, perhaps worried about his Popular Front affiliations and Tenney listings, had been an early signer. But he continued to work with UCLA's resistance, trying to get public figures to speak out against the oath. One of those was Harold Laski, the Leftist leader of the British Labour Party, whom McHenry had come to know while studying in London. On March 20, 1950, Laski wrote him that he found UC's Loyalty Oath "incredible" and the "Sign or Get Out" ultimatum "outrageous," and he expressed his "great pride that the Faculty was overwhelmingly determined to resist this encroachment of Academic Freedom."[45]

Four days later the British socialist, who had suffered from pleurisy for years, died of a collapsed lung.[46] He was only fifty-seven, and it was ironic that he died just one day before the first anniversary of the adoption of the 1949 Loyalty Oath. And that Sproul had proposed that oath to the regents to protect himself from the growing storm of criticism after Laski had been invited to speak at UCLA six weeks earlier.

WARREN APPOINTS THREE NEW REGENTS

With a critical regents' meeting scheduled for March 31, Governor Warren had three vacancies to fill. Only one was unexpected, due to the sudden death of Charles C. Teague, head of an association of fruit growers and a Right-winger as extreme as Neylan. Less than two weeks before he died, Teague had written Sproul that the Loyalty Oath meant that parents could now send their children to the university without fearing that they would be indoctrinated with "the unsound philosophies of communism and socialism." In England socialism had already destroyed freedom, and "the United States had traveled a considerable distance along the same road."[47]

The other positions had opened when the terms of two regents expired on March 1. Mortimer Fleishacker, a liberal San Francisco civic leader who had served thirty-two years on the board, was too old to be reappointed. The other slot was that of Lawrence Mario Giannini, who was politically to the right of Neylan. Mario was the son of A. P. Giannini, who had founded the Bank of Italy and led its successor, the Bank of America, until he died in June 1949. On his death, the son not only took over the business, he was also appointed by Warren to fill the remaining ten months of his father's term on the board.

The most liberal regent was Edward Heller, who had become rich as an investor and financial advisor. During the first three months of 1950 Warren used Heller, who was his friend, to advise the faculty to "delay, delay, delay" rather than to make big decisions related to the oath. The governor foresaw that new appointments on the horizon would shift the board's balance of power and increase the possibility that the oath could be eliminated, or at least modified in important ways.[48]

But it was the governor who delayed. He didn't fill the openings until a week, and in one case one day, before the board meeting. His first appointment, to replace Fleishacker, was Cornelius Haggerty, the head of the AFL in California. The NASE had been urging Warren to choose people from the academic world instead of businessmen. But the union of teaching assistants was pleasantly surprised to learn that someone from organized labor had been made a regent for the first time.

The governor then replaced Teague with Jesse Steinhart, a San Francisco attorney who, like Haggerty, could be expected to side with the liberals. Had he then replaced Giannini with a similarly inclined regent, the board would have had a liberal majority. But Warren's conservative side asserted itself, and he awarded Giannini another sixteen-year term.

Still, the governor had effected a change, albeit a modest one, in the political composition of the Board of Regents. The question remained whether or not it would be sufficient to get the "Sign or Get Out" ultimatum reversed on March 31.

CHAPTER 8

FROM THE GREAT DOUBLE CROSS TO THE ALUMNI COMPROMISE

In that year we went to oath meetings, and talked oath, and thought oath. We woke up, and there was the oath with us in the delusive bright cheeriness of the morning. "Oath" read the headlines in the newspaper, and it put a bitter taste in the breakfast coffee. We discussed the oath during lunch at the Faculty Club. And what else was there for subject matter at the dinner table? Then we went to bed, and the oath hovered over us in the darkness, settling down into a nightmare of wakefulness.

—George Stewart[1]

U CLA ECONOMIST PAUL DODD WAS ONE OF the nation's leading labor-management arbitrators. During World War II he had been on the War Labor Board, and having negotiated waterfront strikes, he was on a first-name basis with Harry Bridges. But his attitude to the radical unionist was more nuanced than that of Hildebrand. He didn't agree with Bridges' politics, but he respected him as a "hard bargainer" and a man who kept his word.

Within the university Dodd put these skills to work as an administrator and as a faculty leader. In 1950 he was the dean of the College of Letters and Sciences, and UCLA's Senate had chosen him to head its anti-oath steering committee.

Much like Berkeley's Clark Kerr, a labor economist who was also a top arbitrator, Dodd believed that behind-the-scenes negotiations was the way to resolve the crisis. This put him at odds with Caughey, who wanted the faculty to confront the regents with principled positions. So for the historian, Dodd's cautious approach was a constant irritant.

The two rivals had similar backgrounds. Both men were born in 1902 in the Midwest. Dodd joined UCLA's faculty in 1928, just two years before Caughey.

During the Depression, when Dodd was studying the economics of health care, he discovered how difficult it was for low-income Californians to get basic services. So he campaigned then to make compulsory health insurance a part of the New Deal. Although he did not succeed, Dodd advocated "socialized medicine" on the Western European model all his life.[2]

This was too much for the American Medical Association. During the 1930s its influential secretary Morris Fishbein called Dodd a communist, and the AMA pressured the California Medical Association to stop cooperating with his research. Then the medical lobby tried to suppress publication of his *Economic Aspects of Medical Services.* Not only that, Dodd was afraid that Sproul would fire him because of the publicity. Instead he got promoted. But the communist charge stuck. Fifteen years later, when Dodd assumed expanded administrative responsibilities at UCLA, he was denied security clearance. Therefore, having been red-baited himself he was skeptical of the charges against the nonsigners and could empathize with them.[3]

Two days before the critical March 31 regents' meeting Caughey spoke to the convention of the AAUP and attacked the regents for violating academic freedom. With the publicity, he became the newest member of Neylan's "enemies list."

This made Dodd nervous, because Caughey, as a member of the Combined Conference Committee, was planning to attend the next board meeting. Dodd hoped that his committee would be able to persuade the regents to rescind, or at least modify, the "Sign or Get Out" ultimatum on March 31. Worried that Caughey's presence, even if he didn't speak, would set Neylan off, he made his colleague remain in their hotel for the entire day. According to Hicks, who recounted the story on his return to Berkeley, Caughey's feelings were very badly hurt.[4]

Unfortunately, sequestering Caughey was another overcautious tactic that didn't work.

THE GREAT DOUBLE CROSS

In 1950 liberals were on the defensive and often felt that they had to prove their patriotism by undergoing humiliating rituals. Even Republicans such as Governor Warren were not immune, as an incident on March 31 demonstrated.

The "who's more anticommunist than thou" ritual began when the ultra-conservative Lieutenant Governor Goodwin Knight expressed his concern about a non–Academic Senate member at UCLA, Miriam Sherman. A piano player in gym classes, she had recently been fired after admitting communist affiliations. To Giannini's question as to why she hadn't been discovered earlier, Knight replied that it was because they didn't have the oath then. He followed with a tirade against the Reds and asked the board's liberals whether they felt "comfortable in their company?"

Victor Hansen, an L.A. attorney and oath opponent, answered, "The greatest victory the Communists ever would obtain would be to continue to have conflict between the Regents themselves and the faculty. That is why the Commies are raising trouble."

Hansen was able to take the provocation and twist it in order to argue the importance of resolving the oath crisis. And to cover his tracks, he ended his comments with the word "commies," a pejorative term that signaled that he was as anti-Red as his conservative colleagues.

Then it was Warren's turn to play the game. The governor stated that he was proud to be a UC alumnus and that he had "three youngsters" on its campuses. And "God willing," in two or three years two more of his children would be Cal students. Then he said, "I would cut my right arm off before I would willingly submit my youngsters to the wiles or infamy of a Communist faculty."[5]

Could even Neylan doubt the loyalty of a man who would cut off his arm, or of a liberal who called Reds "commies"?

With the board taking another look at its "Sign or Resign" ultimatum, Dodd was not alone in expecting that it might be rescinded. For by voting against Red professors in the mail ballot, the faculty had given Neylan and his faction exactly what they had asked for.

It was John Hicks, Berkeley's counterpart to Paul Dodd, who moved that the ultimatum be lifted. But the two men were shocked to hear Neylan speak in favor of keeping the April 30 deadline, reneging on what had seemed to be

a clear-cut promise. A roll call vote resulted in ten favoring ending the ultimatum and ten opposed. The deadlock meant that short of a last-minute mir-
acle the nonsigners would lose their jobs on April 30.

The vote showed that the new appointments had not shifted the balance
of power on the board. By reappointing Giannini, Warren had insured that
the Loyalty Oath, which he personally opposed, would remain in place.

According to Gardner, once the faculty had accepted the "No Communist
Policy" with its vote on Proposition 2, Neylan was no longer interested in the
issue. His concern was to destroy the power of the AAUP's 203 supporters. In
his view they were a "dissident minority" who thought they could block decisions that had been agreed on, and in this way run the university.[6]

Hicks believed that Neylan was "out for blood," and that was why he kept
upping the ante. It wasn't enough to have 80 percent of the faculty in favor of
his policy. Once he got 80 percent, he wouldn't be satisfied until he had 90
percent, and with 90 percent, he would insist on 100 percent.[7]

The following week, Berkeley's Senate, happy to appease the Right-wing regents, took another vote on Regulation 5, the measure written by Hildebrand
in 1934 that argued that communist professors and academic freedom were incompatible. Even though it passed overwhelmingly, the gesture accomplished
nothing. In a little more than a month many firings could be expected.

In the lore of the Loyalty Oath this action of Neylan and his conservative
allies became known as "The Great Double Cross."

This time the reaction at UCLA was immediate, though muted. "Mild indignation" was the phrase the *Daily Bruin* used to characterize the faculty's
mood. Caughey put it this way: "We've been beat over the head so often . . .
we're getting used to it." Wenger, the psychologist who had surveyed faculty
attitudes, was both "amazed and shocked." Dodd reported that he knew eight
to ten colleagues planning to resign. *Bruin* editor Watkins suggested that the
regents were intent on transforming the university into "a polytechnic institute." And Neil Jacoby of the Business School saw UCLA sinking to an academic level as low as that of the University of Georgia.[8]

For the next two weeks Wenger would have nightly faculty meetings at his
house. Contingencies were considered: if a specified number of professors signed
on, there would be mass resignations. Failing that, all deans and department
chairs would step down. In this period (early April 1950), so many Geology

professors sent their resignations to Sproul that the department, one of the nation's best, was now "doomed," according to its chair. There was talk of involving the students, but McHenry warned against a campuswide strike as unnecessarily provocative. Instead he proposed that signers like himself should join with the nonsigners in a "University in Exile." Such a reconfigured UCLA would meet off campus and provide a venue for the rebel faculty members to continue to teach after they were fired.[9]

At Berkeley the reaction of the faculty was one of bewilderment. The Committee of Seven stated that it was now even more determined to rescind the oath. Its leader Hicks said that the Senate would "stand by" the nonsigners. A *Daily Cal* editorial accused the regents of bad faith and predicted that Neylan's "about-face" would unify the faculty. But the student journalist was too optimistic when he declared that the strength of Neylan and his faction was on the wane.[10]

A FRUSTRATED JOHN HICKS TRIES TO RESIGN

In his person and his politics, John Hicks was the consummate middle-of-the-roader, a man who hesitated to challenge authority. Even though he had found the oath irritating and annoying, he was "willing to accept it as a necessary evil."[11] And yet because he represented a faculty that the average Californian considered ultra-radical, Hicks received hate mail. One letter, addressed to "Comrade Hicks," advised him to pray to Stalin when he went to bed. It ended: "Your loyal comrades on the faculty of the University of California . . . have succeeded in establishing the Communistic philosophy as a permanent cog in the wheel of higher education."[12] The chair of Berkeley's History Department was hardly an appropriate target for such abuse, for he personally investigated every new applicant to make sure that no communists would join his faculty.[13]

To a Leftist like Gordon Griffiths, John Hicks was the opposite of a Stalinist. Griffiths considered his fellow historian a "loyal friend" and a man with liberal political instincts, but in 1950 he and his fellow nonsigners were becoming increasingly disturbed by Hicks's tendency to appease the regents. They called him "The Great Compromiser" and "Berkeley's Neville Chamberlain."[14]

For the 1949–1950 academic year, Hicks remained in Berkeley to write, while enjoying the leave from teaching that comes every seven years. He had been pressed into the oath fight against his will, and his responsibilities on the Committee of Seven, along with the campus turmoil, meant that he had not been able to work, thus "wasting" the sabbatical that is every professor's prize. In his autobiography he would write that the year of the oath was "the most traumatic experience of my life."[15]

The historian was stung by the personal attacks from both sides of the political spectrum. Rumors were floating that it was not Hicks himself, but supporters of Harry Bridges who were calling the shots for the Committee of Seven.[16] On the other side the nonsigners were becoming impatient with his condescending attitude. His associate on the Committee of Seven, the popular Stephen Pepper, felt that Hicks had no idea how scornful he was of the beliefs of people like Tolman, Tussman, and tenBroek. Pepper found it ironic that Hicks was offending the very men for whom he had pledged to resign so that they might be able to "express the thoughts he hated."[17]

If the nonsigners were frustrated with Hicks as their main faculty representative, the historian was equally frustrated by the demands of a job he had never wanted. So it came as no surprise when he submitted his resignation as chair of the Committee of Seven. The surprise was that the nonsigners urged him to stay. There was no one available to replace him.

Hicks's failed attempt to resign took place on April 6, 1950, at a meeting of 150 nonsigners and their supporters. Pepper called it "the tensest, most disorganized meeting I had ever seen." Despite the turnout, the nonsigners were "a really demoralized group."[18] But according to Gardner, the entire Berkeley faculty was beset by a hopelessness that expressed itself in resignation and in an inability to act. Looming on the horizon was April 30, the "Sign or Get Out" deadline.

The one hope was Sproul. If he could be persuaded to take a public stand against the oath for the first time, this might influence a regent to vote with the faculty and break the 10 to 10 deadlock. So early in April Senate leaders huddled over how to get the president to act decisively, like a real leader.

Although Wendell Stanley called Harvard president Conant to urge Sproul to speak out, the latter told confidantes that a public statement would provide fodder to the regents who wanted to replace him. And he may have been too depressed to act. Hicks recalled the president as "completely licked, with his tail between his legs, just like a dog that has been beaten."[19]

In that same 1965 interview, the historian expressed wonderment that Sproul didn't resign. But in Hicks's view, the president's temperament, one that Pepper called "rah-rah," made him incapable of admitting defeat. Still, in early April, rumors of an impending resignation were bruited about among the faculty and in the press. Surprisingly the president's job was saved by two of the most Right-wing regents, Dickson and Neylan.[20]

Edward Dickson, the board's oldest and longest-serving member, told Sidney Ehrman that the regents "love Bob Sproul. He has been placed in a most unfortunate position and his reputation is badly battered. We must all endeavor to restore, not only the University's own prestige, but that of our President."[21]

But why did Neylan help to keep Sproul in office just when he might have realized his dream of ousting him? He hadn't changed his views of the man, for he was still referring to him as a "vacillating weakling," the person responsible for "the Loyalty Oath mess." Perhaps by this time Neylan knew that replacing him with Ernest Lawrence was unrealistic. And if Sproul were no longer president, Neylan could no longer control him and make his life miserable.

NO STUDENT STRIKE, BUT ANOTHER MASS MEETING

On April 3, 1950, the NASE polled its membership. Given a choice of sign or get out, 307 voted to get out and only 7 to sign! The group also asked its members to make a formal pledge that they would never sign the oath.

The views of the NASE (and the equally radical GSA) influenced Berkeley's undergraduates. Meeting with the students in small discussion sections, they educated them about the oath in addition to explaining the professors' lectures and the course readings. And given the Senate's timidity, both organizations believed that the students would have to lead the struggle, so they lobbied for a dramatic action such as a campuswide general strike.[22]

Energized by the March mass meeting, student leaders were now receptive to the idea, and plans were made for a walkout of classes. The idea frightened Sproul and the Committee of Seven. They felt that a strike would jeopardize the negotiations going on to persuade the regents to lift the ultimatum. But unable to mobilize enough mass support, the activists decided instead to demonstrate at Sather Gate, the main entrance to the campus. However, Senate leader Frank Kidner talked them into waiting until after the April 21 board meeting.[23]

The growing gloom was reflected in the attendance at the second mass meeting on April 10. Just five weeks after the first gathering, the turnout was much less than half of the earlier event.[24] Still, the growing importance of students in the conflict was acknowledged when NASE leader Leslie Fishman spoke for the student body. With other activists aware that Fishman was a Communist Party member, they were playing a cosmic joke on their unknowing faculty elders. And the not-so-secret Red was enthusiastically applauded when he told the audience that the teaching assistants "would withdraw their services unless the oath was rescinded."

The audience rose to its feet and cheered for several minutes after Arthur Brodeur declared "I will never sign the oath under any circumstances." The ex-communist asserted that "no man can do good work when he is under suspicion; a man is better unemployed," and also spoke to the rumor that Sproul might resign. Lauding him as the "the greatest president in the university's history," he promised that were he forced to leave, he would follow him out the door.[25]

Three days earlier, Dickson, Neylan, and Giannini issued a statement that "the people of California should now know that the Regents constitute the last barrier to the complete domination of the University by a dissident minority of the faculty which demands that a confessed Communist should enjoy the same honors and privileges as the most distinguished and loyal professor." This group had forced the rest of the faculty into "a cold war" and was preparing once again "to intimidate the Regents."[26]

This was the last straw for Hildebrand, who like Hicks and Sproul, was feeling increasingly frustrated. As the featured speaker at the Greek, he heatedly denied any intention to intimidate anyone. And he indicated that he was having second thoughts about his role in promulgating the oath. Having been one of the first faculty members to sign, he now was feeling "rather sorry" that he had done so.

Hildebrand also came to the defense of the president. "Sproul admits to having made a mistake in originally supporting the oath and should not be censured for this mistake." He then pointed out that originally a UC professor had only one offense to be concerned about, that of being a communist. Then came a second offense: failure to sign the oath. And now a third has been added, opposing the regents. "Is docility necessary for a professor?" he asked in conclusion.[27]

UCLA'S STUDENT GOVERNMENT wanted to emulate Berkeley and hold its second mass meeting. But Paul Dodd put his foot down, saying that it would do "more harm than good" for the faculty's cause. So no meeting took place.[28]

Conservative faculty opinion on the Westwood campus was centered in its professional schools, especially Law. On one day in April, the *Bruin* headlined statements in support of the oath by the distinguished jurist Roscoe Pound, then a visiting professor, and by law dean Dale Coffman. As Kantorowicz pointed out, Berkeley's law professors were just as backward in failing to oppose the Regents' Special Oath. Although the university had never faced such a critical legal and constitutional issue, Frank Newman was the only anti-oath leader from Boalt Hall.[29]

At UCLA's April Senate meeting, Morris Neiburger, an associate professor of meteorology, shouted "No" when Dodd moved a vote of confidence in Sproul. In his view the president lacked integrity and had been evasive in never giving his faculty a direct statement regarding his attitude to the oath. And he criticized the Senate for abandoning "all points of principle." Neiburger vowed to "eschew participation in faculty discussions until such time as I see evidence that the merits of a subject, and not expediency, form the basis of faculty discussions."[30]

Meanwhile at Berkeley Stanley was circulating a statement among his fellow scientists. Signed by three Nobel laureates (John Northrop, William Giauque, and Stanley himself), as well as by sixteen other members of the National Academy of Sciences,[31] it said that if the "Sign or Get Out" ultimatum were to be enforced, then "the university will incur, and justly so, the scorn of the academic world." With the institution certain to lose its rank as one of the world's great universities, many of its most distinguished professors would leave and no one of their caliber would agree to replace them.[32]

BY MID-APRIL 1950 the vast majority of the faculty had signed the oath. But it was not clear how many were still resisting the requirement, either actively or passively. Neylan liked to say that the nonsigners were a "mere 12 percent" of the faculty. But Tolman suspected the number was much larger, at least three hundred at Berkeley and UCLA combined, which would make it closer to 20 percent. But there was no way to pin down the precise number, for the president's office, acting on orders of the Board of Regents, wouldn't release the figures.[33]

So Tolman solicited promises from tenured professors that they would continue to hold out. Despite this, the number of holdouts at Berkeley would fall to sixty, as more and more resisters complied with the requirement in the face of the April 30 deadline. And yet in the process, a formerly loose aggregation of people became a unified and cohesive group.

The flagging morale of the resistance was buoyed by outpourings of support from all over the country. With the prospect of mass firings, money was needed to help jobless nonsigners survive. Again Tolman took the lead, writing dozens of letters to colleagues in every academic field who might help out. By mid-April, 245 Stanford professors and other employees had made a sizeable contribution to UC's defense fund, and at Chicago Hutchins got his faculty to agree to donate 2 percent of their monthly salary to support the nonsigners. Also on the Midway sociologist Louis Wirth worked tirelessly to coordinate efforts at other colleges and universities, and committees of support were organized at virtually every major institution in the nation.[34]

With the handwriting on the wall, many resisters began looking for employment at other universities. People who were over sixty-two were advised to retire before the April 30 deadline so that they could keep the pensions and other benefits which would be lost if they were fired.

THE ALUMNI COMPROMISE

For about a month a committee from the Alumni Association had been studying the controversy. To get them more involved, Hicks contacted its chair, Stephen Bechtel of San Francisco's Bechtel Corporation, and arranged meetings between Bechtel, Frank Kidner, Neylan, and himself. In the two weeks before the April 21 board meeting, Bechtel and his committee flew up and down the state to meet with regents, faculty members, influential alumni, and Sproul.[35] The result was a plan known as "the Alumni Compromise."

There were three parts to the proposal. First, the Loyalty Oath was to be rescinded. According to Bechtel's group, it had become a nationwide symbol of "the infringement of the rights of man."[36] But this victory for the resisters was merely a technicality, for the identical wording by which a professor swore he was neither a communist nor a subversive would be attached to the contract that had to be signed if he or she were to remain on the payroll after July 1, 1950. For this reason Hicks would call the new proposal "a distinction without a difference."[37]

The most important part of the package was a procedure to safeguard the jobs of professors expected to refuse to sign the anticommunist proviso in their new contracts. They would no longer be subject to immediate and automatic dismissal. Instead they could explain their unwillingness to sign to a jury of their peers, the members of their campus's Committee on Privilege and Tenure. Privilege and Tenure was one of the Academic Senate's most prestigious committees because it adjudicated the grievances of faculty members who believed that their employment rights had been violated. The proposal stated that Privilege and Tenure would send its recommendations to the president, but the regents would have the authority to make the "final determination" with respect to each nonsigner's fate.

Promising as the plan for hearings appeared, there was no provision at first for graduate student assistants to be offered similar protection.

Stephen Pepper's journal documents the mood of the most involved faculty negotiators, a mood of intense anxiety bordering on desperation, in the days before the regents' meeting of April 21. Even though the Alumni proposal was a compromise, with many objectionable elements, it was all that stood in the way of the mass firings that would take place at the end of the month. So to protect his future, the philosopher accepted a generous offer from Princeton in the event he was forced to leave Berkeley.

Pepper and his committee also worked to get the regents to accept the plan. With Hicks, Kidner, and other leaders, he went into a mode of hyperactivity, following every lead that might have even the slightest chance of influencing the upcoming vote. They were up against a wall, for the week after the board meeting was Spring Break, when it would be impossible to organize a new form of resistance, a Plan B, were Plan A to fall through.

They met with Edward Heller, the regent most firmly in the anti-oath camp. Heller, who reportedly had given up his investment business to devote full time to fighting the oath, told them about the efforts to get Chester Nimitz to the next meeting. The admiral rarely attended sessions of the board, but when he did, he usually sided with the faculty. Someone had tried to convince Secretary of State Dean Acheson that the Loyalty Oath was an "issue of sufficient national implications," hoping he would grant Nimitz a leave from military duty.

They also paid a call on Monroe Deutsch, the retired provost. Having served for almost twenty years, he knew the regents well and might be able to help Hicks formulate a better presentation on April 21. During a long discussion Deutsch kept coming back to the same refrain, lamenting over and over, "How dreadful it was, that a man like Neylan can cause such harm."[38]

That Berkeley's students remained concerned was suggested by the turnout (2,500 according to the *Daily Cal*) at a noon rally on April 19. Sponsored by the Student Progressives, the gathering at the West Gate entrance to the campus heard Left-wing labor lawyer Vincent Hallinan and three members of the ILWU link the oath to the government's "frame-up" of Harry Bridges. Referring to the large (and intimidating) police presence, the fiery Hallinan asked, "Why should students have to hold a meeting such as this under guard of the police?"[39]

The effort to get friendly regents to the meeting paid off, for twenty-two of the board's twenty-four members came to Davis on April 21, 1950. Sproul moved the first of the resolutions that made up the Alumni Compromise, and when Neylan seconded his motion, it was clear that it would have smooth sailing. But Mario Giannini declared that he would resign from the board in protest. Even though a noncommunist statement would still be in the contract, Giannini saw the compromise as a revocation of the Loyalty Oath. When it passed, he predicted that "flags would fly over the Kremlin," with the international communist movement rejoicing. And he added that if the new contract oath failed in its purpose, he would personally "organize 20th Century vigilantes, who will unearth Communists and Communism, in all its sordid aspects."

But no one else saw it that way, and the vote in favor of the Alumni Compromise was 21 to 1.[40]

"Thank God for Giannini," Pepper wrote in his diary. "He absolutely shut up Neylan and Dixon (*sic:* Dickson). How could they claim a victory with Giannini proclaiming defeat from the rooftops?"[41]

In 1950 Pepper was a much venerated elder statesmen on Berkeley's faculty. Born in 1891, he was the son of a talented painter, and became a pioneering student of the philosophical bases of beauty and greatness in art. At Harvard he had studied with William James, and it was his classmate Loewenberg who had brought him to Berkeley as a teaching assistant in 1919. Four years later he became a regular faculty member and one of the most popular teachers on campus.

A close friend of Tolman, Pepper was the most influential member of the Committee of Seven. Unlike its chair, Hicks, he was trusted by the nonsigners. On the night of the regents' meeting, Pepper took his wife to the Black Sheep on Bancroft Way across from the campus "to celebrate."[42] Their steaks, the philosopher wrote, were delicious. But the dinner reminded him of a prisoner's last meal before his execution.[43]

Afterward Pepper returned to the suite that his committee had rented at the Durant Hotel.[44] Today numbers 319 and 320 would be called the nonsigners' situation rooms. For several months they would be filled with professors and the press, as people came and went, planning strategy into the wee hours of the morning. On April 21 it was more crowded than ever. The entire membership of UCLA's combined Steering and Policy Committees had flown to Berkeley in the event that the compromise was voted down and quick decisions had to be made.

Hicks was the last to arrive that evening. As he reported on the Davis meeting, Pepper was struck by the "steely, hard quality" in the historian's face. It had been a meeting at which no one listened to anyone else, so Hicks was especially frustrated. His conclusion: that despite the compromise, the regents were "out for blood." "Those birds damn well would like to see five hundred faculty men dismissed," he said.[45]

Still, Hicks thought that the procedure of the Privilege and Tenure hearings provided hope that the nonsigners' jobs could be saved. To make sure there were no misunderstandings, he dictated a press release late that night about what had been agreed upon. "At the hearing the objection of the faculty member may be clearly stated and there is a guarantee that no man or woman shall be dismissed provided the Committee, the President, and the Regents can find assurance that his inability to sign the contract required arises solely out of good conscience. *Unless such individuals are proved to be members of the Communist Party, a condition we believe cannot be shown in any instance to exist, they will not be dismissed from the University, in spite of their unwillingness to sign the suggested contract.*"[46]

The Alumni Compromise took the pressure off the nonsigners, who were no longer subject to the April 30 ultimatum. They could at least hope that their jobs would be protected by Privilege and Tenure. But as Gardner points out, the "compromise" was a defeat for the faculty that had mobilized to fight the oath. The regents' policy that barred communists from teaching simply because of their political affiliations was now a part of the yearly contract. The compromise had not given any satisfaction to the view that there was something offensive in an oath that was "a political test, an invasion of privacy, and an affront to the academic community." And it certainly did not reinforce the faculty's position that it was the sole authority in personnel decisions.[47] For Caughey, the Alumni Compromise was "a complete defeat."[48]

The gathering at the hotel would last until early morning as the faculty planned its strategy for the Academic Senate meeting. To begin on a positive note, Brodeur was chosen to move a vote of confidence in Sproul, and the Law School's Barbara Armstrong would then ask for an expression of gratitude to the regents who had been friendly to the faculty's cause. It was also decided that Pepper would speak for the Committee of Seven. With Hicks so distrusted, the nonsigners would not react well to his attempt to place a positive spin on the regents' meeting. Pepper was still a nonsigner, and with more authority than almost any other professor, he could make a convincing presentation.

The 750 professors at Wheeler Hall the morning of April 22 matched the number in attendance at the March 7 Senate meeting. Pepper began his speech by expressing his disappointment with the Alumni Compromise. But then he argued that it was not a "total defeat." The regents had recognized the role of Privilege and Tenure, whose hearings should protect the nonsigners. And he urged that "all who can conscientiously do so among the nonsigners should sign."[49] In his view the regents were more likely to protect them if their numbers were not excessive.

Pepper also announced that the Committee of Seven would be replaced by a Committee of Five. This decision had come as a result of sensitive negotiations by Clark Kerr, which had been needed to persuade Hicks and others on his committee to give up their authority. Although Kerr was a Quaker and a pacifist, he had signed the oath without inner qualms. Indeed he hadn't paid much attention to the controversy until he was appointed to this new committee.[50]

Chairing it was Ed Strong, who at the April 22 Senate meeting had asserted the "right of the individual faculty member to decide for himself on the basis of conscience to sign or not to sign." He also warned that if the regents were to dismiss a nonsigner after Privilege and Tenure had determined that he or she was not a communist, this would be considered a violation of the principle of tenure.[51]

Once again Tolman appealed to his colleagues to join him in refusing to sign the new contract. Disagreeing with Pepper, he asserted that "the safety of the conscientious nonsigners from abuse and contumely, lies in numbers." If a great many would refuse, the regents might have to back down. But if the board was successful, it would have gained control from the faculty "over the mechanisms of appointment and dismissal at this university" and would have produced "a group of timorous and cowed men and women in the faculty and among other employees."[52]

Meanwhile the meaning of the Alumni Compromise was being deliberated. Neylan told his friend Griffiths that the hearings of the committee were intended to provide "a way out" only for "people like Quakers" and other "religious or conscientious objectors." Farnham disagreed and tried to counter this interpretation. A similar disagreement took place on the Alumni Committee, where Bechtel said that the "burden of proof" would be on the nonsigners at the upcoming hearings.

These were not good portents for the hearings, or for the nonsigners' fate. And the faculty sensed that dangerous times lay ahead.

THE OATH TAKES ITS TOLL

Fearful of the future of the university, Stephen Pepper, after his April 22 Senate speech, had signed the oath, reasoning that if the regents were to fire many of Berkeley's best professors, the quality of the institution would decline. He also agreed with Regent Heller that Berkeley's liberals should comply with the requirement so that they would be in a position to fight to end it.[53]

The "sign, stay, and fight!" position was gaining ground among the nonsigners. The slogan had been coined by George Stewart. At fifty-five, Stewart had been teaching at Berkeley since 1923, and he was one of its most famous professors because of his best-selling novels. He didn't like the oath, but like Kerr, he had been an early signer, as the issue hadn't moved him.

Still, Stewart wanted to contribute to the fight, so he decided to write a book about the controversy. He began it in April 1950, and in the four months into which he crammed all the research and writing, he enlisted seventy faculty members in his project. Because some were afraid to be known as participants in a work critical of the regents, Stewart organized them into cells in which no one knew all the others, much like "the French organized their *Résistance* during the years of the Nazis."[54]

From the questionnaire Stewart circulated to the faculty, he found only 11 percent of his respondents said that the oath crisis had created problems in their personal lives. But the findings from his focused interviews, a better method for getting peoples' feelings, suggested that the oath had taken a toll on the faculty.[55]

Many professors reported symptoms of nervousness and anxiety. They were smoking more, drinking more, and having difficulty sleeping. Depression and despair were widespread. Ulcers had sent at least two to the university hospital, where one nurse was reported to have commented on the large number of "oath cases" that had come in.

The drop in morale was affecting the ability to work. Professors reported an inability to concentrate on research and a decline in the quality of their teaching. A good example was Jacob Loewenberg, a sixty-eight-year-old professor of philosophy who had taught at Berkeley since 1915 and participated in the Faculty Revolution. Loewenberg, an expert on Hegel, had a reputation as "a brilliant and energetic teacher,"[56] and he was a committed nonsigner. In his dress and manner he radiated a special "elegance" and he spoke with an "impeccable English accent."[57]

No one was hit harder by the oath crisis than Loewenberg. Extremely depressed, he had lost his zest for teaching, which had always been his most satisfying activity. And unless the crisis was soon resolved, he wouldn't be able to face his students. The philosopher's research had also suffered, he hadn't been able to write for a year. One problem was all the meetings, which over-stimulated him. After each one he would play over in his mind everything that had been said. And instead of sleeping at night he would lay awake planning strategy. Dependent on sleeping pills, he had lost his appetite as well. At his age this was affecting his health, already precarious from an operation a few months earlier. After that surgery he had been unable to rest, because all he could think about was the oath.

Loewenberg no longer wanted to see old friends who disagreed with him, so he had withdrawn into a shell. But he was disappointed in himself for being so intolerant.[58]

And his self-respect had been injured, for the regents were treating him as if he were a "laboring man or factory worker." But while the working class was organized, the professoriat was not. So he was now advocating a union, so the faculty could fight for its rights.

Despite the fact that Loewenberg was encouraged by the large numbers of young professors risking their futures by not signing, as well as by the wives' support of their husbands' resistance, he still saw tragedy ahead for the university, a possible disintegration of the institution.

In closing he assured his interviewer that he would never sign the oath, either in its old form or in the new contract. And the last thing he'd ever consider would be to resign, because "that's what they want me to do."[59] His last words, spoken in "a strained tense voice" were: "I am frightened."[60]

Other nonsigners were also feeling alone and isolated. And the mood of those who had signed was not much better; many felt guilty about having succumbed to pressure. So the state of the faculty's morale in May 1950 did not bode well for its ability to engage in a protracted struggle with the regents, should that turn out to be necessary.

THE DAILY CAL KEEPS THE OATH ISSUE ALIVE

After the Alumni Compromise was approved, newspaper headlines suggested that the oath controversy had been resolved. The *Daily Californian* made this mistake for a few days, but by early May it was a leading voice again for a principled academic freedom position.

The student paper kept the issue alive with daily front-page articles, editorials, and letters. Prominent coverage was given to a student body referendum sponsored by the Young Progressives. The issue was whether the hiring and firing of professors should be based on competence and performance alone, without a political test. The ASUC's Executive Committee, still dominated by administration representatives and their student supporters, was able to stop this vote from going forward. The *Daily Cal* also reported that the NASE had hired an attorney to mount a legal challenge to the new contract oath and was circulating a revised compact to its membership. Its TAs and RAs would choose between rejecting the new requirement outright or signing it after striking out the offensive paragraph with the noncommunist disclaimer.[61]

A tongue-in-cheek letter was published from a new student group called "SCUM." The Society for the Conservation of University Morality had voted 237-1/2 to 1/2 to support Giannini. To prove its commitment it was setting up the band of vigilantes the regent had called for to clean out and clear up "our Free University Community."[62] A few days later editor Louis Bell asked why the faculty had lost its fight against the oath. Its mistake, he argued, had been to rely on futile negotiations with the regents. The Academic Senate should have refused the oath in any form when it was offered in 1949.[63]

By this time, Tenney had been replaced as the chair of the state's Little HUAC by Hugh Burns. The Burns Committee, according to the *Daily Cal,* differed from Tenney's group in a "new veneer of politeness." But otherwise the smears and innuendos continued apace during three days of hearings during the second week of May focused on espionage at Berkeley during the 1930s and 1940s. The main targets, physicists Robert Oppenheimer and Joseph Weinberg, had left the area years earlier, but the continued association of the university with subversion was another cross Berkeley's resisters had to bear.

The student paper uncovered a scoop of its own when they publicized a seventeen-page pamphlet about "Red-ucators" at three California universities on May 17. The anonymous authors in the National Council for American Education listed nineteen UC professors in its report. Raymond Birge, the chair of the Physics Department, was included because he had sponsored a dinner for his eminent colleague Edward U. Condon. Aaron Gordon was named a subversive because he once signed a petition. Others in the report were Brodeur, who had actually been a communist, and Tolman, who had affiliated with several Popular Front groups in the 1930s and early 1940s. The chairman of the Senate's new Committee on Academic Freedom, Baldwin Woods, was included, as was William Dennes. Also cited were Max Radin of the Law School and Robert Lowie, one of the nation's most respected anthropologists.

Two former provosts got star billing as Red educators. Monroe Deutsch was charged with having been affiliated with nine subversive organizations. And UCLA's Clarence Dykstra was listed. He had been a member of the American Soviet Friendship Society and had signed a petition circulated by the American Committee for Democratic and Intellectual Freedom.

But "Dyk" did not live to experience this attack. On May 5, 1950, he died from a massive heart attack. Although he had suffered from heart disease for years, Kenneth Starr believes that it was the stress of his testifying before the Tenney Cmmittee that exacerbated his condition and led to his death at the age of sixty-seven.[64] In his first years as provost, Dykstra had to defend himself and his faculty from charges of subversion, and then it was he who took the heat for the events that led to the Loyalty Oath.

For three days the *Daily Cal* published a series of investigative reports on the "Red-ucators" charges. In the last article the exposers were exposed, as feature writer Dick Israel discovered why the officers of the organization had not listed their names. They were known fascists. Indeed the Red-baiting group was led by "the same people who had spread the gospel of Nazism and anti-Semitism prior to World War II."[65]

Neylan was an avid reader of the *Daily Cal*. At the May 26 board meeting he accused the paper of using "smear tactics" against the pro-oath regents. The *Daily Cal* responded that its policy was to eschew all personal attacks. This had not been easy, especially when certain members of the Board of Regents, who had the commercial press at their disposal, engaged in smears themselves.[66]

After his speech at the April 10 mass meeting, Joel Hildebrand had risen to the top of Neylan's sizeable list of enemies. At the same board meeting the regent took another shot at him. Hildebrand, as chair of the Chemistry Department, had given a research job to Robert Hurley, "in full knowledge" that the young man had been branded a security risk by the Atomic Energy Commission.

"What does this reveal about the Senate leader who portrays himself as one of the faculty's most fervent anticommunists?" the regent asked.[67]

Hildebrand countered by accusing Neylan of revealing information that had been classified for security reasons, for the sole purpose of making a personal attack.[68]

By the end of May 1950 the hearings of the nonsigners before Privilege and Tenure were under way. But it would be more than two weeks before the committee's recommendations would be made public.

CHAPTER 9

THE HEARINGS
AT BERKELEY

The faculty's mistake was to wage battle on ideological
grounds. The regents laughed. In order to fight it successfully,
all persons opposed to the oath should have been organized
into a group, such as a labor union, and have used their
collective power to fight the issue.

—Erik Erikson[1]

T HE MOST IMPORTANT PART OF THE ALUMNI
Compromise was the provision that the nonsigners could
request hearings before the Committee on Privilege and Tenure. "P and T," as
it was called, was one of the Academic Senate's key committees. Most powerful was the Committee on Committees, which chose the members of every
Senate panel, including the Budget Committee, whose rulings on promotion
to tenure decided the fate of a young professor. But P and T served as an appeals court for faculty members who felt that their rights had been violated; it
adjudicated cases in which a person had been disciplined, as well as those in
which he or she questioned a personnel decision.

Two members of Berkeley's committee had been partisans in the controversy.
Ralph Chaney was known to provide Neylan with confidential information on
the faculty's attitudes, including reports of Senate meetings. Jacobus tenBroek
was a leading resister. Senate leaders worried that with these men sitting in

judgment, P and T might not be able to reach a consensus. So they decided to ask the entire committee to resign, in order to reconstitute a new panel in time for the hearings scheduled to begin on May 16. The new chair was Stuart Daggett of Economics, an expert on the railroad industry, but its most influential member would be Clark Kerr. The latter was unrivaled among Cal's professors for his powers of persuasion and ability to negotiate difficult settlements.

All six members of the reconstituted committee had signed the oath. And each had voted for the regents' policy of barring communists during the mail ballot two months earlier.[2] This made the group less reflective of the faculty's diversity than the original committee. Loewenberg feared that disbanding the standing committee had been a terrible mistake and that the new P and T would be agents of the Board of Regents.[3]

Fifty-two people from the Berkeley and San Francisco campuses petitioned to be heard. Except for three lecturers, they were all Senate members. Before appearing, each professor wrote a letter to P and T explaining his or her reasons for refusing to sign the noncommunist disclaimer. In the letters, as well as in the hearings, P and T would be looking for statements, either direct or indirect, that indicated that the appellants were not communists and found communism abhorrent.

The fifty-two appellants came from twelve departments, which suggests that resistance to the oath was concentrated in relatively few places. The three largest clusters were Psychology, English, and Mathematics, with six, five, and four petitioners, respectively. But Oriental Languages, a very small department, stood out: three of its six regular faculty members went before the committee. The Business and Medical Schools each contributed three appellants. Two each came from Political Science, Economics, and Art, while there was only one nonsigner each from the Philosophy and History departments.[4]

Most anti-oath leaders went through the procedure. But the hearings provided another chance for resisters to sign. To safeguard their future employment, the Senate leaders Davisson and Pepper had signed in the weeks before the hearings, as did such faculty liberals as tenBroek, Strong, and Griffiths.

For Ed Strong, signing was especially difficult. Telling his fellow nonsigners about his decision was a "touching moment" and "heart-breaking," because the philosopher had been "heart and soul" against the oath, Charles Muscatine recalls. Strong told them that he was sending Sproul a letter of protest and that

if it were ever removed from the file of signed oaths, he would resign. It is striking that the philosopher never mentioned his decision to sign in an oral history
that includes a long section on the oath. The same was true of Griffiths's political autobiography, which suggests how painful the decision was for these men.[5]

The hearings were conducted with deliberation, and it took four weeks for
everyone to be interviewed. And then on June 15 the committee issued its report. After an opening section summarizing the arguments for not signing, a
much longer (and confidential) second part summarized each individual testimony, along with the committee's reasons for recommending that the appellant be retained, or its failure to do so.

The most common reason for not signing was that a "test oath" violated
academic freedom. Second was the idea that the faculty was the body most
competent to judge its own members, and the related point that the oath
threatened tenure rights. The few who thought that the oath involved political
discrimination emphasized that the Communist Party was still a legal organization. One or two people said that some communists might be good teachers
and that the term *communist* was inherently vague. And there were many personal objections. Professors who attested to their years of faithful service asked
almost petulantly how the regents could dare doubt their loyalty.[6]

At the time, the faculty still believed that the regents would retain those
who were open and forthcoming about their motivations. And because none
of the nonsigners were believed to be actual Communist Party members, P
and T looked for reasons to clear the appellants, rather than searching for evidence that would condemn them. However, in contrast to UCLA's Committee on Privilege and Tenure, it did not just focus on whether the appellants'
reasons were satisfactory. Instead the criterion was whether they had established—directly or indirectly—that they were not communists.

In some cases the Daggett committee bent over backward to do this. This
was especially likely if the petitioner was a young scientist with a bright future.
An example was Geoffrey Chew, a twenty-six-year-old nuclear physicist, who
had been a favorite student of both Enrico Fermi and Edward Teller at Chicago.
Chew told the panel that the contract oath subjected professors to "economic
pressures, raised the question of a political test, and invaded the privacy of the
individual in his beliefs." Chairman Daggett, who was not loath to making condescending remarks about his colleagues, called Chew's reasoning "immature

but idealistic." But the committee cleared him, stressing that he had been thoroughly investigated while working at such top-secret facilities as Los Alamos and Berkeley's Radiation Laboratory.

And then there was Chew's colleague, Harold Lewis, whom Robert Oppenheimer had called "the most sought after physicist of his generation." The twenty-seven-year-old Lewis balked at saying anything that might make him an accomplice to the anticommunist hysteria, including a statement that the party was a subversive organization. But because he had been approved earlier to work for the Atomic Energy Commission (AEC), and because Berkeley could not afford to lose such a rising star, he received the committee's imprimatur.

Three overlapping segments of the faculty were over-represented among the petitioners. As might be expected, the largest group was made up of liberal activists. The second category was the émigrés from European fascism. And the third group was made up of women.

LIBERALS, EMIGRÉS, AND WOMEN

Jacob Loewenberg, at sixty-eight the oldest nonsigner, told the committee that he had never joined a political movement and he wouldn't support hiring a communist in the Philosophy Department. But he was refusing to sign on "moral grounds" because of an objection to being assumed guilty until he could prove his innocence. In recommending him for retention, P and T noted his reputation for reacting violently to any form of coercion.

Twenty-nine-year-old English professor and Chaucer scholar Charles Muscatine was one of the youngest resisters. A Navy veteran who had earned a ribbon for valor during the invasion of Sicily and the landing at Salerno, he wasn't particularly political. But he had read a book about how German professors had helped justify genocide, and its impact influenced him to take a stand.[7]

Muscatine explained that he was refusing to sign because a teacher's "highest obligation is to be principled and its worst enemy is expedience." In approving him, P and T took note of his distinguished service as an officer during the war.

Unlike Joe McCarthy and Jack Tenney, the committee did not probe into an appellant's political history. So the former party member Brodeur could tell his questioners with a straight face that he was "outspoken in his scorn of the

Communist Party," and could add without fear of contradiction that "the Party would not venture to try to subvert him." He also stressed how much he loved his country, which he had served in World War I, and that he detested every form of totalitarianism.

In its ignorance of Brodeur's political past, the committee commended him for his "dignity and integrity."[8]

More than a year earlier Brodeur's colleague in English James Caldwell had battled Hildebrand toe to toe, defending the right of communists to teach. But in his statement to the committee he said that they are not "free agents" and that he approved the policy barring them from the academic community. This suggests that the growing storm of McCarthyism had weakened support for the AAUP position among some Berkeley liberals. Still, Caldwell would not sign the oath because "an atmosphere of freedom is vital to a university." And he asked the committee, "How shall we answer the cynical student who accuses us of holding to democracy through fear of losing our jobs?"

Aaron Gordon let his judges know that during the war he had been cleared to inspect "secret documents," and that he had assured Sproul that he was not a communist. In fact the economist had opposed the party all his life and "done battle" in the Berkeley Consumers' Co-op with those he suspected of being Reds. Still, any political oath is objectionable, and Gordon remained hopeful that "reasonable men [could] reach agreement" in the current dispute.

Tolman, the nonsigners' leader, also told the committee that he had been investigated during World War II. Like Gordon, he mentioned his experiences with communists in liberal groups in which they had been a "damned nuisance." But he was resolved not to sign. As a psychologist concerned about the "wave of public hysteria about communists in America," he would not be a party to such a collective psychosis.

Tolman refused to discuss his relationship to the Communist Party. To do so could be interpreted by some of the young faculty members looking to him for leadership as an abdication of their shared conscientious objection to the oath. Had Tolman been a lesser light in the faculty firmament, had he been an obscure lecturer or young assistant professor instead of one of the leaders of his university and profession, this might not have been enough to satisfy P and T. But because he was so eminent and his loyalty taken for granted, they recommended his retention.

OF THE FORTY-SEVEN Berkeley appellants, more than one-quarter were born in Europe. And except for Loewenberg and Peter Boodberg (each of whom had emigrated early in the century), they were refugees from totalitarian regimes. The experience of living in an oppressive society colored their attitudes toward the oath.

When Gian-Carlo Wick was named to fill the position vacated by Oppenheimer in 1948, he was seen as one of the few theoretical physicists capable of equaling the latter's eminence. Only two years later his "Wick theorem" catapulted him to fame.

As a young scientist during the 1930s Wick had been a close associate of Enrico Fermi in Rome. He wasn't as courageous then as his mother, a well-known writer who had defied Mussolini. To keep working he had signed an oath of loyalty to the fascist regime. When faced with a similar decision in 1950 he didn't want "to repeat an act that repelled me as being so much against my liberal principles."[9] Wick told P and T that "any political test is an infringement of academic freedom," and because his loyalty had been affirmed by immigration authorities and by the Radiation Laboratory, the committee cleared him.

Stefan Peters, a forty-year-old professor of insurance, had also lived in Italy—as well as Germany. In both countries he had witnessed the growing power of fascism. To him, loyalty oaths have "tragic consequences," including intimidation and guilt by association. Daggett, P and T's chair, dismissed his fears as "exaggerated," but because of his "sincerity," Peters was recommended for retention.

Ludwig Edelstein was a forty-eight-year-old professor of Greek who had left Germany in 1933. Before coming to Berkeley in 1943 he had taught at Johns Hopkins for ten years and was already famous for his translation of the Hippocratic Oath and his research on ancient medicine. Like most appellants, the Classics scholar assured the committee that he would sign a noncommunist oath for work in agencies that involved national security. But in academic life, political tests are out of place. His most important reason for not signing concerned his integrity as a teacher and his relations with students. For in his courses he covered the rise of science in ancient Greece, an area in which Marxist theories were influential. Would his students trust his critiques of these theories if they knew he had been forced to declare he was not a communist in order to keep his job? he asked.

Ernst Kantorowicz had been the most outspoken refugee against the oath, and the medieval historian was one of the most eminent of Berkeley's resisters. In his testimony Eka repeated some of the arguments he had first made on June 14, 1949. He would not sign the oath because "similar declarations were required of university professors by fascist governments in Europe," soon to be followed by more "extreme abuses." In clearing him of any suspicion of disloyalty, the committee noted that Kantorowicz was "abnormally sensitive to anything which reminds him of his experiences in Germany."

During the second half of the 1950s another emigrant nonsigner would become even more eminent than Kantorowicz. But at the time of the hearings Erik Erikson's first great book, *Childhood and Society,* was still in press.[10]

The forty-eight-year-old Erikson had a joint appointment in Psychology at Berkeley and in the Medical School in San Francisco, where the med students disappointed him with their attitude that the oath was just a "piece of paper." His own stance was a complex one, because he looked at the crisis from two standpoints, that of his "European personality" and his new "American personality." The first told him that the hysteria was a forerunner of fascism, and the United States was on the road to dictatorship and war. But he also knew that American politics was a reflection of the country's unique history.

After a reading program to understand that history, Erikson concluded that the McCarthy Era was similar to the decade between 1910 and 1920, when working-class movements and Left-wing parties were being repressed. The government's attempt to persecute Bridges and Hiss reminded him of the 1921 trial and execution of the anarchists Sacco and Vanzetti.

What's most striking about Stewart's 1950 interview of Erikson is how far to the Left his thinking was. He saw the capitalist system as fundamentally unstable and predicted that it would either be replaced by socialism or degenerate into a dictatorship of the Right. That would lead to war (presumably with the socialist countries), a war that America was destined to lose.

And yet the psychoanalyst was conflicted about the oath. Trained in Vienna's apolitical culture, he didn't feel comfortable taking public positions. And he may have felt personally vulnerable, having taught a course at the Left-wing

California Labor School in 1945. He was also feeling grateful to his adopted country, which had rescued him from fascism. According to biographer Lawrence J. Friedman, it was Erikson's wife, Joan, and his older sons who prevailed on him to stand fast and not sign the contract oath.[11]

The analyst's letter to Privilege and Tenure foreshadowed the concerns with youth, identity, and integrity that would define his life's work. After mentioning that he was not and never had been a communist, he separated himself from other resisters when he said that too much had been made of the oath's threat to the faculty and its academic freedom. For Erikson, the danger to young people and the idealism that is a healthy part of their makeup during this stage in life was more important. Students would notice that "the men who are to teach them to think and to act judiciously and spontaneously must undergo a political test . . . must abrogate 'commitments' so undefined that they must forever suspect themselves and one another. . . . While older people can laugh this off, for young people this produces 'a dangerous rift' between 'the official truth' and those deep and often radical doubts which are the necessary condition for the development of thought."

And then, like Tolman, he noted that psychology studies hysteria, as well as the "tremendous waste in human energy which proceeds from the irrational fear and from the irrational gestures" that make up history. How could he ask his students or the subjects he investigates as a psychologist to work with him, were he to "participate without protest in a vague, fearful, and vindictive gesture devised to ban an evil in some magical way" such as the Regents' Special Oath?[12]

Erikson's publication of this letter in *Psychiatry* was his first public political act. Appearing in 1951 it became a classic document of the struggle against McCarthyism. But even more eloquent was the brief statement of Leonardo Olschki.

The sixty-five-year-old lecturer in Oriental Languages was considered the number one philologist of the romance languages in the world.[13] Olschki was also a historian of the Middle Ages who had written *Marco Polo's Precursors, Machiavelli Scientist,* and *The Genius of Italy.* He wrote P and T:

Gentlemen: I am an old scholar who has never been politically active. Nevertheless I was dismissed by Hitler in 1933 after twenty-five years of teaching at the University of Heidelberg, again by Mussolini after six years of activity at the University of Rome.

Now in a free country, a university which proclaims to protect 'impartial scholarship and free pursuit of truth' is making a political statement the condition for the continuance of my employment.

After having witnessed in other countries the destructive effect of similar compulsory measures on the character of the teachers, the respect of his students, and the standards of academic institutions, I would consider the acceptance of such condition of employment as a betrayal of my professional loyalty and my faith in freedom."[14]

In his memoir *From Berlin to Berkeley,* the sociologist Reinhard Bendix wrote that he signed the oath because he had learned that communists threatened the values of a free society while working with them in the underground resistance against Hitler. Still, he waited until the last minute to comply because the Loyalty Oath also threatened democratic freedoms. Bendix resented having to sign "under duress" and pointedly asked Sproul why fascists were not also excluded from the faculty.[15]

And yet despite Kantorowicz, Erikson, and Olschki, the analogy between McCarthyism and totalitarianism was not universally accepted, even among the refugees from fascism. Bendix didn't subscribe to it, nor did Economics professor Carl Landauer, who had been a Social Democratic member of the German parliament before fleeing Hitler. After signing the oath, Landauer continued to support the resisters, but he argued that his experience taught him that the oath did not portend a totalitarian America.

The European immigrants were a critical part of Berkeley's resistance, for the campus had attracted many more distinguished refugees than UCLA. The idea that their experiences gave them unique insights into what was now taking place in America was an article of faith. With their special moral authority, their views were not easy to dismiss.

And yet this moral authority was not universally accepted. Tussman felt that the emigrants thought they were superior to American-born resisters like himself. And he singled out Kantorowicz for over-dramatizing his youthful history of fighting communists, as well as being vain and pompous.[16]

WOMEN WERE EVEN MORE overrepresented among the resisters than were the emigrants from fascism. At a time when the number of female faculty members with tenure was between 1 and 2 percent, almost 10 percent (three out of thirty-one) of those who would eventually be fired were women. And they would also be overrepresented among those who would resign in protest.[17]

Just to have fashioned a career at such bastions of patriarchy as America's leading universities, women had to be independent spirits, indeed noncomformists. And in this context it is striking that the three women who refused to sign, Emily Huntington, Margaret Hodgen, and Pauline Sperry, all had female companions with whom they shared a house. Since it was a different age, one cannot know whether these relations were overtly sexual, for among the non-signers, only Kantorowicz was open about his sexuality. Still, these women had to be unusually strong in order to counter the mores of their era in this way.[18]

Of Berkeley's three female resisters, only the economist Emily Huntington had a national reputation, as an authority on the cost of living and an expert-advocate for unemployment and health insurance. She attributed this social consciousness to her father, a doctor who treated miners early in his career. Also influential was an event she experienced in 1901 when she was six, during the height of San Francisco's anti-Asian hysteria. One morning Emily went to school to find one of her best friends no longer in class. The Chinese-American girl had been moved to an "Oriental School," and from that day on Hunting-ton would be sensitive to violations of social justice.

When she was a doctoral student at Berkeley, the socialist Jessica Peixotto would be an influential mentor to her.

Emily Huntington came close to signing the oath in the spring of 1950 when she was in Paris on sabbatical leave. On receiving the letter that told her to either "Sign or Get Out," her first inclination was to comply. But when she got to the door of a bank with a notary public, she had an epiphany. "I re-member saying to myself, I cannot sign it," for the memory of "what had been going on on the campus was still vivid."[19] On her return, she aligned herself with the nonsigners, and as one of the faculty's most respected women—she had chaired the Senate's Welfare Committee—she immediately became a leader of the group.

When Huntington appeared before Privilege and Tenure, she was afraid that its members would think she was a communist or a subversive because of her advocacy for the unemployed. But because she was so well known and re-spected, they didn't even probe her reasons for refusing to sign. They asked only about her teaching, research, writing, and public service, so the committee gave her "a clean bill of health."[20]

Like other opponents of the oath who told their stories years later, Huntington omitted facts that suggested any indication of collaborating with the anticommunist *zeitgeist*. For when P and T prepared its report, they noted that she had called the Communist Party a dangerous organization.[21]

Margaret Hodgen also grew up in a privileged California family. Her father was a dentist who pioneered the field of orthodontics. After graduating from Cal in the same 1913 class as Sproul, she inspected working conditions for women in New York factories and served as educational secretary for the Women's Trade Union League, a vaguely socialist organization whose board included Jane Addams and Eleanor Roosevelt. Her concern for women was expressed in her first book, *Factory Work for Girls,* a simply worded exposition of the historical transition from tools to machines that is almost Marxian in its theoretical outlook.[22]

Hodgen returned to Berkeley, where, again like Huntington, she studied with Peixotto. Although her economics dissertation carried on the latter's socialist tradition,[23] her future work would lose its political edge as she became an acolyte of Frederick Teggart and his idiosyncratic approach to social science.

Still, Hodgen would remain a radical in spirit. Her papers reveal that she never considered signing the oath, even in a moment of weakness. And as a classmate of Sproul, she regularly sent him feisty letters protesting his hypocrisy in trying to get her to sign, while claiming to be an advocate of academic freedom. Letters were her forte, for she was too shy and retiring to speak at Senate meetings.

In her letter to Privilege and Tenure Hodgen accused the regents of "reaching for authoritarian control over the institutions of higher learning." Their "demand for submission to a political test for competence in teaching" was like the demands made upon professors in Europe by the fascist regimes. The results of "that earlier surrender by educators and men of learning," she emphasized, "are now spread in ignominy on the pages of history."

Then Hodgen got personal: "I resent the fact that after twenty-five years of honorable service in a high calling, I, with my colleagues of equal or longer service, are suddenly suspect of treason to our country; and are compelled, on pain of dismissal, not only to take an oath to our Constitution, but in addition to confirm that we have not lied in taking that oath. I deplore the resort to economic co-ercion (*sic*) on the part of the Regents; the assumption that scholarship can be bought, that the 'freedom of the mind and spirit' of which they claim to be the steadfast guardians is for sale. This is a personal and a professional affront that I find intolerable."

In conclusion she resorted to the tactic liberals were using to show that they despised communists. "If it be the purpose of the communist conspiracy to foster distrust amongst us and I think it is, the existing situation on the campus may be considered a communist success. If it also be its purpose to stifle free discussion and the fearless pursuit of truth, another success is all but achieved." So that if the regents do not reverse themselves, "the Communists will have won, and by the well-known tactic of suppressing freedom of thought and sowing dissension."[24]

When Hodgen appeared before the committee she made two additional arguments. Once a category of people, even people as despicable as the communists, were proscribed as unacceptable in the academic community, then other categories of people might be ruled beyond the pale in the future. And when she criticized communism in the classroom, her students might believe it was only because she was compelled to do so.

Hodgen's friend Pauline Sperry had been teaching at Berkeley since 1917, and like her she was known for her teaching rather than for her scholarship. Sperry had published only two geometry texts.[25] However she was considered an inspiration by graduate students, who carried on important research.

Sperry's ethical beliefs as a Quaker made her reluctant to sign the oath. But in her testimony she was not as liberal as Hodgen. She stated that communists had no place in the academic community because they did not have "free minds." But Sperry did emphasize that the oath would "destroy one of the things which has made the university great, the atmosphere of trust in each other, a good will, friendliness, and (the protection) from freedom of interference in which we work." Replacing these virtues will be "distrust and cynicism."[26]

In 1950 Sperry had been on the faculty at Berkeley for thirty-three years. Hodgen had been teaching for twenty-five. The fact that both remained associate professors is an indication of the status of women at one of the nation's great universities. While their publication records may have been undistinguished, men with a similar work record would very likely have become full professors. For the "old boys" network would have reasoned that the man's dedication to teaching and contributions to his department were sufficient rationale for promotion.

THE FIVE NOT RECOMMENDED

With Privilege and Tenure under pressure not to recommend all fifty-two appellants for retention, five professors did not get its seal of approval. One was Isabel Hungerland, a distinguished philosopher who had written a book on Hobbes and was also an expert on aesthetics and the social order. The fact that at forty-three she was still an assistant professor, and that her position was in Speech, rather than Philosophy, is another indication of the barriers facing women.

Hungerland refused to make any statement, direct or indirect, with respect to communism. A believer in the AAUP position, and staunchly against guilt by association, she told her all-male questioners that "There's more than one way in which the university can be wrecked, and because of my loyalty to the university, I will not contribute to its slow deterioration from within."

The committee was convinced that Hungerland was not a communist, but she hadn't given them what they felt they needed to exonerate her. In her case and in the others, they did not recommend dismissal. But failing to ask for her retention amounted to the same thing.

An even more distinguished petitioner was Margaret O'Hagan,[27] who had an established reputation as a painter of abstract art, and who had tenure in the Department of Art. Her argument was that the contract oath conflicted with the Fifth Amendment to the Constitution and that all political tests were "abhorrent to the principles of our Bill of Rights." And even though she compared the regents' oath to the regimentation of art in totalitarian societies, this wasn't good enough for the committee, which failed to recommend her retention.

Nevitt Sanford was a social psychologist who had been influenced by John Dewey. Socially conscious, he campaigned for the inclusion of minority groups in higher education and was an early critic of the biases in standardized tests which contributed to their exclusion.

By 1950 he was one of the leading lights in the Department of Psychology, as well as the coauthor of *The Authoritarian Personality,* one of the 20th century's most influential works of social science.[28] In the years he spent studying "the anti-democratic mentality" for this book, he had concluded that Hitler had come to power not primarily because of "the actions of a few evil or misguided men," but rather through the inaction of "good men who told themselves that this was none of their affairs."[29]

A friend of Tolman, Sanford took an even stronger position than the non-signers' leader when he told P and T that "To sign this oath would mean essentially that I believe in authoritarian statism and am willing to approve it. I could not face my students or my conscience if I should do this; and I can contrive no rationalization which I, as a psychologist, cannot see through." And because he was unwilling to clarify his position on the Communist Party, the committee failed to recommend him.

Harold Winkler was the political scientist who had spoken publicly against the dismissal of Irving Fox. He was popular with students for his riveting lectures, as well as his willingness to meet with them off campus to explain the oath controversy. However, Winkler was something of an outsider in the nonsigners' movement. According to an informant who knew him well, he was warmhearted and charming, but also imperious and self-absorbed.[30] A maverick in every way, he was too independent politically and intellectually to sign a loyalty oath.

After getting his Ph.D. at Harvard, Winkler had served for three years on aircraft carriers as a lieutenant commander in the Navy and earned a Bronze Star. Arriving in Berkeley in 1947, he was a charismatic teacher who taught innovative courses such as "Politics and the Novel." His politics were quite radical, but he was also a pragmatist in the tradition of Dewey. Attracted to the Left, he was appalled by Soviet communism, and he was not a joiner.[31]

The political philosopher exemplified a not uncommon academic type: a brilliant thinker who had difficulty formulating his ideas in written form and in compensation channeled his energy into teaching. When he appeared before P and T in 1950, he had no publications to his name. The committee noted that his department's mid-career review had found his "diffusion" of intellectual interests "disturbing."

Harold Winkler was too strong a defender of intellectual freedom to give the panel what it was looking for. He did tell it that he opposed political tests, because with them a university ceases to be a university. He believed in the free competition of ideas, above all to be able to discuss every possible idea in his courses. He hoped that the oath would be tested in the courts, for he was convinced it was unconstitutional.

The committee sent a special report to Sproul about John Kelley, because the facts in his case were "unusually complicated." At thirty-three, Kelley, according to P and T, was "one of the best young topologists in the country," "a mathematical genius." The panel had no doubts as to his loyalty, but still could not recommend his retention.

Kelley's troubles began during the war when he was doing ballistics research at the Aberdeen proving grounds in Maryland. There he was able to solve a mathematical problem with critical military implications; indeed, his supervisor testified that he was the only person in the nation capable of its solution. After the war he continued on as a consultant to the AEC, but on July 1, 1949—just as the oath fight was heating up in Berkeley—the agency refused to extend his contract. Kelley had lost his security clearance, charged with negligence in the storing of classified documents during the war.

The mathematician told the committee that the security status of those documents must have been upgraded after he had last worked on them. He felt that he was the victim of guilt by association, for one of his colleagues at the ballistics research facility had been a former communist. And when he had testified before a New York grand jury on that case, Kelley had sworn that he was not a communist himself.

And yet as a Quaker and an idealistic liberal, he was too principled to make such a statement to P and T. That, the panel told Sproul, was his "great mistake." But perhaps understandable, since Kelley's past had made him "abnormally sensitive to the idea of guilt by association." The committee expressed the hope that Sproul could convince the regents to make an exception by retaining him. His discharge would be "an irreparable loss" to Berkeley's top-rated Mathematics Department, for Kelley was "impossible to replace."[32]

It was now a foregone conclusion that the five professors whose retentions were not recommended would lose their jobs. This infuriated many faculty members, especially those who were still resisting the oath. The nonsigner Ludwig Edelstein spoke out against what he saw as P and T's "extremely formalist" approach, and he called for a reconsideration of these cases.[33]

The most blistering attack came from the Non–Academic Senate Employees. Openly contemptuous of their professor bosses for playing ball with P and T, the NASE saw that committee as "little more than a 'loyalty review board.'"[34]

By this time a procedure had been established to hear nonsigners who were not Senate members. The NASE's appellants were reviewed by a three-person committee chaired by the dean of their particular school. The committee of Felix Rosenthal, the only nonsigner in Architecture, was headed by Dean William Wurster, who supported his resistance. But Rosenthal, a refugee from Nazi Germany, had to dodge tricky questions from law professors on his committee. Although he refused to speak to his position on the Communist Party, he received a favorable recommendation because of his many FBI clearances while working in sensitive positions during the war.[35]

History student Ralph Giesey was questioned by Dean Ed Strong and the chair of his department, John Hicks, who also headed his review committee. He would receive a favorable verdict, but on the advice of mentor Kantorowicz—"It's a matter of your livelihood"—he would eventually sign.[36]

The proportion of nonsigners in the NASE was far higher than on the faculty, and half of them didn't even bother to be heard. Of the eighty-one who did appeal, fifty-eight were reviewed favorably and seven unfavorably. The committee made no recommendations in the remaining cases, because they were not up for reappointment as TAs or RAs.[37]

SPROUL'S "COMPROMISE" ASSAILED BY HUTCHINS

The sacrifice of the five professors who would not cooperate with Privilege and Tenure did not mean that the other Senate appellants were home free. Neylan and his allies were already on record that exemptions to signing the oath were justifiable only on religious or quasi-religious grounds. And more ominously, Stephen Bechtel, the architect of the Alumni Compromise, was upset that the committee had found 90 percent of the faculty nonsigners to be acceptable and thus to be retained. That number was much too large; he would have preferred the ratio reversed, with only 10 percent recommended favorably, or, failing that, no worse than half approved.[38] All this did not bode well for the June 23 regents' meeting, when the committee's recommendations would be presented by Sproul.

The Board of Regents had a crowded agenda that day, most important of which was the president's recommendation that the sixty-two Berkeley and UCLA professors cleared by the Committee on Privilege and Tenure be retained. Sproul warned of the dire consequences that could befall the university were they not to approve his motion: many of the best professors would leave, its brightest prospects would turn down offers, and he also hinted darkly that his own future might be in doubt as well.[39]

Sproul also asked that the six not approved by Privilege and Tenure be removed from the rolls of university employees.[40] He then moved that the 157 non–Academic Senate employees be terminated as of June 30, which was only one week in the future. These were the TAs, RAs, and instructors who had not petitioned for hearings, or had failed to win approval, or were not going to be reappointed.

Underscoring this rather callous attitude toward non–Academic Senate employees, he added 18 new names to the 157 whose dismissal P and T had recommended. They were to be sacrificed in exchange for the board's approval of the 62 nonsigning professors. But Sproul's "tough stance" backfired. Conservative regent Sidney Ehrman was acquainted with several appellants, so he knew they were not communists. And yet to approve them, in his view, would be a nullification of the contract oath. For if 62 were to get through today, what would stop ten times that number from employing the same loophole next year? And Fred Jordan wondered why P and T had protected so many people who were not motivated by "religious scruples."

Before adjourning, the board postponed its decision on the faculty nonsigners until its July meeting. However it was unanimous in voting to terminate the now 175 non-Senate members.[41] By this act the regents had carried out the most massive political purge in the university's history, as well as one of the largest ever in American higher education.

In his June commencement address, Robert Hutchins attacked Sproul for approving the new contract oath and for collaborating in the mass firings. Chicago's chancellor questioned the "fortitude" of his California counterpart, as well as his "qualifications to head a great university." And Hutchins predicted that the University of California would not be a great university much longer.[42]

Immediately after the June 23 session Farnham Griffiths suffered a stroke. Exhaustion and nervous strain were factors in his collapse, but the tension between him and Neylan also contributed to his sudden illness.

For decades Griffiths had been Neylan's personal attorney, and ally on the Board of Regents. Skeptical like his friend about the value of the oath, he had also come to support it. But by the spring of 1950 Griffiths had become anti-oath. One reason was his friendship with Sproul, who often asked him to interview prospective faculty members on his business trips. Even more important was the fact that the regent's son, Gordon Griffiths, had emerged as one of the most militant opponents of the oath.

Neylan did not take this defection lightly and, just as with another former friend, Sproul, he dedicated himself to making Griffiths's life miserable. Gordon believed that the FBI had made available to Neylan the same "thick file" on his Left-wing activities that they had revealed to his father. So Farnham would come to every board meeting fearing that Neylan was going to use his son's political past against him.

The strain would be too much to bear.

Gordon Griffiths, who as a young communist had daydreamed about how remorseful his father would feel when he was imprisoned or shot "as a good soldier of the revolution" now had to deal with his own remorse. "Little did I realize that it would be he rather than I who would someday suffer when the confrontation over Communism would come to a head."[43]

The oath crisis was taking its human toll. On the same day that Griffiths keeled over, Max Radin, a professor of law who had been one of Berkeley's more Left-wing professors, died of a sudden heart attack. Although Radin was retired, he remained active in the oath struggle. His death, like that of UCLA's Dykstra six weeks earlier, was widely attributed to the oath.

Finally there was Dixon Wecter. After a decade of teaching English at UCLA, Wecter had joined Berkeley's History Department. A prolific scholar, he had published nine books by the age of forty-four. A generalist who wrote on a variety of subjects including the Great Depression, Wecter was also a Mark Twain specialist. This expertise had been recognized when he was appointed the executor of the humorist's papers.[44]

Wecter was also active against the oath. Only a little more than a month before the June board meeting he had published an article in the *Saturday Review of Literature* in which he labeled the Board of Regents the "Commissars of Loyalty."[45] Calling the piece "a hodgepodge of libel, slander, and innuendo—wholly untruthful," Neylan charged that its author was engaged in a campaign "to smear the regents." And in his view, an attack on the board was an attack on the university.[46]

On June 24, 1950, one day after the board had met, Wecter died, the victim of a sudden heart attack.[47]

CHAPTER 10

THE HEARINGS AT UCLA

The noncommunist requirement of the regents is a beginning
of the regimentation of the academic mind and an early step
in the destruction of democracy. It is the duty of university
professors to help overcome this, not play into it.

—Donald Piatt[1]

T HE LOYALTY OATH LOOMS LARGE IN BERKELEY'S
institutional memory. Professors on the campus organized
the 50th Anniversary Symposium, and old-timers interviewed for their oral
histories report vivid recollections of the controversy.

But this is not true for UCLA. There was no marking of the anniversary
on the Westwood campus, and what surprised this writer even more was the
relative neglect given to the oath in the oral histories of those professors who
played important roles in it; for example Caughey, Dodd, and McHenry.[2]

One idea why the oath is not as important in its historical memory comes
from Philip Selznick, who transferred from UCLA's Sociology Department to
Berkeley's halfway through the crisis. Selznick was surprised how big an issue
the oath was on his new campus. In the south the faculty was against it, but it
never became the high drama there that he was now witnessing in the north.[3]

In talking to professors from UCLA, Margaret Hodgen was struck by the "mutual confidence and respect between nonsigners and the Senate." Above all, there was no one like Hildebrand and his allies blaming nonsigners like herself for the crisis, jeopardizing Sproul's job, or threatening to ruin the university. There was no concerted effort in the south "to break down the nonsigners" so that they would sign the oath.[4]

Another difference is that UCLA's most vocal nonsigner was incorporated into its Academic Senate leadership. As a member of the Policy Committee and the combined Steering Committee, John Caughey attended meetings of the regents on a regular basis, even if Paul Dodd once all but locked him in his hotel room. At Berkeley, on the other hand, Caughey's militant counterpart Tolman was kept at arms' length from the faculty establishment.

The contrast was summarized by Kerr when he wrote that while the oath divided Berkeley's professors into acrimonious factions, it united UCLA's faculty.[5]

During the first year of the controversy the proportion of nonsigners was actually higher in the south.[6] Although their numbers would eventually decline in comparison to Berkeley, as a percentage of the faculty the twenty-seven UCLA professors who petitioned for a hearing that May was still roughly comparable to the fifty-two faculty members in the north.

Reflecting this greater faculty unity, UCLA's Committee on Privilege and Tenure was not riven by differences in its members' attitudes toward the oath, and so there was no need to dismiss it and reconstitute a new committee. Chaired by Physics professor Joseph Ellis, the panel included Kenneth Macgowan, the friend of Lehman who had founded the Theater Arts Department after a long career as a drama critic and a movie producer. Macgowan had come to the attention of Jack Tenney for championing progressive causes, but he was the only committee member with a liberal political past.[7]

More important, UCLA's panel did not operate in the formalistic and legalistic manner of Berkeley's that had led to the criticisms of Ludwig Edelstein and others. It did not feel the pressure to *not* recommend petitioners in order to placate Neylan and the regents. That's why it approved every single regular faculty member, in contrast to Berkeley, where five Senate members were not recommended.

The twenty-seven Senate members who requested hearings were all approved, as were five lecturers and three visiting professors who were not part of the faculty's governing body.[8] The nonsigners came from eighteen different departments, but as at Berkeley, were concentrated in a few fields. Philosophy was UCLA's most rebellious department, with five petitioners, in large part due to the supportive climate created by its chair Donald Piatt. Next came Social Welfare with three resisters, followed by French, History, and Economics, with two each.[9]

The reasons offered for not signing the oath at UCLA were similar to those offered at Berkeley. They were also as varied as the resisters' special fields. The most common theme was the belief that a political test for employment was a manifestation of authoritarianism. Many appellants expressed the view that loyalty oaths made sense for government employees carrying out sensitive national security work, but in the university they conflicted with academic freedom.[10]

PASTERNAK: A "SACRIFICIAL LAMB"

UCLA's most controversial case was that of Eleanor Pasternak. The sister of Miriam Sherman, the piano player for women's gym classes who had been fired after her communist affiliations had become known, Pasternak also worked in the Women's Physical Education Department as an assistant supervisor. In her hearing before Privilege and Tenure, Pasternak made it clear that she had no sympathy with any form of totalitarianism. But otherwise she would not give the committee what it was looking for, a clear anticommunist statement, or a reasonable substitute for it.[11] The fact that she was not a regular faculty member with Academic Senate status undoubtedly made it easier for P and T not to recommend her.

But before taking such a drastic action the committee made a special effort to clear Pasternak. Troubled that she was unwilling to make more definitive statements, Macgowan asked her for references who could attest to her character and loyalty. He then inquired of at least one reference as to whether she might be in the Communist Party and about her commitment to democratic ideals and the objectivity of her teaching. Unfortunately Macgowan's papers do not include "Martha's" answers, perhaps because they didn't reflect well on the instructor.[12]

Gardner concluded that Pasternak's "reasons for not signing were as legitimate and based on principle and conscience" as the others who were recommended positively."[13] One has to wonder whether she may have been a victim of guilt by association, given her sister's politics. Another factor may have been her obscurity, which meant that her dismissal would not affect the academic standing of the faculty, as well as the fact that she was not known personally to the members of the committee. For John Caughey was just as stubborn in refusing to take a position with respect to the Communist Party, but P and T found reasons to retain the man whom Sproul had called "a major asset" of the university.

Caughey refused to state categorically that he was not a Communist Party member, both in his letter to the Committee on Privilege and Tenure and in his hearing before it. In the committee's words, the historian "stated that he had no desire to deny a lack of sympathy with Communism, that if he were being considered for government service of a secret or special nature, he would answer any questions asked of him; that he had made speeches including statements antagonistic to totalitarianism of any kind, including Russian totalitarianism, along with Nazi and fascist types of totalitarianism, and that 'I abhor the . . . sort of political system whether it be an absolute monarchy with practically no respect for the wishes of the people of the country, or whether it be a totalitarian government without monarchic form but with no regard for the wishes of the people.'" He also told the committee that he considered Russia "a real menace," the principal threat to the United States today.[14]

Because Caughey had been unwilling to state that he wasn't a communist, the letter recommending that he be retained required elaborate justification. In fact, there are ten drafts of this letter in Macgowan's papers, suggesting how hard he had to work to arrive at a statement that would pass muster. What it probably came down to was the "years of intimate professional and social contact" that committee members had had with Caughey, experiences that left them with "absolutely no doubt" that he was not a communist and had never been one.[15] Eleanor Pasternak lacked such a history with the faculty leadership, so she became UCLA's sacrificial lamb.

Another difference between UCLA and Berkeley was the role of the AAUP. In the north it was so uninvolved that Stewart called it "a company union" in bed with the administration.[16] But at UCLA the AAUP spearheaded the resistance, as Caughey and his friend, the historian Charles Mowat, alternated as presidents.

Mowat was born in England in 1911, the son of a historian who was also an Oxford don. Following in his father's footsteps, he got a Ph.D. in history from the University of Minnesota. After briefly teaching there, he joined the faculty at UCLA. While Berkeley's History Department had pioneered in the study of Latin America, the Westwood campus was strong in European, especially British, history. Mowat himself would go on to virtually invent "20th Century British History as an academic pursuit."[17] By 1950 he had published two books, including one on British education during the war, but his most famous works, one on the 1926 General Strike and another on England between the two World Wars, were still ahead of him.

Mowat told the committee that as an immigrant from England he had made sworn statements during his naturalization hearings that were more stringent than the contract oath. He had not perjured himself then, and he asserted his belief in democracy and free enterprise, as well as his opposition to all forms of totalitarianism. But he refused to sign the oath because he found the regents' policy concerning the employment of communists and their procedure for implementing it "inconsistent with the ideal of a university."[18]

In general the nonsigners at UCLA were not as eminent in scholarship as their counterparts from Berkeley. This is not surprising, since UC's flagship campus was ranked in the top five in the nation in academic status. Two notable exceptions to this tendency were Carl Epling and Daniel Popper.

Born in 1894, Epling had served in the army during World War I. The botanist was the world's authority on the mint family, but he was better known for his work with Theodore Dobzhansky that had created a neo-Darwinian synthesis of evolutionary theory. Like Hildebrand at Berkeley, Epling was the chair of the Academic Senate. But he was much more liberal than the chemist. By character a noncomformist, his appearances at regents' meetings had made him another of Neylan's enemies.

Epling told the committee that he was opposed to any dictatorship, "proletarian or otherwise." Although he had come to the attention of the Tenney committee, he denied that he was a fellow traveler. And loyalty oaths in his view "depart[ed] from the principles of jurisprudence on which our Republic is founded." The committee's report mentioned that Epling had emphasized that the totalitarian policy of Communist Russia "had killed" the science of genetics in that country. They also noted that the appellant had held the prestigious position of faculty research lecturer, underscoring his importance to the university.[19]

At thirty-seven Daniel Popper was a Berkeley Ph.D. in astronomy and astrophysics. During the war he had carried out top-secret research at the Radiation Laboratory. He became UCLA's first stellar astronomer in 1947, and by the time of the oath crisis had discovered the orbits of several stars in binary systems.[20]

Popper told the committee that "loyalty checks departed from the American tradition and they have troubling totalitarian implications.'" Although the vast majority of his colleagues shared his views, their failure to protest actively had already lowered the university's standing "in the eyes of thinking men." The astrophysicist predicted that the requirement's harmful impact would only accelerate, as many scholars would leave, others would refuse to come, and the faculty's morale would plummet.[21]

In 1950 future university president David Saxon was a little known assistant professor of Physics. Since he was not "a political person" no one would have expected him to defy the regents. But gradually he found to his surprise that he was determined not to sign. More than thirty-five years later Saxon still wasn't sure how he got to that point. But the issue got him aroused, and he began speaking at Senate meetings. Yet his response, Saxon stresses, was "personal and individual," and he never became a member of any anti-oath group.[22]

Saxon told the committee that he had been given total clearance during the war when he worked on a classified project at MIT and had undergone a security review by the Atomic Energy Commission (AEC). If called to work on a government project requiring a noncommunist oath, he would have no qualms about signing it. But as he told the panel, he was rejecting the oath tied to his contract because he saw it as an encroachment of academic freedom and as a dangerous expression of guilt by association. The competence and objectivity of a professor should be judged only by his faculty peers.

P and T's chair Joseph Ellis also chaired Saxon's department, so he knew him well. In his report to Sproul, he noted that Saxon deplored Communist Party tactics in Russia and was particularly disturbed by that country's denial of academic freedom. Ellis was moved by his colleague's statement that because of the oath he now regretted taking a job at UCLA.[23]

Another resister was Kenneth Roose of Economics. Roose was born in 1921 to a religious family, and the antiwar stance of his church "rubbed off" on him, both in Kansas where he was born and in North Hollywood where his family moved when he was seven. Already a pacifist as a teenager, in 1942 he became a conscientious objector and spent the war working as a statistician for the Forest Service in Southern California. These were the events in his past that led him to become a nonsigner.[24]

Ecstatic to be teaching in the city where he had grown up, with his wife and children comfortable in a house walking distance from UCLA, Roose had no desire to leave. His prospects were bright, for his early work on business cycles, inspired by his mentor Joseph Schumpeter, was highly regarded.

But the oath fired him up, and although he was not important enough to serve on a Senate committee, he began to take part in the resistance. Like Caughey, who became his friend, Roose was critical of the way in which UCLA's old guard leadership was fighting the oath. In his view, the "legalistic" approach of Dodd and Grant failed to sufficiently emphasize the oath's implications for civil liberties, including the freedoms of speech and association.

Interviewed more than fifty-five years later, Roose recalled that his two-hour hearing was a friendly one, as the committee refrained from asking him directly about communist associations. The most important question concerned his economic philosophy. As a Keynesian the young assistant professor supported the New Deal and similar full-employment policies, but he also made it clear that he was against the redistribution of wealth. As for Marxism, he "was strongly opposed to the Communist doctrine in the subject of economics," and he did not believe that a communist could be objective in teaching his field.[25]

Roose's principal reason for not signing was an opposition to political tests for employment. He also believed in defending everyone's civil liberties, without exception. Even with his doubts about communists, he continued to hold the AAUP position. Finally, when asked about Franco and his government, he responded deftly that he was against totalitarianism "in all its forms." In recommending his retention, the committee concluded that Ken Roose was "a man of deep convictions."[26]

A third young assistant professor was Abraham Kaplan, one of five philosophers who had petitioned for a hearing. Although never hounded by investigating committees, Kaplan had a radical past. He expressed his idealism in a commitment to making philosophy accessible to the common man and the priority he gave to teaching.[27]

Kaplan told the committee that he had already been cleared by the Air Force and the AEC while doing "secret work" at the Rand Corporation. "Opposed to totalitarianism in all forms," he would sign loyalty oaths for those agencies. But what angered him about the contract oath was its "premise of universal guilt," requiring an individual to plead his or her innocence. And since a communist would not hesitate to sign, the oath's implementation victimized "those whose principles make them the most uncompromising opponents of the totalitarian control of thought and action for which Communism stands."[28]

Morris Neiburger was the meteorologist who had been the only faculty member to vote "no confidence" in Sproul. An associate professor with tenure, he told the committee that it was "a serious error" to require a political test for employment. Were he to work for the government, he would have no qualms about signing a non-communist oath. Although he was opposed to all forms of totalitarianism (including the Soviet Union, which he viewed as a police state), his conscience would not permit him to sign the Regents' Special Oath.[29]

UNDERLINED IN RED

In the same folder in the archives of the Bancroft Library that includes the summary report of UCLA's Committee on Privilege and Tenure, as well as its letters to Sproul on each individual appellant, there is also a four-page memorandum titled "Confidential." Without a signature or other clues to its authorship, the document lists the "subversive" organizations and conferences that took place in Los Angeles during the 1940s. Underneath each listing are the names of the faculty members reported as participants, either in the press or by the Tenney Committee. *And the names of the nonsigners who petitioned for a Privilege and Tenure review are underlined in red.*[30]

UCLA's P and T committee took this information seriously. For the campus was faced with a problem that Berkeley didn't have. While Tolman was the only nonsigner in the north who had come to the attention of Tenney's committee, at least five of the 18 Senate members at UCLA still resisting the oath had received this kind of publicity, earning them red underlines on that confidential document. Two of them, Donald Piatt and Hugh Miller, were professors of philosophy, and the third, David Appleman, was an associate professor of soil science.[31]

Donald Piatt had received his Ph.D. in 1925 from the University of Chicago, where he had studied with John Dewey. Like his mentor, he became a pragmatist, and would write papers on the history of that quintessentially American philosophy. Because of this work he was made president of the American Philosophical Association for 1948–49. He also chaired his department for ten years, including the period of the oath crisis.

On the Westwood campus Piatt was best known for his inspired teaching. It was common for an undergraduate student to say that one of his classes was the best he or she had ever taken. He was equally devoted to his graduate students, and many of them became well-known philosophers in the Deweyian tradition.[32]

Don Piatt was selfless in his support of student organizations. He was the faculty's liaison to the organization of UCLA's teaching and research assistants, and he didn't hesitate to support the most radical students. He had been a faculty sponsor of the American Youth for Democracy, the Communist Party's youth organization, and as late as 1947 had lectured at the Peoples Education Center (PEC). All of which had brought him to the attention of Tenney and his committee.

In his appearance before P and T, Piatt made it clear that he was against all forms of "dictatorship of opinion."[33] Like other appellants, he'd have been willing to sign a noncommunist oath for a position that was vital to national security. But he was one of a very few willing to state his opposition to the regents' 1940 policy of excluding communists from the faculty. To Piatt that was "guilt by association." If an individual professor were to advocate overturning the government by force and violence, that would constitute grounds for dismissal.

For Piatt, the regents' requirement was "a symptom of the social and moral climate in which we live," a climate marked by "fear and anxiety," which during the era of the Cold War had affected the "thinking and feeling" of most of the people of the world. The duty of a professor, as he saw it, was to help overcome such a debilitating climate, and not to give in to it.

California's test oath reminded Piatt, just as it had Kantorowicz, Hodgen, and Olschki, of how Europe's professors had been subjected to similar requirements. Since that had been a critical step in the rise of totalitarian dictatorships, he feared that the oath might foreshadow "a beginning of the regimentation of the academic mind as an early step in the destruction of democracy" in America.[34]

Piatt's testimony posed a problem for the committee, given his Popular Front connections and the criticisms that had been leveled at him because of his political history. They wrote Sproul that they had taken this into account, and were satisfied with his candid answers to their questions about his Left-wing activities. In 1950 it took courage for UCLA's Committee on Privilege and Tenure to assert that the charges of Tenney had no bearing on their own investigation.

The panel was swayed by Piatt's statement that he was against the "ideal of a classless society" and had lectured against Marx's tenet that the state was the executive committee of the ruling class. Certainly, they concluded in recommending his retention, "No Communist would entertain such sentiments."[35]

Born in 1891, Hugh Miller had been on the committee that organized the 1943 Writers Congress. He specialized in the relations between philosophy, science, and religion. In speaking to P and T he was more circumspect than Piatt. And much more conservative: he assured them that he was a strong supporter of the regents' noncommunist policy. He stressed that he was not now and never had been a communist, nor had he ever had any connections with front groups.[36]

David Appleman may have been P and T's most difficult case. Born in a shetl in Tsarist Russia in 1899, he had taught Hebrew to monks in the old country. After immigrating to the United States he graduated with honors from Berkeley in 1927 and eight years later earned a Ph.D. in Nutritional Science with a dissertation on *chlorella vulgaris,* an important green alga.[37]

After joining UCLA's faculty, Appleman became active in progressive causes, with the result that he would earn more "Tenney listings" than almost any other UC professor. One concerned a 1945 talk on "Soviet Advances in Agricultural Research" delivered at a conference on American-Russian Cultural Exchange. The soil scientist was also a regular lecturer at the PEC, and as late as 1948 he sponsored a peace conference organized by the Hollywood chapter of the Council on the Arts, Sciences, and Professions, an organization widely considered to be a communist front group. So it's no surprise that Appleman was called to testify before California's Little HUAC in 1948. On that occasion he swore under oath that he was not a party member, nor even a subscriber to the West Coast equivalent of *The Daily Worker, People's World.*

During the late 1940s, Soviet geneticist Trofim Lysenko had rocked the world of science by proclaiming that acquired characteristics could be inherited, a theory which challenged the accepted approach to evolution. This put the not inconsiderable number of Western scientists who were either communists or fellow travelers in a quandary. Would they side with the new dogma coming out of the Soviet Union or with the consensus of the scientific community? Most likely it was the Lysenko affair that led to Appleman's disillusionment with the USSR, and if he had once been a communist, he was no longer in the party at the time of the oath controversy.

In his testimony to P and T the soil scientist reiterated his distaste for the Soviet Union and its innovations in agriculture. The Russian government's policy of choosing scientists on the basis of loyalty to the regime rather than competence had led to "tragic results" in his discipline. Underscoring his commitment to free inquiry, he told the committee that he had resigned from the organizations he once belonged to that did not share this value.

In approving Appleman, the committee stressed how he had served the university loyally for seventeen years and how his personal contacts had helped the university gain an unusually large endowment![38]

A great deal of the credit for the fact that UCLA's most Left-wing resisters got favorable recommendations must go to Paul Dodd. For it was the powerful dean who took the findings of his Privilege and Tenure committee and packaged them in a report to Sproul that emphasized each petitioner's loyalty and importance to the university.

PART III

WAR IN KOREA
AND VICTORY
IN THE COURTS

CHAPTER 11

KOREA CHANGED
EVERYTHING

Chicago law professor to Chancellor Hutchins: "If the trustees fire Lovett, you'll receive the resignations of 20 full professors tomorrow." Hutchins: "Oh no I won't . . . my successor will."[1]

O N   J U N E   1 ,   1 9 5 0 ,   A T   A   T I M E   W H E N   T H E Committee on Privilege and Tenure was halfway through its interviews, something remarkable took place three thousand miles away. On the floor of the U.S. Senate, Margaret Chase Smith gave a speech that brought hope to the nonsigners and their allies. At fifty-three, the Maine Republican was the only woman in the upper house, and on that day she became the first legislator to break the rules of senatorial clubbiness and put Joe McCarthy in his place.

Smith said that the Senate had been "debased to the level of a forum of hate and character assassination" and had become "a platform for irresponsible sensationalism." Those "who shout the loudest about Americanism" too often ignore its basic principles, which are "the right to criticize, the right to hold unpopular beliefs, the right to protest, and the right to independent thought." She concluded by stating that she still hoped for a political change in the November elections, but she did not want "to see the Republican Party ride to victory on the Four Horsemen of Calumny—Fear, Ignorance, Bigotry, and Smear."[2]

Brave as was the senator's speech, it neither silenced McCarthy nor slowed the winds of anticommunism. At the University of California, the June 15 report by Privilege and Tenure had provided hope, but many remained fearful that the regents would not be satisfied with the six professors the committee had offered up in sacrifice. The result was a wave of resignations that swept Berkeley and UCLA in late June. Those who quit were mostly young instructors and assistant professors who had not put down roots and who had become fed up with the chaos, the uncertainty, and the wounded academic freedoms at the university. But several established professors also resigned at this time, including Erik Erikson and Lawrence Powell, the archivist for whom a library at UCLA would one day be named.

Even more significant in its impact was the nationwide boycott of the university. A questionnaire that the new Senate Committee on Academic Freedom had sent to department heads revealed that an impressive number of prospective faculty members had refused offers because of the oath. Raymond Birge, chair of Physics, reported that "we cannot induce a single first-class theoretical physicist to accept a job at Berkeley." But it was not just the idealistic young who were turning down the university. Two of the three most eminent scholars in sociology, Robert Merton and Paul Lazarsfeld, both at Columbia, each said no to visiting professorships, at UCLA and Berkeley, respectively.[3] Many worried that the status of the university as the nation's leading public university was in jeopardy.

AARON GORDON'S NEW PLYMOUTH

As one of Berkeley's leading liberals, Robert Aaron Gordon was a staunch opponent of the oath. Assigned the most important speech at the March mass meeting, he had refuted Neylan's arguments point by point. On June 21 Gordon left Berkeley for professional meetings in the east. After completing that business, he took a train to Detroit, where he had arranged to pick up a new Plymouth sedan. In the decade following World War II, you could save money by buying your vehicle in Detroit, close to the assembly lines of America's Big Three automakers.

Gordon was planning a leisurely drive across the country, a chance to relish some solitude, a rare pleasure for him in a year of crises. But the second day of his trip was Sunday, June 25, 1950, and that was when he heard the news on his car radio that North Korean troops had crossed the 38th parallel, the border between that communist nation and South Korea, an ally of the United States. For a few hours the world was uncertain whether this was just another of the nuisance raids that periodically interrupted the fragile peace between the two Koreas. But by midday it had become clear that it was a full-scale invasion, not a border dispute, and that evening the UN's Security Council met in emergency session to call for the withdrawal of North Korean troops. Two days later Truman told the nation that he was sending American fighter planes and warships to help the South Korean army—ground troops would follow within the week. It was imperative, the president said, to keep that nation from being swept into the Soviet-Chinese orbit. But the North Koreans were meeting little resistance as they swept through the south; Seoul, South Korea's capital, fell on June 29th.

Aaron Gordon's son Robert J. Gordon, today an economist at Northwestern, told me that his father was "devastated" by the outbreak of war.[4] And though he could not know all its implications at first, he did know, long before he arrived in Berkeley, that everything had changed for the nonsigners. The holdouts would be excoriated as unpatriotic, as giving comfort to the enemy—charges, however unjustified, that would resonate with a public that, even before Korea, was hostile to them.

While en route, Gordon decided that he would sign the oath before the June 30 deadline. And the first thing he did in Berkeley, after showing his family their new automobile, was to call his friend Clark Kerr. Kerr strongly supported his decision, for he felt that the new international situation would make the stance of the nonsigners untenable.

It is difficult for those who did not live through that time to understand how the outbreak of war transformed the political atmosphere. Of course, even before June 25, 1950, anticommunist hysteria infected the nation, and Joe McCarthy, whose crusade now bore his name, had become more and more emboldened. But when the Cold War turned hot, "Communists were no longer merely the advocates of a strange ideology; they would now be seen to belong to the party of the enemy."[5]

The nation rallied behind its troops, and unlike in Vietnam a generation ago or Iraq today, the initial opposition to the war would be limited to a tiny band of communists and "fellow travelers." And these opponents did not then know all the dangers they were facing. For it would be revealed in 2007 that in early July 1950 the FBI's J. Edgar Hoover had sent the White House a plan to suspend habeas corpus and incarcerate in military prisons the twelve thousand Americans he considered disloyal and subversive.[6]

But that wasn't all that made the situation of the nonsigners precarious. In 1950 many Americans made little or no distinction between liberals, even anticommunist ones, and communists. So as the pressure for a not-to-be-questioned patriotism ratcheted up, the effect spilled over on liberals, especially those like the nonsigners, who for reasons most Americans could not understand, were refusing to state that they did not belong to the party of our nation's enemy.

THE NONSIGNERS' ZERO HOUR

On Thursday, June 29th, just a day before the deadline, Berkeley's nonsigners met. In a letter to her friend Pauline Sperry, Margaret Hodgen reported that the attendance was high. It was the resisters' "zero hour," and there were many "friendly signers" present.[7]

And yet the mood was grim. Ewald Grether, dean of the School of Business, set the tone by urging that every nonsigner immediately comply. Given the war, they would soon be dismissed if they continued to hold out. And then he chided the resisters for endangering Sproul's job.

Aaron Gordon then took the floor and informed a hushed audience that because of Korea he was going to sign. Until that moment, his fellow resisters had no idea of his intentions, so the defection was a serious blow. The economist would rise later to read a letter from Hildebrand, who reiterated how the stubbornness of the nonsigners was harming the university and putting Sproul in a difficult position. And if the president were forced to resign? "He would be replaced by a McCarthy, either Senator or Charlie."[8]

"The only way to avert this," the chemist continued, "would be for the nonsigners to assert that in view of the state of war with Communism in which our nation is now plunged, they consider it their duty to remove all grounds of suspicion, whether reasonable or not, that they have any connection or sympathy with our enemies. Even (if) most, if not all, nonsigners have felt their course was for the good of the University, is this not the time to accept on that matter the decision of the vast majority of their colleagues? We do not want the University to be 'saved' by a victory of John Francis Neylan over Robert Gordon Sproul."

And then Hildebrand concluded on a personal note, confessing how he had tried to keep himself "free from bitterness over the past trying year." "But if the worst is allowed to happen by persons who could have prevented it, I am going to end my service to the university in bitterness."[9]

After such heavy artillery it was up to Tolman to rally his troops the best he could. He began by refusing to let Gordon, Grether, or Hildebrand dictate the terms of the debate. For "war or no war," the oath remained a political test and an example of guilt by association. Both were threats to the way of life that we were fighting for in Asia.[10] Then he presented a sober picture of the future, stating that "those who continued to resist could expect . . . dismissal, 'smears' in the press, difficulty in finding good jobs, and criticism from signing colleagues, some of whom would consider nonsigners to be 'stiff-necked malcontents.'"

Because he was near retirement himself, he could "indulge in the sin of self-righteousness and in the luxury of an untrammeled conscience."[11] But to his younger comrades whose family and economic circumstances would make loss of their jobs catastrophic, he gave the permission to sign.

Tolman's words, as well as those of others who declared that they were standing firm, boosted the morale of the nonsigners. Hodgen wrote Sperry that speakers like Grether and Edward Strong had tried to "create depression" among them and that others had engaged in the tactics of divide and conquer by circulating a rumor that everyone would be fired except those who had served in the military. Trying to maintain some optimism, she expressed the hope that only four or five people would break ranks and sign the oath.[12]

Tolman's predictions proved more accurate than hers. In the days and weeks after the beginning of the war, the number of nonsigners declined precipitously. And the remaining holdouts were subjected to abuse and slurs that painted them as unpatriotic and disloyal.[13] In an attempt to counter such charges, Tolman had to protest that the nonsigners supported "wholeheartedly" the American military action in Korea, and added that "it is just in such minutes of crisis that it is more imperative than ever to stand firm for the freedoms which distinguish democracy from totalitarianism." Even earlier a group of UCLA's nonsigners had professed their loyalty.[14]

And in a letter explaining why he was resigning from Berkeley's Department of Physics, Geoffrey Chew informed his chair that in the charged political climate of wartime the majority of the faculty was now looking upon the nonsigners as "lepers who must keep out of sight."[15]

It did not help that the United States and its South Korean ally were losing the war, even after American soldiers entered the fray under the command of Douglas MacArthur, the general who had been the hero of World War II in the Pacific theater.

BUSY AS EVER, NEYLAN KEPT ON the offensive with a barrage of letters. In one sent on July 6, 1950, he called Sproul "a vacillating weakling." Even worse was the faculty, for it tried his patience "to sit and listen to some of these arrogant little men who feel that they are the modern representations of Aristotle, Euclid, and Socrates. They have no sense of humor or of proportion."[16]

And in a note to Sidney Ehrman, he informed his fellow regent that ten of the sixty-two holdouts had already signed, and more were soon to follow. With glee Neylan cited the defection of Berkeley's Gordon and Caldwell, as well as Miller and Epling of UCLA.[17]

In the weeks before the July 21 regents' meeting, there was a rush to sign. The list included many who had been valiant resisters. Albert Elkus, a distinguished composer and conductor who had virtually created Berkeley's Music Department, wrote Sproul explaining that his position as chair was too important to give up and that at sixty-six he was too old to begin a new life at another university. His objection to a political test for employment was as strong as ever, but he was signing the contract nevertheless. "The present international crisis," Elkus wrote, made it imperative that differences be put aside in favor of cooperation.[18]

Others who signed in this period included Berkeley's Walter Horn, an immigrant from fascism and a respected art historian, as well as most of the remaining resisters from UCLA, including Appleman, Kaplan, and the philosopher Donald Kalish. An exception was Kenneth Roose, who, rather than sign the oath, left a comfortable situation in Los Angeles to teach at Oberlin.

Although his signing received no publicity, Erik Erikson also complied with the requirement so that he could keep his research position, thus vitiating the moral weight of his resignation from the Department of Psychology.[19]

Howard Bern was a young assistant professor of Zoology in 1950, and like his friend the biochemist Howard Schachman, he considered himself one of the "Young Turks" in the forefront of the fight against the oath. On the day before the regents were expected to fire the holdouts, Bern ran into Schachman on the Berkeley campus. Each was on his way to sign the oath, and as Bern recalls, "We had some sad words to say to each other."[20]

Joe Tussman, who had been the only faculty member to argue publicly that communist professors could be assets to a university, recalls a day in early July when he ran into Jack Kent on campus. "Joe, I got something to tell you, we're all signing," Kent said, and then he mentioned the names of several professors who had been stalwart holdouts.[21]

"I felt, my God, these guys have all signed (and) with various excuses." And the philosopher continued, "I felt absolutely stripped of support. (But) I was married, and I had a young son, and I had no money."[22] The idea of signing was so painful that Tussman would postpone the inevitable for more than six weeks.

Daniel Popper felt "humiliation and disgust" when he signed his contract. UCLA's leading astronomer complied because he became "afraid," after seeing "the faculty of a great university brow-beaten into submission."[23]

THE NONSIGNERS ORGANIZE AND GET A LAWYER

On July 6, 1950, the nonsigners for the first time set up a formal organization. The Group for Academic Freedom (GAF), which represented the resisters from the Northern Section of the Academic Senate,[24] began with thirty-one members. Tolman was elected chairman, and Walter Fisher, an assistant professor of Agricultural Economics and an expert on the price of lemons, was the secretary-treasurer. Rounding out the executive committee were Emily Huntington, Gian-Carlo Wick, Harold Winkler, and Charles Muscatine—who would soon replace Fisher as secretary.

The GAF began with an ambitious agenda. One goal was raising money to help professors facing the loss of their jobs, as well as for non-Senate employees in a similar bind. Public relations was another priority, for it was important to make the issues raised by the oath understood around the country.[25] But first and foremost was the need for a legal strategy.

With the controversy in its sixteenth month, it had become clear that there was no chance that the nonsigners' jobs might be saved by the regents. Their only hope now rested in the courts. Tolman and his Law School friends were convinced that the oath was unconstitutional and could be overturned through a legal challenge. So the GAF asked Kent to find a lawyer for them.

As an undergraduate at Cal, Jack Kent had been active at Stiles Hall. Like Gordon Griffiths and Kenneth May, with whom he became friends, he had a conservative family background. The 1930s radicalized him, although unlike the other two, he never became a communist. But the reason why, he liked to tell people, is that no one had ever asked him to join the party.[26]

Kent graduated with a degree in architecture, but never practiced his profession. In his view architects worked only for the rich. In 1948, after serving two years as head of San Francisco's planning department, he was brought to Berkeley to set up a new Department of City and Regional Planning.

During the first year of the oath crisis Kent had been one of the hardest working of the nonsigners. While elder statesmen such as Tolman and Kantorowicz made dramatic speeches at Senate meetings, the daily work of organizing was carried out by "Young Turks" such as Griffiths, Muscatine, Tussman, and Kent—who was the only one of the four with the security of tenure. Just days before the June 30 deadline, Kent had signed the contract oath "against his will."[27] He signed because he knew that dismissals were coming, and he did not want to lose the chance to build his new department. As Tolman kept saying to his son-in-law and daughter Mary, one martyr in the family was enough.[28]

And yet Jack Kent, like many others, felt guilty for deserting his comrades. It was painful to leave the group, for in the year of the oath the nonsigners had forged a solidarity that was unique in an academic culture based on individualism and competition. Charles Muscatine recalled how "deeply bound together emotionally" the nonsigners were, still marveling fifty years later that "we all (had) become wonderfully close to one another."[29]

The bonds between the resisters were strengthened by activities off campus. Kent was one of many liberal professors in the "Little Thinkers" discussion group, and he also acted in the university's Drama section. Not only that, most of the nonsigners lived close to one another in the Berkeley hills, and with their children going to the same schools, they attended PTA and other meetings together.

Kent resolved to stay close to those still carrying on the fight and to do all he could do to advance their cause. First he helped the GAF get organized, and then he researched California's law firms to find an attorney.[30]

There were more than a dozen Left-wing lawyers in Los Angeles and the Bay Area in 1950 who would have jumped at the chance to take such a case. But to have an attorney who could be accused (and with some justice) of being a communist would have been the kiss of death. So Kent narrowed his search to law offices that were in the mainstream. And considering the political climate, it was to be expected that few would be interested in the nonsigners' case. But even he was surprised when only two out of the fifteen firms he contacted would even talk to him about a possible interest.

Fortunately all Kent needed was one lawyer willing to buck public opinion. He found him in Stanley Weigel, a graduate of Stanford Law School. Weigel was a registered Republican who was strongly committed to civil liberties. He agreed to take the case as an individual, for his partners in the San Francisco law office of Landels and Weigel felt that it would be bad for business if they represented Berkeley's resisters. In a 1989 oral history, Weigel explained why Kent had so much difficulty. Almost every firm had represented the Bank of America at one time or another, and they wanted to keep the state's most powerful business as a prospective client. With a Giannini on the Board of Regents, it would involve a conflict of interest to represent Berkeley's dissident faculty.[31]

Considering how pessimistic Weigel was about the nonsigners' prospects, his acceptance of their case is all the more impressive. He would tell the GAF that his chances of winning were less than 1 in 3 in view of the judicial climate. He cited a judge of the District Court of Appeals who had congratulated the City of Los Angeles for requiring a loyalty oath of its employees. He mentioned Learned Hand, a distinguished jurist with a liberal record, who had recently decided, in the case of the twelve communists being tried under the Smith Act, that "advocacy rather than action," was a sufficient basis for guilt. And most ominous for Weigel was the fact that the Supreme Court had just upheld the Taft-Hartley Act, including its loyalty oath for union leaders.

And if that wasn't discouraging enough, the attorney told the group that were they to lose in court, it would be a "fatal blow to academic freedom."[32] But impressed with his frankness and commitment to civil liberties, the GAF decided to go ahead with a suit, pinning their last hope on a Republican lawyer.

CAUGHEY AND KERR CONFRONT NEYLAN

In the weeks before the July 22 regents' meeting, the anticommunist hysteria was so shrill that it was easy to assume it had reached its crescendo and nothing new could arise. But things kept happening that could only increase the nonsigners' pessimism. Birmingham became one of the first American cities to rule that it was illegal to be a member of the Communist Party. Not only that, the Alabama steel center gave party members forty-eight hours to leave town if they wanted to stay out of jail. The city council then made it a misdemeanor "to communicate or associate voluntarily with communists." In comparison, all Detroit's city fathers did was to ban the sale of the *Daily Worker* and other "subversive publications" from its newsstands.[33]

But the biggest event in mid-July was the arrest of Julius Rosenberg on the charge of having passed atomic secrets to the Soviet Union. Less than a month later, his wife, Ethel, would also be arrested as a co-conspirator. For three years "the Rosenberg case" would be the *cause celebre* of the communist Left, who portrayed the couple as freedom-loving progressives with young children whose persecution was a reflection of anti-Semitism.

The July board meeting was critical. Privilege and Tenure's recommendation to retain the sixty-two professors who had refused to sign the contract oath would then be voted on. In the days before, a new Senate committee (Academic Freedom), as well as individual faculty members, tried to influence the most flexible of the "unfriendly regents" to change their position.[34]

Sproul reported that more than half of the non–Academic Senate's resisters had complied since the June board meeting, as well as twenty-three of the original sixty-two faculty nonsigners. He then moved that the six professors not approved by P and T be fired, as well as all the NASE employees who had not signed. Again the idea was that such a "tough stance" would convince some regents to accept his recommendation to retain the remaining thirty-nine professors. For if they were dismissed, it would have been better "not to have granted the privilege of hearings before the Committee" in the first place.[35]

Neylan disagreed. In a characteristically long speech, he emphasized that recent signers included Kent, Gordon, and Caldwell, the very men who had fought hardest against the requirement. If they had seen the light, why couldn't the other holdouts abide by the decision of the vast majority of their colleagues?

Earl Warren, who was now working to resolve the crisis, had invited several Senate members to speak to the regents. The most memorable presentations were made by Caughey and Kerr.

In an eloquent and emotional statement, the leader of UCLA's nonsigners began with an appeal to reason. Since both sides were equally devoted to the university, "we should be able to find a way out of this great and tragic misunderstanding." The oath had not "exposed one traitor," nor "improved a patriot." And as he had told P and T, it was reminiscent of the tactics of totalitarianism, which he abhorred.

The test oath, Caughey continued, silences "functioning and vocal minorities," which are essential to a democratic republic. And above all it is detrimental to "the free pursuit of truth."

In closing, the historian told Neylan why he would not follow the path of Gordon and Kent. Were he to do so, it would suggest a lack of sincerity in his original stand; it would be interpreted as an act of fear; and it would show a lack of confidence in the Committee on Privilege and Tenure and in Sproul.[36]

If the regents' meeting was Caughey's big opportunity to plead the nonsigners' case, it was also Neylan's chance to deflate him. Referring back to Caughey's appearance before the board in January when he had defended the AAUP position, he asked, "Is it true you're not in accord with the policy of excluding communists from the university?" "Yes," was the answer, and twice he affirmed that he continued to believe that. But then he assured the board that he also favored the Regents' 1940 policy, which barred Reds from the university.

Regent Chester Nimitz pushed Caughey on the contradictions in his position. The historian replied that as a University of California employee he was subject to the rule of eliminating communist professors, so he would help enforce it if necessary. But it was not "the ideal way" to approach the problem. His answer, he noted, might appear as "equivocation."[37]

William Prosser, the conservative dean of Berkeley's Law School and a member of the Privilege and Tenure committee, was sitting behind Clark Kerr, P and T's youngest member. Feeling that only senior faculty should address the regents, Prosser grabbed Kerr by his coattails in an effort to make him sit down before he could speak. But the economist held fast to the seat in front of him, which was occupied by a heavy-set man.[38]

The dean gave up and Kerr, looking directly at Neylan, asked him, "Can the regents, in good faith, close a channel which they themselves opened for nonsigners?" And then he added that they were "the most independent spirits" on the faculty, so independent that they would never follow party discipline. And he concluded by asking whether the board, in its attempt to rid the university of communists, really wanted to fire the nonsigners "only for their sense of independence."[39]

Prosser asked the regents why his committee had even bothered to conduct hearings for an entire month. Was it all "sound and fury signifying nothing, an entirely meaningless gesture . . . to permit a safety valve to blow off steam?" But neither he nor the other speakers changed anyone's mind. With the board deeply split, the fate of the nonsigners was still in doubt. Farnham Griffiths had not yet recovered sufficiently from his stroke to return. Since he was now voting with the faculty, his presence might have made the difference.

Just before the roll call on the motion to confirm the appointments, Regent Norman Sprague, a wealthy physician, got sick and left the room. Since he voted with Neylan, the nonsigners would have a chance unless he returned in time.

Asking for a voice vote, the board's secretary polled each regent in alphabetical order. Every one of the first four voted against Sproul's recommendation, including John Canaday, who was the board's newest member, having recently become the president of the Alumni Association. An unknown quantity, the fact that he had lined up with Neylan was a bad omen.

After labor leader Haggerty and liberal investor Heller voted, the tally was 4 to 4. Then Neylan's group regained the lead, although the prospects were more promising for the nonsigners after they got the votes of William Merchant, president of the Mechanics Institute, who previously had been anti-faculty, and Nimitz, whose support had been anticipated, but was not certain.

The votes of Neylan and Ed Pauley made it 9 to 6 against the president's motion. But four of the last five board members were expected to support Sproul and the nonsigners. The fifth vote, that of Sprague, who had left the meeting, would result in a 10 to 10 deadlock.

Roy Simpson, California's superintendent of public instruction, voted aye, and then the secretary called out "Norman Sprague." He was not in the room, so the votes which followed, those of Sproul, Steinhart, and Warren, produced a 10 to 9 victory for the motion and the nonsigners.

But Neylan changed his vote from nay to aye, and now as member of the majority he had the right to ask that the decision which upheld the nonsigners' jobs be reconsidered at the next board meeting. This clever parliamentary maneuver in effect suspended the regents' action. The reprieve for Tolman and his comrades had lasted only a few minutes.[40]

There had been no disagreement about the fate of those who had not been recommended by P and T. The motion to dismiss them was carried unanimously, as was the one to fire the nonsigners who were non–Academic Senate employees.[41]

HIGH IN THE HILLS OVERLOOKING the Berkeley campus a huge concrete letter "C" had been a symbol of the university for half a century. On the Monday after the board meeting, students on their way to class were astonished to see that the white marker had been painted black. Two anonymous graduate students would take credit, and they made it clear to the *Daily Cal* that they were grieving the death of academic freedom, as well as the teaching and research assistants who had been fired.

The editorial that Monday was titled "A Day of Mourning."[42]

CHAPTER 12

REGENTS FIRE THE NONSIGNERS

Who passes into anonymity, the thousands of gray faces who stay on to fill their little cubbyholes in Berkeley? Or the forty who said to hell with you guys—we move out and stand firm for what we believe in? Who loses—those who stay and teach a course on how to design a good garden at the cost of liberty? Or the forty who become a symbol of liberty and carry the fight with them wherever they go? What's more important to teach students, facts or freedom?

—Lawrence Halprin[1]

DURING AUGUST 1950 THE SOUTH KOREAN army was suffering defeat after defeat at the hands of Communist North Korea. It looked as if the forces of the United States and its ally might be pushed into the sea, resulting in a "stunning defeat."[2]

Neylan played on America's anxieties about the war in his editorials in the *San Francisco Examiner*. In one typical screed, published shortly before the August 25 board meeting, he contrasted the patriotic Californians who were dying for freedom in Korea with the faculty's "dissident minority," who wanted the university to be "neutral observers in the fight of civilization against barbarism." Neylan urged the parents of those brave soldiers to let President Sproul know their views on the oath.

The Hearst paper's rival, the *San Francisco Chronicle*, had been the only major newspaper in California to support the faculty's anti-oath stand. But even in the liberal Bay Area, the morning daily was out of touch with public opinion, as four hundred subscriptions had been cancelled due to its coverage of the crisis. After receiving two thousand letters protesting the *Chronicle's* liberal stance and only ten in support, by mid-summer 1950 the paper was no longer giving Berkeley's resisters the sympathetic press it had earlier.[3]

The Academic Assembly, the new name of the former NASE, tried to take up the slack. In an effort to explain the issues to a larger public it mailed out an information booklet on the controversy to more than five hundred college and university papers across the country. But its impact was miniscule compared to that of syndicated columnists such as Raymond Moley, who charged in *Newsweek* that a group of faculty members at the University of California was "spreading communism among the students."[4]

Meanwhile Joel Hildebrand was publishing his "A Final Appeal to the Nonsigners," which argued that it was their patriotic duty to unite with the rest of the faculty and take a stand against communism. And although Hicks was now writing angry letters to Bechtel, the architect of the Alumni Compromise, he felt that Sproul's job was in jeopardy if the resistance continued. So he implored Tolman to comply with the requirement. Even UCLA's nonsigners were feeling the heat. Charles Mowat rebuked Paul Dodd for exerting so much energy trying to get him to sign, rather than mobilizing the faculty to pressure the regents to uphold their July vote.[5]

By the late summer the great majority of the faculty was tired of the controversy; they wanted it resolved immediately. Apathy, fear, insecurity, weariness, and confusion were the words the head of a key Senate committee used to sum up the prevailing mood.[6] As the epidemic of resignations continued, recruiting remained difficult. Robert Penn Warren, who in 1950 was arguably the nation's leading man of letters, turned down Berkeley's Department of English, because the actions of the regents "would reduce the academic community to the level of hired hands" who served at the whim of men "whose acquaintance with intellectual life and its responsibilities" was minimal.[7]

The Group for Academic Freedom met on August 21, four days before the regents were scheduled to convene. Their attorney, Weigel, reported that the outlook for the board meeting looked bleak, and that the nonsigners should decide that very evening if they were going to comply with the requirement or continue to hold out. Twelve declared their intention to keep fighting, two said that they were going to sign, and five were undecided. It was at this meeting that Joe Tussman announced his intention to sign.[8]

On the day he turned in his signed oath to the secretary in the president's office, Tussman was "virtually in tears. It was a very difficult moment for me."[9] He knew that the remaining nonsigners would view his action as a betrayal, just as he had considered those who had complied before him. Signing made him feel "like a disgrace," and he was so ashamed that it would be fifty years before he could even talk about it.[10]

But on August 24, 1950, the philosopher made a public statement, charging that he had been "coerced by economic pressure." And in an open letter to Governor Warren, he asserted his continuing opposition to the oath.[11]

Like the defections of Strong and Gordon, Tussman's signing was a major blow to the resistance, for he had been the man whom many had consulted for advice on how to carry on the struggle. Erik Erikson, for example, would call him to ask whether a meeting was important enough to attend, and even whether he should sign or continue to resist.[12]

But from another point of view, the fight had long been over for Tussman. He had battled for the principle that communists should not be banned from the academic community because of their political beliefs and associations, and once the faculty had repudiated that position in the mail ballot, the philosopher's heart had no longer been in the anti-oath struggle.

NEYLAN WINS AGAIN

Twenty-two of the twenty-four regents were present for the August 25 meeting. The absentees were Giannini, whose resignation had not yet been accepted, and Nimitz. The admiral's presence would have meant one more vote for the faculty, but this loss was countered by the return of Farnham Griffiths, who had recovered enough from his stroke to attend.

Wasting no time on formalities, the board immediately took up Neylan's motion to reconsider the July vote that had saved the jobs of the nonsigners. Realizing that they lacked the votes to defeat it, the strategy of the liberal minority was to challenge it on procedural and legal grounds. Regent Victor Hansen raised a point of order challenging Neylan's motion, and Warren then asked the

attorney for the board whether it was in order. The latter replied that reconsideration was indeed proper on procedural grounds, but that it was not valid
on legal grounds. Because the regents' actions at the July meeting had been an
executive decision, it was final and not subject to review.[13]

The board's attorney, Warren, and Regent Jesse Steinhart drew on their
knowledge of legal precedents with respect to the employment of public officials.
In challenging their reasoning, Ehrman argued that a faculty member was not
a public official like a governor. For him faculty members were employees of
the regents and had no more rights to their jobs than the university's gardeners.

The complicated arguments changed no one's minds, for when Neylan's
motion to reconsider the one of Sproul's that would have restored the nonsigners' jobs, the Warren faction could only get ten of the twenty-two votes cast.[14]

The president then noted that twenty-seven more non–Academic Senate
employees had signed. And after reading the names of the professors who had
complied since the last meeting, he moved that the remaining thirty-two holdouts be retained.

Before the vote Edward Heller read excerpts from the Privilege and Tenure
committee's report on Arthur Brayfield, a Berkeley assistant professor of education. The liberal regent asked whether there was any reason to suspect that
such a person was a communist. Ehrman said no, but retaining him would
still be "a great injustice" to the 99 percent of the faculty who had signed.

Ehrman's statement, and a similar one by Regent Arthur McFadden, that
the issue was discipline and not communism, was more significant than it
might appear. For as one of the newest regents, labor leader Haggerty, then
said, "There is no longer an impugning of those individuals as Communists.
It is now a matter of demanding obedience to the law of the Regents." When
Heller asked whether everyone agreed that none of the professors on the list to
be fired were being accused of being Reds, McFadden confirmed this, and no
one contradicted him.[15]

It was now on record that the regents were going to fire thirty-two professors for refusing to conform to their policies, rather than for their subversive
politics. Such an admission might become important for a court of law, were
the nonsigners to go forward with their plans to sue.

When Sproul's motion came to a vote, it was defeated by the same 12 to 10
margin. Neylan then moved to give the thirty-two professors ten days to change

their minds and sign the contract oath. He also moved that each faculty member who resigned be given one year's severance pay. The contradictions involved did not escape Warren, who noted that "we are discharging these people, not because they are Communists, or suspected of being Communists, but because they are recalcitrant. So we give them ten days to sign up and work next year for a salary, but if they continue to be recalcitrant, we will give them a year's pay without working."[16]

The verdict of Berkeley's student paper was that the faculty had failed and that the fight was over. But one good thing came out of it. The student body got an education, the *Daily Cal* editorialized, on the gap between what professors say and what they do.[17] Similarly, UCLA's *Daily Bruin* would deplore that the battle was over, the faculty vanquished, and "all that remains of the oath fight is an attempt to save a few noble souls . . . Post Mortem concluded. May the oath never rest in peace."[18]

The night after the board meeting the nonsigners got together to consider the regents' actions. They also awarded Tolman a "doctor's degree in Academic Freedom." Invoking "all liberty loving people," the plaque called him a "great leader, a genius in human relationships," and "a never failing inspiration."[19]

Three days later when the GAF's executive committee met, attorney Weigel asked the nonsigners to declare their intentions again. The first to respond was Emily Huntington, who stated that she was considering signing, but were she to do so, she would donate between one quarter and one half of her income to the group as long as the money was needed. When Weigel asked whether her determination to continue the fight had weakened, she replied "definitely not." Then Loewenberg and Tolman stated that they would neither sign nor resign, although the latter added that he was considering a position that had been offered him at Chicago.[20] Neither Edelstein nor Wick would consider signing, but they also might take jobs elsewhere. And all the others present were planning to hold out.

As the meeting closed, the attorney declared that his chances of winning in court had "measurably improved" because the issue of communism "was effectively knocked out of play by the brilliant work of Regent Heller. Not even Neylan can bring communism back in."[21]

Six of Berkeley's nonsigners would take advantage of the ten-day grace period to comply. The list included two men from Psychology, Warren Brown and Robert Harris; Anthony Morse of Mathematics; and James Hopper, who taught at the Medical School in San Francisco. The other two were Huntington and Brodeur.[22]

In an oral history interview more than twenty years later, Huntington explained that she signed because she could not face the disruption that would result from losing her job. The economist had created a life with Dorothy Williams, with whom she would live for thirty years, that centered on their Berkeley home and garden. Signing the oath was "a very sad day," and "her most fervent hope at the time" was that her comrades would not consider her to be "a traitor to the cause" about which she had felt so deeply.[23]

The nonsigners had an agreement that were one of them to break ranks, they were to inform their attorney. So Huntington met with Weigel in an interview which was "formal and courteous." And although she could feel his great disappointment, she was not prepared for what happened later. The lawyer called her that evening to ask "if a regent had gotten to her." She then called Tolman, who was as shocked and disgusted as she was. But his words comforted her: "Emily, whatever were your reasons, they were your own, and honest, and it is shocking that anyone would think that you could possibly have been 'reached' by a regent."[24]

Tolman, according to Huntington, never uttered a single word of "disrespect or bitterness toward a signer," and she never admired a man as much as she did "the guide and mentor" of the nonsigners. But more than twenty-one years later, she was still feeling the hurt from Weigel's question.[25]

Perhaps even more, Huntington regretted that in giving up her resistance, she had separated herself from those "who fought the fight to the end." And she would have been "a much prouder person" had she not abandoned them. For in her view the nonsigners saved the university from disaster.[26]

For Muscatine, Huntington's signing was "tragic," an irreplaceable loss to the nonsigners. But when Brodeur complied a few days later, the Chaucer scholar felt betrayed. His colleague in English had encouraged him to join the fight, and it was Arthur who had proclaimed at the April mass meeting that he would never ever sign. But Brodeur had been given the chance to build a new Scandinavian languages department, and he could not let that opportunity slip away.[27]

"I wanted the university saved from a political test," Brodeur explained. "I knew how the universities of Germany had gone, and how whatever freedoms

Germany had went with them. That ground was cut out from under my feet by the Senate's actions of last March; the very overwhelming majority, which until then had refused to accept a political test, suddenly went overboard for one."[28]

Unlike Brodeur, Anthony Morse made no excuses. His action, wrote the highly regarded mathematician, was a disservice not only to those "patriots" who were continuing to resist, but also to his country. He feared that the time would soon come when he and his colleagues would be afraid to express this kind of admiration for the nonsigners. But he needed to remain on his job, even though the University of California had become a "second-rate institution."[29]

TWENTY NONSIGNERS SUE THE REGENTS

In late August the nonsigners authorized Weigel to go ahead with the lawsuit. His "show cause" order in effect forced the regents to defend the legality of their failure to confirm the appointments of the professors who did not sign. Twenty resisters joined the suit when the attorney filed a petition with the District Court of Appeals on August 31, 1950.[30]

The eight nonsigners who continued their resistance but did not participate in the legal action were the three holdouts from UCLA (Caughey,[31] Mowat, and Saxon), three members from the group that had not been cleared by Privilege and Tenure (Winkler, Sanford, and Kelley), as well as Olschki from Berkeley and Hans Weltin, a physicist on the Santa Barbara campus. In addition, three of the dismissed professors resigned: Fisher, O'Hagan, and Pasternak. Finally, two who were out of the country during the summer, Stephen Enke of UCLA and Isabel Hungerland of Berkeley, indicated they would sign on their return.[32]

Weigel believed that his case would be stronger if his clients met their classes when the semester began. So Tolman and several others taught their scheduled courses, even though they knew they would not be paid.[33] But on September 14 Sproul informed department heads that this must stop. And despite the fact that the dismissals were being challenged in court, none of the nonsigners could teach during the 1950–51 academic year, nor could they continue to serve on the committees of their graduate students working on advanced degrees.

Of the fifty-five courses that were cancelled, nine were in English, six in Psychology, and five in Oriental Languages. (The chair of the latter department, Peter Boodberg, resigned so that he would not have to inform Olschki that he could no longer teach.) In addition, Mathematics, Education, and Business each had four classes that were not offered, while History, Philosophy, and Physics each cancelled three courses.[34]

In protest of Sproul's decision, many departments decided not to replace their fired colleagues and to place asterisks after the listings of the discontinued classes in the following year's directory.

On learning of the president's move, Tolman wired Hutchins that he would be arriving in Chicago for the start of the autumn quarter.

At UCLA, however, most of the nonsigners' courses continued to be offered. Caughey was particularly upset that emeriti professors had been called out of retirement to teach his and Mowat's seminars.[35] And his graduate students had been left "high and dry." He had at least a dozen doctoral students, many of whom had been working under him for four years or more, including some who had come from places as far away as Italy to study with him. Now it was uncertain whether they would ever finish their degrees.[36]

However, there was one thing that made Caughey happy. Not only had he and Mowat received checks for July and August, UCLA's Senate's fundraising group, the Committee for Responsible Government, had accumulated such a large surplus that it was able to help their colleagues at Berkeley, where the number of resisters was much greater.[37]

Meanwhile, across the country university faculties were protesting to the Board of Regents. At Princeton's Institute of Advanced Studies, ten professors— including Albert Einstein, John Von Neuman, Erwin Panofsky, and Robert Oppenheimer—called on the Academic Senate to hang tough in its resistance. A similar letter from Columbia included the signatures of Jacques Barzun, Richard Hofstadter, and C. Wright Mills.

And there was no letup in the boycott against the university. Edward Teller, one of America's preeminent scientists, had accepted a position at UCLA and fallen in love with a house nearby, but the oath had made him rethink leaving Chicago. "I must continue to act in such a way that I should be able to look myself in the eyes while shaving," the father of the H-bomb concluded.[38] And Cora DuBois, a distinguished anthropologist who had been selected to replace Robert Lowie, wrote that her refusal of Berkeley's offer might be "a futile gesture," but not to make it would be the beginning of "personal and social degradation."[39]

An even more eloquent refusal came from Lawrence Halprin. Although he would become one of the nation's most famous landscape architects, in 1950 he was just starting out in his career. Berkeley had offered a teaching position to him, as well as to several other young architects, and this had sparked a spirited debate in the profession. This is how Halprin placed the issue in a letter to one of his teachers:

Who passes into anonymity, the thousands of gray faces who stay on to fill their little cubbyholes in Berkeley? Or the forty who said to hell with you guys—we move out and stand firm for what we believe in? Who loses—those who stay and teach a course on how to design a good garden at the cost of liberty? Or the forty who become a symbol of liberty and carry the fight with them wherever they go? What's more important to teach students, facts or freedom?[40]

On September 19 Aaron Gordon took the unusual step of postponing his Economics 1 lecture for ten minutes to talk about the oath. For years he had been proud to teach at the University of California, he told his 950 students in Wheeler Hall. But "no longer . . . Today I am ashamed to stand before you and I feel apologetic that I haven't been fired. The Communists saved my job by marching into South Korea." And he explained that he had signed because he was afraid that "the fight for academic freedom might become confused with disloyalty."

Gordon's students responded to this breach of classroom protocol with "overwhelming applause." And in its featured editorial, the *Daily Cal* also congratulated him for his remarks. But Neylan was not amused. In an *Examiner* editorial titled "Abuse of the Classroom," he asked, "We wonder who, if anybody, gave Gordon permission to use his class room as a forum to present a one-sided argument and a vicious attack on the Regents?" A few years later he would single out Gordon as "a clown" and "a ham actor."[41]

THE YEAR OF THE OATH

The Year of the Oath by George Stewart was scheduled to appear on October 1. Because it was expected to bring more national attention to the crisis, and even influence its outcome, Doubleday began running ads for it in June. But

Neylan already knew what to expect. With his spies on the faculty, he was aware that Stewart was fiercely anti-oath.

Hoping to influence the English professor to produce a more balanced treatment, the regent offered him the records of all board meetings, including those from its closed-door executive sessions. Stewart did not answer Neylan directly. Instead he informed Sproul that he was declining the offer because the standing orders of the Board of Regents forbade direct contact with faculty members. And were he to accept it, he then would have to use the records of other regents, which "might interfere with our freedom of action as scholars."[42]

For Neylan this was beyond belief. So he made the same offer to Stewart's publisher. But when Doubleday's West Coast editor refused to make the short trip to the regents' office to look at the material, Neylan decided to wash his hands of the matter.[43]

Still, after *The Year of the Oath* was released early, Neylan was one of the first to buy a copy. At the September 22 board meeting he told his colleagues how Stewart and the publisher had refused his offer, which made it clear to him that the book was not scholarly research, but an addition to the best-selling author's long list of fiction. But that didn't make it harmless. In fact the book was an important reason the nonsigners continued to hold out, "misled by a work that was being used maliciously to the detriment of the university." Neylan then read passages that were "false and dishonest," including a footnote that said that all of the regents' records were not available to the authors![44]

Neylan could have been even more critical. Most of the book's 141 pages of text consisted of anecdotes and imagined conversations, with relatively little use of Stewart's own rich interviews. Since the English professor looked upon the writing of the book as an underground act as dangerous as the French resistance, he did not use the names of his collaborators, nor even those of professors like Tolman and Hildebrand.

In his review of *The Year of the Oath,* Tussman praised the chapter on the regents for its careful research, although he argued that the main point was not the lack of representativeness Stewart bewailed, but the fact that the board wielded authority that more properly belonged to the Academic Senate. The philosopher also faulted the book for presenting the faculty as more militant than it was, and ignoring the fact that the Senate's timid leaders met the regents with "cap in hand." Stewart also underplayed the bitterness of factional conflict among the faculty. Tussman did feel that the work captured the flavor of the crisis, though in an oral history more than fifty years later he would call the book "superficial."[45]

The *New York Times* assigned the book to Sidney Hook, a professor of philosophy at New York University and a renowned expert on Marxism. It was Hook's position that those who express unpopular doctrines that are merely heretical should be protected by the Bill of Rights, but that those who engage in conspiracies against the democratic way of life forfeit such protection. Since the Communist Party was a conspiracy, he did not object to the arrest and conviction of its leaders under the Smith Act.

Hook's essay "Heresy Yes, Conspiracy No!" appeared in the *New York Times Magazine* at a critical moment, for it immediately reframed the debate in a way harmful to the nonsigners. If the Communist Party was a conspiracy, and even worse, one linked to hostile foreign powers, and not a heresy, then the argument that the oath was a violation of academic freedom could be dismissed.[46]

A former communist who had become the anticommunist camp's leading intellectual, Hook was well placed to review Stewart's book. He had been a visiting professor at Berkeley during the summer of 1950, despite the fact that America's intelligentsia was virtually united behind the boycott on accepting positions at the University of California.[47] This gave him the authority to assert that "the faculty of the University of California is as free to teach and reach conclusions in any field of study as any faculty in the country," and to chide Stewart for hysterical exaggeration. He also took issue with the author's comparison of the oath to those required by Hitler and Mussolini. For Hook, a loyalty oath per se did not violate academic freedom. However he did feel that the Regents' Special Oath was "ill-considered," and the board's decision to flout the recommendation of an Academic Senate committee and fire the nonsigners was even worse.[48]

BERKELEY'S FACULTY MOVES LEFT

UCLA and Berkeley liberals coordinated their strategies for their late September Senate meetings. The goal was to present a united front with hard-hitting motions criticizing the regents, instead of the mild words of censure expected from their P and T committees.

Meeting a day earlier than their northern counterparts, a group of UCLA's liberals moved a sharp condemnation of the regents who had voted to dismiss the nonsigners. But "elder statesmen" such as Grant and Dodd warned against their strong language and succeeded in passing a moderate substitute resolution that "deplored" the board's action in dismissing "competent and loyal" members of the faculty and thanked the regents who had supported the nonsigners.[49]

The next day seven hundred professors were present at the outset of Berkeley's Senate meeting. The session would last four hours, the longest yet. The Committee on Academic Freedom reported first, warning how the regents' actions had "severely damaged" the university's reputation, and that assistant professors and graduate students were losing their enthusiasm for academic careers. Then it was Privilege and Tenure's turn. The committee regretted the regents' failure to accept its recommendations, but expressed the hope that the faculty and the board could still reach an agreement on tenure. When its chair Stuart Daggett moved that the resolution be submitted to a mail ballot, so that all members of the Northern Section could vote on it, two liberals, Lawrence Harper of History and Jerzy Neyman of Mathematics, maneuvered to table the motion. Neyman was one of Berkeley's most Left-wing professors, a statistician who had caused a commotion a few months earlier when he had inveighed against accepting the Alumni Compromise.

The stage was set for the liberals to unite around a much stronger motion that had been prepared by Monroe Deutsch, who, though retired, was playing a more active role in the controversy. In introducing it, the ex-provost engaged in the formal oratorical style that once graced Academic Senate meetings. "People at other universities have tenure," he intoned, "but not you. People in state colleges have tenure, but not you. People in elementary and secondary schools have tenure, but you do not have it."

The Deutsch resolution thanked each regent who had supported the president, but charged that the board had "grossly violated" its own resolution, "broken faith with the Senate," and failed to honor the principle of tenure. And it condemned "such actions on the part of the *bare majority* of the Board."[50]

Sproul, alarmed by the impact of his former assistant's words, warned the assembly "not to draw lines of battle between the regents and the faculty." To do so would result in great harm to the university and to the Senate. The non-signers' case was in the courts, and that's where it should be debated and decided, the president concluded.

By the time the Deutsch resolution came to a vote, two-and-a-half hours had been devoted to its discussion. It was getting late, and many professors had left the meeting. The remaining members were able to pass the measure decisively.[51]

The Senate's actions so disgusted the conservative historian Raymond Sontag that he resigned in protest from the powerful Committee on Committees.[52] Hildebrand also blasted the body's procedures. In his view, the Deutsch resolution was illegal because it had violated the Senate's rules that required all new business to be announced in advance. And he saw the events of September 26, 1950, as a replay of the November 1949 meeting when the tenBroek and Adams resolutions had been passed by the most die-hard liberals after many of their colleagues had gone home to dinner. Finally, the maneuver to eliminate the mail ballot meant the disenfranchisement of not only those Berkeley professors who left early or hadn't attended in the first place, but of the entire faculty from the Davis campus.[53] Had all the members of the Northern Section cast their ballots, instead of the less than five hundred in the room when the vote was taken, the Deutsch resolution probably would have been defeated.

Even so, Berkeley's faculty was moving toward the Left. That day the Senate easily passed a measure instructing Privilege and Tenure to reconsider its earlier decision not to recommend the retention of the six least cooperative nonsigners.

And John Hicks, who had been the soul of caution as chair of the Committee of Seven, was now saying that the dismissal of the nonsigners was an act of "vigilante justice: give a man a fair trial and then hang him!"[54] Then there was the head of Berkeley's math department. A self-styled conservative, Charles Morrey had voted against the tenBroek resolution in November. But as his own faculty and grad students became more militant in resisting the oath, their passion influenced him. On October 4, 1950, he wrote an open letter explaining why he was now working with the faculty radicals.[55]

The official voice of Berkeley's student government, the Executive Committee of the Associated Students, was split between a liberal minority in favor of the strong academic freedom positions of the *Daily Californian* and a cautious majority that did not want to antagonize the administration. After the Senate meeting the liberals prepared a statement in support of the Deutsch resolution that condemned the regents for arbitrarily dismissing professors and supported the right of the faculty to make its own personnel decisions. What made Ex Com's statement distinctive, at a time when similar condemnations of the regents were being issued daily, was its emphasis on the student body.

Because forty-three classes had been cancelled, many undergraduates had had to revise their entire schedules. Classrooms were already crowded, but now they were jammed beyond capacity. For many students it was no longer possible to get the courses they needed for their degrees. And many graduate students had been forced to start over with new advisors.

Finally, the degrees received from the university in the future were likely to be diminished in their academic worth, since the prestige of the institution had been seriously damaged.[56]

Ex Com's conservatives, led by the dean of students and faculty representative Ralph Chaney, both of whom were voting members of the board, were at first able to postpone a vote on the statement in favor of the Deutsch resolution. But they couldn't stop the liberal members from setting up tables and collecting signatures in support of the statement. Although many students were afraid to take a stand, in the course of a week the initial timidity wore off. Eventually close to three thousand signatures were collected, as well as $365 to help the fired professors. The student body's reaction turned Ex Com around enough to pass the statement on October 18 by a vote of 12 to 10 and to authorize its publication in the *Daily Cal*.[57]

MEANWHILE THE TIDE seemed to have turned in Korea. A daring invasion by U.S. marines on September 15 of amphibious landing crafts on a beachhead at Inchon had been successful. As a result of the surprise assault, United Nations troops were able to break out of their quagmire at Pusan and go on the offensive. In a few days the marines had surrounded Seoul. The capital fell on the 26th of September, and by October 1, the South Koreans had crossed the 38th parallel into North Korea.

CHAPTER 13

WARREN'S NEW OATH: WORSE THAN SPROUL'S?

The bravest, most high-minded and most steadfast group . . . willing to sacrifice everything for a principle.

—Stanley Weigel (on the nonsigners)[1]

The imposition of any more conclusive test than the constitutional oath would be the forerunner of tyranny and oppression.

—California District Court of Appeals[2]

ALTHOUGH EARL WARREN WAS A LIBERAL Republican who had been elected with bipartisan support, his hatred of communism and communists was as strong as that of his friend Sproul; recall how the two had cooperated to spy on student radicals during the 1930s. And although California's governor occasionally spoke out against McCarthy's methods, he accepted the senator's goals and was not averse to employing his tactics when it suited him.

On August 4, 1950, Warren warned that it was necessary to prepare for the almost certain deployment of sabotage by members of the Communist Party. Two days later, on the fifth anniversary of the launching of the first nuclear weapons on Japan, the governor pandered to popular fears of a third world war when he stated that "only Joe Stalin himself knows whether an atomic bomb is to fall on the California target areas."[3]

Patrick McCarran was *not* a liberal Republican. One of McCarthy's closest allies, the Nevada senator headed a subcommittee on internal security, which had allowed him to pursue investigations of subversion during the administrations of Roosevelt and Truman. After refurbishing the defunct Mundt-Nixon bill on national security, McCarran introduced it in the Senate in August. Passed by the House as the McCarran-Walter Act, it required members of the Communist Party to register with the attorney general. Even more disturbing was a provision that called for the rounding up of domestic communists in the case of a national emergency, with the wartime incarceration of Japanese Americans serving as its precedent.

Back in California, Earl Warren was looking ahead to the November election, where he was being challenged by James Roosevelt, FDR's eldest son. The liberal Democrat had attacked the Truman Doctrine and spoken out against loyalty oaths and other vehicles of repression, and he was running well in the polls. Warren needed the visibility of the governorship if he were to remain a top prospect for the 1952 presidential nomination. So his reelection to an unprecedented third term was an imperative.

But because the governor's defense of the university's nonsigners had become a "political liability," he could not count on the support of the conservatives in California's GOP.[4] The Right-wing press, for example, the *Los Angeles Times,* had distorted his position, portraying him as defending the right of communists to teach, when his opposition to the oath was based instead on the principle of academic tenure. The conservatives supported Lieutenant Governor Goodwin Knight, who had challenged Warren for the nomination. Were the Right wing to sit out the election, Warren's chances would be slim.

Needing to move to the Right, his response was an even tougher line on communism. So in early August the governor called a special session of the California legislature to deal with domestic subversion. This emboldened the extremists of his party. State Senators Tenney and Burns, as well as Assemblyman Harold Levering, prepared a series of draconian bills in the weeks that followed. Needing their support, Warren entered into negotiations with his former adversaries.

Before the special session of the legislature on September 21, the front-page news was the congressional debate on the McCarran-Walter Act. Its repressive language would inspire state and local governments to adopt their own laws against the communist threat. In August, the city of Los Angeles followed L.A. county in adopting loyalty programs for its employees. By the fall, three Northern California cities, Oakland, Richmond, and Berkeley (not yet a liberal bastion), followed suit. And then on September 18 the National Security Resource Board (NSRB) made it a requirement that civil defense workers disclaim all subversive affiliations.

President Truman recommended that the states adopt the NSRB's oath as a guideline for their own civil defense employees. That encouraged Warren to go even farther. Stating that he was "only following the recommendations of the federal government," on September 21 the governor asked that *all* state employees be required to sign an oath. Unlike the Regents' Special Oath, which contained a disclaimer of communist affiliations only in the present, Warren proposed that people attest to their loyalty over a five-year period, arguing that the Soviet Union had been America's enemy since V-J Day.

While Warren was consulting with Burns and Levering on the wording of his oath, Truman vetoed McCarran-Walter, stating that the measure "moves in the direction of suppressing opinions and belief (and) would make a mockery of the Bill of Rights." But such was the mood in the nation that even a Democratic congress overrode his veto.

On September 26 the California legislature, with only two dissenting votes in the Senate and five in the Assembly, passed the new oath as part of the Levering Act. Another measure in the State Senate approving the recent firing of the nonsigners who had refused to comply with the Regents' Special Oath passed by a vote of 27 to 5. The upper house also proposed an amendment to the state constitution that would bar subversives from public employment and strip away their voting rights.[5]

The Levering Act's loyalty oath was both similar to and different from the Regents' Special Oath. It contained almost identical language with respect to its disclaimer of membership in any party or organization advocating the overthrow of the federal or state government "by force or violence or other unlawful means." But the "Sproul-Hildebrand" oath was only concerned with present memberships and activities. The new requirement covered the past five years and also outlawed future affiliations. Not only that, everyone who signed it had to list present and past memberships in the organizations on the attorney general's list, which now totaled 157. And unlike the regents' oath, stiff penalties were proscribed for those who would commit perjury in signing it.

Applied to all public employees, the Levering oath did not discriminate against university professors as the regents' oath did. But a consensus soon emerged that it was more intrusive and generally worse than the old one. Curiously, Tolman and Caughey disagreed, swayed by the fact that professors were no longer singled out as a suspect class. The UCLA historian actually signed the Levering Act oath for "tactical reasons" on the day after he was fired by the regents. He was scheduled to deliver a lecture series sponsored by University Extension, so it was sign or cancel.[6]

Because they were state employees, even the regents were subject to the new oath. At their October session, fourteen board members signed, to great fanfare. But not Neylan. He opposed the Levering Act, arguing that Warren and the legislature had infringed on the board's jurisdiction. Ironically, the new more arduous oath was defended by the most liberal regents, who saw it as an opportunity to overturn the earlier requirement that had created so much havoc in the university community.

With the regents still bitterly debating the legality of the new oath, compliance at first was slow. On October 23 the regents sent out a reminder that the deadline was November 2. And yet by October 27 only 38 percent of Berkeley's employees had signed and a bare 21 percent at UCLA.[7]

THE FUNDAMENTAL ISSUE

On October 8, Kantorowicz brought together his thoughts in a pamphlet he called *The Fundamental Issue*. He envisioned a wide circulation for his self-published work, but Weigel convinced him to wait before making it public. The attorney worried that its fiery tone could backfire on the nonsigners' court case. Still, many copies were circulated underground.

Neylan viewed the tract as part of a "campaign of libel and slander" against the regents. What most infuriated him was Eka's citing the German historian Theodor Mommsen's words that "It is far easier to dethrone a cabinet minister than it is to dismiss a full professor." This was true in Imperial Germany, Kantorowicz continued, "and it is true also in this country, and the Regents of the University of California will have to learn a lesson, whether they like it or not."[8]

Eka called the oath and the sanctions the regents used to enforce it "one of the most ruthless attacks on the academic profession" ever. The result was the virtual end of tenure and trial by jury. And he quoted Plutarch, "Children are to be deceived with toys, men with oaths."

Since he remained politically conservative, nothing would have been easier than to sign the oath and "sit back, tend my garden, books, and manuscripts. However, where a human principle, where *Humanitas* herself is involved, I cannot keep silent."[9]

At the October board meeting Neylan attacked Kantorowicz's pamphlet, just as he had Stewart's book a month earlier. And having heard that the regent had stated that he "brought no luster to the university," the medieval historian had the GAF's secretary send Neylan a list of his publications, public lectures, and other honors. And he became another addition to the regent's enemies list, his special bete noir.

Kantorowicz was a visiting professor at Harvard during the 1950–51 academic year. Although the nonsigners' diaspora had not yet begun, Tolman was already teaching at Chicago. And offers were pouring in for Loewenberg, after his department chair had written to colleagues around the country about him.

With most of the nonsigners unemployed, the faculty focused on raising money for their salaries. On September 26, Berkeley's Academic Senate had urged every professor to donate 2 percent of his or her monthly paycheck (before deductions) for this purpose. Eventually the vast majority, seven hundred faculty members, would contribute.[10]

At UCLA, 175 professors had pledged $13,000, and because there were so few faculty nonsigners in the Southern section, most of the surplus was sent to Berkeley. Among the other universities who helped were the University of Chicago, which had kicked in $1,500, and Brown, Minnesota, and Wisconsin, each of which had contributed $1,000. Fundraising at Harvard was anemic in comparison; there only $388 would be collected.[11]

With a quarter of the fundraising income reserved to help unemployed teaching assistants and other grad students, the task of raising $6,000 each month for Berkeley's nonsigners was daunting. To make it happen, a committee of friendly signers chaired by Milton Chernin of Social Welfare was set up. Every department had a fundraising representative, and in many, not a single professor refused to contribute. In addition to this effort, Ben Lehman, who was married to wealth, made generous donations to the fund, and Tolman called upon his rich contacts. In another irony of the oath controversy, the faculty support of the nonsigners was greatest after they lost their jobs, and organizing to provide for their salaries would be its most impressive achievement.[12]

During the fall of 1950 the Senate continued to move toward the Left. On October 9 the body instructed Privilege and Tenure to change its recommendations on the six professors who had been the first to lose their jobs, and the committee did so. However, at the November meeting, the Senate voted down a motion by Jerzy Neyman to commend Stewart for his book, along with others such as Caughey who had published articles on behalf of the faculty cause. But UCLA did pass a similar resolution sponsored by its Privilege and Tenure committee.[13]

EARL WARREN EASILY DEFEATED Roosevelt in November. In a Republican sweep, the race that would prove most historic was Congressman Richard Nixon's election to the United States Senate. His opponent, Helen Gahagan Douglas, was one of the nation's leading liberals, and the future president would coast to victory by means of an unprecedented Red-baiting campaign. The GOP picked up five seats in the Senate and twenty-eight in the House of Representatives, leaving the Democrats with a narrow majority.

On November 13 Weigel filed a brief challenging the regents' appeal. The nonsigners' attorney argued that the Loyalty Oath was unconstitutional and that the appointments that had been made at the July board meeting, only to be overturned by Neylan's maneuver, were not revocable. Furthermore, the requirement of a special declaration of loyalty violated California's constitution, which stipulated that "no other oath, declaration, or test" could be added to its own Constitutional Oath. The Regents' Special Oath, the lawyer argued, violated that document in a second fashion, for it stated that the university "shall be kept free from all political or sectarian influence." Then Weigel added that the dismissal of the nonsigners was a breach of the ordinary law of contracts, for the regents had abrogated their implicit contract with the Committee on Privilege and Tenure. The last violation charged concerned the right to tenure.[14]

The deadline for signing the Levering Act oath had been extended to November 15. Three days later, the state controller's office reported an almost total compliance with the new regulation. At the University of California, only eleven members of the Academic Senate had failed to sign, along with seventy-six employees who were not Senate members.

The fight against the Regents' Special Oath had exhausted the faculty. Neither at Berkeley nor at UCLA was any stomach left to fight the Levering Act. That's why the attempt to build a movement against the new oath fell to the students. And to the most radical Leftists among them, those who had supported Wallace in 1948. Along with six other members of the Student Progressives, Burt Wolfman took the lead, hiring radical attorney Vincent Hallinan to contest the oath in court. Then the group began a campaign to collect signatures protesting the new oath. But as Wolfman would tell a meeting of the ASUC, most students were afraid to sign, even though they were "overwhelmingly against the oath."[15]

Despite such efforts, no significant movement materialized against the Levering Act and its oath.

IN THE FALL OF 1950 the belief was widespread among both opinion leaders and ordinary citizens that communism on the world stage might win out over capitalism and democracy. Although the North Atlantic Treaty Organization provided a military deterrent against Soviet expansion in Europe, neither it nor the Marshall Plan had greatly weakened the communist parties in Italy and France. It was a realistic possibility that free elections might send one or even both of these nations into the Russian orbit. However it was in Asia where the most serious threats existed.

In Indochina a liberation movement led by the communist-leaning Ho Chi Minh was winning military victories against the French colonial armies. While France was retreating in Southeast Asia, in the center of the continent the Chinese Communists had invaded the independent republic of Tibet, and had declared it to be a part of China. However in Korea the momentum had shifted in favor of the armies of South Korea and the United States.

On October 1 South Korean troops had crossed the 38th parallel, entering North Korean territory. Less than three weeks later MacArthur's Eighth Army captured Pyongyang, the capital of the communist nation. As the general continued his sweep across North Korea, pushing back its undermanned and underequipped army, Mao Tse Tung feared that he would invade the Peoples' Republic of China. So in late October, five hundred thousand Chinese troops came to the aid of their neighbor, crossing the boundary between the two countries. A South Korean division was overwhelmed and American troops were driven back again.

But in late November, UN armies went on the offensive, arriving at the Yalu River. This set the stage for the biggest battle of the five-months-old war. When MacArthur underestimated the size and the military capacity of his enemy, his forces were routed. Although Truman was upset with his general's handling of the war, the president kept quiet for the moment, and on November 26, 1950, announced that he was considering the use of nuclear weapons in Korea.

The year ended with the Americans and the South Koreans in full retreat. With morale at a low on the battlefield and the homefront, the Korean War and America's president were becoming more and more unpopular.

ON DECEMBER 22, STANLEY WEIGEL made his final arguments before the District Court of Appeals in Sacramento. The hearings in the case that was now known as *Tolman* v. *Underhill* lasted three hours;[16] the attorney was expecting a decision early in 1951.

Acting on complaints from customers, Berkeley's student bookstore removed copies of the Far Left weekly the *National Guardian* from its news racks. The move engendered protest, and the Store Committee of the ASUC voted unanimously to chide the manager and make the paper available again.[17]

At UCLA the Anthropology Department took the lead in organizing a series of speakers to mark Negro History Month. With the crackdown on "controversial speakers" still in force, the administration, after sending the names to the FBI, eliminated nine of the ten recommended experts as too radical. Several weeks later it acted once more against the *Daily Bruin*. The administration-dominated Student Executive Board fired the top editors and replaced them with its handpicked choices. In protest the newspaper's staff resigned en masse.[18]

DIASPORA OUT OF BERKELEY

By early 1951 a climate of fear had crept into the nation's classrooms, especially among teachers in the social sciences and humanities. According to Berkeley's Margaret Hodgen, professors had become afraid to offer objective appraisals of Karl Marx and his theories, lest their loyalty be questioned. This meant that college students, without the experience of hearing Marxism subjected to scientific scrutiny, were now seriously disadvantaged. Without the tools to assess the ideas of communism, they might be more vulnerable to its appeals, the nonsigner asserted.[19]

"Karl Marx and the Social Scientists" appeared in the *Scientific Monthly* in April, the same month that Hodgen learned that she had been granted a fellowship from the Huntington Library for the 1951–52 year. She was already working in the Huntington when she got the news. Tolman and Kantorowicz had also left Berkeley for visiting professorships at Chicago and Harvard, respectively. And early in 1951 Eka accepted what would turn out to be a permanent position at the Institute for Advanced Study in Princeton. Similarly, Wick, one of the nation's leading theoretical physicists, accepted an offer from Carnegie Tech.

The diaspora out of Berkeley gathered even more steam when several of the younger resisters received attractive offers. Not yet as eminent as his colleague Wick, the still highly regarded physicist Harold Lewis was considering a research position at the Princeton Institute. The Chaucer scholar Charles Muscatine was preparing to take a job at Wesleyan, while Arthur Brayfield was on his way to Kansas State, where he would become acting chair of Psychology. Another young psychologist, Hugh Coffey, was looking at a visiting lectureship with Harvard's Department of Social Relations. The same school made Harold Winkler an assistant professor, prompting the *Daily Cal* to editorialize, "Harvard, in contrast to California, is still willing to judge a man upon his own merits rather than upon his willingness to crawl upon his knees."[20]

UCLA's Mowat took a position at the University of Chicago, while physicist Saxon found a research job with the Bureau of Standards on the Westwood campus. During the fall Caughey had supported his family with funds from UCLA's Committee on Responsible University Government. But in the winter, a grant from the Rockefeller Foundation allowed the historian to get off "relief."[21]

IN THE FIRST HALF OF 1951, the Senate's Committee on Academic Freedom (CAF), established in 1950 to study the oath's impact on the university, assumed the leadership of Berkeley's resistance. And it took an especially aggressive stance in defense of faculty rights after Wendell Stanley replaced Baldwin Woods as its chairman.

At Earlham College, Stanley had won all-state honors in Indiana as the captain of the football team. He would have become a coach had he not discovered chemistry at the University of Illinois. A specialist in viruses, he would publish 150 scientific papers on the topic, and be awarded a Nobel Prize in 1946.

Always looking for opportunities to increase its prestige in the sciences, in 1948 Berkeley lured Stanley by creating a new virus lab for him to head. During the years of the oath controversy he also chaired the Department of Biochemistry.

Along with English professor James Caldwell, Stanley provided the vision that made the CAF's much-awaited report a special document. Released on February 28, *The Consequences of the Abrogation of Tenure* was full of facts—the 26 Senate members who had been "ejected" from the faculty, the 157 non-Senate employees recommended for dismissals, and the 37 professors who had resigned rather than sign the contract oath. The committee also noted that the actions of the regents had been protested by more than 1,200 professors in more than forty colleges and universities, as well as by twenty professional societies.[22]

The oath and the dismissals had greatly weakened several key departments, especially at Berkeley. In psychology there hadn't been so much faculty discontent in twenty years, as the loss of several senior members had dealt it an "enormous blow." The morale of graduate students was particularly low. Many of the best Ph.D. candidates had transferred to other universities, or simply dropped out, while the quality of new applicants had plummeted.[23]

The CAF took special note of the forty-seven people who had turned down offers at Berkeley and UCLA. The list involved such luminaries as the cybernetics pioneer Norbert Wiener, Howard Mumford Jones of English, the writer Robert Penn Warren, and Rudolf Carnap, whom the report called one of America's three most brilliant philosophers. The refusal of an even more illustrious candidate took place too late to be included. Ralph Bunche, preparing to leave the United Nations to join the academic world, told Berkeley's Political Science Department that he could not accept such an offer until the threats to tenure created by the regents' actions of August 1950 were resolved.[24]

In concluding, the committee wrote that "a great university, famous for its scientific and humane accomplishments, for its devoted service to the State, and for the prideful regard in which it was held by the citizens, has in the space of about six months, been reduced to a point where it is condemned by leading scholars and learned societies as a place unfit for scholars to inhabit." And it warned that unless this was rectified, the University of California would be fated "to continue a tragic course toward bankruptcy in those resources of repute, intellectual power, and integrity, which are its essential treasures."[25]

The report would influence opinion both within and outside the university. In its lead editorial, the *San Francisco Chronicle* hailed it as an "indispensable document" and warned that unless the faculty and the regents came to an agreement on the issue of tenure, the "progressive decline" of the university might one day be seen as the "worst disaster ever experienced by American education."[26] And in addition to a news story, the *Daily Cal* ran in-depth feature stories for three days on the report's findings.[27]

"THE FORERUNNER OF TYRANNY AND OPPRESSION"

On April 6, 1951, the Third District Court of Appeals handed down a unanimous decision in favor of the nonsigners in *Tolman* v. *Underhill*. The judges cited Justice Robert Jackson's statement that "the freedom to differ" was not meant for trifling matters, but for those issues "that touch the heart of the existing order," as well as an earlier decision that asserted that the principle that political orthodoxy could not be enforced by government officials was "a fixed star in the constitutional constellation." And in a sentence that went to the heart of the controversy, they asserted that "The imposition of any more conclusive test than the constitutional oath would be the forerunner of tyranny and oppression."[28]

Because the Constitutional Oath was "the highest loyalty" that could be demanded of a citizen, the court ruled that the regents had overreached in requiring their special oath. In addition, it accepted Weigel's argument that the university must be kept independent of political and sectarian influence. However, it did not take a position on such larger issues involved as whether the dismissals were an infringement of academic tenure or whether the regents' actions at their July 1950 meeting were irrevocable. That was when they had approved Sproul's motion to retain the nonsigners in their jobs.[29]

Still, the decision was all that could be hoped for, as the court ordered the university to reinstate the nonsigners. That evening Weigel filed a writ asking the regents to restore their employment.

The lawyer hailed the decision as a sign that the tide was turning against the "dangerous and Un-American trend" of loyalty oaths and the larger repression. Less grandiose, the *Daily Cal* saw the court's ruling as a return to sanity "over the hysterical orthodoxy which parades under the American flag and forgets the things the flag stands for." The paper also expressed gratitude to the eighteen litigants, whose courage served as an example to people trying to stop the destruction of civil liberties.[30]

The ruling made headlines in the *Washington Post* and the *New York Times*.[31] Its importance was sensed immediately, as victories for free speech and academic freedom were so rare in the early 1950s. Kantorowicz, living in Washington, D.C., while teaching at Harvard, noted that it had awakened his "sleepy" town, as the news was being broadcast on the radio day and night.[32] And in Los Angeles an exultant Caughey said that the decision should become required reading in the American History and Institutions course that every UC undergraduate had to take.

On the Saturday night after the decision, the Group for Academic Freedom celebrated at the Shattuck Hotel in Berkeley. As Sperry wrote to her friend Hodgen, "the champagne flowed copiously and the caviar and the Roquefort disappeared as the evening wore on." Time after time the excited partygoers raised their glasses, as one toast after another was offered. Edelstein hailed "a country where such a decision was still possible," while others praised Tolman for his "unselfish leadership" and their lawyer for his courage in taking the case. Weigel, in turn, declared that it was the nonsigners who deserved all the credit. They were "the bravest, most high-minded and most steadfast group he had ever known . . . willing to sacrifice everything for a principle."

The attorney then told his clients that the chances of the regents' appealing the decision were "50-50." But if they were to do so, he assured the GAF members, they would win their case in California's Supreme Court.[33]

On April 13 a hastily called unofficial meeting of the Academic Senate unanimously passed a resolution introduced by Carl Landauer expressing "profound gratitude" to the nonsigners for their contributions to the faculty's welfare. Although there is no record of the number in attendance, and it can be assumed that such a motion would have been diluted had the entire Senate voted on it, the resolution was still a remarkable turnaround. For over a year the resisters had been reviled for their stubbornness in fighting for a hopeless cause and standing firm for dubious principles. In the process they had threatened Sproul's job, and after the outbreak of the Korean War they had been branded disloyal and unpatriotic. And now the Senate was lauding them.[34]

ON THE NIGHT OF THE NONSIGNERS' victory party, regents' chairman Edward Dickson announced that the board would appeal the decision. But such an action was by no means certain in a body that was split down the middle and at a time when many wanted the controversy laid to rest. Still, both sides began mobilizing immediately.

Hugh Burns, the new chair of the Committee on Un-American Activities, proposed a resolution to the state Senate urging that the state's attorney general and legislative counsel help the regents prepare their appeal. It passed 25 to 0. And a group of liberal alumni that included Monroe Deutsch urged the board to let the decision stand, as did Berkeley's student leaders.

The regents were not due to meet until April 20, but their main counsel, Eugene Prince, was concerned that the board's position might be weakened were he to wait that long. So he filed a petition for a rehearing on the morning of the meeting. During the session Steinhart's motion to withdraw the appeal passed by 11 to 10, after Warren made a moving appeal to accept the court's decision. The nonsigners had a right to have their lives settled, and it was not good for the university to continue to be "a guinea pig" on the issue.[35]

Again Neylan switched his vote so that the matter could be reconsidered at the May meeting.

With the pro-oath leader too ill to attend that session, the liberal regents were able to block Prince's appeal once more. But a majority of the board was not needed; any one member could file an appeal as an individual. So when Ehrman, who had standing as an attorney in Los Angeles, filed his petition, the issue was before California's Supreme Court. If they did not accept it by June 5, the decision of the lower court would stand, and the nonsigners would have their jobs back.

But this was not the end of the Byzantine drama. The State Supreme Court first denied Ehrman's appeal, and then reversed itself. Acting on its own, it agreed to decide the constitutionality of the Regents' Special Oath, along with several related cases, including a number of challenges to the Levering Act.[36]

ON THE DAY BEFORE the court decision, a New York judge handed down death sentences to Julius and Ethel Rosenberg. A few days later, on April 11, Truman removed MacArthur as the commander of UN troops in Korea and named General Matthew Ridgway to replace him.

The course of the war had gone back and forth during the first three months of 1951. The Chinese and North Koreans had recaptured Seoul on January 4, only to lose control of the capital in March. MacArthur himself had zigzagged, telling the Chinese that he was willing to discuss a ceasefire, and then when the offer was rejected, threatening to bomb some of their big cities. Fears of World War III, already at a high pitch, were rekindled; American school children were being taught to hide under their desks at the sign of a blinding light. But the president assured the nation that he was pursuing a "limited war."

And yet in the political climate of 1951 the general was more popular than the president. MacArthur was greeted as a hero on his return, and Right-wing Republicans saw him as their best bet to be the next president. There was talk of impeaching Truman; instead Senator Nixon introduced a bill to censure him.

On May 8 the United States detonated the first hydrogen bomb on an unpopulated atoll in the South Pacific. The leader of the scientists who had developed it was Edward Teller. By this time he had decided not to accept UCLA's offer.

In June the U.S. Supreme Court, by a vote of 6 to 2, upheld the Smith Act convictions of the top leadership of the Communist Party. They began their prison terms, except for four who went into hiding. Later in the month, the second tier of the party's leadership was indicted, followed by the arrests of the "third-string" in August. Needless to say, there would be no more bail for communist functionaries, and for the next five years those who were not in prison would operate underground.

THE NEW HEAD OF California's little HUAC, Hugh Burns, was even more Right-wing than Jack Tenney. While the latter only targeted a few projects associated with the university and the UCLA professors affiliated with them, Burns attacked the University of California as an institution in his June 1951 report. Because it had only a vague policy against communism, rather than an "efficient screening unit," he charged that Sproul and his university's apathy in dealing with the red menace amounted to "aiding and abetting" an international conspiracy.[37]

In rebutting these charges, the president stated that most of the committee's sixty-page section on the university dealt with events from the 1930s and the war. He did not mention the new material, including a 1949 article by Sidney Hook that explained why "members of the professoriat constitute the strongest and most influential group of Communist fellow-travelers in the United States,"[38] as well as the long section of the report devoted to the Loyalty Oath.

Burns used Stewart's *The Year of the Oath* to summarize the controversy, before blasting the author for his unkind words about Jack Tenney. Then he ridiculed the book's sympathetic description of dismissed TA Irving David Fox and the author's naiveté about the communist problem at the university.[39] Next came a long section on Edward Tolman.

The Burns report charged that the nonsigners' leader had subscribed to the Communist Party paper *Peoples' World* in 1939, and had also belonged to five front organizations. Although these affiliations were not dated, most of the groups were active during the late 1930s and early 1940s, for example organizations supporting Republican Spain and its civil war refugees. Burns emphasized that Tolman, along with Paul Robeson, Albert Maltz of "the Hollywood Ten," Anna Louise Strong, and other well-known Leftists, had signed an open letter sponsored by the *New Masses* (the Communist Party's cultural magazine) protesting HUAC's investigations. He wondered how the Academic Senate could have selected such a man to lead the fight against the oath, for he either knew "exactly what he was doing in lending his name, his prestige, his financial contributions, and his time" to important front organizations, or if he wasn't smart enough to know this, he had no business teaching at the university.[40]

The report also charged that there were Communist Party student clubs at Berkeley and UCLA. The most sensational material concerned a member who had been murdered because he was about to defect and reveal the party's secrets. Before his death the young man had written (approvingly) to his parents that there were articulate communists in all his classes who contested the bourgeois ideology of their professors.[41]

On Weigel's advice, Tolman responded immediately, protesting that he had always been "a loyal American citizen," but was also "fed up with vague innuendos." There wasn't "a shred of truth" in Burns's allegations. "Unalterably opposed to communism," he had, like most Americans, belonged to many organizations, but "never knowingly to any subversive ones."[42]

Three days later, Yale honored the Berkeley psychologist as "a valiant defender of the freedom of the mind" who had "served your country in its hour of need." Yale had marked the 250th anniversary of its founding by awarding honorary doctorates to twenty-five leading scholars, including Tolman.[43]

The Senate's Committee on Academic Freedom issued a blistering critique of the Burns Report, calling it "false," "shocking," and "utterly misleading." The CAF emphasized how it had not backed up its charges by naming a single communist faculty member, nor one so-called communist organization on campus, and thus had done a "great disservice" in undermining public confidence in the university. But the liberal group also paraded its anticommunist credentials by pointing out that Berkeley's faculty had been the first of a major university to bar communists.[44]

Coming to the Burns' Committee's defense, Neylan published a letter that condemned the CAF's report as "distorted and malicious" and took Sproul to task. In a glaring breach of etiquette, he charged his former friend with "undermining" and then trying to "wipe out" the policy of excluding communists from the faculty. Then it was Hugh Burns's turn to accuse the faculty and Sproul of "a malicious distortion" of his report. A few days later, he announced that a full-scale investigation of communist infiltration at the university would begin in the fall.[45]

Meanwhile the State Supreme Court began hearings on the oath cases it had agreed to review. And when attorneys Weigel and Prince made their arguments to the justices in *Tolman* v. *Underhill*, almost 350 people jammed the chambers in San Francisco to hear them. It was the most crowded gallery in the court's history.[46]

DURING THE SUMMER of 1951 most of the faculty nonsigners who were not already employed found new jobs. Edelstein returned to Johns Hopkins, the university that had welcomed him as a refugee from fascism. Brewster Rogerson went to Princeton as a visiting lecturer, and Kelley was hired at Tulane. Tolman accepted an offer from Yale that had been proffered shortly after he had been awarded an honorary doctorate there. And when Loewenberg decided to spend a year at Columbia, Sperry became the only one without work or income.

By this time four faculty committees were engaging in fundraising. The $36,000 raised by the Group for Academic Freedom went primarily to pay its lawyer's fees. As more people found jobs, some of the money raised by the Senate's fund-raising committee would also be used to reduce the debt to Weigel. Two committees had been set up to help graduate students. In addition to the one that took care of those NASE members who had resisted the Regents' Special Oath, there was a new group assisting those who were refusing to sign the Levering Act's oath. However, because donations were coming in slowly, after an initial 65 percent of their normal salaries, the aid for grad students had fallen to only 45 percent.[47]

Goodwin Knight had been reelected as California's lieutenant governor in 1950. In a speech to the San Jose Junior Chamber of Commerce on August 7, he accused the nonsigners of "following the direct dictates of the Kremlin."[48] To the GAF, this was libelous, so the group made plans to sue him. Hodgen pledged $75 to defray expenses and then drafted a reply to the lieutenant governor in which she affirmed her right to come to her own conclusions about Marxism and communism without being told by any administrative body how she should teach. "Were I to yield to the demands of the board of Regents," then "I would place myself in the company of Soviet teachers who teach not what they believe is right, but what an insolent clique forces them to teach."[49]

By August 1951, William Benton of Connecticut, the U.S. Senate's most consistent critic of Joe McCarthy, could no longer bear to be in the same chambers with him. He therefore introduced a resolution calling for McCarthy's expulsion. His effort failed, as America's number one Red hunter counterattacked with a libel suit charging slander. But Benton's courage may have inspired Truman to finally speak out against "the scaremongers and hate-mongers," whose stock in trade was "character assassination" and whose motto was "guilt by association." The president called on "every American who loves his country" to "rise up and put a stop to this terrible business."[50]

There was now hope on the Board of Regents. Warren had made three new appointments in 1951, so that by the August meeting, his liberal faction had a solid majority.[51] That's why they were able to defeat a Neylan notion to reject the Academic Senate's "memorial" asking the board to rescind the oath. In the course of a bitter debate, the regent threatened to bury the memorial so deep that no one would ever find it. But even though the oath was not eliminated in August, the time when Neylan could get his way by bullying others was long past.[52]

THE DEMISE OF THE REGENTS' SPECIAL OATH

In late summer and early fall, the Committee on Academic Freedom, led by Stanley and Caldwell, took the lead in challenging the contract that professors had to sign for the 1951–52 academic year. Although it was the same wording they had complied with the year before, the April court decision had renewed the faculty's courage. So Stanley complained to Sproul that the way in which salary and rank were stipulated amounted to "a denial of tenure." Although he and Caldwell eventually signed their contracts, many others did not, so that by the end of August there was a whole "new crop of nonsigners."[53]

At the October 19 regents' meeting Sproul announced that forty-eight teachers, including twelve Senate members, had not accepted appointments because of the oath. They had all signed the Levering Act's oath and were continuing to teach, despite the fact that they hadn't been paid in almost two months. The unexpected revolt gave a new urgency to the Loyalty Oath issue, setting the stage for a resolution by Donald McLaughlin to rescind it. When McLaughlin was appointed in June 1951 to fill Giannini's long-vacant seat, *The Daily Californian* and many Berkeley students were disappointed. For months the paper had campaigned to convince Warren to replace the banker with Monroe Deutsch.

But McLaughlin may have been the ideal person to bridge the gap between the faculty and the regents. A mining engineer and businessman, he had taught at Berkeley as well as Harvard, where he was serving on its Board of

Overseers. He had also been in the liberal minority on the Bechtel committee that had fashioned the Alumni Compromise.

In the course of a heated debate, the conservative bloc argued that McLaughlin's resolution had not been properly circulated in advance. But the outnumbered Neylan faction couldn't stop it, and it passed 12 to 8. Then Regent Brodie Ahlport changed his vote so that the decision could be reconsidered at the next meeting. Knowing that he was defeated, Neylan and five of his allies didn't even appear for this vote on reconsideration. So on November 16, when that motion was decisively defeated and McLaughlin's resolution became official policy, *the hated Loyalty Oath was off the books.*

And yet there was no jubilation among the nonsigners. The regents voting against the old oath had argued that the Levering Act was a better tool for eliminating communists. Even McLaughlin had insisted that the new oath be retained as the vehicle of choice for enforcing the regents' anti-Reds policy.[54]

The war in Korea was almost eighteen months old, with fourteen thousand American soldiers killed in action. For much of 1951 there had been a virtual stalemate on the battlefield. A Chinese offensive in April had been followed by an American one in May. Then in June, overtures by Secretary of State Dean Acheson and Jacob Malik, the Soviet ambassador to the United Nations, gave rise to hopes for a ceasefire. By late July, armistice negotiations had begun in earnest. After some progress, they were suspended, only to be resumed again. As the year ended, there were critical issues unresolved, including the boundary between the warring parties and what to do about the prisoners of war on both sides.[55]

ON NOVEMBER 23, 1951, Neylan addressed San Francisco's Commonwealth Club. Because Monroe Deutsch had spoken to the group three weeks earlier, he used his talk to bewail how the ex-provost had changed, saying that the loyalty oath had transformed him from a reasonable man to an embittered militant.[56] Then he excoriated both Deutsch and Sproul for "cringing" before a minority of the faculty, whom he characterized as petty "campus politicians" doing the bidding of the AAUP. For Neylan, the group was a "sinister organization, a nemesis which can destroy any American university."

The regent's next targets were Stewart and Kantorowicz, whose writings he saw as part of a "campaign of terror" against the regents. He made only one reference to the court decision, asking, "If Mr. Tolman and his associates now accept appointments (and) if they now execute the same type of statement in the Levering Oath, are they martyrs or mountebanks?"[57]

Neylan also revealed that he had been planning to resign from the board after almost twenty-five years of service. But he had changed his mind, deciding that he would no longer turn "the other cheek under a barrage of slander and libel churned out in a pressure campaign by men determined to rule or ruin the university."[58]

CHAPTER 14

MCCARTHY DEFEATED, BUT HIS -*ISM* LINGERS ON

A war that went on and on and on.

—David Halberstam[1]

B Y APRIL 1952 A YEAR HAD PASSED SINCE THE decision in *Tolman* v. *Underhill.* The nonsigners' jobs were still in limbo, and further delays could be expected, as the court kept asking for additional briefs to study. But the Group for Academic Freedom did get an unexpected present that spring when the American Civil Liberties Union awarded it a Citation for Distinguished Service in the Cause of Academic Freedom.[2]

In 1952 the Republicans' prospects of ending twenty years of Democratic rule had never looked brighter, as Truman and his party were bogged down in an increasingly unpopular war. Illinois Governor Adlai Stevenson emerged as the Democratic frontrunner, but the Republican race was wide open. Four UC regents were in the thick of the politicking before the Republican Party's nominating convention. Farnham Griffiths, who in 1948 had headed a Democrats for Warren organization, changed his registration so that he could work more effectively for his friend. Sproul was also a Warren supporter. But despite his now impeccable anticommunist credentials, Warren remained a dark horse. The early favorite was the conservative senator from Ohio, Robert Taft.

Neylan was a Taft supporter. He and Warren fought even harder for control of the California delegation to the Republican convention than they had on the Board of Regents. But the Taft-Warren battle became moot in April 1952 when Dwight Eisenhower asked Truman to be relieved of his post as supreme commander of American and NATO forces in Europe. "Ike" lost little time in making his ambitions clear, and the popular general was a strong favorite to beat Stevenson in November. The liberal governor was considered an "egghead," a reputation that in 1952 was the kiss of death. For McCarthyism was driven in large part by the strong currents of anti-intellectualism in the American tradition.

FOR YEARS SPROUL HAD BEEN CRITICIZED for an unwillingness to delegate authority. Weakened by his handling of the oath, in 1952 he had to relinquish some of his powers when two new chancellors were appointed to lead the university's largest branches. Berkeley had not had a provost since Deutsch's retirement in 1947, and UCLA was still being run by committee, two years after the death of Dykstra.

The choices for the new posts reflected the distinct political cultures of Northern and Southern California, as well as divisions on the Board of Regents. Raymond Allen, who as president of the University of Washington had fired several professors in 1948 because of their Left-wing politics, took over at UCLA. Indeed it was his sterling history of anticommunism that had made him attractive to regents such as Dickson and Neylan.[3] Berkeley's new chancellor was Clark Kerr. Unlike Allen, Kerr was considered a liberal, but he was equally opposed to communism and communists. It was the labor arbitrator's skill at negotiating agreements between various factions of the faculty during the oath controversy that made him a popular choice.

In his first semester as chancellor Kerr spoke out against the Levering oath. Soon he was involved in another controversy. Sproul had agreed to provide Burns and his committee with the names of candidates for new faculty positions, just as he had his predecessor Tenney. To facilitate this, each UC branch had to appoint a "contact man" with the Senate panel. The rumors that Kerr had assumed the role caused a stir on the Berkeley faculty, but he steadfastly denied involvement.[4]

To the nonsigners, it must have seemed as if their case was dragging out as long as the war in Korea. In that conflict, negotiations had stalled for much of 1952 over how to resolve the prisoner of war issue: a significant number of the captives were reluctant to return to their communist homelands. During the summer, in an attempt to induce more concessions, the U.S. Air Force engaged in heavy bombing of the enemy's infrastructure and the North Korean capital, Pyongyang. Then, shortly after the communists rejected the UN's final offer in October, Eisenhower announced that he would fly to Korea to end the impasse if he were elected in November.

ON OCTOBER 17, 1952, the California Supreme Court finally acted on the regents' appeal of the decision that the lower court had handed down eighteen months earlier. For Tolman, Weigel, and the lawyer's other clients, it was good and bad news. On the one hand, the decision that had restored their jobs was upheld, which meant that they could return to teach. But none of the larger issues upon which the lower court had spoken so eloquently were addressed: there was no mention of academic freedom, free speech, or the right to tenure. Its "positive" decision was based on the narrowest of grounds, the fact that the Levering Act and its oath—which the court upheld the same day by a similar 6 to 1 majority—superseded the Regents' Special Oath, making the latter moot.[5]

The nonsigners had won their case in the courts after a legal battle of more than two years, but it was a pyrrhic victory. Tolman was disheartened by the decision, and wondered whether the long struggle had been worth the cost. Hodgen tried to console him, arguing that good had "come out of all the confusions and distress." For their resistance, she suggested, was "the first shot, and after all, it was heard pretty well around the world."[6]

After Neylan, along with the rest of the board, decided not to appeal to the U.S. Supreme Court, the once powerful regent took a rosy view of the outcome. In his oral history he called the court's reasoning a "very statesmanlike job," and as for Weigel's claim that it was a victory for the nonsigners, he almost "fell out of his seat" when he heard that.[7] In his view the Tolman group was made up of "gullible people" who had been led astray. He was now feeling sorry for them, because "They stand alone and I don't know what they are going to do."[8]

On November 4 Eisenhower (with Nixon as his running mate) won by a landslide in the Electoral College, garnering 442 votes compared to only 89 for Stevenson and John Sparkman. "Ike" also received a hefty 55 percent of the popular vote. The Republicans took over Congress, winning the House of Representatives by a mere eight seats and wresting control of the Senate by only one. In California the voters affirmed anticommunism in a big way. The Levering Act, with its loyalty oath, was on the ballot as a constitutional amendment, and the measure was approved by 69 percent of the state's voters.[9]

Although the USSR was close to testing its own hydrogen bomb, optimism that the dreaded weapons might never be used increased in March 1953, following the unexpected death of Soviet Premier Stalin. Despite uncertainties about the locus of power in a new Kremlin, the death of Russia's supreme leader led to a "thaw" in Soviet-American relations. As a result, the stalled negotiations in Korea resumed, and on July 27 an armistice was signed, ending more than three years of conflict.

As president, Eisenhower had a style that was more low-key and laissez-faire than that of his Democratic predecessor. However, he failed, either through words or actions, to alleviate the hysteria of anticommunism. This was a disappointment to civil libertarians, who had hoped that the president might deploy his popularity to counter the climate of McCarthyism. But when the Wisconsin senator, always looking for another pillar of the establishment whose patriotism he could impugn, smeared George Marshall, a silent Ike did not even defend his fellow general.

LESS THAN HALF THE NONSIGNERS RETURN

In his first year as chancellor, Kerr's priority was to eliminate the year-to-year contract, so that members of the faculty who had reached the ranks of associate and full professor would have job security. With a solid majority of the regents now pro-faculty, the board accepted his plan for "continuous tenure." And it even permitted student organizations to invite anyone to speak on the campus—except communists or other radicals.[10]

Change was taking place in the Academic Senate also. Members of the old guard such as Hildebrand, Lehman, and Hicks were now seen as equivocators. Having failed to fight hard during the critical first year of the oath controversy when militancy might have succeeded, they were no longer trusted. Younger, more liberal professors, many who had been active as "friendly signers," replaced them on key Senate committees.

After the October 1952 decision, Kerr personally invited Berkeley's faculty nonsigners to return to the campus, assuring them that they would not be discriminated against.[11] Those who had commitments elsewhere for the 1952–53 academic year would not come back until the fall of 1953. There was concern about their reception by the faculty, but Muscatine reported that he and his comrades were received warmly.[12]

Caughey found returning to UCLA "a jolt." Unlike Muscatine, he had spent the interim doing research rather than teaching. Out of the classroom for so long, he had to start over memorizing his lecture notes. Not only that, the resistance leader had problems getting back some of the classes he had taught for twenty years, as they had been assigned to younger instructors.[13] And it didn't help that Neylan was now making him a prime target: the regent not only labeled him "the most distinguished propagandist of them all," he also accused him of working "both sides of the street" for having signed the Levering Act's oath in October 1950.[14]

Of the twenty-one remaining faculty nonsigners, only nine would teach again at the University of California. There were five who retired: Loewenberg, Olschki, Hodgen, Sperry, and, soon after his return, Tolman. The eight who resigned to carry on their academic careers at other universities included three of Berkeley's most illustrious scholars, Kantorowicz, Wick, and Edelstein, as well as UCLA's Mowat.[15]

Harold Winkler returned from Harvard in what could have been his last year as an assistant professor, for Political Science was due to review him in an "up-or-out" decision. His prospects were bleak, not having published a book or even an article. Just before his department met to decide his fate, Winkler reportedly told students at the Hillel Foundation that "there was something wrong with a young person . . . who is not idealistically inspired to the point of belonging to a communist, socialist, anarchist, or other similarly inspired group."[16] The man was no flaming radical himself, but he liked to shake up complacent students.

Winkler's alleged statement caused a stir in the press, and according to Kerr, "some regents reacted violently to the news." Berkeley's new chancellor feared that if the board fired Winkler, an aroused faculty would come to his defense, and a new loyalty oath crisis might ensue. So he visited Neylan to urge him not to support Winkler's dismissal. By this time his department had voted down his promotion, so he would be leaving anyway. The tactic worked. At the next board meeting, only Edward Dickson voted to fire the maverick professor.[17]

Kerr may have averted another crisis by keeping a potentially volatile episode quiet. Sproul called him in 1953 about three members of the Senate who had signed the Regents' Special Oath when they were members of the Communist Party. More than three years later they were still teaching and still in the party. Because the professors had perjured themselves, the president expected Berkeley's chancellor "to take the necessary action." So Kerr visited them and worked out an agreement in which they would quietly resign from the faculty. In return the chancellor kept the news from becoming public.[18]

KENNETH MACGOWAN, THE CHAIR of UCLA's Department of Theater Arts, had been planning to spend the summer of 1953 traveling in Europe. But the State Department refused his passport application. This did not surprise the former Hollywood producer, for two years earlier Tenney Committee charges of affiliation with communist front groups had resurfaced to prevent him from participating in a panel sponsored by Pasadena's Board of Education, as well as in other events. Macgowan mounted a campaign to save his trip, enlisting the support of UCLA's Chancellor Allen, as well as Nelson Rockefeller, for whom he had worked during the war. He was ultimately successful in gaining his passport, but not in winning the coveted Fulbright Fellowship he had applied for. Its sponsor, the liberal Senator William Fulbright, had become one of McCarthy's targets, so the agency was being especially careful about who they selected.[19]

Since the State Supreme Court's narrow ruling had not addressed the matter of back pay, surprising and disappointing the litigants, Kerr also lobbied the regents to grant the nonsigners their lost salaries. But the board resisted, as Neylan and Goodwin Knight, who in 1954 was finally elected governor, were bitterly opposed to the idea. So Weigel sued the regents once again. In December 1954, an amicable settlement was worked out for five of the twenty-one nonsigners who were teaching at other universities. But it would be another year and a half before the lawsuit was settled out of court for the remaining resisters.

And yet even after the final agreement in May 1956 there were still loose ends not yet tied up. Several nonsigners balked at returning that portion of their back pay that was needed to cover Weigel's expenses. That is why the Faculty Fund for Financial Assistance did not close its books until 1957. At that date it reported that all the contributors had received the compensation they had been promised when collections began in 1950. After the nonsigners gave back that part of their back pay that constituted an overpayment, when the salaries they had earned elsewhere were figured in, the fund was able to return to each contributor almost 45 percent of his or her original donation.[20]

THE DOWNFALL OF MCCARTHY

Two events that took place in 1954 would have major effects on American society and politics. In June the U.S. Supreme Court ruled in *Brown* v. *Board of Education* that racial segregation in public schools was unconstitutional. It would take more than a year for the decision's import to be seen, when the modern civil rights movement was ushered in with the bus boycott in Montgomery, Alabama, that began in December 1955.

The significance of McCarthy's investigation of the U.S. Army in 1954 was almost immediately apparent when the counsel for the military, Joseph Welch, became the first defense lawyer to aggressively confront America's leading Red hunter. Although Edward R. Murrow's television specials had begun to shift public opinion against him, Welch's dramatic questions, "Have you no sense of decency sir, at long last?" and "Have you left no sense of decency?" had a remarkable resonance. Along with McCarthy's overreaching in going after the army in the first place, his confrontation with Welch sent his political stock into a nosedive.[21]

The demise of the once powerful demagogue emboldened faculty liberals. In a letter to Sproul, Hildebrand bemoaned the fact that there were now Berkeley professors advocating that there should be communists on the faculty! And yet as late as 1955 the chemistry professor was advising the president on the political purity of prospective faculty members. He assured Sproul that the Nobel Prize–winning chemist Harold Urey may have made questionable statements on matters outside his expertise (for example on "the legalities of the Rosenberg case"), but unlike Linus Pauling, he never supported pro-Soviet peace conferences, and was "altogether conscientious and loyal."[22]

John Francis Neylan was a McCarthy supporter, so one wonders whether the latter's demise was a factor in his decision to retire as a regent in 1955. Seventy years old, he had served for twenty-eight years. He stated that he wanted to spend his time writing his memoirs and speaking publicly about higher education. But for Robert Gordon Sproul, who had outlasted his nemesis as president of the university, the end of the once powerful regent's reign was a personal vindication. And in a surprising move, Governor Knight replaced Neylan with Thomas Storke, a liberal Santa Barbara publisher who had consistently spoken out in defense of civil liberties.

During the second half of the 1950s, McCarthy the man and the politician would no longer dominate American politics. The shift in the political climate would be reflected in the courts when the Smith Act convictions of Communist Party leaders were reversed in 1958. And yet the impulse of anticommunism would linger on for at least a decade. Professors at the University of California, as well as all other state employees, would have to sign the anticommunist declaration of the Levering Act until 1967, when that law was finally struck down by the California Supreme Court. The case that overturned it was *Vogel* v. *California,* for it was a Quaker named Bob Vogel who had sued the state. John Caughey applauded the court for its "fortitude" in admitting that its earlier decision upholding the Levering Act had been a mistake.[23]

CHAPTER 15

HOW THE OATH CHANGED A UNIVERSITY, A NATION, AND PEOPLE'S LIVES

The decision in *Tolman* v. *Underhill* confirming the non-signers in their post was a hollow victory. . . . Theirs had been a futile struggle.

—David Gardner[1]

Perhaps it's self-aggrandizing, but my feeling is that these decisions [in *Tolman* v. *Underhill*] helped turn the tide against McCarthyism.

—Stanley Weigel[2]

I've always felt that some day I'd get very old and very gray, and somebody would see me in the university library and they'd say, "Who is that little old lady over there?" The reply would be, "That's Mrs. Sproul." The voice: "What on earth is she doing?" And then I'd say, "I'm trying to find out what the Loyalty Oath was all about."

—Ida Wittschen Sproul[3]

DURING THE 1950S PAUL LAZARSFELD WAS one of the many distinguished professors who, because of the Loyalty Oath, said no to an attractive offer to teach at the University of California. The sociologist, a Viennese-born Jewish immigrant, was also one of Columbia's most eminent faculty members. He was a pioneer of an important methodology in his field (survey research), had refined the best technique for analyzing its results (multivariate analysis), and was also an expert in the study of communications.

In the spring of 1955, Clark Kerr received a phone call from Columbia. It was his friend Lazarsfeld, who in analyzing the data from an interview study of American social scientists had discovered that the proportion of Left-wing professors at Berkeley was twice that of any other major public university.[4]

Berkeley's chancellor was not surprised by this revelation, but even so, it was an astonishing finding. For only six years earlier, before the Loyalty Oath rocked the institution, the faculty at Berkeley, including its social science professors, had been moderate to conservative in its political outlook. That such a dramatic turnaround had taken place in so short a time could only have been because of the oath and the resistance to it.

This made sense to Kerr, for he had personally observed many of his colleagues move toward the Left during the controversy. And as he would write more than forty years later, the oath also "radicalized the faculty" because it made Berkeley an attractive place for Left-leaning instructors and assistant professors to come to teach, and for similarly minded graduate students to study. Kerr also argued that the controversy created an anti-administration mentality among professors at Berkeley. They could not forget how it had been President Sproul who had proposed the oath in the first place, and how he had equivocated rather than providing strong leadership, even after he had come to oppose the requirement.

Kerr's perspective is provocative but also self-serving. UC's former president used the "radicalization" of his faculty to explain its support for student rebels during the Free Speech Movement, an event that along with other unrest at Berkeley during the 1960s would doom his tenure as the university's top administrator.[5] And his analysis is also one-sided, as historian Robert Cohen has emphasized.

The oath crisis may well have radicalized a *segment* of the faculty and attracted some Left-leaning young professors and grad students to the campus. But in making it clear that control over university governance resided in the Board of Regents (and not in the Academic Senate) and that conservative legislators in Sacramento could always set limits on the faculty's vaunted autonomy, it made other professors more fearful. The best examples are Berkeley's Chancellor Edward Strong and Kerr himself. The two men were important figures in the resistance, but fifteen years later as top administrators their over-cautious and vacillating leadership was the major reason why a containable protest escalated into the most massive student rebellion in American history.[6]

During the oath crisis the Academic Senate and its leaders talked tough, but never followed through with action. How often did they threaten mass resignations, or symbolic ones by spokesmen such as Hicks and Hildebrand? But threats and tough talk continually dissipated into calls for more negotiation and compromises with the Board of Regents.

Not only that, the overwhelming majority of the faculty chose to sign the oath rather than to mount a principled resistance. In this sense the nonsigners were not only a "dissident minority" (to use one of Neylan's favorite epithets), but a miniscule one. Furthermore, the Senate, to the extent that it did fight for the nonsigners, was concerned primarily with its own members and virtually abandoned the much larger group of grad student resisters.

If there was one lesson the faculty learned from the years of the oath, it was the need for organization. Berkeley's nonsigners were able to hold out and eventually win in court because they were tightly organized. The mobilization of "friendly signers" was also pivotal, as was the effort to raise money for the lost salaries of fired professors and graduate students. At UCLA the faculty's campaign to raise money for salaries was even more successful, but its once sizable nonsigners' movement dissipated because it was not organized.

In the years following the oath UCLA did not experience even the partial faculty radicalization that occurred at Berkeley. From being the more liberal campus (if only marginally), it became the more conservative of UC's two largest branches. The fact that the oath was not a big issue in the south explains why the Westwood campus never became a magnet for Leftist professors and graduate students. In addition, the L.A. region couldn't compete with the Bay Area as a center of the new youth culture. There was nothing in the southland to attract the young comparable to San Francisco's Beat writers and coffee houses, followed by the "flower children" and hippies.

During the 1960s it became clear that Berkeley was the place "where it was happening." But fifteen years before that now trite expression became part of hip discourse, it was the Loyalty Oath that first established the connection between Berkeley and political resistance in America's cultural imagination.[7]

DID BERKELEY'S RESISTANCE TURN
BACK MCCARTHYISM?

If it is not easy to sort out the effects of the Loyalty Oath on the university, it's even more difficult to assess its impact on the larger political climate of McCarthyism. Opinions diverge sharply; the absence of consensus is not surprising since the question involves highly subjective speculations, often based on personal bias, rather than on facts.

One of the more extravagant claims was made by Stanley Weigel, who stated that the nationwide publicity received by the favorable court decision "helped turn the tide against McCarthyism."[8] But the key word in his assertion, "helped," is too vague to be useful: one could just as well argue that every statement made by every public figure or even ordinary citizen against an act of repression in the late 1940s and early 1950s helped turn back McCarthyism. But Weigel wants us to believe that his clients had a significant impact on the political climate, and to me this exaggerates their historical role.

The events that did turn the tide against the anticommunist hysteria were international ones. The death of Stalin led to a thaw in the Cold War and made possible an end to the Korean conflict. Perhaps if Stalin had not miscalculated in assuming that the United States would not come to the aid of South Korea, then, without a Korean war, the resistance at Berkeley might have had some of the historical impact Weigel claimed for it.

John Caughey also resorted to careless wording when he wrote that "the California resistance is sometimes credited with preventing a nationwide epidemic of test oaths for teachers. It certainly promoted an awareness of academic freedom and alerted scholars to the need for (its) staunch defense."[9] The phrase "is sometimes credited" suggests the weakness of Caughey's claim. While not implausible, his statement is impossible to prove.

More modest assessments have been made by Margaret Hodgen and Ellen Schrecker. After the controversy was resolved, the Berkeley nonsigner consoled Tolman that their resistance was not in vain, for it was the "the first shot" and it was heard throughout the nation. A generation later, Schrecker, a historian of McCarthyism, argued that the oath controversy showed that it was possible for university professors to fight back against repression. Since America was not a totalitarian state, resistance, though extremely rare, could be mounted, and even more remarkably, succeed.

In my view the best way to assess the nonsigners' resistance is not through such ambitious and ultimately indemonstrable claims, but to place their actions in the context of the behavior of academic men and women at the time. Here Howard Zinn's summary is useful. According to the radical historian, "the silence of the academy in regard to Cold War foreign policy in the 1950s was matched by its passive acceptance of the Cold War's equivalent on the domestic scene: the firings, the black-listings, the attacks on unions, the FBI harassments. University administrations and their faculties found a way to justify each of these assaults on traditional American liberties because of the communist threat."[10]

Because the nonsigners' movement was unique, it inspired faculties all across the country. Professors responded with an unprecedented display of moral, political, and financial support. For highly individualistic academic men and women, the solidarity of the professoriat in support of the UC resistance was almost as remarkable as the actions of the nonsigners themselves.

We are left then with David Gardner's oft-quoted assessment that the controversy was a vain and futile episode in the history of the University of California.[11] Forty years after the publication of *The California Oath Controversy*, the president emeritus's conclusion seems less valid than it may have appeared at the time. With a renewed interest in the McCarthy Era on the part of historians and journalists, the civic courage of those who resisted repression has finally received the attention it deserves. Gardner called the actions of Berkeley's resisters counterproductive, but in the least they helped maintain the morale of liberal professors in a difficult period and may also have contributed, if only modestly, to the eventual restoration of a less hysterical political climate.

John Francis Neylan believed that the controversy taught the general public that communism at the university was a real danger that required action on the part of the institution. Gordon Griffiths also stressed the educational effects of the crisis, but from an opposite standpoint. For the Marxist historian, the struggle at Berkeley and UCLA made professors all over the country more aware of the importance of academic freedom and the need to defend it.

The claims of Neylan and Griffiths only appear to be contradictory, but both men may be correct. The Loyalty Oath and the resistance to it resonated with different publics in different ways. The California citizens that the regent had in mind were more likely to believe that many professors were indeed communists, above all the nonsigners, "who must have had something to hide." For the so-called common folk, the idea of academic freedom made little sense. And yet as Griffiths argued, the resistance made college teachers more aware of the importance and the vulnerability of their cherished value.

This suggests another of the oath's consequences: it widened the already considerable abyss between the worldviews of academic people and the larger citizenry, especially in California.

WINNERS AND LOSERS

Which participants came out of the conflict as winners and who were the big losers? Unlikely as it may seem, the winners were the two groups that fought each other most doggedly, the nonsigners and the conservative regents led by Neylan. The losers were the faculty, especially Berkeley's Academic Senate, and above all President Sproul.

Tolman and his followers prevailed for several reasons. Believing so firmly in the rightness of their cause, they were able to hold out longer than might have been expected, even though their numbers dropped drastically after the outbreak of war in Korea. But the score of those nonsigners who continued to fight back had both a strong organizational structure and outstanding leadership. They were fortunate to have a man like Tolman at the helm. As one of the nation's top psychologists, his academic prestige was considerable. But even more important was a personality marked by a quiet warmth, an unassuming bearing, and a sincere concern for people and their welfare, above all his youthful followers. The Group for Academic Freedom was also lucky to be able to draw on the legal skills of Stanley Weigel, as well as to have a cadre of "Young Turks" willing to do the day-to-day work of keeping their resistance alive.

It is remarkable that Neylan and his regential allies were able to grind out victory after victory for a year and a half despite the fact that they were opposed by two of the state's most popular figures, Governor Warren and President Sproul, for most of this time. Perhaps the most important reason was that the *zeitgeist* was on their side. The pervasiveness of the anticommunist hysteria put liberals constantly on the defensive.

Another advantage for Neylan and his faction was ideological consistency. His three closest allies on the board, Giannini, Dickson, and Knight, were extremists who shared his belief that the fight against the oath was a communist plot. True believers, with an unshakeable passion for their cause, they had a single-mindedness that not even Heller, the board's most liberal member, could match. And the latter's main allies, Sproul and Warren, were politicians who had to please a number of constituencies, so they could not afford ideological consistency.

The Right-wing regents were better organized than the liberals, in large part due to Neylan's hard work and boundless energy. In an era before faxes and e-mail, he maintained daily contact with his allies through letters and phone calls. The Neylan group was always prepared, primed to act quickly and decisively. To ensure that they were united they caucused early in the morning before each board meeting.

Neylan fought his enemies vigorously, but he also had limits. Privy to classified intelligence, he knew that two of his adversaries, Tolman and Deutsch, had histories of affiliation with communist front organizations. Indeed, they had appeared in the public reports of California's little HUAC. And yet he never once red-baited Tolman or Deutsch.

But aside from this, Neylan was willing to employ any tactic, any trick, no matter how duplicitous, to gain his objectives. It was this ruthlessness that most struck Ben Lehman the day the regent talked about replacing Sproul with Ernest Lawrence.[12] Believing totally in his cause, the regent never saw the contradiction between what he said and what he did. So he would complain constantly about how the press sided with the "dissident minority" and unfairly impugned him and the Board of Regents, while of the dozen or so daily papers in the state, only the *Chronicle* and the low-circulation *San Francisco News* opposed the oath. And at the time he was decrying this press "bias," he was writing unsigned editorials for the *Examiner* and other Hearst papers, which couched the oath controversy as part of the struggle between civilization and barbarism.

But if Neylan won many more battles than he lost, it was above all due to the force of his will and the power of his intelligence. Faculty observers at regents' meetings reported how he wore down the opposition by hammering away with the same arguments and dominating the discussion by his constant talk, so that it was hard for anyone else to speak. And this was all calculated, for in the last analysis Neylan simply outsmarted Sproul, Warren, and the liberals on the board. Hicks called him "one of the cleverest men I've ever met."[13]

And yet the regent's tactics could backfire. His relentless bullying of Sproul evoked sympathy for the embattled president. And because Neylan so often engaged in ad hominem attacks on his opponents, there were times when the policy issues under debate were overshadowed by the emphasis on the personal.[14]

In the long run, Neylan's bullying created a backlog of resentment, not only with the liberals but also with middle-of-the-road regents. By late 1950 the board was solidly against him. From the one person who had wielded the most control over the affairs of the university, he became during his final years a man without power or authority.

JOEL HILDEBRAND EXPERIENCED a similar decline. From the single most powerful member of the Academic Senate and the professor closest to Sproul, he would lose this influence because of the way he misled the faculty in the early stages of the controversy. And rather than becoming an advocate of faculty unity as did Paul Dodd, his middle-of-the-road counterpart at UCLA, he continuously questioned the motives and patriotism of the nonsigners, badgering them to sign for the good of the university and the sake of the president's job. Not only that, Hildebrand complained incessantly about their recalcitrance; they were making his last years as a professor miserable.

The faculty also comes off as a loser in the conflict. While a tiny band of nonsigners was carrying on their resistance, Berkeley's Senate was taking pride in the fact that it was the first faculty at a major university that had voted to exclude communists from its ranks. Hicks even boasted that they were starting a trend.

Tolman summed up the lessons of the struggle in a 1951 speech. Of the many reasons for the collapse in the once high number of resisters, most important was economic pressure. Then came the Korean War, which led to a "more vivid realization of what it would mean to be without jobs." Finally, there was "sheer fatigue." The faculty's intrinsic weaknesses were also critical. It was not organized for decisive action, and it was also hamstrung by lack of money. But its fatal mistake was assuming that the regents were "reasonable men" with whom negotiation was possible. Only too late would it realize that the board held all the power.[15]

A year earlier a blunt analysis of why the faculty failed came from an editor of UCLA's *Daily Bruin.* After the 1950 firings, Gene Frumkin wrote that the faculty was "vanquished" and that its defeat was the result of a "naiveté" expressed on two key occasions. The first was voting to bar Reds from teaching on the mistaken belief that this would appease the regents. The second error was to put its trust in the hearings, the naïve belief that Neylan and his allies would honor the recommendations of the Privilege and Tenure committees.

What it finally came down to, the editorial continued, was "the unwillingness of the faculty to risk anything stronger than a few, a very few, tough-sounding words." The result was a great disappointment to the students who had supported their professors, having assumed that as a group they were as brave as an Albert Einstein. In reality UC's professors were timid souls, concerned first and foremost with their economic security.[16]

However, in the later stages of the conflict, as the old-guard Senate leadership was replaced, the faculty began to redeem itself. Once the nonsigners had lost their jobs, committees at both UCLA and Berkeley organized to support them financially and were effective in this endeavor. And once leadership was assumed by a new Academic Freedom Committee, the Senate acted more vigorously, as was reflected in that group's important February 1951 report on the abrogation of tenure.

Even though that was too little and too late, in the long run the faculty regained some of the authority and control it had relinquished to the regents during the conflict. Serving on the board in 1965, Elinor Heller, the widow of Edward Heller, reported that because of the battles over the oath the regents had a better understanding of the academic perspective than they did during her husband's tenure. Fewer board members think that "the faculty should just do as they are told," she added.[17]

BEFORE HIS SERIES OF BLUNDERS in 1949, Robert Gordon Sproul was the most popular president in the history of the University of California. A major figure on a national scale, he was considered one of America's leading educators and was also seen as a potential Republican vice-presidential candidate in 1952.

The years of the oath changed this. Sproul's faculty might have forgiven him for his initial mistakes had he asserted himself as a strong leader and worked to modify or rescind the requirement. But the president's commitment to anticommunism was stronger than was his commitment to academic freedom. In addition, his fears about his own job security kept him from speaking out. The result was that in his negotiations with the faculty and the regents, Sproul was inconsistent, even equivocating.

After the oath crisis the president lost so much power and prestige that he was subject to demeaning treatment by the regents. The conservative bloc wanted to get rid of him, but after November 1950 they had become a minority on the board. It was ultimately his popularity with the alumni that saved him. But with the faculty, the oath had "just destroyed" his influence.[18]

Even though Sproul would live to be eighty-four, in his wife's view the controversy took ten years off his life. But for Ida Sproul what was even more tragic was that the crisis made many people believe that the president had done lasting harm to the university. He so loved the University of California, she stated, that he wouldn't have done anything to hurt it "for all the rice in China."[19]

EARLIER CHAPTERS HAVE DETAILED the conflict's toll in heart attacks, strokes, and nervous breakdowns, as well as the uprooting of the lives of those who were fired or who resigned. And not to be minimized are the effects on those who signed the oath. Their lives may not have been disrupted, but as psychoanalyst Norman Reider noted of his oath patients, choosing expediency over principle did violence to their psyches. No one has put this better than Norman Mailer, who wrote that "every stale compromise to the authority of any power in which one does not believe" undermine's one's very manhood, or in gender neutral language, one's human dignity.[20]

The oath controversy affected everyday life at the university. In the late 1940s one of the most popular events on the Berkeley campus was a weekly Poetry Hour, at which members of the English Department read their favorite poems to rapt audiences of students, professors, and staff. In 1950 this cultural tradition was cancelled. With so many of its professors fired as nonsigners, English no longer had the personnel to keep it going.[21]

Especially at Berkeley, the crisis brought about personal animosities, poisoning collegiality in many departments. And these bad feelings persisted long after the conflict was resolved. "Among us old faculty members," Joe Tussman recalled in 2004, "for years grudges remained, although they were not openly expressed. You remember [that] that guy signed too early. . . . You remember perfidious actions of your colleagues. They ran very deep and sometimes were never forgiven, never forgotten."[22]

For John Hicks the years of the oath were the worst years of his life. Not only was his university falling apart, but because of the demands of his Senate leadership he was unable to write his books. Hildebrand too felt bitter about the conflict. In his eyes the stubbornness of Tolman and his followers were making the final years of his teaching career miserable. The oath took a heavy toll on Jacob Loewenberg also. Like many others, he could not do his research, teach up to his standards, or even sleep at night.

On the other hand, for many young resisters, being part of this fight was a peak life experience. At eighty-six, UCLA's Ken Roose looked back at his refusal to sign as one of the three things he was most proud of in his life. For Berkeley professors such as Muscatine and Griffiths, their participation in the struggle was a formative experience, one that turned them into scholar-activists and affected the contours of their later careers.

The professors who risked their jobs and futures for an ideal did not turn back the anticommunist hysteria of post–World War II America. But without their bravery the Loyalty Oath at Berkeley and UCLA would have been just one out of hundreds of examples of the policing of the free expression of academic men and women during the McCarthy Era. And not, as Kerr and Meiklejohn have stated, the single most important controversy in the history of higher education in the United States.

THE 1999 SYMPOSIUM

The marking of the oath's 50th anniversary in 1999 was an extremely significant event, with two days of panels and discussions devoted to the crisis. In his welcoming address, Berkeley Chancellor Robert Berdahl did not hesitate to challenge the "melancholy conclusion" of Gardner's book, even with the president emeritus in the audience. Rather than being a "futile interlude" in the university's history, Berdahl argued, the crisis was "a defining moment," and it would serve for years as a point of reference for the values "essential to a free university."[23]

Ellen Schrecker, the authority on McCarthyism, was the keynote speaker. Placing the events at Berkeley and UCLA in the larger context of the Cold War and anticommunism, she also noted that the professors fired by the regents got their jobs back, while those dismissed at Washington never did.

President Emeritus David Saxon recalled the atmosphere at UCLA during the conflict. He emphasized that nonsigners like Caughey and himself had no organization, had no group activities, and made no effort to persuade people to follow their example—in contrast to the activism of their counterparts at Berkeley. In 1999 he was proud of his own resistance, but admitted that there were times when he felt he had been a naïve young man.

Clark Kerr galvanized the audience with his memories of Neylan and his discussion of the controversy's critical crossroads. He also noted that he had paid little attention to it during the first year, having signed the oath without inner qualms.

But the conference's highlights were provided by those faculty members who had fought against the oath. Eighty years old and in failing health, Gordon Griffiths came from Seattle to meet with his old comrades. The chance to reminisce about his role in the struggle was especially meaningful to him, and he had so much to say that the organizers awarded him two speaking slots. That was when Griffiths argued that the resistance at Berkeley encouraged the professoriat "to think that the fight against tyranny was not hopeless," and in doing so it "contributed to the education of people throughout the country."[24]

Howard Bern noted that women professors, though miniscule in numbers, were conspicuous among those who refused to sign, a point missed by Gardner and Stewart, as well as in contemporary accounts. But it was Charles Muscatine who charmed the audience with his colorful remembrances of his fellow nonsigners. Explaining why he didn't hesitate to return, despite a good job at Wesleyan, he asked how he could not rejoin a faculty that was capable of resisting the oath. And he attributed the victory at Berkeley to the fact that it had such a "pool of extraordinary people," who whether liberal or conservative, exhibited a "kind of openness" (and) a "kind of integrity" that made it possible for him and his comrades to hold out so long.

In introducing the final audience discussion, Berkeley historian David Hollinger expressed the hope that it might be able to unite Gardner's analysis of the controversy with the belief of most of the speakers that the struggle had been a positive episode in university history. Although this did not happen, the lively discussions and impressive attendance over the two days suggested that the Loyalty Oath was not "ancient history," but rather a cautionary tale that remained alive in the hearts and minds of the members of Berkeley's academic community.

FROM THE LOYALTY
OATH TO THE FREE
SPEECH MOVEMENT

The two crises made the university freer, bringing changes
that evoked admiration from those who cherished freedom.
But both also sparked fear from those who equated such
freedom with disorder and subversion.

—Robert Cohen.[1]

IN THE TWO YEARS BEFORE THE ONSET OF
the 1960s the president who had proposed the Loyalty Oath
and the professor who had opposed it most vigorously had buildings named
for them. In 1958 the regents' vote was unanimous to christen the old Administration Building Sproul Hall. A year later Clark Kerr, who had replaced Sproul
as president that same year, would have a much tougher time convincing the
board to call the new Education-Psychology building Tolman Hall. To Edwin
Pauley, the oil magnate who had assumed Neylan's mantle as the board's leading anticommunist, the psychologist remained a traitor. Still, Kerr convinced
a majority of the regents to honor the psychologist with a building, just as he
had persuaded them to grant him an honorary doctorate while he was still
alive.[2]

Tolman Hall was too far from the flow of traffic to play a role during the Free
Speech Movement (FSM), but Sproul Hall would be its epicenter. Only forty

feet away from the corner of Bancroft and Telegraph, the main thoroughfare for students on their way to class and the library, Sproul Hall, along with the steps up to it and the plaza below, became the site of the most massive student protest in American history.

There has been no shortage of explanations why a free speech movement broke out at Berkeley in 1964. Rather than being a comprehensive survey of these theories, this epilogue focuses on connections between the FSM and the Loyalty Oath, with a special interest in the people who participated in both.

The simplest thesis linking the FSM to the oath is that a confrontation that dramatic was needed to complete the unfinished business from the earlier conflict.[3] Even though Kerr had eliminated a few of the restrictions limiting freedom of speech for students and faculty, others remained. Most important was a rule that prohibited students from engaging in political activities on university property.

For years student groups had circulated their leaflets on the north side of Bancroft Way, directly across the street from Telegraph Avenue's coffee shops and bookstores. But in July 1964, university administrators learned that the *Oakland Tribune* had discovered that the twenty-six by forty foot strip between Sproul Hall and the corner of Bancroft and Telegraph—the site of the "Sather Gate tradition" of free speech—belonged to the campus rather than to the city of Berkeley. Instead of negotiating with student groups for a solution to the problem, a vice-chancellor, Alex Sheriffs, declared that it was a violation of the law to carry out political activities in that space. And with the approval of Edward Strong, who had become Berkeley's chancellor in 1961, police were called on October 1, 1964, to arrest the offenders.

To avoid arrest, Jack Weinberg, a nonstudent civil rights worker, went limp. He was then dragged away and locked in a police car that had driven onto that disputed piece of property. A throng of supporters gathered around the vehicle, and it was on top of this police car that philosophy major Mario Savio spoke to the crowd. The twenty-one-year-old Savio had just returned from Mississippi, where he had been a volunteer in the Freedom Summer campaign to register black voters. He and Weinberg, along with other FSM leaders, were passionate about the cause of racial justice. They wanted Berkeley's student body to take a stand in support of civil rights, and having risked their lives in the Deep South, they were impatient with what they saw as the pettiness of the university's rules regulating political activity.

For the remainder of October and November the FSM held rallies almost daily. There were inspiring speeches and the emergence of new leaders as the support from the student body continued to grow. Some faculty members advocated the students' cause openly on Sproul Steps, while others engaged in negotiations with the administration. Academic Senate meetings were consumed with the crisis.

But no dramatic event would take place until early December, when in the course of eight days the campus would experience a sit-in in Sproul Hall followed by mass arrests (December 1 and 2); a convocation in the Greek Theater addressed by Clark Kerr, who after his own speech refused Mario Savio's request to address the crowd (December 7); and the coup de grace, the Senate meeting of December 8 at which the faculty unequivocally supported student rights for the first time.

A SECOND EXPLANATION for the FSM focuses on the administrative errors that allowed a protest that could have been contained, even settled, in its early stages to escalate into a mass uprising. This is the thesis favored by people close to Sproul. The ex-president's son and his long-time secretary, Agnes Robb, as well as many other "Old Blues," remain convinced that had he been in office he would have drawn upon his personal style of leadership to defuse the crisis. Ben Lehman is clear on this point. Had Sproul been at the helm during the FSM, he would have made a major address to the students: "one bellowing, jocose speech, and kidded them to death." And he would never have called the police to arrest students on December 1, Robb insists, but would instead have sat down much earlier with Savio, Weinberg, and other leaders to forge a compromise that would have satisfied them and saved face for the university.[4] For in October 1964 the nascent movement was not yet interested in bringing down the institution. Its goal was a simple one: to secure the right to lobby for civil rights without restriction.

Sproul of course was long retired; his interests in 1964 were in Republican politics, in which he had been an advocate of Nelson Rockefeller's candidacy.[5] But his strong aversion to student radicals and his inability (or unwillingness) to defuse the oath crisis in its early stages don't give us much assurance that he could have settled the 1964 conflict. Still, the leadership styles of Strong and Kerr, the one characterized by rigidity, the other by bureaucratic aloofness, certainly exacerbated the situation.

It's ironic that Strong, who in 1948 had testified on behalf of the right of an avowed communist to teach, would light the fires of faculty discontent sixteen years later by denying a position to an acting assistant professor of German he considered to be a party member. Eli Katz was a Yiddish scholar who had defied HUAC in 1958 by not answering questions about his political affiliations. Without any real evidence, Strong became convinced that Katz was a communist who had committed perjury in signing the Levering Act oath. That's why he denied the German Department's request to regularize the appointment.

Strong may be the best example of a Berkeley professor who rather than being emboldened by the oath fight became instead more fearful and rule-bound.[6] His decision in the Katz case put him on a collision course with the liberal faculty, and especially with other veterans of the oath crisis. For it was Howard Schachman and Jacobus tenBroek, key members of the Senate's Academic Freedom Committee, who fought to retain Katz.

Another example was Kerr. Although he claimed to have disagreed with Strong about enforcing the rule against petitioning on campus property, he stood by his chancellor until much too late. More attuned to the faculty than to students, his words and actions were as important as Strong's in widening the chasm between the FSM and the administration. First there was his statement in early October that 49 percent of the movement's "hard core" was sympathetic to Mao and Castro.[7] An even greater disaster for the administration was Kerr's refusal to allow Savio to speak at the Greek Theater on December 7. As a result, fifteen thousand people witnessed the police assaulting the FSM leader and dragging him away.[8]

According to Kerr, Strong's decision of September 14, 1964, to limit political advocacy on the Bancroft strip, his own failure to overrule it, and Sproul's proposal of the Loyalty Oath were the three greatest "administrative blunders" in university history.[9]

For Clark Kerr, the FSM was a "popular front" between students and faculty in which the Academic Senate's support for the movement was the critical link. But why, the ex-president asks, did a free speech movement break out at Berkeley and not at Harvard, Yale, or Columbia? His answer is that it was the Loyalty Oath's radicalization of a critical mass of the faculty and the magnet it threw out to attract Left-leaning young professors to the campus that explains the FSM.

The problem with this theory is that the Free Speech Movement would have been a historic event even if the Academic Senate had never thrown its weight in favor of rescinding restrictions on political activity. The faculty's support for the student rebels came late in the game, suggesting the limits of Kerr's analysis.

Still, his ideas may help explain why so many oath resisters played a prominent role in the 1964–65 events. When the Senate's support for unfettered political expression finally manifested itself on December 8, the critical resolution passed overwhelmingly that day had been drafted by tenBroek. In the weeks before, impassioned speeches in favor of the political liberties of students had been made by his friend Tussman, as well as by such other oath veterans as Frank Newman, David Rynin, and Kenneth Stampp. And there was no one on the faculty more dedicated to the student cause than John Kelley and Charles Muscatine. Because they had been nonsigners, the two had a distinctive cachet among their colleagues, and they spoke with a unique authority at Senate meetings.

According to Muscatine, in 1964 the faculty "naturally gravitated to the folkways that we had developed during the loyalty oath." The essential one was communication. Having been secretary of the Group for Academic Freedom, he set up the same kind of "telephone tree" to bring liberal faculty to their first meetings that he had used fifteen years earlier.[10] The result was a faculty caucus, The Committee of Two Hundred, whose support of student free speech would prove critical.

Still, Kerr has exaggerated faculty radicalization. For the first three months of the controversy, most professors and the Senate itself were reluctant to take a stand. What finally forced them to be decisive was the sit-in in Sproul Hall on December 1–2, which led to the largest mass arrest of students in the history of an American university.

Kerr's ideas do help explain why there was no similar movement at UCLA. In his view the faculty and the administration were more united in the south during the years of the oath, so that an oppositional mentality never developed among a substantial group of professors. And because the resistance to the Loyalty Oath was much less dramatic, the Westwood campus never became a magnet for liberal faculty and graduate students. However, the difference between the two student bodies was even more important. UCLA was still a commuter college in 1964, and its students did not live in one concentrated neighborhood that was walking distance from the campus. After class they got into their cars and dispersed throughout the region. The result was that it lacked anything like Berkeley's densely populated south campus neighborhood, with its Telegraph Avenue catering to the tastes of college youth.[11]

The Kerr thesis also misses the point that not all veterans of the earlier crisis were part of the 1960's Left. Anti-oath leader Aaron Gordon, for example, stood mostly on the sidelines during 1964–65 out of personal loyalty to his friend the president. Another Kerr friend, the sociologist Seymour Martin Lipset, who in 1950 was adamant that he would not return to Berkeley from a visiting appointment at Columbia as long as he had to sign an oath, was among the most pro-administration of Berkeley's professors during the FSM. In 1964 he also believed that the uprising was destroying the university.

Lipset, along with his close associate Reinhard Bendix, was part of the conservative bloc that subscribed to the "Weimar thesis." Viewing the revolt as a symptom of instability in society, this perspective was favored by a number of refugees from fascism, the same group that had produced the most nonsigners in 1950. To an old socialist like Carl Landauer, Berkeley's student rebellion was out of control, evoking memories of the breakdown of social order in Weimar Germany that paved the way for Hitler. At Senate meetings these conservatives harped upon the Weimar theme, imploring their colleagues to support the administration lest popular fears of revolution would bring the Right to power in California and the United States.[12]

Unlike others who were radicalized by the oath struggle or the unrest of the 1960s, Joe Tussman never wavered in his liberal outlook. Remaining faithful to his mentor Meiklejohn, he spoke out in 1964 against all restrictions on the political activities of students. As chair of the Philosophy Department, he worked hard to find a solution to the crisis. Tussman was also one of the faculty members who got up in the middle of the night to witness the arrest of the students who were sitting in at Sproul Hall on December 1 and 2.

A few days later at the Greek Theater, he broke with Kerr and other chairmen by calling for Savio's immediate release from police custody. And then at the crucial December 8 Senate meeting, it would be Tussman who seconded the motion that led to the resolution of the conflict.

Joe also had good relations with Mario Savio, who spoke publicly for the philosopher's experimental college. And he was close to the Committee of Two Hundred, even though he was not a core member of the group. But while he supported the rebels' goal of free speech, he had mixed feelings about their methods, especially the sit-ins, which he considered "coercive."[13]

With the exception of a few refugees and Kerr's friends, there was a striking consistency between attitudes toward the students' cause and earlier positions on the oath. Although he had retired, Hildebrand was one of the fiercest critics of the student movement, and he also lobbied against efforts for educational reform that followed in its wake, above all the experimental college started by Muscatine.[14] Sproul's old friend grew more conservative with age; in 1972 he would label the then avant-garde practice of organic farming a "superstitious cult."[15]

Jacob Loewenberg had been the oldest nonsigner. Returning to Berkeley for his retirement, he was able to finish several books. But his favorite pastime was sitting in the sun on a bench near his old office. The old iconoclast had been contemptuous of his friend Tolman for "selling out" when the latter accepted an honorary doctorate. But a few years later he didn't refuse a similar honor.[16]

The FSM reconciled Loewenberg to the university. The uprising spoke to his rebellious instincts, and the actions of Kerr and Strong confirmed his anti-administration bias. Then, when the Senate overwhelmingly supported free speech on December 8, 1964, Loewenberg could finally applaud a faculty which had so disappointed him fifteen years earlier.

The FSM signaled a shift in the locus of protest to students from its faculty base during the years of the oath. It also broke down the fears on the part of both students and faculty that had remained from the McCarthy Era.[17] Martin Roysher's insight thus supports the idea that the FSM helped complete the Loyalty Oath's unfinished business.

However none of these theories are satisfactory as an explanation of the student revolt. Each has a kernel of truth, but in every case the impact of the old crisis on the later one was at best marginal. That's because the FSM was sui generis, a reflection of the unique spirit of the 1960s. Since its leaders were committed to racial equality, it can be seen as the critical link between the civil rights and the student movements.[18] And when one compares the two rebellions, the biggest difference lies in the larger political climate. Because the McCarthy Era put such a damper on dissent, the oath did not lead to similar protests on other campuses. But because the 1960s were so open to social change movements, the FSM inspired student revolts on campuses all over the country, indeed throughout the world. But none that followed compared in scope or import, until 1968, the year of Columbia's rebellion and above all the events of May in Paris.

LIKE THE LOYALTY OATH the FSM had ripple effects. Perhaps most important was the core of faculty and student activists it produced. FSM veterans began organizing protests against the Vietnam War almost as soon as the free speech crisis was resolved. Although the campus peace movement was primarily sparked by younger faculty and grad students, two of its most vigorous activists were the former nonsigners Kelley and Muscatine. And at Seattle Gordon Griffiths would devote the remainder of his career to working for peace and other causes.

Student draft resisters counseled by John Kelley would be fortunate if their court cases were heard by Stanley Weigel. The nonsigners' attorney had been appointed a federal judge by Kennedy in 1962. He remained a Republican, but never lost his sympathy for those who challenged authority. While other judges imposed prison sentences on those who refused to serve, Weigel usually recommended probation or community service.[19]

Despite the traditional split between town and gown, both the oath and the FSM helped changed the politics of the city of Berkeley. In 1950 Berkeley was still a conservative small town. Over the next decade and a half, it would begin its transformation into one of the nation's more Left-wing cities. Radicalized by the oath crisis, Jack Kent became part of the new liberal majority in the city council during the late 1960s, only to be replaced by even more Left-leaning representatives. John Kelley and his wife, Ying Lee, would be major figures in the city's antiwar movement during the Vietnam era.

The FSM brought about new leadership for the university administration, first at Berkeley, then statewide. Strong resigned as chancellor in 1965, having taken most of the blame for the administration's failures during the student revolt. Kerr held his job for two more years, but he was gravely wounded by the crisis. Just as Neylan had campaigned to oust Sproul during the first year of the oath, Regent Pauley was determined to get rid of Kerr. But unlike Neylan, who imposed some limits on his behavior, with Pauley it was no holds barred.

With informants on the CIA and the FBI, he had the latter agency feed him confidential information on the political activities of Berkeley faculty, students, and even his fellow regents.[20] The oil magnate was also able to have the university revert to its practice during the McCarthy Era when Sproul asked the FBI to report on the political history of every person offered a faculty position. But after the FSM, which infuriated Pauley, he became obsessed with Kerr. In a letter to the FBI, Pauley called the president "a communist or a communist sympathizer."[21]

In January 1967 Pauley finally succeeded, when the regents voted 14 to 8 to dismiss the president.[22]

IN 1986, SEVENTEEN YEARS BEFORE Clark Kerr would die at the age of ninety-two, the University of California named one of its prime sites for residence halls and athletic facilities the Clark Kerr campus. It took longer for it to recognize the former president's adversary. That had to wait until Mario Savio's death in 1996 at the age of fifty-three. And then in 1997, Sproul Steps, where one man's oratory had nearly brought down a university, became the Savio Steps.[23]

IF THE LOYALTY OATH controversy first identified Berkeley as a center of political resistance, it was the Free Speech Movement which solidified that association in America's cultural imagination. The crisis of the McCarthy Era produced a cadre of faculty activists who fifteen years later were able eventually to convince the overwhelming majority of their less-involved colleagues to support the students' demands for unrestricted political expression.

But the oath's impact was double-edged. It also produced timidity and caution in a university administration made even more fearful of how conservative regents and legislators might react to student activism. An irony is that the administrators, Strong and Kerr, whose rigidity and fearfulness most contributed to the FSM's victory, had been two of Berkeley's most fearless professors for much of the oath crisis. Another is that it took thirty years and one of the most dramatic uprisings in American history to rid the university of the restrictions on student freedoms that had been put in place after the San Francisco General Strike of 1934.

ACKNOWLEDGMENTS

THIS BOOK COULD NOT HAVE BEEN WRITTEN
without the existence of the Bancroft Library of the University of California at Berkeley and its voluminous collections of papers from the participants in the oath crisis. David Farrell, the chief archivist, was especially helpful, but every one of the Bancroft's librarians went out of their way to help me find what I needed.

I also relied heavily on the unpublished manuscripts that are part of the Bancroft's affiliated Regional Oral History Project. These oral histories have been indispensable for my research, and I am especially indebted to ROHO's director, Lisa Rubens, who furnished me with manuscripts to read during the four months in 2005 when the Bancroft was closed for retrofitting.

At UCLA's Charles Edward Young Research Library, special collections archivists Charlotte Brown and Monique S. Leahy were enormously patient with my many requests. They made my trip to Los Angeles pleasant as well as productive.

I am also indebted to Salgu Wissmath for making it possible for me to sit in the office of the *Daily Californian* at Berkeley, where I was able to read back issues of the student paper in their original print editions, saving time as well as my eyes from not having to use the microfilm machine.

I'm grateful to Diane Sprouse and the Committee on Research on the Berkeley campus for funds to pay my research assistant and for much-needed computer equipment. Over the years I have also enjoyed small grants from the COR, which paid for photocopying, books for my research library, and cartridges for my busy printer. I'd like to take this opportunity to also thank the staff of the Department of Sociology at Berkeley, especially Judy Haier and Sue Thur. I am pleased to acknowledge "Baker," a service of the university library that magically delivered the books I needed to my office mailbox, thus saving me hours of trudging around campus.

But most of all, this book could not have been written without the survivors of the oath years who granted me their time, their memories, and their insights. I was fortunate to have completed two interviews with philosopher Joseph Tussman just weeks before he died at age ninety-one in October 2005. With his uncanny recall for the events of fifty-five years earlier, I was hoping that Joe would live until ninety-five or one hundred, or at least until he could critique my manuscript. I am also grateful to a member of the nonsigners group, English professor Charles Muscatine, for granting me my first interview, for pointing out inaccuracies in my manuscript, and for his enthusiastic support of my project.

Thanks also to Mary Tolman Kent, who provided information both on her father Edward Tolman and on her late husband Jack Kent—as well as many other helpful courtesies. Marian Sproul Goodin, the daughter of President Sproul, shared with me her memories of her father, as well as of Regent John Francis Neylan and other important personages.

Since I first met Kenneth Roose in 2005, only days after beginning work on this book, the economist who left UCLA rather than sign the oath has been an unfailing resource. On a dozen occasions he shared his memories of the crisis on the Westwood campus, provided documents attesting to his own role and that of his colleagues, and assured me that my book was worth the effort. I also learned valuable information about the mood at UCLA in the late 1940s and early 1950s from my old teacher and colleague Philip Selznick.

Leon Litwack was kind enough to take time from his busy schedule to talk about his role as a student leader at Berkeley during the oath crisis and to share his memories of the student movement at the time. Clancy Sigal and George Garrigues gave me a greater understanding of student attitudes at UCLA.

David Nasaw shared his knowledge of John Francis Neylan's relations with William Randolph Hearst. Professor David Griffiths of Reed College went out of his way to provide me with a copy of the unpublished manuscript of Gordon Griffiths, as well as his reflections on his father. Robert J. Gordon took time out from busy professional meetings to talk to me about his father, Robert Aaron Gordon. David Tussman kindly provided me with a photo of his father Joseph Tussman, and Nina Fishman verified for me that the young man in another photo was indeed her dad, Leslie Fishman.

Robert Cohen provided trenchant criticisms of the manuscript on two occasions that helped me immeasurably in improving the final product. I am also grateful to the historian for his help with the epilogue on the Free Speech Movement. At various stages of the book's development I benefited from valuable feedback from David Farrell, Tim Beneke, Charles Muscatine, Mary Tolman Kent, Lisa Rubens, Leon Litwack, Joa Suorez, and Joseph Lam Duong. The latter's work as a research assistant was very helpful.

I have greatly appreciated the aid of President of the University Emeritus David Gardner. Even though we disagreed at times in our interpretations of events, Gardner never failed to answer my many questions.

Above all I have been extremely fortunate in having such a great editor as Kate Wahl of the Stanford University Press. In my many years of writing I have never found an editor who has combined such enthusiastic support for my work with such a remarkable critical sense. Her reading of the manuscript at a crucial moment resulted in almost a hundred suggestions for revision, and to my amazement virtually every one of them made sense. She also made good choices in soliciting comments from experts whose reviews were instrumental in strengthening the final versions of the book. Her assistant, Joa Suorez, has also been extremely helpful. And David Horne of Classic Typography did a superb job of copyediting.

Last, but not least, I could not have written this book without the daily support of my wife Karina Epperlein.

REFERENCE MATTER

NOTES

PREFACE

1. James T. Patterson, "The Enemy Within," *Atlantic Monthly* digital edition, October 1998.

2. Clark Kerr, *The Gold and the Blue: A Personal Memoir of the University of California, 1949–1967,* Vol. 2 (Berkeley and Los Angeles: University of California Press, 2003), p. 28. Kerr, who is also the source of the statistics on the number of professors fired, notes that the thirty-eight non-University of California professors who were dismissed came from twenty-five different institutions.

3. The Meiklejohn quote comes from Joseph Tussman, *Philosopher and Educational Innovator,* oral history interviews conducted by Lisa Rubens, Disk 5, November 4, 2004, p. 40, Regional Oral History Office, Bancroft Library, University of California, unedited raw transcript in author's possession.

4. Ellen Schrecker, remarks at the 50th Anniversary Symposium on the Loyalty Oath, University of California, Berkeley, October 1999. An online transcript of her remarks may be found at http:sunsite.berkeley.edu/uchistory/archives—exhibits/loyaltyoath/symposium/program-

5. *Save San Francisco Bay Association 1961–1986,* interviews with Barry Bunshoft, Esther Gulick, Catherine Kerr, and Sylvia McLaughlin, Regional Oral History Office, Bancroft Library, University of California, 1987.

6. Kerr, *The Gold and the Blue,* Vol. 2, pp. 43–44. I say "predominantly white" because student movements at historically black colleges preceded those at Berkeley.

7. For the idea of Berkeley in the cultural imagination, I am indebted to Joseph Lam Duong.

8. Hubert Park Beck, *Men Who Control Our Universities* (Morningside Heights, N.Y.: King's Crown, 1947), p. 77 and table 19, p. 190. The author found that among the fourteen largest state universities, UC had the highest proportion of trustees (30 percent) who held major offices or directorships in one or more of the nation's four hundred largest businesses. His data were from 1934–35, but there is no reason to think that the makeup of the regents was significantly different fifteen years later.

9. Robert Cohen, *When the Old Left Was Young: Student Radicals and America's First Mass Movement, 1929–1941* (New York: Oxford , 1993), pp. 99–105.

10. Hildebrand told David Gardner in 1965 that he had drafted Regulation 5. David P. Gardner, *Papers,* 1949–2005, Series 8, Loyalty Oath Controversy, Research Materials, Carton 13, Folder 7, Bancroft Library, University of California. His role is confirmed by C. Michael Otten, *University Authority and the Student* (Berkeley and Los Angeles: University of California Press, 1970), p. 124.

11. In 1874 Ezra Carr, a professor of chemistry in the School of Agriculture, was dismissed because of policy differences with President Daniel Coit Gilman. However, there was also evidence that Carr lacked competence in his scientific field. See Verne A. Stadtman, *The University of California 1868–1968* (New York: McGraw-Hill, 1970), pp. 76–77.

12. For the Regents' actions in 1940, see David P. Gardner, *The California Oath Controversy (Berkeley, Calif.: University of California Press, 1967), Appendix A;* John Neylan, *Politics, Law, and the University,* oral history interviews conducted by Walton Bean and Corinne Gilb in 1954, Regional Oral History Office, Bancroft Library, University of California, 1961. Both the 1940 policy and the May firing are discussed in Chapter 2.

13. See Chapter 3, note 35, for a portion of the AAUP statement, which appeared in its Spring 1948 *Bulletin.*

14. Norman Reider to Edward Tolman, August 28, 1950, in Gardner, *Papers,* Carton 11, Bancroft Library, University of California.

15. Gardner, *The California Oath Controversy.*

16. Ibid., pp. 244–51.

17. Allen Weinstein and Alexander Vassiliev, *The Haunted Wood: Soviet Espionage in America—the Stalin Era* (New York: Random House, 1999), chapter 3.

18. Martha Dodd, *The Searching Light* (New York: Citadel Press, 1955). That the novel is about Berkeley is apparent from the many similarities in the storyline, and the fact that Joseph Tussman told Lisa Rubens when he was being interviewed for his oral history that he had provided Dodd with the background on the Loyalty Oath when they met in 1950. Tussman, *Philosopher and Educational Innovator,* Disk 5, p. 43.

CHAPTER I

1. Robert M. MacIver, *Academic Freedom in Our Time* (New York: Columbia University Press, 1955), p. 43.

2. Testimony before the State of Illinois Seditious Activities Investigating Committee, April 21, 1949, as quoted in Carey McWilliams, *Witch Hunt: The Revival of Heresy* (Boston: Little, Brown, 1950), p. 224.

3. Clark Kerr, *The Gold and the Blue: A Personal Memoir of the University of California, 1949–1967,* Vol. 2 (Berkeley and Los Angeles: University of California Press, 2003), p. 28.

4. The most thorough discussion of the history of academic freedom in America is Richard Hofstadter and Walter P. Metzger, *The Development of Academic Freedom in the United States* (New York, Columbia University Press, 1955). See also Ellen Schrecker, *No Ivory Tower: McCarthyism and the Universities* (New York, Oxford University Press, 1986), chapter 1.

5. Erich Fromm, *Escape from Freedom* (New York: Holt, Rinehart & Winston, 1941), pp. 32–35.

6. The leading spokesman for this position was the philosopher Sidney Hook, who already during the 1930s was urging university faculties to purge themselves of communists. Schrecker, *No Ivory Tower,* esp. chapter 1.

7. Walter P. Metzger, "Organization, Loyalty, and War," in Hofstadter and Metzger, *Development of Academic Freedom,* pp. 468–506.

8. Alonzo L. Hamby, *Beyond the New Deal: Harry S. Truman and American Liberalism* (New York: Columbia University Press, 1973), chapter 6. The term *fellow traveler* was widely used in mid-century America to refer to a person who was not an actual member of the Communist Party, but who was sympathetic nevertheless to communism.

9. Hannah Arendt, *The Origins of Totalitarianism* (New York: Schocken Books, 1951).

10. Abbott Gleason, *Totalitarianism: The Inner History of the Cold War* (New York: Oxford University Press, 1995), p. 3.

11. Hamby, *Beyond the New Deal,* pp. 104–105.

12. Ibid., p. 115.

13. For Hamby, the historian of the Truman administration, this gave liberalism a moral integrity that was lacking during the years when its emphasis was only antifascism. Hamby, *Beyond the New Deal,* pp. 279–82.

14. Ibid., chapter 10.

15. Haynes Johnson notes that there is a consensus among scholars that it was Truman who instituted "the repressive climate that culminated in the McCarthy era." He specifically cites Executive Order 9835 and the Attorney General's List as the two measures that legitimized anticommunism. Haynes Johnson, *The Age of Anxiety: McCarthyism to Terrorism* (Orlando: Harcourt Brace Jovanovich, 2005), p. 128.

16. Ellen Schrecker, *Many Are the Crimes: McCarthyism in America* (Boston: Little, Brown, 1996), p. 144.

17. Ibid., pp. 220–21.

18. As Howe put it some years later, "The sudden upsurge of McCarthyism was to prove a crucial test for the intellectuals." Irving Howe, "Ideas in Conflict," in Irving Howe, *A Margin of Hope* (San Diego: Harcourt Brace Jovanovich, 1982), pl. 206, as quoted in Johnson, *Age of Anxiety,* pp. 130–31.

19. It was a given that a husband's career took precedent, for a woman's responsibility was to support her man. Erving Goffman, the most eminent professor in Berkeley's Sociology Department during the 1960s and the world's leading scholar on interpersonal interaction, told Arlene Kaplan Daniels when she was a married graduate student that "You're not really a professional. You're only a housewife looking for pin money." Arlene Kaplan Daniels, "When We Were All Boys Together: Graduate School in the Fifties and Beyond," in Kathryn P. Meadow Orlans and Ruth A. Wallace, *Gender and the Academic Experience;*

(Lincoln: University of Nebraska Press, 1994), p. 33. This volume documents the oppressive atmosphere in the Sociology Department at Berkeley for women grad students during the 1950s and 1960s, a department one would expect to be relatively egalitarian. It's possible that the situation was even worse for women during the 1950s and 1960s because of the backlash against the breakthroughs that they had made as a result of the manpower short-ages in World War II. After World War I, women in the academic world were so few in numbers that they could be patronized as novelties.

20. Kenneth Starr, *Inventing the Dream: California in the Progressive Era* (New York: Oxford University Press, 1985), p. 274ff.

21. George R. Stewart et al., *The Year of the Oath: The Fight for Academic Freedom at the University of California* (New York: Doubleday, 1950), pp. 108–116. Among the many anachronisms Stewart cites is the reservation of an ex officio position for the director of San Francisco's Mechanics Institute. In 1868 it was an important organization, with the largest library in the area, but by 1950 it was noted primarily for the world-class chess tournaments it sponsored. Stewart also argued that it made sense to mandate a representative for Cali-fornia's farmers at one time, but by the middle of the 20th century, organized labor, science, and medicine had become even more deserving of seats on the board.

22. The philanthropist and benefactor of the university, Phoebe Apperson Hearst (mother of William Randolph), had served from 1899 until her death in 1919, and two other women had followed her.

23. Stadtman, *The University of California,* p. 36, and note 1, p. 535.

24. Walter Heller, the board's most liberal member, was the grandson of a pioneering San Francisco merchant who had left Germany in 1850, when many German Jews were in-fluenced by the revolutionary spirit of the "Forty-Eighters." Heller was also the nephew of the most senior Jewish regent, Sidney Ehrman, who was conservative but was still consid-ered pro-faculty. The final "Jewish seat" was occupied by Mortimer Fleishacker until he re-signed in March 1950 and was replaced by another German Jew, Jesse Steinhart.

25. According to G. William Domhoff, author of *The Bohemian Grove and Other Re-treats* (New York: Harper and Row, 1974), there had been German Jewish members of the Bohemian Club in the late 19th and early 20th centuries. However, long before 1950, a tacit "gentleman's agreement" served to keep Jews out. This exclusionary policy would be re-versed in the 1970s. Author's phone conversation with Bill Domhoff, October 7, 2007.

26. Kenneth Starr, *Embattled Dreams: California in War and Peace, 1940–1950* (New York, Oxford University Press, 2002), pp. 315–16.

27. During the first year of the crisis, regents based in the San Francisco Bay Area voted for the Academic Senate's position by a ratio of 3 to 1, while those from the Los An-geles region opposed the faculty by a ratio of 4 to 1. See Stewart, *The Year of the Oath,* p. 54.

28. Neylan was so worried about Warren's appointments—and potential appoint-ments—that he accused him of plotting to "pack" the Board of Regents just as Roosevelt had attempted to "pack" the Supreme Court with jurists favorable to his policies during the 1930s.

29. Richard Hofstadter, *The Paranoid Style in American Politics and Other Essays* (New York: Alfred A. Knopf, 1965), p. 31.

30. Daniel Bell, ed., *The New American Right* (Garden City, N.Y.: Doubleday, 1964), an update of the original edition, which appeared in 1955.

31. Michael P. Rogin, *The Intellectuals and McCarthy: The Radical Specter* (Cambridge, Mass.: The M.I.T. Press, 1967). Curiously, Rogin did not cite his fellow Berkeley political scientist Nelson Polsby, who had convincingly deflated the populist interpretation of McCarthyism seven years earlier. In this 1960 article, as well as in a later one in the 1980s, Polsby adds an additional cause of the phenomenon: the political climate of the times. He used public opinion data to undermine the Hofstadter-Bell thesis and to argue, like Rogin, that McCarthy was a creature of the Republican Party leadership, which used him for its own purposes against Truman and the Democrats. For me, Polsby's most interesting finding was that the demagogue's support among the American people was much weaker than commonly believed. But the Republican elites capitalized on the misperception of the Wisconsin Senator's power in order to narrow the confines of the political debate. See Nelson Polsby, "Toward an Explanation of McCarthyism," *Political Studies* VIII, no. 3 (1960): pp. 250–271; and "Down Memory Lane with Joe McCarthy," *Commentary* 75, no. 2 (February, 1983): pp. 55–59.

CHAPTER 2

1. John Caughey, *In Clear and Present Danger: The Crucial State of Our Freedoms* (Chicago: University of Chicago Press, 1958), p. 28.

2. Wheeler served as president from 1899 to 1919. In the decade before he arrived, the institution was transformed from a small college of four hundred students to a mid-sized university with almost five times that number attending. C. Michael Otten, *University Authority and the Student* (Berkeley and Los Angeles: University of California Press, 1970), p. 40. Berkeley's faculty more than tripled in number during his tenure, an indication of his role in creating a world-class university. John Aubrey Douglass, *The California Idea and Higher Education* (Stanford, Calif.: Stanford University Press, 2000), p. 122.

3. Douglass, *The California Idea and Higher Education,* pp. 102ff.

4. Agnes Roddy Robb, *Robert Gordon Sproul and the University of California,* interviews conducted by Harriet Nathan, 1996, pp. 40–41, Regional Oral History Office, Bancroft Library, University of California. The president's long-time personal secretary stated that "Mr. Sproul was ahead of the Women's Lib Movement."

5. Robert Nisbet recalled that she was also known as having been a "stunning beauty." Robert Nisbet, *Teachers and Scholars: A Memoir of Berkeley in Depression and War* (New Brunswick, N.J., Transaction, 1992), p. 67.

6. "Emily Huntington," Academic Senate, University of California, *In Memoriam,* 1971, University of California Digital Archives.

7. Nisbet, *Teachers and Scholars,* pp. 68–70.

8. For her insights on the relation between anti-Semitism in San Francisco and the Berkeley campus, I'm indebted to Marian Sproul Goodin. Author's interview, October 26, 2005. Tape in my possession.

9. Nisbet, *Teachers and Scholars,* p. 67, specifically mentions Benjamin Kurz, Benjamin Lehman, and James Hart. Historians often had similar biases to those of literary scholars.

Leon Litwack has informed me that anti-Semitism was rife in Berkeley's History Department through the 1950s, the legacy of Herbert Bolton's prejudices.

10. Barrows would publish a history of the Philippines based on his tenure as head of the school system in Manila and his service as director of the Bureau of Non-Christian tribes. He also wrote a work of anthropology based on his travels in Africa, *Berbers and Blacks: Impressions of Morocco, Timbuktu and the Western Sudan* (London: Century, 1927).

11. David Barrows, *Memoirs,* Bancroft Library, University of California, pp. 142ff.

12. University of California, *In Memoriam,* "David Barrows," April 1958.

13. David P. Barrows, "Are Berkeley Socialists Bolshevists? A Reply to an Invitation of the Berkeley Local Socialist Party of California to Renew the Debate on the Revolutionary Soviet Government, 1919, and the correspondence between Barrows and the Socialist Party in Barrows," *David P. Barrows Papers,* Bancroft Library, University of California.

14. For the dispute about Wheeler's pro-German stance and the "ardent neutralist" characterization, see Stadtman, *The University of California,* esp. chapter 7. Wheeler is defended by Joel Hildebrand, as well as by Robert Nisbet. See Joel Hildebrand, *Chemistry, Education, and the University of California,* interview conducted by Edna Tartaul Daniel, 1962, p. 131, Regional Cultural History Project, Bancroft Library, University of California; and Nisbet, *Teachers and Scholars,* pp. 189–190. On the other hand, philosophy professor George Adams is clear that the president was pro-German. George P. Adams, *Correspondence and Papers, 1950–1960,* oral history interview, Box 2, Centennial History Project of the University of California, Bancroft Library. Perhaps the most balanced account appears in Barrows, *Memoirs,* p. 149.

15. It is striking that no one has commented that this was UC's first loyalty oath. Stadtman, *The University of California,* p. 195.

16. The special status of Berkeley's Academic Senate is mentioned by Nisbet, *Teachers and Scholars,* p. 49, as well as by two professors who were teaching at the time. See Stephen C. Pepper, *Art and Philosophy at the University of California 1919 to 1962,* interview conducted by Suzanne B. Riess, 1963, pp. 93–94, Regional Cultural History Project; and William R. Dennes, *Philosophy and the University Since 1915,* interview conducted by Joann Dietz Ariff, Regional Oral History Office, Bancroft Library, University of California.

17. Dennes, *Philosophy and the University,* p. 36. Verne Stadtman, a historian of the University of California, stresses Barrows's "high-handed" manner and problems with the faculty. Stadtman, *The University of California,* pp. 246 ff. But philosophy professor Jacob Loewenberg has written how pleasantly surprised he was at how scrupulously Barrows adhered to the democratic norms of the academic community. Loewenberg provides one of the best retrospective accounts of the Faculty Revolution in which he participated. See his *A Faculty Revolution and Reminiscences, May 12, 1967,* manuscript in The Centennial History Project, Box 3, Bancroft Library, University of California.

18. James A. C. Grant, *Comparative Constitutional Law at UCLA,* interviews conducted by Steven J. Novak, 1989, Oral History Program, UCLA. Available at both the Bancroft and Young libraries, University of California.

19. In this period Edward Dickson was the only board member from Southern California.

20. Kerr, *The Gold and the Blue,* Vol. 1, pp. 157–58.

21. Douglass, *The California Idea,* p. 141.

22. Kerr, *The Gold and the Blue,* Vol. 1, p. 330.

23. George Garrigues, *Loud Bark and Curious Eyes: A History of the UCLA Daily Bruin, 1919–1955,* Internet Edition, 2001.

24. Dean E. McHenry, *Childhood, Education, and Teaching Career,* oral history interviews conducted by Elizabeth Spedding Calciano, Vol. 1, 1972, pp. 87–88, University of California, Santa Cruz.

25. According to his assistant George Pettitt, Sproul spent much of his time flying back and forth from Berkeley to Los Angeles. George Pettitt, *Twenty-Eight Years in the Life of a University President* (Berkeley and Los Angeles: University of California Press, 1966), p. 34.

26. For the "too Rotarian" criticism, see Robb, *Robert Gordon Sproul,* p. 10. The faculty's distrust of Sproul is confirmed by George P. Adams, as well as Ben Lehman, who adds that many were concerned that he was not an intellectual. See George P. Adams, *Correspondence and Papers,* oral history interviews of June 11, 1956, in University of California Centennial History Office; and Benjamin Lehman, *Recollections and Reminiscences of Life in the Bay Area from 1920 Onward,* interview conducted by Suzanne B. Riess, 1969, p. 279, Regional Oral History Office, both at the Bancroft Library, University of California.

27. Roger W. Lotchin, "John Francis Neylan: San Francisco Irish Progressive," in *The San Francisco Irish—1850–1976,* ed. James P. Walsh (San Francisco: Irish Literary Society, 1978), p. 91. For the background material on Neylan I am indebted primarily to Lotchin and to Neylan's own oral history, *Law, Politics, and the the University of California,* interviews conducted by Walton Bean and Corrinne Gilb, Regional Oral History Office, Bancroft Library, University of California.

28. Lotchin, "John Francis Neylan," pp. 91ff; and Neylan, *Law, Politics, and the University of California,* pp. 91ff.

29. Lotchin, "John Francis Neylan," pp. 91ff.

30. Lehman, *Recollections,* p. 262.

31. Barrows, *Memoirs,* pp. 222ff. Barrows also glossed over the fact that California's Communist Party had advised its members in the union to vote against a general strike, believing that it was premature. Nisbet, *Teachers and Scholars,* p. 51.

32. As Kevin Starr writes, "The bound volumes of the Bay Area newspapers published in mid-July 1934 reveal today just how blatantly the publishers and editors followed Neylan's suggestion. San Francisco is depicted as a city on the verge of armed insurrection." Kevin Starr, *Endangered Dreams: The Great Depression in California* (New York: Oxford University Press, 1996), p. 115. In a telegram to Hearst, who had urged him to act, Neylan boasted that he had broken the strike more totally than the British government had done with its general strike in 1926.

33. The most important provision was an end to the "shapeup," the corrupt practice by which workers were given jobs. It was replaced by joint labor-management control of the hiring halls. It wasn't a complete victory for the rebels, because Bridges had wanted total control of hiring. Neither did he win all the wage increases the union had sought. But the union, which would secede from the East Coast–based International Longshoreman's Association to form the new International Longshoremen's and Warehouse Union (ILWU) did get the acceptance of coastwide labor standards and the six-hour day. Starr, *Endangered Dreams.*

34. Robert Cohen, *When the Old Left Was Young: Student Radicals and America's First Mass Movement, 1929–1941* (New York: Oxford , 1993), pp. 100–101. There was a precedent for such spying in the university's history. After the Red Scare of 1919–1920, the Board of Regents, in cooperation with the American Legion, had set up a network of student spies on the Berkeley campus. Otten, *University Authority and the Student,* p. 103.

35. Cohen, *When the Old Left Was Young,* p. 101.

36. Interview of Joel Hildebrand, Centennial History Project, University of California, June 22, 1965. Hildebrand had become concerned about communism at the University of California in the early 1930s. By 1933 he had begun clipping articles from the newspapers about the threat of subversion at Berkeley and UCLA. After the 1934 strike, Harry Bridges became his personal *bete noire,* as the radical union leader would be for so many others. What particularly galled Hildebrand were student groups who wanted to invite Bridges to the campus to talk about world peace. The chemist, who did not shrink from expressing his own views on politics and other fields outside his professional domain, felt that Bridges *might* have something to say about the labor movement, but certainly not on world affairs.

37. "I was the one who drafted Regulation 5," recalled Hildebrand when he was interviewed by David Gardner on June 22, 1965. David P. Gardner, *Papers, 1949–2005,* Series 8, Loyalty Oath Controversy Research Materials, Carton 13, Folder 7, Bancroft Library, University of California. The chemist's role is confirmed by Otten, *University Authority and the Student,* p. 124. The latter's discussion of Regulation 5 is the most comprehensive I've seen.

38. To me, this language seems more appropriate for a university official in Mussolini's Italy or Hitler's Germany than at the University of California in 1934. *Records of the Northern Section of the Academic Senate,* Box 16, Bancroft Library, University of California. Although Sproul was against totalitarianism, his capitalization of *State* in the memorandum makes one wonder whether his astuteness in local and national politics extended to the international level.

39. Otten, *University Authority and the Student,* pp. 120–25. Regulation 5 was revised in 1944 by Sproul without any substantive changes. It was not until 2003 that President Richard Atkinson issued a version whose language reflects more modern understandings of the relationship between values and scholarship. In the present version it is acknowledged that it may be appropriate for professors to be motivated by deeply felt beliefs. The language about using the classroom to convert has been eliminated, as well as the unfortunate wording about the university being the creature of the state. See the letter of Berkeley law professor Robert Post to Richard Atkinson, March 12, 2003. Post drafted the revision for President Atkinson. Records of the Academic Senate of the University of California, Northern Section.

40. Robert G. Sproul, "Problems of an American University," *School and Society* (May 30, 1936): pp. 723–24, as cited in Cohen, *When the Old Left Was Young,* pp. 104ff.

41. Ibid. p. 119.

42. Ibid.

43. Ibid. Otten, *University Authority and the Student,* p. 110, notes that it was the communist-led National Student League that had proposed the debate. Partisan motivations may have also been behind Moore's decision, for the provost was a member of the Central Committee of the Republican Party in Los Angeles.

44. Cohen, *When the Old Left Was Young,* p. 120.

45. Ibid. p. 118. Like many men of the Far Right, Moore had difficulty distinguishing between liberals and communists. The economist Paul Dodd, who later would become UCLA's powerful dean of letters and sciences, recalls the provost's fear of "liberal tendencies" and how every time they met on campus, Moore would discourse on how communist students were ruining UCLA's reputation. Paul A. Dodd, *Patient Persuader,* interviews conducted by Thomas Bertonneau, UCLA Oral History Program, 1985, p. 13, Bancroft Library, University of California.

46. Otten, *University Authority and the Student,* pp. 110–11.

47. Stadtman, *The University of California,* p. 272.

48. Cohen, *When the Old Left Was Young,* pp. 203–204.

49. Sproul's son said that in the 1930s the *San Francisco Examiner* was trying to get rid of his father, thinking that he was "too easy on all these left-wingers." Robert Gordon Sproul Jr., *The Robert Gordon Sproul Oral History Project,* interviews conducted by Suzanne B. Riess, 1984–1985, Vol. 1, p. 166, Bancroft Library, University of California.

50. No one, including Clark Kerr, a keen observer of both Sproul and Neylan, has been able to explain what caused the falling out. Kerr did state that the bad blood between the two former friends was the single most important cause of the oath crisis. Kerr, in the *Robert Gordon Sproul Oral History Project,* Vol. 2, p. 611.

51. Gordon Griffiths, *Venturing Outside the Ivory Tower: A Political Autobiography,* unpublished manuscript, Version 1, 2002, pp. 7–8, available from The Library of Congress. The memoir exists in two forms. Version 1 is a typescript that includes the names of Berkeley's secret communists (including J. Robert Oppenheimer), and Version 2 is a longer, more polished computer version that describes the club but omits the names of its members. Oppenheimer was long suspected of being a communist, and in the McCarthy Era he would lose his security clearance because of his past affiliations and activities. The memoir by Griffiths comes the closest to providing hard evidence for Oppenheimer's Communist Party membership, but as I elaborate further on in the text of this chapter, it falls short of being conclusive. Ibid., Version 1, pp. 25–28. It may be of interest that the Russian "handlers" of Soviet espionage agents in the United States were clear that the physicist was a party member. Allen Weinstein and Alexander Vassiliev, *The Haunted Wood: Soviet Espionage in America—the Stalin Era* (New York: Random House, 1999), pp. 183–85.

52. Charles V. Jones, Philip C. Enros, and Henry S. Tropp, "Kenneth O. May 1915–1997," *Historica Mathematica* II, no. 4 (November 1984): pp. 359–79.

53. The elder Griffiths would become the club's president in 1939.

54. Griffiths, *Venturing Outside the Ivory Tower,* pp.7–8, Version 1.

55. The account of Griffiths' return to the United States, and his role as a conduit to the secret cell, is taken from *Venturing Outside the Ivory Tower.*

56. Kai Bird and Martin J. Sherwin, *American Prometheus: The Triumph and Tragedy of J. Robert Oppenheimer* (New York: Alfred A. Knopf, 2005), pp. 135–37.

57. The Soviet Union was the only nation that provided money and arms to the Republic.

58. Barrows, *Memoirs,* p. 227.

59. Lawrence was a close friend of Neylan, who used his clout on the Board of Regents to help raise money for the physicist's projects, including his pioneering cyclotron. Bird and Sherwin, *American Prometheus,* pp. 126–27.

60. Gregg Herken, *The Brotherhood of the Bomb: The Tangled Lives and Loyalties of Robert Oppenheimer, Ernest Lawrence, and Edward Teller* (New York: Henry Holt, First Owl Books Edition, 2003), pp. 31–32. The basis for Herken's statement that it was Oppenheimer who wrote these broadsides (both of which can be found at Berkeley's Bancroft Library) is an interview in 2000 with his then graduate student, the physicist Phillip Morrison, as well as letters to Oppenheimer from Haakon Chevalier.

61. Otten, *University Authority and the Student*, pp. 127–31.

62. "Minutes of the Board of Regents," University of California, October 11, 1940, in Gardner, *Papers*, Carton 9.

63. In firing May, Berkeley's Math Department was disciplining the most brilliant student it had ever seen, as much a prodigy in his field as Oppenheimer and Lawrence were in physics. And after a long interlude as a Communist Party functionary, he would go on to become one of the 20th century's most innovative American mathematicians. See Jones, Enros, and Tropp, "Kenneth O. May."

64. Although he kept this information from his fellow regents, Neylan's empathy for the graduate student may have been related to the fact that his two daughters had been close friends with May (and another Red, Stanley Moore), while undergraduates at Cal. Neylan, *Politics, Law, and the University, of California*, oral history interviews conducted by Walton Bean and Corrine Gilb, draft manuscript, in Gardner, *Papers*, Carton 13, Folder 7, pp. 235–37.

65. Gardner, *The California Oath Controversy (Berkeley, Calif.: University of California Press, 1967)*, Appendix A.

66. In 1999 at the 50th Anniversary of the Loyalty Oath Symposium, a Berkeley professor emeritus of biochemistry, Howard Schachman, also made this observation.

At UCLA during this period it was Southern California's Right-wing press and public opinion that enforced conformity. In 1940 Bertrand Russell, notorious as an advocate of sexual liberation, was teaching on the Westwood campus; calls for his ouster escalated until he resigned. *The Hartford Sentinel*, April 30, 1940, reported that a suit was filed in Los Angeles to force Russell's removal from UCLA. In addition, the Supreme Court of the State of New York intervened to stop his appointment at the City College of New York. Only too happy to see him leave UCLA, Robert Gordon Sproul joined such luminaries as Albert Einstein, John Dewey, and Robert Hutchins in a protest against the interference of the judiciary in university affairs. File of clippings collected by Joel Hildebrand for the University of California Centennial, in Centennial History Project, *Correspondence and Papers*, Box 4. After the CCNY position fell through, the philosopher wanted to return to UCLA, but Sproul blocked his reappointment.

CHAPTER 3

1. Haynes Johnson, *The Age of Anxiety: McCarthyism to Terrorism* (Orlando: Harcourt Brace Jovanovich, 2005), p. 128.

2. David P. Gardner, *The California Oath Controversy (Berkeley, Calif.: University of California Press, 1967)*, p. 281, note 13.

3. Robert Nisbet, *Teachers and Scholars: A Memoir of Berkeley in Depression and War* (New Brunswick, N.J.: Transaction, 1992), p. 200.

4. Ibid., pp. 198–199.

5. Gordon Griffiths, *Venturing Outside the Ivory Tower: A Political Autobiography*, unpublished manuscript, Version 1, 2002, p. 27, available from The Library of Congress. The historian recalls that Senator Truman predicted that "the Germans would slice through the Russians like a knife through butter."

6. Ibid., pp. 29–30.

7. Ibid., p. 33, Version 1.

8. Author's interview with Marian Sproul Goodin, the daughter of President Sproul, October 25, 2005. Tape in my possession.

9. George Garrigues, *Loud Bark and Curious Eyes: A History of the UCLA Daily Bruin, 1919–1955*, Internet edition, 2001, chapter 8.

10. I owe the insight about Neylan's Pacific realm orientation to David Nasaw, the biographer of William Randolph Hearst. David Nasaw, e-mail to the author, September 14, 2005. The Hearst press had popularized the "Yellow Peril" shibboleth, the idea that gained currency at the turn of the century, that white America was being inundated by Chinese and Japanese immigrants.

11. John Neylan to Robert Sproul, May 1, 1945, John Francis Neylan, *Papers*, Box 157, Folder 12, Bancroft Library, University of California.

12. No one has been able to explain why one of Sproul's best friends and a close ally would become his worst enemy. But a Berkeley philosophy professor has mentioned another event that soured the regent on the president. Stephen Pepper learned from a controller in the business office that Sproul had deceived the Board of Regents concerning the existence of funds that were under his control, and that had infuriated Neylan. Stephen C. Pepper, *Art and Philosophy at the University of California, 1919 to 1962*, interview conducted by Suzanne B. Riess, 1963, p. 264, Regional Cultural History Project.

13. Gregg Herken, *The Brotherhood of the Bomb: The Tangled Lives and Loyalties of Robert Oppenheimer, Ernest Lawrence, and Edward Teller* (New York: Henry Holt, 2002), p. 371.

14. In an influential book, *Fear, War, and the Bomb: Military and Political Consequences of Atomic Energy*, published in 1948, P. M. Blackett wrote that since the Japanese were virtually defeated by August 1945, "The atomic bombings were not so much the last military act of the Second World War as the first major operation of the cold diplomatic war with Russia now in progress." Pages 139–40 in the 1949 American edition of the original British publication, as cited in Kai Bird and Martin J. Sherwin, *American Prometheus: The Triumph and Tragedy of J. Robert Oppenheimer* (New York: Alfred A. Knopf, 2005), p. 389 and note, p. 657.

15. Allen Weinstein and Alexander Vassiliev, *The Haunted Wood: Soviet Espionage in America—the Stalin Era* (New York: Random House, 1999), pp. 300ff.

16. Griffiths, *Venturing Outside the Ivory Tower*, Version 2, pp. 48–56. Griffiths never explicitly states when or why he quit the party. In their preface to his memoir, his children say it was in the mid-1940s. They also note that he remained a Marxist and a progressive activist all his life.

17. Johnson, *The Age of Anxiety*, p. 73.

18. Tony Judt, *Postwar: A History of Europe Since 1945* (New York: Penguin Press, 2005), p. 127.

19. Ellen Schrecker, *Many Are the Crimes: McCarthyism in America* (Boston: Little, Brown, 1996), chapter 8. A more positive view of the loyalty board's procedures comes from J.A.C. Grant, a UCLA political science professor. Grant, who served on the board's western district, said that many of its members were University of California professors. Aware of the lack of due process in the loyalty board's operations, they worked to improve its fairness and "cleared a lot of people" who had been wrongfully charged. James A. C. Grant, *Comparative Constitutional Law at UCLA,* interviews conducted by Steven J. Novak, 1989, Oral History Program, UCLA, Bancroft Library, University of California.

20. Alonzo L. Hamby, *Beyond the New Deal: Harry S. Truman and American Liberalism* (New York: Columbia University Press, 1973), pp. 387–388.

21. According to Jno. U. Calkins, who was the Board of Regents' attorney in 1949, Joel Hildebrand utilized the wording in this noncommunist oath as a model for California's Loyalty Oath. Jno. U. Calkins to David Gardner, May 26, 1965, in David P. Gardner, *Papers,* 1949–2005, Series 8, Loyalty Oath Controversy, Research Materials, Carton 12.

22. David Caute, *The Great Fear: The Anti-Communist Purge Under Truman and Eisenhower (New York: Simon & Schuster, 1978),* pp. 341–42.

23. For a discussion of the 1948 war scare, see Richard M. Freeland, *The Truman Doctrine and the Origins of McCarthyism: Foreign Policy, Domestic Policy, and Internal Security, 1946–48 (New York: New York University Press, 1985), pp. 277–280.*

24. The screenwriters and producers who became known as the "Hollywood Ten" after they were indicted for contempt of court and blacklisted from the industry took another tack. They invoked the First Amendment's guarantee of freedom of speech to justify their refusal to talk about their political associations and to name those of others. This led to their being charged with contempt of court, convicted, and sent to prison.

25. Noam Chomsky, "The Cold War and the Transformation of the Academy," in R. C. Lewontin, ed., *The Cold War and the University* (New York: New Press, 1997), p. 29.

26. Six years earlier, investigations of CCNY and Brooklyn College by the Rapp-Coudet Committee of New York's state legislature had led to the firing of twenty faculty members and the resignations of eleven more who had been accused of being communists. Ellen Schrecker, *No Ivory Tower: McCarthyism and the Universities* (New York, Oxford University Press, 1986), pp. 75–83.

27. Carey McWilliams, *Witch Hunt: The Revival of Heresy* (Boston: Little, Brown, 1950), pp. 219–21.

28. Clarence Dykstra to Robert Sproul, February 23, 1949, Gardner, *Papers,* Carton 9.

29. Notes on the University of Washington's 50th Anniversary Commemoration of the 1948 firings. Internet article; available at www.washington.edu/newsroom/news/1998archives.

30. McWilliams, *Witch Hunt,* pp. 216–17.

31. Gardner, *The California Oath Controversy,* pp. 11–13.

32. Harold Bergstein, "UC Professor Defends Phillips' Stand," *Daily Californian,* March 4, 1949, p. 4.

33. Edward W. Strong, *Philosopher, Professor, and Berkeley Chancellor 1961–1965,* interviews conducted by Harriet Nathan, 1992, p. 116, Regional Oral History Office, Bancroft Library, University of California. Strong found himself on the FBI's blacklist after subscribing for a year to the West Coast Communist daily, *People's World.* In his oral history he

explains that he did so in order to help a down-and-out friend who was selling "P.W." to get back on his feet. Ibid., pp. 154–55.

34. Nisbet, *Teachers and Scholars*, pp. 134–35. See also Strong, *Philosopher*, pp. 41–45.

35. "If a teacher, as an individual, should advocate the forcible overthrow of the government or should incite others to do so, if he should use his classes as a forum for communism, or otherwise abuse his relationship with his students for that purpose; if his thinking should show more than normal bias or be so uncritical as to evidence professional unfitness, these are the charges that should be brought against him. If these charges should be established by evidence adduced at a hearing, the teacher should be dismissed because of his acts of disloyalty or because of professional unfitness, and not because he is a Communist. *So long as the Communist Party in the United States is a legal political party, affiliation with that party in and of itself should not be regarded as a justifiable reason for exclusion from the academic profession.*" The entire statement appeared in the spring 1948 issue of the *AAUP Bulletin*. The emphasis is mine.

36. Edward Strong to Joel Hildebrand, March 7, 1949, in Joel Hildebrand, *Papers*, "Year of the Oath" file, Box 1, Bancroft Library, University of California.

37. Ibid.

38. James Caldwell to Joel Hildebrand, January 26, 1949, Hildebrand, *Papers*.

39. Joel Hildebrand to James Caldwell, February 9, 1949, Hildebrand, *Papers*.

40. The editorial board of the *Spectator*, which was published at Stanford, included two Berkeley liberals, George Stewart of English and Dixon Wecter of History, as well as California's finest novelist, Wallace Stegner, then teaching at Stanford. The same issue that published Hildebrand's essay included an article by Carey McWilliams, the editor of the *Nation* and America's foremost liberal spokesman.

41. Joel Hildebrand, "The Communist Party and the Academic Profession, *Pacific Spectator* (Spring 1949).

42. Hildebrand's essay is not cited in any of the books on the Loyalty Oath, nor in any of the magazine articles written about the crisis. This is an indication of how his role has been underestimated.

43. Joel Hildebrand to Robert Sproul, March 18, 1949, in Hildebrand, *Papers*, "Year of the Oath" file.

44. See, for example, John Francis Neylan, "Loyalty Oaths and Academic Freedom," Address to the Commonwealth Club, San Francisco, California, November 23, 1951, Bancroft Library, University of California.

45. Lawrence J. Friedman, *Identity's Architect: A Biography of Erik Erikson* (New York: Scribners, 1999), p. 244.

46. Joel Hildebrand to Dean A. R. Davis, College of Letters and Sciences, January 26, 1949, in Hildebrand, *Papers*, Box 1, Bancroft Library, University of California.

47. Tolman had met with Sigmund Freud during a visit to Vienna in 1932. However, on his return he chose a Jungian for his therapist, having found Freudianism too intimidating.

CHAPTER 4

1. Kenneth Roose to Sally Thomas, University of California Digital History Project, June 1, 2005, copy of e-mail in author's possession, p. 5.

2. "Minutes of the Board of Regents," University of California, March 25, 1949, Executive Session. Transcript in David P. Gardner, *Papers,* 1949–2005, Series 8, Loyalty Oath Controversy, Research Materials, Carton 9, Bancroft Library, University of California.

3. Kenneth Macgowan to R. B. Shipley (Head of State Department's Passport Division), May 25, 1955, in Kenneth Macgowan, *Papers,* Loyalty Oath folder, File 3, Correspondence on U.S. State.

4. R. E. Combs, Chief Counsel of California's State Senate Committee on Un-American Activities, to R. L. Frick, October 12, 1948, in Macgowan, *Papers,* Folder 1, Correspondence re: University of California Loyalty Oath, 1949–1951.

5. David Caute, *The Great Fear: The Anti-Communist Purge Under Truman and Eisenhower* (New York: Simon & Schuster, 1978), pp. 341–42.

6. Carey McWilliams, *Honorable in All Things: Memoirs of Carey McWilliams,* interviews conducted by Joel Gardner, p. 208, Charles Young Research Library, Special Collections, UCLA.

7. Caute, *The Great Fear,* and David P. Gardner, *The California Oath Controversy (Berkeley, Calif.: University of California Press, 1967),* p. 9.

8. Gardner, *The California Oath Controversy,* p. 9.

9. McWilliams, *Honorable in All Things,* p. 210.

10. Edward L. Barrett Jr., *The Tenney Committee: Legislative Investigation of Subversive Activities in California* (Ithaca, N.Y.: Cornell University Press, 1951), pp. 121–22.

11. Ibid., pp. 138–39.

12. Kenneth Macgowan to R. L. Frick, October 12, 1949, in Macgowan, *Papers.*

13. The sixty-two-year-old Dykstra had wanted to retire in Southern California, where he had established roots. Dean E. McHenry, *Childhood, Education, and Teaching Career,* oral history interviews by Elizabeth Spedding Calciano, Vol. 1, 1972, pp. 316–22, University of California, Santa Cruz, available at Bancroft Library.

14. Paul A. Dodd, *Patient Persuader,* interviews conducted by Thomas Bertonneau, 1985, p. 170, UCLA Oral History Program, available at Bancroft Library.

15. Upton Close, "Closer-Ups," *Newsletter of Upton Close,* Vol. 1, No. 2, December 10, 1945, UCLA University Archives Record Series No. 359, Chancellor's Office, Administrative Files, 1939–1959, Box 207, Charles Young Research Library.

16. McHenry, *Childhood,* p. 343. Other members of the organizing committee were Carey McWilliams, the Left-liberal editor of the *Nation,* and UCLA anthropologist Harry Hoijer.

17. Edward L. Barrett Jr., *The Tenney Committee: Legislative Investigation of Subversive Activities in California* (Ithaca, N.Y.: Cornell University Press, 1951), pp. 119–21.

18. McHenry, *Childhood,* p. 348. However, after Clark Kerr became president of the University of California he named his friend McHenry the first chancellor of the new Santa Cruz campus in 1965.

19. *Los Angeles Times,* February 21, 1946, Centennial History Project, clippings in Joel Hildebrand's files.

20. In addition to McHenry, six professors were identified, including two anthropologists: Harry Hoijer and Ralph Beals; the sociologist Leonard Bloom (who later changed his name to Broom); the psychologists Franklin Fearing and Howard Gilhausen, and the soil scientist David Appleman. *West Los Angeles Independent,* June 20, 1947.

21. *The Santa Monican,* June 27, 1947.

22. Kevin Starr, *Endangered Dreams: The Great Depression in California* (New York: Oxford University Press, 1996), p. 325.

23. *Los Angeles Times,* April 3, 1948, clippings from the Hildebrand files of the Centennial History Project, Bancroft Library, University of California.

24. Ibid. In one of his most famous speeches, Franklin Roosevelt had spoken of four freedoms that he considered to be the birthright of all people in the world. They were the freedom of speech, the freedom of religion, freedom from want, and freedom from fear.

25. However, three East Bay cities, Oakland, Richmond, and the then conservative town of Berkeley, did follow L.A.'s example in 1950.

26. James A. C. Grant, *Comparative Constitutional Law at UCLA,* interviews conducted by Steven J. Novak, 1989, p. 255, Oral History Program, UCLA, Bancroft Library, University of California.

27. Caute, *The Great Fear,* p. 429.

28. Harvard's record during the McCarthy Era was not without blemishes. At first its president, James B. Conant, much like Chicago's Hutchins, vigorously spoke out against the anticommunist hysteria. But then, unlike the Chicago chancellor, he accepted the idea of eliminating the fellowships and teaching jobs of graduate students who were accused of subversion. He did, however, hold the line against HUAC, insisting that Harvard professors would be judged only as scholars and not for their political views. Laura Nader, "The Impact of the Cold War on Anthropology," in R. C. Lewontin, ed., *The Cold War and the University* (New York: New Press, 1997), pp. 110ff.

29. McHenry, *Childhood,* p. 336.

30. Gardner, *The California Oath Controversy,* pp. 14–16.

31. Benson had been personally recommended by Washington's President Raymond Allen.

32. McHenry, *Childhood,* p. 335.

33. "Report on Forum," a three-page letter in the form of a memorandum from Clarence Dykstra to Robert Gordon Sproul, February 23, 1949, UCLA documents on the Loyalty Oath, in the Bancroft Library, University of California. The emphasis is mine.

34. Ibid. UCLA's provost goes on to say that he would not approve communist speakers in a partisan, uncontrolled setting.

35. McHenry, *Childhood,* p. 338, uses the term *gunshy.*

36. The quotation, which includes Gardner's emphasis, is from Gardner, *The California Oath Controversy,* pp. 19–20. His source is a letter from Dykstra to the Board of Regents on March 27, 1949.

37. McHenry, *Childhood,* p. 343.

38. Ibid., p. 338.

39. Interview of (Regent) Edwin Pauley by David Gardner, April 28, 1965, Gardner, *Papers,* Carton 13, Folder 7.

40. Clarence Dykstra to Robert Sproul, March 27, 1949, Gardner, *Papers,* Carton 9. It is also true that Laski's Harvard talk, originally scheduled at the Law School, had to be moved off campus.

41. Gardner informs us that Sproul would later tell Dykstra that he had been misunderstood and had never instructed that the invitation to Laski be withdrawn. Regent Neylan takes Dykstra's position and not Sproul's on the facts of the case.

42. For the theory of "the deal," see the letter from Berkeley historian Walton Bean to David Gardner, Gardner, *Papers,* Carton 12.

43. "Minutes of the Board of Regents," March 25 1949.

44. Clark Kerr, remarks at the 50th Anniversary Symposium on the Loyalty Oath, University of California, Berkeley, October 1999.

CHAPTER 5

1. Robert MacIver, *Academic Freedom in Our Time* (New York: Columbia University Press, 1955), p. 8.

2. Clark Kerr in *The Robert Gordon Sproul Oral History Project,* interviews conducted by Suzanne B. Riess, 1984–1985, Vol. 2, p. 611. Kerr goes on to say that another factor was a "vendetta of some of the Southern regents against Sproul over whether UCLA was getting its fair share."

3. David P. Gardner, *The California Oath Controversy* (Berkeley, Calif.: University of California Press, 1967), p. 24.

4. The rule that unanimous consent of the board was required for the discussion of new business not announced in advance had been insisted upon by Neylan, who stated that Sproul liked to spring things on the board at the last minute, issues they weren't prepared to discuss, and this was his antidote for that practice. John Francis Neylan, *Politics, Law, and the University,* oral history interviews conducted by Walton Bean and Corinne Gilb, draft in David P. Gardner, *Papers,* 1949–2005, Series 8, Loyalty Oath Controversy, Research Materials, Carton 13, Folder 7, p. 237, Bancroft Library, University of California.

5. Gardner, *The California Oath Controversy,* pp. 24–27.

6. David Gardner interview with Edwin Pauley, April 28, 1965, Gardner, *Papers,* Carton 13, Folder 7.

7. Neylan, *Politics, Law, and the University,* p. 269.

8. Hildebrand and Lehman were the two most important members of Sproul's Advisory Committee, as well as close friends of the president, so it is telling that they weren't consulted. Stephen Pepper was a highly respected professor of philosophy and a long-time leader of the Academic Senate.

9. Benjamin H. Lehman, *Recollections and Reminiscences of Life in the Bay Area from 1920 Onward,* interview conducted by Suzanne B. Riess, 1968, pp. 276–77, Regional Oral History Office, Bancroft Library, University of California. According to J.A.C. Grant, Sproul did consult in advance with the UCLA member of his advisory committee, Martin Huberty, who reportedly told him that the faculty would like the oath. James A. C. Grant, *Comparative Constitutional Law at UCLA,* interviews conducted by Steven J. Novak, 1989, pp. 191–95, Oral History Program, UCLA.

10. See, for example, Neylan, *Politics, Law, and the University,* p. 241, where the regent said "I wouldn't give you the paper it was written on."

11. Clark Kerr, *The Gold and the Blue: A Personal Memoir of the University of California, 1949–1967,* Vol. 2 (Berkeley and Los Angeles: University of California Press, 2003), p. 38.

12. Neylan, *Politics, Law, and the University,* p. 235.

13. Hutchins's opening statement immediately became a classic in the literature of intellectual freedom and in the same year was included with the writings of Milton and Jefferson in Howard Mumford Jones, *A Primer of Intellectual Freedom* (Cambridge: Harvard University Press, 1949).

14. Carey McWilliams, *Witch Hunt: The Revival of Heresy* (Boston: Little, Brown, 1950), pp. 221–29.

15. That Sproul did not fully "know the academic mind" has been advanced by professors at both UCLA and Berkeley as an explanation for his miscalculations in proposing the oath. A possible flaw in this interpretation is that Hildebrand would become a cosponsor of Sproul's oath, and that there were presidents such as David Barrows who had been on the faculty and yet were even more anticommunist than Sproul.

16. Joseph Tussman, *Philosopher and Educational Innovator,* oral history interviews conducted by Lisa Rubens, 2005, Disk 1, p. 49, Regional Oral History Office, Bancroft Library, University of California, unedited raw transcript in author's possession.

17. Ibid.

18. Ibid., Disk 4 (00:27–58) and (0021:212); and author's interview with Tussman, August 15, 2005, tape in my possession.

19. Gardner, *The California Oath Controversy,* pp. 29–31. In a memo to President Sproul, Pettitt explained that he had not published the wording of the oath because the regents had not instructed him to do so. He assumed that since it was drawn up in an executive (that is, closed) session that it was not to be made public. And he was also afraid that its publication would encourage the State Legislature to pass one or more of the Tenney bills aimed at the university. Undated memorandum from George Pettitt to Sproul, in the Sproul Papers (Administrative Records), in Gardner, *Papers,* Carton 9.

20. Tussman, *Philosopher and Educational Innovator,* Disk 5, p. 31; and author's interview with Tussman, August 15, 2005, Berkeley, tape in my possession.

21. Ibid.

22. Benbow Ritchie, "Edward Chace Tolman," *Biographical Memoirs,* National Academy of Sciences, 1964, Vol. 37. Tolman had been a student of William James at Harvard, and his classic work was *Purposive Behavior in Animals and Men.* He also analyzed humankind's proclivity to destroy itself in *Drives Toward War.*

23. Author's interview with Tussman. See also Tussman, *Philosopher and Educational Innovator.*

24. When Clark Kerr became Berkeley's first chancellor in 1952, his priority was to establish the principle of continuous tenure. Clark Kerr, remarks at the 50th Anniversary Symposium on the Loyalty Oath, University of California, Berkeley, October, 1999.

25. *Daily Bruin,* front page articles of April 4, April 5, April 14, and May 24, 1949. The feature articles on the regents appeared on the front page of the second section under Irving Shimer's byline on May 25 and June 1.

26. Michael Burawoy and Jonathan Van Antwerpen, interview with Kenneth Bock, Grass Valley, California, June 21, 1999. Copy of tape in my possession.

27. John Francis Neylan to (fellow regent) Fred Jordan, October 5, 1949, Box 179 of the Neylan Papers, in Gardner, *Papers,* Carton 10.

28. Gardner, *The California Oath Controversy*, p. 32.

29. Edward Condon was a leading physicist who had been hounded by Un-American Activities Committees, and Judith Coplon was being tried on charges of espionage.

30. These are just some of the headlines listed in George Stewart et al., *The Year of the Oath: The Fight for Academic Freedom at the University of California* (New York: Doubleday, 1950), p. 55.

31. Interviews with Mary Tolman Kent and Deborah Tolman Whitney in *The Loyalty Oath at the University of California, 1949–1952,* Regional Oral History Office, Bancroft Library, University of California. Nisbet considered Tolman, along with Ernest Lawrence and Alfred Kroeber, one of the three poorest undergraduate lecturers among Berkeley's most eminent professors. Robert Nisbet, *Teachers and Scholars: A Memoir of Berkeley in Depression and War* (New Brunswick, N.J.: Transaction, 1992), p. 135–36.

32. Gardner, *The California Oath Controversy*, p. 33.

33. Gordon Griffiths, *Venturing Outside the Ivory Tower: A Political Autobiography,* unpublished manuscript, Version 2, 2002, p. 63, available from The Library of Congress.

34. My paraphrase of his letter, which is quoted in full in Alain Boureau, *Kantorowicz: Stories of a Historian,* trans. Stephen G. Nichols and Gabrielle M. Spiegel (Baltimore and London: John Hopkins Press, 2001), pp. 12–13. Besides Boureau, my sources on Kantorowicz in Germany include Robert L. Benson and Johannes Fried, eds. *Ernst Kantorowicz: Erträge der Doppeltagung* (Stuttgart: Franz Steiner Verlag, 1997); and Harmut Lehmann and James J. Sheehan, eds. *An Interrupted Past: German Refugee Historians in the United States After 1933* (Washington D.C. and Cambridge, U.K.: German Historical Institute and Cambridge University Press, 1991), esp. the articles by Robert E. Lerner and Michael Kater.

35. Norman F. Cantor, *Inventing the Middle Ages: The Lives, Work, and Ideas of the Great Medievalists of the Twentieth Century* (New York: William Morrow, 1991), p. 98.

36. Stewart, *The Year of the Oath*, p. 90.

37. The entire statement may be found in Gardner, *The California Oath Controversy*, pp. 34–36.

38. Griffiths, *Venturing Outside the Ivory Tower,* Version 2, p. 64, is making a distinction similar to the one between local and cosmopolitan orientations that Robert Merton and Alvin Gouldner would introduce in sociology a decade later. During the course of the oath crisis, the conservative and moderate faculty tended to be "locals," in Gouldner's sense, the liberals and radicals "cosmopolitans." See Alvin Gouldner, "Cosmopolitans and Locals: An Analysis of Latent Social Roles," *Administrative Science Quarterly* 2, no. 3 (December 1957–March 1958): pp. 281–306.

39. My emphasis. Ernst Kantorowicz to Robert Sproul, October 4, 1949, and Kantorowicz to Frank Kidner, December 1949. Both letters may be found in Group for Academic Freedom, *Papers,* Box 1, Bancroft Library, University of California. The letter to Sproul also appears in Kantorowicz's bookler *The Fundamental Issue,* published privately in 1950. On the advice of the lawyer for the nonsigners, who feared its publication might jeopardize their court case, it was never circulated at the time. However, with its lively underground circulation, it would infuriate John Francis Neylan. See John Francis Neylan, "Loyalty Oaths and Academic Freedom," Address to the Commonwealth Club, San Francisco, California, November 23, 1951, Bancroft Library, University of California. Kantorowicz was the

person most responsible for promoting the analogy between California's Loyalty Oath and European totalitarianism. This issue would become an important part of the debate in the months that followed, and it would divide the faculty, with even some refugees from the regimes of Hitler and Mussolini arguing that the analogy was misleading.

40. Gardner, *The California Oath Controversy,* p. 37.

41. Ritchie, "Edward Chace Tolman," pp. 315–16.

42. Neylan, *Politics, Law, and the University,* pp. 238–39.

43. Ibid., p. 239.

44. Ibid.

45. Ibid., pp. 247–48. Neylan was also a member of a special Regents' Committee on Communist Activities, which was working up its own resolution on the subject of Red professors. The group was united on the policy of barring them from teaching, but in none of their drafts was there even a mention of the Loyalty Oath. Until Sproul, to whom they had sent the resolution for his editing, inserted the March 25 requirement!

46. Neylan, *Politics, Law, and the University,* p. 241.

47. Gardner, *The California Oath Controversy,* p. 39.

48. Stewart, *The Year of the Oath,* p. 30, quotes the revised disclaimer: "That I am not a member of the Communist Party, or under any oath, or party to any agreement, or under any commitment that is in conflict with my obligations under the oath." See also Gardner, *The California Oath Controversy,* pp. 45–46. I have not been able to determine who was responsible for the addition of the Communist Party disclaimer. In his 1951 speech to the Commonwealth Club, Neylan says it was Hildebrand who insisted on it. See Neylan, "Loyalty Oaths and Academic Freedom." But a few years later in his oral history Neylan said that he believed the idea came from his fellow conservative regent Edward Dickson. See draft of Neylan, *Politics, Law, and the University* in Gardner, *Papers,* Carton 13, Folder 7, p. 244.

49. Neylan, *Politics, Law, and the University* in Gardner, *Papers,* Carton 13, Folder 7, pp. 242–44. It was at the same meeting that Lieutenant Governor Goodwin Knight made a statement that would become a part of the Loyalty Oath lore. He went on record against Phi Beta Kappa, the honorary fraternity whose condemnation of California's oath had been a headline in the newspapers ten days earlier, and added that he was glad that the fraternity had never rushed him when he was a college freshman! This remark evoked applause from many of the regents and a good part of the audience, for they were as ignorant as Knight about the meaning of a Phi Beta Kappa key. An ultra-conservative, Knight was the most fervent pro-oath regent during the months that Neylan remained skeptical of the requirement.

50. Gardner, who is very protective of Hildebrand in his *California Oath Controversy,* writes that the latter did fairly represent faculty opinion, but his own interviews belie this. Gardner, interviews of Berkeley Senate leader Frank Kidner and UCLA's J.A.C. Grant in Gardner, *Papers,* Carton 13, Folder 7.

51. Gardner, *The California Oath Controversy,* p. 47.

52. Stewart, *The Year of the Oath,* p. 30. In fairness to Hildebrand and Lehman, their jobs had been made more difficult because of the ambiguities defining their roles. Some people had left the June 14 meeting believing that the Advisory Committee had been entrusted with the power to act on its own, while others believed that their responsibility was only to consult and that they needed the Senate's approval before committing the faculty

to a position. The author of *The Year of the Oath* saw this as a crucial "parliamentary mistake" that would come back to haunt the faculty, injuring its cause almost fatally.

53. Lehman, *Recollections*, pp. 268–71, and esp. 269–70, where he is quoted as saying, "I always thought that Alexander Meiklejohn and the rest made too much fuss about it," "it" being the academic freedom issues of the Loyalty Oath.

54. "Regents Affirm Stance on Oath," *Daily Bruin*, June 28, 1949, p. 1.

55. Bob Lyhne, "Wrong Yardstick," *Daily Californian*, July 14, 1949, p. 8.

56. Sproul's action is even more surprising considering that he and Farnham Griffiths were close friends. Later, when the president wanted to overturn the oath, Griffiths would support him, and after the regent's son Gordon became a leader of the nonsigners, he would be one of the most consistent anti-oath members of the board. His son's role would pose a conflict of interest, so Griffiths often would have to recuse himself from voting.

57. Neylan, *Politics, Law, and the University*, p. 241.

58. Gardner, *The California Oath Controversy*, pp. 50–51.

59. He also encouraged professors to get receipts of their notary fees so that the university could reimburse them. Robert Sproul to Margaret Hodgen, dated July 16, 1949, in the Hodgen file, Group for Academic Freedom, *Papers*, Folder 7, Bancroft Library, University of California.

60. Stewart, *The Year of the Oath*, p. 31.

61. Ibid., pp. 31–32.

CHAPTER 6

1. Norman Mailer, *Advertisements for Myself* (New York: G. P. Putnam, 1959), p. 222.

2. John Walton Caughey, Norris Hundley Jr., and John A. Schutz, *The American West, Frontier & Region* (Los Angeles: Ward Ritchie Press, 1969).

3. Interview with John and La Ree Caughey conducted by Ron Grele, June 5, 1981, unedited draft, p. 36ff, Charles Young Research Library, UCLA.

4. Ibid., p. 5.

5. The historian's phrasing suggests that he might have suspected Sproul's involvement in the oath's origins, even though that fact would not be public knowledge for months. John Caughey to Robert Sproul, July 10, 1949, UCLA University Archives Record Series No. 359, Chancellor's Office, Administrative Files, 1936–1959, Box 239, Folder 105, Charles Young Research Library.

6. UCLA University Archives Record Series No. 393, Loyalty Oath Controversy, 1945–1968, Box 2, Folder 84, Charles Young Research Library.

7. Memorandum, "Confidential," "UCLA Faculty Members named as Reds," dated June 21 (no year, no author), in David P. Gardner, *Papers*, 1949–2005, Series 8, Loyalty Oath Controversy, Research Materials, Carton 12, Folder 19, Bancroft Library, University of California.

8. "TAs Oppose Oath Plan, Regents' Stand," *Daily Californian*, September 16, 1949, p. 1.

9. Nina Fishman, "Leslie Fishman," March 18, 2008, guardian.co.UK.

10. Douglas Dowd to author, May 13, 2008 e-mail in my possession.

11. Interview with Ralph Giesey in *The Loyalty Oath at the University of California, 1949–1952*, Regional Oral History Office, Bancroft Library, University of California, pp. 35–36.

12. Frank Finney, "Forum Participants Denounce University's Oath Requirement," *Daily Californian*, September 16, p. 4. Like many Reds at the time, Doyle would leave

school to go into industry. In 1952 we were fellow workers at Gardner Electric, a trans-former plant in Emeryville, California. Later he would marry Dorothy Doyle, a novelist who would document her party experiences in *Journey Through Jess.*

13. Years later, as president of San Jose State University, Bunzel would be one of the na-tion's first prominent neo-conservatives.

14. Of the eighty-three NASE members who would be dismissed as nonsigners, 21 per-cent were female, in contrast to about 10 percent of the faculty fired. And yet not one of these women could be counted among the group's leadership. Author's calculation from the list in Agnes R. Robb to David Gardner, December 22, 1964, Gardner, *Papers,* Carton 13, Folder 4. Her memo has eighty-four names, but one is ambiguous in gender.

15. David P. Gardner, *The California Oath Controversy (Berkeley, Calif.: University of California Press, 1967),* p. 55. On the Davis campus near Sacramento, where many of the fac-ulty did research on behalf of agro-business, 70 percent had signed. In the three years of the crisis there would be virtually no opposition to the oath by the faculty at Davis. Gardner, *The California Oath Controversy,* p. 55.

16. Ibid,. pp. 55–56.

17. Benjamin Lehman, letter to UCLA Advisory Committee, as quoted in Gardner, *The California Oath Controversy,* p. 58.

18. Ibid.

19. Ibid., pp. 59–60.

20. Various articles from the *Daily Californian,* September 15 through October 15, 1949. The news stories and editorials have been placed online by the Loyalty Oath digital project of the Bancroft Library.

21. George Arnsen, "Daily Bruin Appointments to Be Debated," *Daily Californian,* September 15, 1949, p. 1. A few months later Sigal would be forced out, after having re-placed Garst as editor-in-chief.

22. Clancy Sigal, "Northern Section Struck a Major Blow for Academic Freedom," *UCLA Daily Bruin,* editorial, p. 1, September 21, 1949.

23. "Minutes of the Academic Senate," Southern Section, September 22, 1949, Los An-geles, in UCLA University Archives Record Series No. 393, Loyalty Oath Controversy, Records, 1945–1968, Box 1, Folder 21, Charles Young Research Library.

24. William Ray Dennes, *Philosophy and the University Since 1915,* interview conducted by Joann Dietz Arff, 1969, p. 95, Regional Oral History Office, Bancroft Library, University of California.

25. His only scholarly work was a study of Thomas Carlyle's conception of the hero. Toward the end of his life he was writing about Native American languages.

26. Lehman was one of the few white Americans not a radical or even a liberal who was far ahead of his time with respect to race relations. At Harvard he had befriended the one African-American in his class, Alain Locke, who would become a leader of the Harlem Renaissance. He was particularly close to the singer Roland Hayes and would sponsor the poet Langston Hughes for a Rosenwald Fellowship.

27. Benjamin Lehman, *Recollections and Reminiscences of Life in the Bay Area from 1920 Onward,* interview conducted by Suzanne B. Riess, 1969, p. 47, 116ff, and 147–48, Regional Oral History Office, Bancroft Library, University of California.

28. It was a precedent-shattering meeting, for university regulations mandated that all contact between the faculty and the board be mediated through the president.

29. Dennes, *Philosophy and the University,* p. 103.

30. Gardner, *The California Oath Controversy,* pp. 65–67.

31. Ibid., p. 67.

32. Lehman, *Recollections,* pp. 255–56 and p. 261. Neylan reports that both Lehman and Hildebrand were "shell-shocked" when they learned the truth about the oath's origin. John Neylan, *Politics, Law, and the University,* oral history interviews conducted by Walton Bean and Corinne Gilb, Regional Oral History Office, Bancroft Library, University of California, p. 249.

33. Lehman, *Recollections,* pp. 259–62.

34. Ibid., pp. 262–67. Some of the details on Lehman's letter come from Box 185 of the Neylan papers, in David Gardner, *Papers,* Carton 10.

35. Amt Froshaug, "Ex Committee Passes Oath Resolution, "*Daily Californian,* October 11, 1949, p. 1.

36. "TAs Strongly Protest Oath Policy Statement of Regents," *Daily Californian,* October 10, 1949, p. 4.

37. Gardner, *The California Oath Controversy,* pp. 74–75, 80–81.

38. Gordon Griffiths, *Venturing Outside the Ivory Tower: A Political Autobiography,* unpublished manuscript version 2, 2002, p. 15, and interview with Howard Bern by Germaine LaBerge, in *The Loyalty Oath at the University of California, 1949–1952,* Regional Oral History Office, Bancroft Library, University of California, 2004, pp. 13.

39. Gardner, *The California Oath Controversy,* pp. 81–82.

40. "Oath Talks Will Drag into November," *Daily Californian,* October 21, 1949, p. 1.

41. George F. Taylor to Jim Corley, November 3, 1949, UCLA University Archives Record Series No. 359, Chancellor's Office, Administrative Files, 1936–1959, Box 239, Folder 105, Charles Young Research Library. If undergraduates at Berkeley were not that concerned about the Loyalty Oath, they had good reason to be excited about their football team. When the Bears beat UCLA 35 to 21 that day, they took over first place in the Pacific Coast Conference. Ranked as the fourth best team in the country, they were trying to repeat Cal's undefeated 1948 season.

42. Robert Sproul, Speech to the American Bankers Association, San Francisco, November 1, 1949, in Gardner, *Papers,* Carton 10. See also Gardner, *The California Oath Controversy,* pp. 76–77.

43. Gardner, *The California Oath Controversy,* p. 77.

44. Griffiths, *Venturing Outside the Ivory Tower,* Version 2, p. 134.

45. Gardner, *The California Oath Controversy,* pp. 82–83. My emphasis. The meeting lasted almost four hours instead of the usual ninety minutes or so. The tenBroek resolution passed by a vote of 148 to 113, which suggests that a third or more of the original four-hundred-plus professors had gone home.

46. Ibid., pp. 80–83.

47. Ibid., p. 85. On the Davis campus every one of the faculty had signed!

48. Ibid., pp. 86–87.

49. The data come from Gardner's summary of the poll results, in *The California Oath Controversy,* p. 290, note 45, and also the file of Daniel Popper, in UCLA University Archives

Series No. 393, Loyalty Oath Controversy, 1945–1968, Box 2, Folder 30, Charles Young Research Library. The committee included one expert on survey research design, the social psychologist Richard Centers.

50. Fearing was a Popular Front liberal who had served as an editor of the *Hollywood Quarterly* and had been active in the Hollywood Writers Congress. Those acts, along with being on the committee that had welcomed Hewlett Johnson, the "Red Dean" of Canterbury, to Los Angeles, had earned him several mentions in Tenney's reports.

51. Daniel Wilner and Franklin Fearing, "The Structure of Opinion: A Loyalty Oath Poll," *Public Opinion Quarterly* (Winter 1950): pp. 729–43. The students were questioned between November 14 and December 10, 1949.

52. Stephen C. Pepper, *Art and Philosophy at the University of California, 1919 to 1962*, interview by Suzanne B. Riess, 1963, p. 262, Regional Oral History Office, Bancroft Library, University of California.

53. Gardner, *The California Oath Controversy*, p. 89.

54. Ibid.

55. Six days earlier, in a letter to Ben Lehman, Neylan had likened the "radical minority" at Berkeley that was claiming a "complete victory" after the passage of the tenBroek resolution to the minority of communists that had brought Poland and Czechoslovakia into the Soviet camp. John Neylan to Benjamin Lehman, December 7, 1949, in Gardner, *Papers,* Carton 10.

56. Report of the Academic Senate's Combined Conference Committee (Davisson-Grant) on meeting with Neylan, December 13, 1949. Gardner, *Papers,* Carton 10. See also Gardner, *The California Oath Controversy,* pp. 87–89.

57. Stephen C. Pepper, *Journal,* in Gardner, *Papers,* Carton 13, Folder 14.

58. Gardner, *The California Oath Controversy,* pp. 91–93, and Stewart, *The Year of the Oath,* pp. 41–46.

59. Alva Senzek, "Fight Against Loyalty Oath Opened Again By TAs," *Daily Californian,* February 9, 1950, p. 4. For the account of the January 11 meeting, see UCLA University Archives Record Series No. 393, Loyalty Oath Controversy, Records, 1945–1968, Box 1, Folder 81, Charles Young Research Library.

CHAPTER 7

1. Clancy Sigal, editorial, *Daily Bruin,* January 6, 1950, p. 1.

2. When the vote took place on April 25, only 676 students voted for Sigal to return as editor, while 2,272 opposed his reinstatement. George Garrigues, *Loud Bark and Curious Eyes: A History of the UCLA Daily Bruin, 1919–1955,* Internet Edition, 2001.

3. Clancy Sigal, "30 Editorial," *Daily Bruin,* January 6, 1950, p. 1., as cited in Garrigues, *Loud Bark,* Chapter 9.

4. In 1950 everyone in Berkeley from the Center to the Left, as well as many nonpolitical people, belonged to "the Co-op," which was ahead of its time in providing healthy eating alternatives and in environmental consciousness. Besides several groceries, there was also a Co-op gas station, a credit union, and one of the nation's first natural food stores.

5. David P. Gardner, *The California Oath Controversy (Berkeley, Calif.: University of California Press, 1967),* pp. 94–95.

6. Ibid., pp. 98–103.

7. Haynes Johnson, *The Age of Anxiety: McCarthyism to Terrorism* (Orlando: Harcourt Brace Jovanovich, 2005), pp. 13ff. Truman, to his credit, ignored the outcry, and Acheson would serve as secretary of state until Eisenhower became president in 1953.

8. John Neylan, *Politics, Law, and the University,* oral history interviews conducted by Walton Bean and Corinne Gilb, Regional Oral History Office, Bancroft Library, University of California, p. 252. The regent was also encouraged by the Harry Bridges case. At this time (early 1950) he believed that the U.S. government would succeed in convicting the labor leader for perjury and then deport him to Australia. But Bridges, like Robert Oppenheimer, was never convicted of anything. He would remain a radical all his life, unlike the famous scientist who became quite conservative.

9. Clark Kerr used the "twisting in the wind" phrase in his contribution to *The Robert Gordon Sproul Oral History Project,* interviews conducted by Suzanne B. Riess, 1984–1985, Vol. 2, p. 612, Bancroft Library, University of California.

10. Johnson, *Age of Anxiety,* p. 13.

11. "UC Regents Right on Loyalty Oath," *San Francisco Examiner,* February 27, 1950, p. 1.

12. *San Francisco Chronicle,* February 28, 1950.

13. The data on each paper's circulation and position on the oath may be found in David P. Gardner, *Papers, 1949–2005,* Series 8, Loyalty Oath Controversy, Research Materials, Carton 11, Bancroft Library, University of California. However three of the nation's most prestigious papers, the *New York Times,* the *Washington Post,* and the *Christian Science Monitor,* were strongly anti-oath.

14. Kantorowicz to Strong, February 28, 1950. Gardner, *Papers,* Carton 10. See also Gardner, *The California Oath Controversy,* p. 120.

15. "New Drive May Finance Oath Fight," *Daily Californian,* March 3, 1950, p. 1.

16. The historian's early work was influenced by Frederick Jackson Turner, the theorist of the American frontier, and Hicks would teach the same courses on the American West that Turner had taught at Wisconsin, before he left Madison for Berkeley in 1942. John D. Hicks, *My Life with History: An Autobiography* (Lincoln: University of Nebraska Press, 1968), pp. 145–46, 158.

17. Gardner, *The California Oath Controversy,* p. 119, quoting a letter from Hicks to Frank Newman of the nonsigners' Steering Committee. Meanwhile the Conference Committee was trying to make it clear that the faculty was not defending communism or communists. The regents do have a right to fire communists, they emphasized. But "virtually to a man, the faculty protests the Regents' right to wreck the University by firing men for no other reason than non-signing of a particular oath, created by the Regents, without the Regents ever bothering to investigate whether these men are in fact Communists or otherwise disloyal." More than eight hundred members of the faculty would sign this statement.

18. George Stewart et al., *The Year of the Oath: The Fight for Academic Freedom at the University of California* (New York: Doubleday, 1950), p. 24. See also Kenneth Starr, *Embattled Dreams: California in War and Peace, 1940–1950* (New York, Oxford University Press, 2002), p. 327. Both sources quote the *San Francisco Chronicle* of March 1, 1950.

19. Bill Doyle, "As I See It," editorial, *Daily Californian,* February 28, 1950, p.7.

20. Author's interview with Leon Litwack, Dec. 20, 2005. Tape in my possession.

21. *San Francisco Chronicle,* March 7, 1950, p. 1. The *Chronicle* offered 8,000 as the attendance, while the student newspaper, the *Daily Californian,* estimated "close to 10,000." Jeannie Hamilton, "Large Crowd Hears Oath Issues Aired," *Daily Californian,* March 7, 1950, p 1.

22. *San Francisco Chronicle, March 7, 1950.*

23. *San Francisco Chronicle,* March 7, 1950; Hamilton, "Large Crowd Hears Oath Issues Aired"; and the *Berkeley Daily Gazette,* March 6, 1950, p. 1. Before the upcoming Senate meeting Strong circulated a memorandum among his fellow nonsigners that cautioned against playing into Neylan's hands. It was critical, he urged, not to give the impression that the opposition to the oath was coming from a "dissident minority." Because the split between those professors who upheld the AAUP position and those who did not was "irreconcilable," the group should forebear from debating the issue on the Senate floor. The goal should be to showcase the faculty's unity in opposing the oath.

24. Statement of Paul Dodd at press conference, March 7, 1950, in UCLA University Archives Record Series No. 393, Loyalty Oath Controversy, Box 2, Folder 35, Charles Young Research Library.

25. Hal Watkins, editorial, *Daily Bruin,* March 8, 1950, p. 8.

26. Caughey talked about his unhappiness two months later when he was interviewed by Berkeley's George Stewart. See George Stewart, Interview Transcript no. 18 for *The Year of the Oath,* in Gardner, *Papers,* Carton 10.

27. Gardner, *The California Oath Controversy,* pp. 132–34. For Davisson's collapse, see "UC Oath Alternative Drafted," *Westwood Hills Press,* March 9, 1950, p. 8, continuation of front-page story. The article notes that it was lack of sleep and "nervous strain" that felled Davisson, forcing him to cancel a scheduled appearance at UCLA's Senate meeting.

28. Hildebrand's perspective was based in turn on the ideas of the political philosopher Arthur Lovejoy, who had published his position in the Summer 1949 issue of the *American Scholar.* In an interview fifteen years later Hildebrand took pride in his authorship of the argument against Proposition 2 and his overall role in the oath crisis. Gardner's interview of Joel Hildebrand, June 22, 1965, Gardner, *Papers,* Carton 13, Folder 7.

29. Stewart, Interview Transcript no. 2 (anonymous associate professor) in Gardner, *Papers,* Carton 10.

30. In addition to Berkeley, the Northern Section included the much smaller faculties on the Davis campus and at the Medical School in San Francisco. Professors at Santa Barbara and the Scripps Institute at La Jolla voted in the Southern Section, of which UCLA was by far the largest segment.

31. Gardner, *The California Oath Controversy,* p. 138.

32. Stewart, Interview Transcript no. 17 ("Professor 20 plus years at the university"), in Gardner, *Papers,* Carton 10. This interview can be clearly identified as that of Caughey.

33. Liberal Berkeley professors were also affected. Several who had strongly supported the AAUP in 1949 in their dialogues with Hildebrand would compromise that position a year later when they were interviewed by the Privilege and Tenure committee.

34. Ralph Works Chaney, *Paleobotanist, Conservationist,* interview conducted by Edna Tartaul Daniel, 1960, p. 168, Regional Oral History Office, Bancroft Library, University of California.

35. Stephen Pepper called him Neylan's "boy scout" and "stooge," while Gardner more delicately referred to him as an "intermediary." See Pepper, *Journal,* p. 20, in Gardner, *Papers,* Carton 13, Folder 14; and Gardner, *The California Oath Controversy,* p. 130.

36. Jeannie Hamilton, "Faculty Sets New Oath Stand," *Daily Californian,* March 23, 1950, p. 1.

37. *Daily Bruin,* March 24, 1950, p. 1.

38. Stewart, Interview Transcript no. 17, in Gardner, *Papers,* Carton 10.

39. Joseph Tussman, *Philosopher and Educational Innovator,* oral history interviews conducted by Lisa Rubens, Disk 5, 2004, pp. 53–55, Regional Oral History Office, Bancroft Library, University of California, unedited raw transcript in author's possession.

40. Ibid., pp. 44–46.

41. But Winkler was out of touch with faculty opinion. On March 30 he would predict that if Fox were not granted a rehearing "a considerable number of the faculty will resign." Dick Israel, "Reinstatement of Fox Urged at Public Protest Meeting," *Daily Californian,* March 31, 1950, p. 1.

42. Jeannie Hamilton, "TA Meeting Has Unexpected Guests: Notetakers Cause Uproar, Flee," *Daily Californian,* March 13, 1950, p. 1.

43. Newsletter No. 1 of UCLA's Non-Academic Senate Employees, April 12, 1950, p. 1, in UCLA Archives Record Series No. 393, Loyalty Oath Controversy, Box 2, Folder 81, Charles Young Research Library.

44. *Daily Bruin,* March 15, 1950, p. 1.

45. Letter of Harold Laski to McHenry, March 20, 1950, in Gardner, *Papers,* Carton 10.

46. Isaac Kramnick and Barry Sheerman, *Harold Laski: A Life on the Left* (New York: Penguin, 1993), p. 577.

47. Teague to Robert Sproul, as quoted in the *UCLA Daily Bruin,* March 7, 1950.

48. Although it was illegal for a regent to meet directly with faculty members, Heller had found a way around the rule. He would dine at the home of his friend Lawrence Sears, who taught at Mills College in Oakland. After the meal, Cal professors would drop by to exchange ideas with Heller. The regent would advise them to sign the oath, so they could keep their jobs and fight against it, and also to delay big decisions. David Gardner, interview of Elinor Raas Heller, 1965, pp. 8–10, in Gardner, *Papers,* Carton 13, Folder 7.

CHAPTER 8

1. George Stewart et al., *The Year of the Oath: The Fight for Academic Freedom at the University of California* (New York: Doubleday, 1950), p. 9.

2. Paul Dodd, *Patient Persuader,* interviews by Thomas Bartonneau, 1985, pp. 41ff, UCLA Oral History Project.

3. Ibid., pp. 38–40.

4. Stephen C. Pepper, *Journal,* pp. 9ff., in David P. Gardner, *Papers,* Series 8, Loyalty Oath Controversy, Research Materials, Carton 13, Folder 14, Bancroft Library, University of California.

5. Transcript of portion of Regents Meeting of March 31, 1950 Pertaining to the Loyalty Oath, Gardner, *Papers,* Carton 10.

6. Gardner, *The California Oath Controversy (Berkeley, Calif.: University of California Press, 1967),* pp. 143–44.

7. David Gardner interview with John Hicks, May 7, 1965, in Gardner, *Papers,* Carton 13, Folder 7.

8. "Regents Keep Special Oath: Sign or Resign Elicits Howls," *Daily Bruin,* April 3, 1950, p. 1. Jacoby was quoted in the *Westwood Hills Press,* April 6, 1950, p. 8.

9. Dean McHenry to Alfred Longveil, April 10, 1950, in UCLA University Archives Record Series No. 393, Box 2, Folder 67, Charles Young Research Library.

10. "Regents Retain Loyalty Oath, Faculty Resolutions Are Tabled," *Daily Californian,* April 3, 1950, p. 1. The editorial, "Not in Good Faith," appears on p. 6 in the same issue.

11. John D. Hicks, *My Life with History: An Autobiography* (Lincoln: University of Nebraska Press, 1968), p. 283.

12. Letter from Carl Mote Jr. to John Hicks, in the University of California Centennial History Office, *Correspondence and Papers, 1950–1960,* Box 1, Bancroft Library, University of California.

13. John Hicks to Frank Kidner, March 1950, in Gardner, *Papers,* Carton 10.

14. Gordon Griffiths, *Venturing Outside the Ivory Tower: A Political Autobiography,* unpublished manuscript, Version 2, 2002, pp. 31–33, available from The Library of Congress.

15. Hicks, *My Life with History,* p. 287.

16. Coincidentally the Bridges Defense Committee, like the Committee of Seven, was using the Durant Hotel for its headquarters. See letter of John Hicks to the manager of the Durant Hotel, August 18, 1950, in John Hicks, *Papers,* Committee of Seven files, Bancroft Library, University of California.

17. Pepper, *Journal,* pp. 94–95.

18. Ibid.

19. David Gardner interview of John Hicks, May 7, 1965, p. 17, in Gardner, *Papers,* Carton 13, Folder 7. Stephen Pepper believes Sproul would not speak out because that would have been an admission that he had been wrong in proposing the oath and that Neylan had been right in opposing it. Pepper didn't think Sproul was a "big enough man" to make such a gesture, but had he done so, he would have become "a national figure of major proportion." Stephen C. Pepper, *Art and Philosophy at the University of California, 1919 to 1962,* interview by Suzanne B. Riess, 1963, p. 265, Regional Oral History Office, Bancroft Library, University of California.

20. Gardner, *The California Oath Controversy,* pp. 146–49.

21. Dickson to Ehrman, Box 177 of Neylan Papers, in Gardner, *Papers,* Carton 10.

22. "NASE Resolution Asks Graduate Students to Counter Loyalty Oath," *Daily Californian,* April 5, 1950, p. 1.

23. Pepper, *Journal,* p. 12.

24. Neylan's estimate of 2,500 is probably on the low side because of his bias. Others suggest the crowd was between 3,000 and 4,500. The last figure, from the *Daily Cal*'s news story, was probably somewhat exaggerated. See Jeannie Hamilton, "Oath Assailed at Protest Rally," *Daily Californian,* April 11, 1950, p. 1.

25. Hamilton, "Oath Assailed." See also Lawrence Harper, *Papers,* University of California Centennial History Office, *Correspondence and Papers, 1950–1960,* Box 1, Bancroft Library, University of California.

26. *Daily Bruin,* April 10, 1950, p. 1, and Stewart, *The Year of the Oath,* p. 39. Kenneth Macgowan found the regents' statement "hysterical," a sign of desperation. Kenneth Macgowan,

Papers, Loyalty Oath folder, File 3, Correspondence and notes re: the University of California Loyalty Oath controversy, circa 1949–1951.

27. Harper, *Papers.* Neylan called Hildebrand's speech "disgraceful." John Neylan to Chester Nimitz, April 14, 1950, in Gardner, *Papers,* Carton 10.

28. "UCLA Protest Meeting on Oath Ultimatum Cancelled," *Daily Californian,* April 18, 1950, p. 2.

29. Kantorowicz to Stanley, April 7, 1951, in Gardner, *Papers,* Carton 11. The young Richard Jennings was also a supporter of the nonsigners. For the Pound and Coffman statements, see *Daily Bruin,* April 13, 1950, p. 1.

30. Neiburger to Dodd, April 13, 1950, in UCLA University Archives Record Series No. 393, Box 2, folder 36, Charles Young Research Library.

31. In 1950 Berkeley had five Nobelists, all scientists. Herbert Evans, the discover of Vitamin E, was outspoken in his support of the oath. Ernest Lawrence kept a low profile on the issue but he told his intimates that he'd gladly sign the oath every morning. He was also beholden to Neylan for funding his Cyclotron, and he considered the regent a friend.

32. "Alumni Committee Attempts Settlement of Oath," *Daily Californian,* April 17, 1950, p. 1.

33. Stewart confirms the idea that there were three hundred nonsigners at this point. *The Year of the Oath.*

34. Ibid., pp. 39–40.

35. "Alumni Committee Attempts Settlement of the Oath," *Daily Californian.*

36. *Report of the American Association of University Professors on the Loyalty Oath Controversy at the University of California* (Washington, D.C.: AAUP, 1951), p. 25.

37. Hicks, *My Life with History,* p. 285.

38. Pepper, *Journal,* p. 44.

39. Jack Russell, "Hallinan Heard at West Gate," *Daily Californian,* April 20, 1950, p. 1.

40. Gardner, *The California Oath Controversy,* pp. 154–57. For the Giannini quote, see the *San Francisco Chronicle,* April 22, 1950, or the *Daily Californian,* May 1, 1950, p. 1.

41. Pepper, *Journal,* p. 88.

42. The Black Sheep was Berkeley's most expensive eating place in the era before such gourmet restaurants as Chéz Panisse, or the latter's early forerunner, the Pot Luck.

43. Pepper, *Journal,* pp. 89ff.

44. The committee's decision to spend money on the hotel on Durant and Bowditch, two short blocks from the campus, was based on the need to avoid the conflict of interest that unfriendly regents might charge them with were they to have used university offices and secretaries for the purpose of fighting the oath.

45. Pepper, *Journal,* p. 93.

46. Gardner, *The California Oath Controversy,* p. 160. The emphasis is Gardner's.

47. Ibid., p. 157.

48. John Caughey, "A University in Jeopardy," *Harpers* 201, no. 12 (November 1950): pp. 72–75. Fifteen years later Hicks would use almost identical language, calling it a "complete surrender." David Gardner interview with John Hicks. But in 1950 he tried to put the best construction on the Alumni Compromise.

49. Gardner, *The California Oath Controversy,* p. 161.

50. Clark Kerr, remarks at the 50th Anniversary Symposium on the Loyalty Oath, University of California, Berkeley, October 1999.

51. The other members of the Committee of Five were Gordon of Economics, Harry Wellman of Agriculture, and H. B. Gotaas of Engineering. Gardner, *The California Oath Controversy,* pp. 162ff.

52. Ibid.

53. Even Congressman Richard Nixon, who was running in 1950 to be a senator from California, had urged the faculty to sign the oath and then fight it through legal channels. At a Sather Gate rally on April 13, Nixon said there was no contradiction between his opposition to the Loyalty Oath and the strident anticommunist provisions of the Mundt-Nixon (later the McCarran-Walter) Act, which he was then sponsoring. "Nixon: 'Sign Under Protest and Fight Oath Through Channels,'" *Daily Californian,* April 14, 1950, p. 1.

54. Stewart, *The Year of the Oath,* p. 11. However an inner circle of five met regularly. See George Stewart, *A Little of Myself,* interview conducted by Suzanne B. Riess, p. 176, Regional Oral History Office, Bancroft Library, University of California.

55. Forty-two members of the faculty were asked about how the crisis had affected their states of mind and the routines of daily life, and twenty-eight of these summary interview transcripts can be found in Gardner, *Papers,* Carton 10.

56. The quote comes from a note by George Stewart to David Gardner, when he loaned him his interview transcripts. Among the twenty-eight summaries, three besides Loewenberg's can easily be identified. One is UCLA's Caughey, the other two are both Berkeley psychologists: Erik Erikson and Else Frenkel-Brunswick.

57. Author's interview with Joseph Tussman, August 29, 2005, who added that Loewenberg's manner was also somewhat pompous. Tape in my possession.

58. Loewenberg had also observed a defensiveness in those colleagues who signed the oath, indicated by the fact that they went into "over-elaborate explanations" of their reasons. George Stewart, Interview Transcript No. 15 ("Mr. A.") for *The Year of the Oath,* in Gardner, *Papers,* Carton 10.

59. Stewart, Interview Transcript No. 15 (Mr. A.) (Loewenberg).

60. The only thing that gave Loewenberg relief from the pressures of the oath was talking to like-minded people. So the interview with Stewart provided a much-needed opportunity to unburden himself.

61. Reports of the referendum controversy can be found in front-page news stories in the *Daily Californian* on April 21 and May 2, 1950, along with stories on May 18, p. 2, and May 23, p. 12. The NASE stories appeared on p. 1 on April 22 and (after Spring Break) on May 2. On May 16 the NASE changed its name to the Academic Assembly.

62. Letter from five students, *Daily Californian,* May 2, 1950, p. 8.

63. Louis Bell, "Still a Chance," *Daily Californian,* May 8, 1950, p. 6.

64. Kenneth Starr, *Embattled Dreams: California in War and Peace 1940–1950* (New York: Oxford University Press, 2002), p. 323.

65. The pamphlet was first summarized, with the names of the "subversive" professors, in a guest editorial by Kenneth Green, *Daily Californian,* May 17, 1950, p. 12. The three feature articles by Israel appeared in the same source on May 18 (p. 12), May 22 (p. 6), and May 23 (p. 8.)

66. "John Francis Neylan and the 'Daily Cal,'" *Daily Californian,* May 29, 1950, p. 12.

67. "Trap Door Charged: Oath Controversy Flares Up Again," *Daily Californian,* May 29, 1950, p. 1.

68. According to Hildebrand it would be years before Hurley could find another job. David Gardner, interview of Joel Hildebrand, June 22, 1965, pp. 20–21, in Gardner, *Papers,* Carton 13, Folder 7.

CHAPTER 9

1. George Stewart, Interview Transcript No. 5, May 8, 1950 (an "Associate Professor of Medicine," identifiable as Erik Erikson), in David P. Gardner, *Papers,* Series 8, Loyalty Oath Controversy, Research Materials, Carton 13, Folder 7, Bancroft Library, University of California.

2. David P. Gardner, *The California Oath Controversy (Berkeley, Calif.: University of California Press, 1967),* p. 172.

3. Jacob Loewenberg, *A Faculty Revolution and Reminiscences, May 12, 1967,* manuscript in The Centennial History Project, Box 3, p. 15, Bancroft Library, University of California.

4. My calculations are taken from the list of petitioners listed in the *Report of the Committee on Privilege and Tenure,* University of California, Berkeley, June 15, 1950. Gardner, *Papers, Carton 12, Folder 19.*

5. See Edward W. Strong, *Philosopher, Professor, and Berkeley Chancellor 1961–1965,* interviews conducted by Harriet Nathan, 1992, p. 116, Regional Oral History Office, Bancroft Library, University of California; and Gordon Griffiths, *Venturing Outside the Ivory Tower: A Political Autobiography,* unpublished manuscript, 2002, available from The Library of Congress. Both versions of the latter's work have the same account of the Loyalty Oath. The point about Strong's meeting with the nonsigners comes from Charles Muscatine, *The Loyalty Oath, The Free Speech Movement, and Education Reforms at the University of California, Berkeley,* an oral history interview conducted by Germaine LaBerge, 2000, p. 37, Regional Oral History Office, Bancroft Library, University of California.

6. The general summary, as well as the assessments of all the individual faculty members that follow in this chapter, are taken from *Report of the Committee on Privilege and Tenure,* University of California, Berkeley, June 15, 1950, in Gardner, *Papers,* Carton 12, Folder 19.

7. The book was Max Weinrich, *Hitler's Professors: The Part of Scholarship in Germany's Crimes Against the Jewish People* (New York: YIVO, 1946). Charles Muscatine, *The Loyalty Oath,* p. 6, and author's interviews with Muscatine, 2005. Tapes in author's possession.

8. I am not suggesting that the committee, had it known that Brodeur was an ex-communist, should have recommended that he not be retained. I am just pointing out the ironies of Brodeur's testimony, as well as a certain hypocrisy in his stance.

9. Maurice Jacob, "Gian-Carlo Wick 1909–1992," *Biographical Memoirs,* Vol. 77, 1999, National Academy of Sciences.

10. Even though he was relatively unknown in 1950, there is more information about Erikson and the oath than almost any other professor, because his interview by George Stewart is so recognizable.

11. Lawrence J. Friedman, *Identity's Architect: A Biography of Erik Erikson* (New York: Scribner, 1999), pp. 246–48.

12. Ibid. Erikson's statement of June 1, 1950, is published in full, with a discussion of the historical context, in Robert Coles, *Erik H. Erikson: The Growth of His Work* (Boston and Toronto: Little, Brown, 1970), pp. 155–158.

13. Charles Muscatine offered that assessment during his talk at the 50th Anniversary Symposium.

14. Statement of Leonardo Olschki to the Committee on Privilege and Tenure, Gardner, *Papers,* Carton 12, Folder 19.

15. Reinhard Bendix, *From Berlin to Berkeley: German-Jewish Identities,* paperback ed. (New Brunswick, N.J.: Transaction, 1990), p. 286; and Bendix to Robert Sproul, May 15, 1950, and October 5, 1949, in Gardner, *Papers,* Carton 12, Folder 19.

16. Author's interview with Tussman, August 15, 2005. Tape in my possession. See also Joseph Tussman, *Philosopher and Educational Innovator,* oral history interviews conducted by Lisa Rubens, Disk 5, November 4, 2004, pp. 50–51, Regional Oral History Office, Bancoft Library, unedited raw transcript in author's possession.

17. While the books on the Loyalty Oath take account of the role of the Europeans, it is curious that neither Gardner nor Stewart, nor anyone who wrote articles about the crisis at the time, mentions the special role of women. Even in all the retrospective accounts, only one person, the zoologist Howard Bern, has recognized this. Howard Bern, remarks at the 50th Anniversary Symposium on the Loyalty Oath, University of California, Berkeley, October 1999.

18. Although she was not a nonsigner, mention should be made of Barbara Nachtrieb Armstrong, a distinguished law professor who was probably the woman most active in the Academic Senate. A strong supporter of the resistance, it was she who had offered the resolution of gratitude to the friendly regents at the April 22 Senate meeting.

19. Emily H. Huntington, *A Career in Consumer Economics and Social Insurance,* 1971, p. 79, Regional Oral History Office, Bancroft Library, University of California.

20. Ibid. p. 81.

21. Like many others, she added that she would have no qualms signing an oath if it were required for work that was essential to the nation's defense. *Report of the Committee on Privilege and Tenure,* June 15, 1950, Gardner, *Papers,* Carton 12, Folder 19.

22. Margaret Hodgen, *Factory Work for Girls* (New York: The Women's Press, 1920).

23. Published in 1925 as *Workers Education in England and the United States* (London: Kegan Paul, Trench Traebner; New York: E. P. Dutton), the book includes as frontispiece an anonymous poem that is a paean to the common man and a polemic against the powerful. Ending with the wish that "fishers, choppers, and ploughmen" should constitute state power, it could have been written by Hodgen herself.

24. Margaret Hodgen, letter to the Committee on Privilege and Tenure, May 28, 1950, Hodgen file, Group for Academic Freedom, *Papers,* Bancroft Library, University of California.

25. "Pauline Sperry," University of California, *In Memoriam.* Unlike the other two women, Sperry did not leave her papers to the archives, nor become the subject of an oral history. Therefore relatively little is known about her.

26. *Report of the Committee on Privilege and Tenure,* University of California, Berkeley, June 15, 1950, in Gardner, *Papers,* Carton 12, Folder 19.

27. She was also known as Margaret Peterson.

28. Else Frenkel-Brunswick, Daniel Levinson, Theodor Adorno, and R. Nevitt Sanford, *The Authoritarian Personality* (New York: Norton, 1950). When the senior author was interviewed by Stewart in May 1950, she told him that she had just signed the oath so that she could keep working on the research project. She also made pointed remarks about the oath as a symbol of a new American totalitarianism.

29. R. Nevitt Sanford to Robert Sproul, undated, but evidently written in September 1949. Gardner, *Papers,* Carton 9.

30. Author's interview with Henry Elson, November 30 2006. Tape in my possession.

31. Thanks to the gracious cooperation of his son, Dr. Matt Winkler, as well as conversations with Sam Bloom and Henry Elson, I received much more biographical information on Harold Winkler than I was able to use.

32. *Special Report to President Robert Gordon Sproul from the Committee on Privilege and Tenure on the Case of John L. Kelley,* June 15, 1950. Gardner, *Papers,* Carton 12, Folder 19. Kelley's Department of Mathematics was not only number one in the nation, it may also have been Berkeley's most radical department. Two months earlier, in April 1950, its faculty had voted to support either a strike or a mass resignation in the event that the regents did not approve the Alumni Compromise. Professors who were Academic Senate members voted 16 to 8 for such a strong response, while the support of the department's lecturers and instructors for these measures was 9 to 1! Math's graduate student teaching and research assistants voted 30 to 10 in favor. Letter of Professor Charles B. Morrrey Jr., chairman of the Department of Mathematics, to the Committee of Seven, April 17, 1950. Gardner, *Papers,* Carton 10.

33. Statement of Ludwig Edelstein, in Gardner, *Papers,* Carton 12, Folder 19.

34. Gardner, *The California Oath Controversy,* p. 178.

35. "Felix Rosenthal, Non-Signer," letter to the organizing committee of the 50th Anniversary Symposium, available at sunsite.berkeley.edu/uchistory/archives—exhibits/loyaltyoath.

36. Interview with Ralph Giesey by Germaine LaBerge, in *The Loyalty Oath at the University of California, 1949–1952,* Regional Oral History Office, Bancroft Library, University of California, pp. 136–37. Giesey would also report that the majority of resisters in the History Department were Eka's students.

37. Gardner, *The California Oath Controversy,* pp. 177–78.

38. Statement of Stephen Bechtel in Robert Gordon Sproul, *Papers,* Administrative Records, June 10, 1950, in Gardner, *Papers,* Carton 10.

39. Gardner, *The California Oath Controversy,* pp. 178–79.

40. In addition to the five from Berkeley already discussed, there was a sixth from UCLA. I will examine the case of UCLA's Eleanor Pasternak in the next chapter.

41. Gardner, *The California Oath Controversy,* pp. 180–82.

42. "UC Firings Are Assailed by Hutchins," *San Francisco Chronicle,* June 25, 1950, p. 1.

43. Griffiths, *Venturing Outside the Ivory Tower,* Version 1, pp. 41–42, and for the second quote, Version 2, pp. 28ff.

44. One of Sproul's coups as president had been to secure the papers of Mark Twain for Berkeley. Wecter's expertise and his nine books are mentioned in "Dixon Wecter, Twain Expert, Dies Suddenly at 44," *Daily Californian,* June 30, 1950, p. 1.

45. Dixon Wecter, "Commissars of Loyalty," *Saturday Review of Literature* XXXIII, no. 14, May 13, 1950.

46. An undated newspaper clipping in Joel Hildebrand, *Papers,* Box 1, Loyalty Oath file, Bancroft Library.

47. Wecter, Radin, and Griffiths, along with Malcolm Davisson and Clarence Dykstra, were not the only casualties of the oath crisis. Ben Lehman said that one of his colleagues in Berkeley's English Department (George Potter, who died in 1954) suffered a heart attack from the stress of the controversy. And Right-wing conservatives could also suffer. Neylan wrote that the death of his fellow regent Teague was oath-related.

CHAPTER 10

1. Letter of UCLA's Committee on Privilege and Tenure to Robert Sproul on Donald Piatt, May 25, 1950, in David P. Gardner, *Papers,* Series 8, Loyalty Oath Controversy, Research Materials, Carton 12, Folder 19, Bancroft Library, University of California.

2. In the case of Caughey, part of the reason may be that he was interviewed with his wife La Ree. Their oral history focused on the American Civil Liberties Union, the organization in which they served as leaders in the years after the oath. But this doesn't explain why none of UCLA's oral history interviewers evidenced any serious interest in the oath conflict. At Berkeley it was a major concern for everyone.

3. Author's interview with Philip Selznick, June 10, 2005. Tape in my possession.

4. Margaret Hodgen to Pauline Sperry, July 1, 1950, Hodgen file, Group For Academic Freedom, *Papers,* Folder 7 of 7 folders.

5. Clark Kerr in *The Robert Gordon Sproul Oral History Project,* interviews conducted by Suzanne B. Riess, 1984–1985, Vol. 2, p. 649, Bancroft Library, University of California. The "incredible unity" of the UCLA faculty during the oath crisis is confirmed by Education professor Paul Sheats, who contrasts that unity with the discord that took place in the 1960s. Paul H. Sheats to Robert Vosper, December 20, 1968, in UCLA University Archives Record Series No. 393, Loyalty Oath Controversy, Records, 1945–1968, Box 1, file 5, Charles Young Research Library.

6. Speaking at the March 6 mass meeting, Aaron Gordon noted that there were 200 Senate members from Berkeley and 150 from UCLA who had not yet signed. Since Berkeley's faculty was about twice the size of UCLA's, the proportion in the south was much higher.

7. David P. Gardner, *The California Oath Controversy (Berkeley, Calif.: University of California Press, 1967),* p. 171, where the author refers to Macgowan as Morganson.

8. Gardner, *The California Oath Controversy,* p. 174.

9. Summary *Report of the UCLA Committee on Privilege and Tenure,* June 13, 1950, Gardner, *Papers,* Carton 12, Folder 19.

10. Ibid.

11. UCLA Committee on Privilege and Tenure Report on Eleanor Pasternak, June 1950.

12. Letter of Macgowan to "Dear Martha," June 9, 1950, in Macgowan, *Papers,* Correspondence and Notes re: the University of California Loyalty Oath Controversy circa 1949–1951, UCLA Special Collections, No. 887, Box 67, Folder 2.

13. Gardner, *The California Oath Controversy,* p. 175.

14. Letter of UCLA's Committee on Privilege and Tenure to Robert Sproul on John Caughey, in Gardner, *Papers,* Carton 12, Folder 19.

15. Memorandum of Dean Paul A. Dodd, June 22, 1950, Summary of Loyalty Oath Hearings and Recommendations, in Gardner, *Papers,* Carton 12, Folder 19.

16. George Stewart et al., *The Year of the Oath: The Fight for Academic Freedom at the University of California* (New York: Doubleday, 1950), p. 103.

17. The quotation above and the biographical material is from Walter L. Arnstein, "The MWCBS at Fifty: Reflections and Recollections," a speech delivered at a meeting of the Midwest Conference on British Studies, Ann Arbor, Michigan, October 23, 2004.

18. Letter of UCLA's Committee on Privilege and Tenure Robert Sproul on Charles Mowat, June 5, 1950, in Gardner, *Papers,* Carton 12, Folder 19.

19. Letter of UCLA's Committee on Privilege and Tenure, Academic Senate Southern Section, to Robert Sproul on Carl Epling, June 1, 1950, in UCLA Archives Record Series No. 83, Box 2, Folder 33, Charles Young Research Library.

20. "Daniel M. Popper, Astrophysicist," University of California, *In Memoriam,* 1999.

21. Statement of Daniel Popper to UCLA's Committee on Privilege and Tenure, May 11, 1950, UCLA Archives Special Collections, Box 1, Folder 32.

22. David S. Saxon, *University of California President,* interviews conducted by James V. Mirk and Dale E. Treleven 1986–1993, Vol. 1, p. 116, Oral History Program of UCLA. When the university's nonsigners took legal action in 1950, Saxon would not be a part of their suit.

23. Letter of UCLA's Committee on Privilege and Tenure to Robert Sproul on David Saxon, May 25, 1950, Gardner, *Papers,* Carton 12, Folder 19.

24. The biographical material on Roose comes from a variety of sources. Most important was a May 2005 interview by the University of California Digital History Project, which I attended. Besides my notes on this interview, additional information came from e-mails and letters exchanged with Roose that remain in my possession.

25. For his testimony, see letter of UCLA's Committee on Privilege and Tenure to Robert Sproul on Kenneth Roose, June 5, 1950, in Gardner, *Papers,* Carton 12, Folder 19.

26. Ibid.

27. In 1968 *Time Magazine* would name Kaplan one of America's ten best teachers.

28. Letter of UCLA's Committee on Privilege and Tenure to Robert Sproul on Abraham Kaplan, May 26, 1950, in Gardner, *Papers,* Carton 12, Folder 19. Some of the information on Kaplan comes from the author's interview with Philip Selznick, June 2005. Tape in my possession.

29. Letter of UCLA's Committee on Privilege and Tenure to Robert Sproul on Morris Neiburger, in Gardner, *Papers,* Carton 12, Folder 19.

30. *Confidential,* Memorandum, June 21, 1950, in Gardner, *Papers,* Carton 12, Folder 19.

31. The other two, Epling and Neiberger, have already been discussed.

32. "Donald Piatt," Academic Senate, University of California, *In Memoriam,* May 1968, University of California Digital Archives.

33. A phrase that would seem to be original with him, in not so subtly identifying loyalty oaths with totalitarian regimes.

34. Letter of UCLA's Committee on Privilege and Tenure to Robert Sproul on Donald Piatt, May 25, 1950, in Gardner, *Papers,* Carton 12, Folder 19.

35. Ibid.

36. Letter of UCLA's Committee on Privilege and Tenure to Robert Sproul on Hugh Miller, May 29, 1950, in Gardner, *Papers,* Carton 12, Folder 19.

37. "David Appleman," University of California, *In Memoriam,* 1995.

38. Letter of UCLA's Committee on Privilege and Tenure to Robert Sproul on David Appleman, May 24, 1950, in Gardner, *Papers,* Carton 12, Folder 19.

CHAPTER 11

1. Milton Mayer, *Robert Maynard Hutchins: A Memoir* (Berkeley and Los Angeles, University of California Press, 1993).

2. Haynes Johnson, *The Age of Anxiety: McCarthyism to Terrorism* (Orlando: Harcourt Brace Jovanovich, 2005), pp. 177–82. Johnson notes that Smith's bold action encouraged a few other elder statesmen of her party to speak out against McCarthy, but the criticism soon fizzled out, especially after the onset of the war in Korea on June 25.

3. The third person, Harvard's Talcott Parsons, was, along with Chicago's Louis Wirth, a national leader in raising awareness and funds for California's nonsigners. See the letters from various department heads to Baldwin Woods, chair of the Committee on Academic Freedom and Tenure, in David P. Gardner, *Papers,* 1949–2005, Series 8, Loyalty Oath Controversy, Research Materials, Carton 10, Bancroft Library, University of California.

4. The story about the drive back from Detroit comes from the author's interview with Robert J. Gordon, San Francisco, February 3, 2006. Tape in my possession.

5. Gordon Griffiths, *Venturing Outside the Ivory Tower: A Political Autobiography,* unpublished manuscript, Version 2, 2002, p. 42, available from The Library of Congress. The term *McCarthyism* was coined by Herb Block, when he used it as a caption for one of his cartoons in March 1950.

6. Tim Weiner, "A 1950 Plan: Arrest 12,000 and Suspend Due Process," *New York Times,* December 23, 2007, p. 30.

7. Margaret Hodgen to Pauline Sperry, July 1, 1950, in the Hodgen file,, Group for Academic Freedom, *Papers,* Bancroft Library, University of California.

8. With this comment Hildebrand was attempting to live up to his reputation as one of the faculty's great wits. Charlie McCarthy was a household name in the 1940s and 1950s, for he was the dummy of the popular ventriloquist and comedian Edgar Bergen. Joel Hildebrand, "A Final Appeal to the Nonsigners," Hildebrand, *Papers,* Box 1, file on the Loyalty Oath, Bancroft Library, University of California.

9. Hildebrand, *Papers.*

10. Griffiths, *Venturing Outside the Ivory Tower,* Version 2, pp. 42–43.

11. Gardner, *The California Oath Controversy,* p. 183.

12. Margaret Hodgen to Pauline Sperry, July 1, 1950.

13. Nancy Innis, "Lessons from the Controversy Over the Loyalty Oath at the University of California," *Minerva* 30 (1992): pp. 337–65.

14. "Regents to Meet Today on Contracts," *Daily Californian,* July 21, 1950, p. 1; "UCLA's Oath Objectors Assert They're Loyal," *Los Angeles Times,* July 8, 1950, p. 1.

15. Geoffrey Chew to Raymond Birge, July 24, 1950, in Gardner, *Papers,* Carton 10.

16. John Neylan to Franklin Hichborn, July 6, 1950, in Box 178 of the Neylan Papers, in Gardner, *Papers,* Carton 10.

17. John Neylan to Sidney Ehrman, July 10, 1950, in Box 178 of the Neylan Papers, in Gardner, *Papers,* Carton 10.

18. Elkus to Robert Sproul, July 15, 1950. Gardner, *Papers,* Carton 10.

19. Lawrence J. Friedman, *Identity's Architect: A Biography of Erik Erikson* (New York: Scribners, 1999), p. 250.

20. Interview with Howard Bern conducted by Germaine LaBerge in 1999, in *The Loyalty Oath at the University of California, 1949–1952*, Regional Oral History Office, Bancroft Library, University of California, p. 12.

21. Author's interview with Joseph Tussman, August 29, 2005. Tape in my possession.

22. Joseph Tussman, *Philosopher, and Educational Innovator*, oral history interviews conducted by Lisa Rubens, 2004, Disk 5, pp. 56–57, Regional Oral History Office, Bancroft Library, University of California, unedited raw transcript in author's possession.

23. Daniel Popper to Robert Sproul, July 27, 1950, in Gardner, *Papers*, Carton 10.

24. The nonsigners at UCLA also met in early July. Much less organized than the group at Berkeley, it was their first meeting. By July 19th the number who had not complied on the Westwood campus was estimated to be between twelve and fifteen, as a much higher proportion of holdouts in the south had signed just in the past month.

25. Gardner, *The California Oath Controversy*, pp. 183–84.

26. This probably exaggerates Kent's radicalism. Though a staunch liberal, he was not a fellow traveler, nor even a Leftist. He and Mary had considered voting for Wallace in 1948, but after hearing him speak, they had cast their ballots for Truman instead. Author's interview with Mary Tolman Kent. Tape in my possession.

27. Jack Kent to David Gardner, September 30, 1965. Gardner, *Papers*, Carton 13, Folder 8.

28. Author's interview with Mary Tolman Kent. Tape in my possession.

29. Charles Muscatine, *The Loyalty Oath, The Free Speech Movement, and Education Reforms at the University of California, Berkeley*, an oral history interview conducted by Germaine LaBerge, 2000, p. 23, Regional Oral History Office, Bancroft Library, University of California.

30. Jack Kent to David Gardner.

31. Weigel mentioned A. P. Giannini specifically, but the bank's founder had died more than a year earlier. His son Mario had resigned but remained on the board because Warren had not accepted the resignation. Even with such inaccuracies, his point has merit, as Neylan and several other regents had close ties with the Bank of America. See Stanley A. Weigel, *Litigator and Federal Judge*, interviews conducted by William A. Fletcher, 1990, p. 50, Regional Oral History Office, Bancroft Library, University of California.

32. Notes of the meeting of the Group for Academic Freedom with Stanley Weigel, recorded by Charles Muscatine, August 3, 1950, Group for Academic Freedom, *Papers*, Box 1, Bancroft Library, University of California.

33. "Misguided Patriots," *Daily Californian*, July 21, 1950, p. 8.

34. Gardner, *The California Oath Controversy*, p. 185 and p. 301 (note 62).

35. Ibid., p. 186, and Gardner, *Papers*, Carton 10.

36. "Minutes of the Board of Regents," University of California, July 21, 1950, in Gardner, *Papers*, Carton 10. See also Gardner, *The California Oath Controversy*, pp. 186–87.

37. Neylan then quoted President Truman about how much was at stake in the war with communists in Korea, implying that Caughey was lacking in patriotism, and that he was an equivocator. "Minutes of the Board of Regents," July 21, 1950.

38. Clark Kerr, remarks at the 50th Anniversary Symposium on the Loyalty Oath, University of California, Berkeley, October 1999.

39. Gardner, *The California Oath Controversy,* pp. 187–88.

40. "Minutes of the Board of Regents," July 21, 1950.

41. Gardner, *The California Oath Controversy,* p. 189.

42. Greg Arnstein, "A Day of Mourning," *Daily Californian,* July 28, 1950, p. 12; and "Regents Debate: Fire 9 Profs," *Daily Californian,* July 28, 1950, p. 9.

CHAPTER 12

1. Lawrence Halprin to the chair of Berkeley's Landscape Architecture Department, no date, but filed with other early September 1950 letters in David P. Gardner, *Papers,* 1949–2005, Series 8, Loyalty Oath Controversy, Research Materials, Carton 11, Bancroft Library, University of California.

2. David P. Gardner, *The California Oath Controversy,* (Berkeley, Calif.: University of California Press, 1967), p. 198.

3. Gardner, *The California Oath Controversy,* p. 304, note 88.

4. "Action Pressed on 'Oath' Front," *Daily Californian,* August 11, 1950, p. 1, and the *Los Angeles Times* story of August 22, 1950, which headlined Monroe Deutsch's refutation of Moley's charges.

5. Charles Mowat to Paul Dodd, August 18, 1950, in John Hicks, *Papers,* Committee of Seven file, Bancroft Library, University of California.

6. Baldwin Woods, chair of Berkeley's Academic Senate Committee on Academic Freedom, to Robert Sproul, August 21, 1950, cited in Gardner, *The California Oath Controversy,* p 196–97.

7. Robert Penn Warren to Robert Sproul, August 11, 1950, in Gardner, *Papers,* Carton 10.

8. Gardner, *The California Oath Controversy,* p. 197.

9. Joseph Tussman, *Philosopher and Educational Innovator,* oral history interviews conducted by Lisa Rubens, 2004, Disk 6, p. 57, Regional Oral History Office, Bancroft Library, University of California, unedited raw transcript in author's possession.

10. Ibid., p. 64.

11. "Two Profs Sign Loyalty Statement," *Daily Californian,* August 25, 1950, p. 1.

12. Author's interview with Joseph Tussman, August 29, 2005. Tape in my possession.

13. Gardner, *The California Oath Controversy,* pp. 198–99.

14. Ibid., pp. 200–201. With the main motion to reconsider before the board, Warren read a telegram from Nimitz saying that were he present he would oppose it.

15. Ibid., pp. 200–201.

16. "Minutes of the Board of Regents,"University of California, August 25, 1950. Gardner, *Papers,* Carton 11. See also "Regents Reverse July Stand: Revive 'Sign-Resign' Demand," *Daily Californian,* Sept. 1, 1950, p. 1.

17. "Failure," *Daily Californian,* September 1, 1950, p. 8.

18. The *Daily Bruin*'s editorial was quoted in the *Daily Californian,* October 2, 1950, p. 8.

19. I thank Mary Tolman Kent for showing me the plaque. The full text, from which I have excerpted only a few quotes, appears in Gardner, *The California Oath Controversy,* p. 305–306.

20. Chicago's Chancellor Hutchins personally made the offer to Tolman as a gesture of support for California's nonsigners.

21. "Minutes of the Board of Regents," August 25, 1950.

22. "Six More Profs Accept Contracts," *Daily Californian,* September 12, 1950, p. 12.

23. Emily Huntington, *A Career in Consumer Economics and Social Insurance,* interviews conducted by Alice G. King, 1969–1970, p. 80, Regional Oral History Office, Bancroft Library, University of California, 1971. According to Charles Muscatine, it was her partner, a lawyer, who forced the decision. Author's interview with Muscatine. Tape in my possession.

24. Huntington, *A Career,* pp. 84–85.

25. Ibid., p. 84.

26. Ibid., pp. 84–85.

27. Author's interview with Muscatine.

28. Arthur Brodeur to Brewster Rogerson (secretary of the Group for Academic Freedom), in Gardner, *Papers,* Carton 11.

29. Anthony Morse to Robert Sproul, September 7, 1950. Gardner, *Papers,* Carton 11.

30. Gardner, *The California Oath Controversy,* pp. 203–204.

31. Later Caughey tried to join the lawsuit, but Weigel did not want the technical complications of such a change. This freed the UCLA historian to speak out and write about the oath; the litigants had to keep silent.

32. Letter from the assistant secretary of the Board of Regents to Robert Gordon Sproul, Sept. 11, 1950, in Gardner, *Papers,* Carton 11. See also "Minutes of the Board of Regents," September 22, 1950.

33. Edward Tolman to Robert Hutchins, September 13, 1950, in Gardner, *Papers,* Carton 11, as well as the letter of Edward Strong (chair of Sociology and Social Institutions) to Margaret Hodgen, instructing her to meet her classes. Hodgen file, Group for Academic Freedom, *Papers,* Folder 1, Bancroft Library, University of California.

34. Gardner, *Papers,* Carton 11.

35. "The reality," he would write a Berkeley Senate leader, "is that I have been displaced." John Caughey to Wendell Stanley, February 21, 1951, in Gardner, *Papers,* Carton 11.

36. "Total Casualty List at UCLA Disclosed for the First Time," *Westwood Hills Press,* September, 21, 1950, p. 10.

37. John Caughey to Kenneth Roose, October 3, 1950. Copy of letter in my possession.

38. Edward Teller to Robert Brode, September 20, 1950, in Gardner, *Papers,* Carton 11.

39. DuBois also referred to "the supine role of intellectuals in pre-Nazi Germany" and the "miserable moral position of intellectuals in the USSR." Cora DuBois to Robert Gordon Sproul, September 27, 1950. Gardner, *Papers,* Carton 11.

40. See note 1.

41. "Prof Attacks Regents: Gordon Blasts 'Oath' Dismissals," *Daily Californian,* September 20, 1950, p. 1; *New York Times,* article of September 24, 1950, which quotes both the *San Francisco Chronicle*'s account of the incident and the *Examiner* editorial. For Gordon as a "ham actor," see John Neylan, *Politics, Law, and the University,* oral history interviews conducted by Walton Bean and Corinne Gilb, Regional Oral History Office, Bancroft Library, University of California, p. 299.

42. George Stewart to Robert Sproul, July 25, 1950, in John Neylan, *Papers,* Box 180, File: Year of the Oath, Bancroft Library, University of California.

43. Neylan, *Papers,* Box 180. Neylan told Doubleday that the war in Korea and the communist danger at the university made it imperative that the book should be a truthful account and not "a campaign of misrepresentation." He also wrote letters to his fellow regents informing them what had happened.

44. Bob McGuigan, "New Activity in the 'Oath' Dispute," *Daily Californian,* September 25, 1950, p. 1; and Gardner, *Papers,* Carton 11. See also the regent's marked-up copy of *The Year of the Oath* in Neylan, *Papers,* Box 184.

45. Joseph Tussman, review of George Stewart, *Year of the Oath, Journal of Legal Education* 3, no. 3 (Spring 1951), pp. 467–68. Despite its 1951 publication, the review appears to have been written shortly after the book appeared, since there is no mention of the nonsigners' court case. The "superficial" comment appears in Tussman, *Philosopher and Educational Innovator,* Disk 5, p. 51.

46. Sidney Hook, "Heresy Yes, Conspiracy No!" *New York Times Magazine,* July 9, 1950. The philosopher would further develop his position in a book of the same name published by John Day in 1953. Tussman discussed the critical role of Hook's formulation in author's interviews with Tussman, August 29, 1950. Tape in my possession.

47. Arthur Schlesinger Jr., whose 1949 book *The Vital Center* had become the bible of American liberals who wanted to combat the communist Left as well as the reactionary Right, was another prominent intellectual who did not honor the boycott. After the death of Berkeley historian Dixon Wecter, he had recommended one of his Harvard Ph.D. students to replace him. Carl Bridenbaugh to Wendell Stanley, March 8, 1951, in Gardner, *Papers,* Carton 11.

48. *New York Times Sunday Book Review,* October 1, 1950. The most favorable review was written by best-selling novelist and Berkeley alumnus Irving Stone, who called Stewart's book "a brilliant and searing study." "Trusted Arms Among the Ivy: Review of *The Year of the Oath,*" *Saturday Review of Literature,* September 30, 1950, p. 12. The dean of American historians, Henry Steele Commager, called *The Year of the Oath* "important" in the October 15 issue of the *New York Herald Tribune,* but he devoted most of his essay to a book on internal security by Walter Gellhorn.

49. Caughey used the term *elder statesmen* in his report on the meeting to Kenneth Roose. See John Caughey to Kenneth Roose, October 3, 1950. For the resolution that was passed, see the *Faculty Bulletin,* Vol. 20, no. 5, November 1950, pp. 44–45, in Gardner, *Papers,* Carton 11.

50. Emphasis mine. *Faculty Bulletin,* pp. 44–45.

51. It was a voice vote, so there is no exact tally. But Brewster Rogerson, who had replaced Muscatine as the secretary of the Group for Academic Freedom, estimated that the ayes outnumbered the nays by almost 2 to 1.

52. Copy of letter of Raymond Sontag to "Dear Colleagues," September 28, 1950, in Gardner, *Papers,* Carton 11.

53. Joel Hildebrand to Robert Sproul, October 5, 1950, and his four-page memorandum, both in Gardner, *Papers,* Carton 11.

54. John Hicks, Press release, July 30, 1950, in Gardner, *Papers,* Carton 10.

55. Charles Morrey, letter to the members of the Committees on Academic Freedom and Privilege and Tenure, October 4, 1950, in Gardner, *Papers,* Carton 11.

56. "Ex Com Statement of September 27," *Daily Californian,* October 23, 1950, p. 6.

57. See the *Daily Californian:* "Students Aid Non-Signers Loyalty Fight," October 10, 1950, p. 1; "Ex-Com Supports Faculty," October 12, p. 1; and "Ex-Com to Publish Policy Statement in Oath Dispute," October 19, p. 1.

CHAPTER 13

1. Pauline Sperry to Margaret Hodgen, April 9, 1951, in Hodgen file, Group for Academic Freedom, *Papers,* Bancroft Library, University of California.

2. Summary of the April 6, 1951, court decision in David P. Gardner, *Papers,* 1949–2005, Series 8, Loyalty Oath Controversy, Research Materials, Carton 11, Bancroft Library, University of California.

3. Earl R. Long, "Earl Warren and the Politics of Anti-Communism," *Pacific Historical Review* 51, no. 1 (February 1982): pp. 61 passim. I have based much of my account of Warren during the summer and fall of 1950 on this article.

4. Ibid., p. 58.

5. Gardner, *Papers,* Carton 11.

6. John and La Ree Caughey, interview conducted by Ron Grele, June 5, 1981, unedited draft, pp. 18–19, Charles Young Research Library, UCLA.

7. David P. Gardner, *The California Oath Controversy (Berkeley, Calif.: University of California Press, 1967),* p. 221.

8. John Neylan to Edwin Pauley, May 8, 1951, in Gardner, *Papers,* Carton 11. Neylan underlined the Mommsen quote and Kantorowicz's commentary on it in the printed version of a speech he would make more than a year later. See "Loyalty Oaths and Academic Freedom," address to the Commonwealth Club, San Francisco, November 23, 1951, Bancroft Library, University of California.

9. *The Fundamental Issue* also included Kantorowicz's speech at the June 14, 1949, Academic Senate meeting, as well as his letter to Sproul explaining why he could not sign the oath. The pamphlet was never distributed, for the author would discard all his copies after the nonsigners won their case in court. It was not published until the early 1990s, in a German edition. The first English publication appeared in 1999 in connection with the university's celebration of the 50th anniversary of the oath. It is available at http://sunsite.berkeley .edu/ucalhist/archives_exhibits/loyaltyoath/symposium/kantorowicz.

10. Faculty Committee on Financial Assistance, letter to its contributors, September 18, 1957, summarizing seven years of fund-raising before disbanding. Gardner, *Papers,* Carton 12.

11. *Report of the Treasurer of the Faculty Fund-Raising Committee,* September 26, 1950, to March 26, 1951, in Gardner, *Papers,* Carton 12.

12. In October alone, 350 professors made donations at Berkeley, meeting that month's target. Faculty Committee on Financial Assistance, letter to its contributors, in Gardner, Carton 12. It helped that six nonsigners didn't require assistance. The list included Winkler, who was independently wealthy, Tolman, who was teaching in Chicago, Kelley, Sanford, Hans Lewy, and Leonard Doyle.

13. Gardner, *Papers,* Carton 11.

14. The five arguments were listed in a historical summary of the controversy prepared by Tolman for the Group for Academic Freedom. See "Report on the Controversy at the University of California," December 1, 1950, p. 4, in Gardner, *Papers,* Carton 11.

15. Jenette Inglis, "Levering Act Meets ASUC Opposition," *Daily Californian,* November 20, 1950, p. 1. Also see the article in the *San Francisco Chronicle,* November 18, 1950, summarized in Gardner, *Papers,* Carton 11. For the lawsuit, see Gardner's summary of an October 31, 1950, *Berkeley Gazette* article, ibid., and one from the *Daily Californian,* which noted that the students' lead attorney also represented Harry Bridges.

16. Gardner, *Papers,* Carton 11. Robert M. Underhill was the regents' secretary, so his name served as a shorthand for the board as a whole.

17. G. T. Scharrenghausen, "Guardian Cannot Be Banned, ASUC Store Manager Told," *Daily Californian,* January 9, 1951, p. 1.

18. C. Michael Otten, *University Authority and the Student* (Berkeley and Los Angeles: University of California Press, 1970), pp. 145–46, and 150–51.

19. Margaret T. Hodgen, "Marx and the Social Scientists," *Scientific Monthly* LXXII, no. 4 (April 1951). In the body of the article the author discussed Marx's philosophy of historical change and subjected it to a devastating critique. However, her essay added little to Marxian criticism, for Hodgen was not a first-rate social theorist. In a one-sided reading she failed to give the founder of historical materialism credit for any contributions to social science. It is ironic that it was precisely in this period that Marx began to enjoy a resurgence in sociology, and when two of her colleagues in Sociology and Social Institutions were writing a much more balanced interpretation of his theories. See "Karl Marx's Theory of Social Classes," by Reinhard Bendix and Seymour Martin Lipset, in Bendix and Lipset, *Class, Status, and Power* (Glencoe, Ill.: Free Press, 1954). Hodgen had sent a draft of her piece to Weigel to make sure that nothing in it might jeopardize their court case. The lawyer responded by praising the article and suggesting changes that would minimize the possibility that an unfriendly reviewer might lift sentences out of context. Hodgen file, Group for Academic Freedom, *Papers.*

20. "Harvard Wins Out," *Daily Californian,* February 19, 1951, p. 6. In addition, English instructor Edwin Fussel received a one-year appointment at Pomona College in Southern California. Mathematician Hans Lewy was supporting himself doing research for the Navy at nearby Stanford, while Stefan Peters and Leonard Doyle were putting their business training to work in the private sector.

21. John Caughey to Wendell Stanley, February 21, 1951, in Gardner, *Papers,* Carton 11.

22. Gardner, *The California Oath Controversy,* pp. 228–29.

23. Undated letter of Psychology chair Clarence Brown to James Caldwell, in Gardner, *Papers,* Carton 11; and *Report of the the Trustees of the Fund for Non-Academic Senate Employees,* by Joseph Fontenrose, March 27, 1951, in Gardner, *Papers,* Carton 11.

24. Peter Odegard to Stanley, January 9, 1951, in Gardner, *Papers,* Carton 11. Bunche went to Harvard.

25. See *Interim Report of the Committee on Academic Freedom,* summarized in Gardner, *Papers,* Carton 11; and Gardner, *The California Oath Controversy,* pp. 228–30.

26. "Dire Aftermath of Oath," *San Francisco Chronicle,* March 5, 1951, p. 16.

27. Dick Hotter, "Faculty Report Hits 'Oath,'" *Daily Californian,* March 2, 1951, p. 1.

28. Summary of the April 6, 1951, court decision in Gardner, *Papers,* Carton 11.

29. Gardner, *The California Oath Controversy,* pp. 230–31.

30. "Sanity Wins Out," editorial in the *Daily Californian,* April 7, 1950, p. 1; and Bob McGuigan, "Court Voids Regents' Oath," ibid. By this time two of the litigants had dropped out, reducing the number from twenty to eighteen.

31. On the following Sunday, the *Times* devoted an editorial to how "the famous oath" had driven "scholars of integrity" away from the University of California and lowered its national prestige. *New York Times,* April 8, 1951, in Gardner, *Papers,* Carton 11.

32. Ernst Kantorowicz to Wendell Stanley, April 7, 1951, in Gardner, *Papers,* Carton 11.

33. Pauline Sperry to Margaret Hodgen, April 9, 1951.

34. Bob McGuigan, "Faculty Calls for 'Oath' Peace," *Daily Californian,* April 16, 1951, p. 1. Other sponsors of the resolution included Caldwell and Gordon. There are no official records of this meeting, according to the summary of it by David Gardner, in Gardner, *Papers,* Carton 11.

35. Bob McGuigan, "'Oath' Rehearing Asked by Regents," *Daily Californian,* April 30, 1951, p. 1. See also American Association of University Professors, *A History of the University of California Loyalty Oath,* in Gardner, *Papers,* Carton 12.

36. Four main arguments made up the regents' appeal. First, the lower court had not cited sufficient legal precedent for its decision. Second, the nonsigners' jobs were not protected, as the court had suggested, because they were not "officers of public trust," like the governor of the state. Third, the court did not have the jurisdiction to rule on the case. And finally, the Regents' Special Oath was not an infringement of either tenure or academic freedom. Gardner, *Papers,* Carton 11.

37. California State Legislature, *Sixth Report of the Senate Fact-Finding Committee on Un-American Activities,* 1951.

38. Ibid., p. 39, citing Sidney Hook, "Academic Integrity and Academic Freedom," *Commentary,* October 1949, pp. 329–39.

39. Ibid., pp. 68–85. The discussion of Stewart's book ends with the statement that "the members of the academic senate seem only concerned with their own personal problems and somewhat outraged at the bruises they feel are being inflicted on the supersensitive carcass of what they refer to as academic freedom."

40. Ibid., pp. 92–94.

41. Ibid., pp. 101–52.

42. Public statement of Tolman, June 8, 1951, Group for Academic Freedom, *Papers,* Box 2.

43. "Yale Honors Professor Fired Over Oath," *Los Angeles Daily News,* June 12, 1951, p. 13; and *New York Times,* June 12, 1951, as cited in Gardner, *Papers,* Carton 11.

44. Statement by the University of California Faculty on the Burns Report, in Gardner, *Papers,* Carton 11.

45. *San Francisco Examiner,* June 24, 1951, as summarized in Gardner, *Papers,* Carton 11.

46. Bob McGuigan, "Supreme Court Hears 'Oath' Case," *Daily Californian,* June 22, 1951, p. 1.

47. Milton Chernin, Report of Faculty Fund-Raising Committee, in Gardner, *Papers,* Carton 11.

48. Hodgen file, Group for Academic Freedom, *Papers,* Folder 3.

49. Hodgen's scribbled draft of this letter may be found in the Hodgen file, ibid. Apparently the letter was never sent, nor did the Group for Academic Freedom follow through on its plan to sue Knight.

50. Haynes Johnson, *The Age of Anxiety: McCarthyism to Terrorism* (Orlando: Harcourt Brace Jovanovich, 2005), pp. 221–27.

51. Farnham Griffiths had resigned in June 1951 due to ill health. And Mario Giannini's seat was finally filled. Donald McLaughlin, his replacement, would turn out to be key in resolving the crisis. See Gardner, *The California Oath Controversy,* p. 233.

52. Dick Israel, "Neylan Denounces Professors' Plan," *Daily Californian,* August 31, 1951, p. 1. See also the summary of the August 24, 1951, meeting of the Board of Regents in Gardner, *Papers,* Carton 11; and the letter from Ewald Grether to Wendell Stanley, August 27, 1951, in Gardner, *Papers,* Carton 11.

53. Ewald Grether to Robert Sproul, September 28, 1951, and Edward Tolman to William Hay, September 30, 1951, both in Gardner, *Papers,* Carton 11. The "new crop" phrase was Tolman's. By October 12, eighteen regular faculty members, plus two instructors and six lecturers, had not returned their contracts. In addition, thirteen graduate assistants and thirty miscellaneous employees had not complied. By the end of the month they still had not been paid for October, and their November salaries were in doubt. Gardner, ibid.

54. My summaries of the October and November regents' meetings are taken from Gardner, *The California Oath Controversy,* pp. 234–38.

55. Max Hastings, *The Korean War* (New York: Simon & Schuster; Touchstone, 1987), pp. 348–49.

56. In a letter six weeks later he spoke again of Deutsch, who "over a long period of years (was) the smiling, genial scholar when he met with the Regents. I never had an unkind word with him personally, and I was never so badly fooled in any human being." John Neylan to Marian Hooker, February 5, 1952, in Gardner, *Papers,* Carton 11.

57. John Neylan, "Loyalty Oaths and Academic Freedom," Address to the Commonwealth Club, San Francisco, November 23, 1951, Bancroft Library, University of California.

58. Ibid. See also "Neylan Calls Professors' Group Sinister," *Los Angeles Times,* November 24, 1951.

CHAPTER 14

1. David Halberstam, *The Coldest Winter: America and the Korean War* (New York: Hyperion, 2007), p. 2.

2. David Gardner, *Papers,* 1949–2005, Series 8, Loyalty Oath Controversy, Research Materials, Carton 11, Bancroft Library, University of California.

3. Clark Kerr, *The Gold and the Blue: A Personal Memoir of the University of California, 1949–1967,* Vol. 1 (Berkeley and Los Angeles: University of California Press, 2003), p. 48.

4. David Gardner interview with Clark Kerr, Gardner, *Papers,* Carton 13, Folder 7.

5. David P. Gardner, *The California Oath Controversy* (Berkeley, Calif.: University of California Press, 1967), pp. 242–44.

6. Margaret Hodgen to Edward Tolman, January 1, 1953, in the Hodgen file, Group for Academic Freedom, *Papers.* In the same letter Hodgen said that she would probably sign

the Levering Act's oath, because her "soul" was not as involved in it. But after telling Weigel that she would sign, she retired instead.

7. John Neylan, *Politics, Law, and the University,* oral history interviews conducted by Walton Bean and Corinne Gilb, Regional Oral History Office, Bancroft Library, University of California, p. 232.

8. "Regents Kill Oath Appeal," *Daily Bruin,* November 3, 1952, p. 1.

9. There were 2.7 million votes for the measure and only 1.2 million opposing it. Gardner, *The California Oath Controversy,* p. 250.

10. Kerr, *The Gold and the Blue,* Vol. 1, p. 140, 146. The ban against "controversial speakers" was still being enforced even against those who were fiercely anti-communist. In October 1951 Max Schactman, the nation's leading Trotskyist, had not been allowed to speak at Berkeley. When the ban on communist speakers was finally lifted in 1963, the Communist Party had been virtually defunct for seven years. Ibid., Vol. 2, p. 163.

11. Clark Kerr to Margaret Hodgen, Hodgen file, Group for Academic Freedom, *Papers.*

12. Charles Muscatine, *The Loyalty Oath, The Free Speech Movement, and Education Reforms at the University of California, Berkeley,* an oral history interview conducted by Germaine LaBerge, 2000, p. 31, Regional Oral History Office, Bancroft Library, University of California, p. 31.

13. Interview with John and La Ree Caughey, conducted by Ron Grele, June 5, 1981, unedited draft, Charles Young Research Library, UCLA, p. 15.

14. "Regents Turn Over Back Pay Wrangle to Supreme Court, *Daily Bruin,* February 16, 1953, page 2.

15. For those who did return, salary and rank were adjusted to make up for the lost years. David Saxon and Hugh Coffey came back as associate professors with tenure, while John Kelley was promoted to full professor.

16. The quotation comes from C. Michael Otten, *University Authority and the Student* (Berkeley and Los Angeles: University of California Press, 1970), p. 147. While Otten doesn't identify the speaker, Kerr's discussion of the case makes Winkler's identity clear.

17. Kerr, *The Gold and the Blue,* Vol. 2, pp. 131–32.

18. Ibid., pp. 57–58. Writing almost forty years later, Kerr claimed that he could no longer remember the names of the three involved.

19. Kenneth Macgowan, *Papers,* Collection 887 of Special Collection, Box 678, folder: "Correspondence and Notes re the University of California Loyalty Oath," Charles Young Research Library, UCLA.

20. Final Report of Faculty Committee on Fundraising, September 18, 1957, in Gardner, *Papers,* Carton 12.

21. The McCarthy-Welch confrontation is described in detail in Haynes Johnson, *The Age of Anxiety: McCarthyism to Terrorism* (Orlando: Harcourt Brace Jovanovich, 2005), pp. 419–427. The quotations appear on p. 424.

22. Joel Hildebrand to Robert Sproul, undated letter circa 1954, and letter dated June 10, 1955, in Joel Hildebrand, *Papers,* Bancroft Library, University of California.

23. Interview with John and La Ree Caughey, p. 12.

CHAPTER 15

1. David P. Gardner, *The California Oath Controversy* (Berkeley, Calif.: University of California Press, 1967), p. 250.

2. Stanley A. Weigel, *Litigator and Federal Judge,* interviews conducted by William A. Fletcher, 1990, p. 52, Regional Oral History Office, Bancroft Library, University of California.

3. Ida Wittschen Sproul, *The President's Wife,* interviews conducted by Suzanne B. Reiss, 1980–81, p. 290, Regional Oral History Office, Bancroft Library, University of California.

4. Clark Kerr, *The Gold and the Blue: A Personal Memoir of the University of California, 1949–1967,* Vol. 2 (Berkeley and Los Angeles: University of California Press, 2003), pp. 42–44. The results would be published three years later in Paul Lazarsfeld and Wagner Thielens Jr., *The Academic Mind: Social Scientists in a Time of Crisis* (Glencoe, Ill.: Free Press, 1958).

5. Kerr's discussion of the relation between the two upheavals in *The Gold and the Blue,* Vol. 2, pp. 42–43, is sketchy and indecisive, in contrast to the much stronger statement of his thesis in both his remarks at the 50th Anniversary Symposium and his contribution to the *Robert Gordon Sproul Oral History Project.*

6. Robert Cohen, personal communication, April 2008. For a more extended analysis of the links between the Loyalty Oath and the Free Speech Movement, see the Epilogue, which follows this chapter.

7. I am indebted to Joseph Lam Duong for the concept of Berkeley in the cultural imagination.

8. Weigel, *Litigator,* p. 52.

9. John W. Caughey, *In Clear and Present Danger: The Crucial State of Our Freedoms* (Chicago: University of Chicago Press, 1958), p. 151.

10. Howard Zinn, "The Politics of History in the Era of the Cold War," in R. C. Lewontin, ed., *The Cold War and the University* (New York, New Press, 1997), pp. 48–49.

11. Gardner, *The California Oath Controversy,* pp. 250–51.

12. With regard to another of his enemies, Neylan stated that Edward Heller "has been flirting with Communists for God knows how long," and was providing funds for the non-signers' campaign. Draft version of Neylan, *Law, Politics, and the University,* oral history interviews conducted by Walton Bean and Corrine Gilb, p. 239 in David P. Gardner, *Papers, 1949–2005,* Series 8, Loyalty Oath Controversy, Research Materials, Carton 13, Folder 7, Bancroft Library, University of California.

13. David Gardner interview with John Hicks, May 7, 1965, Gardner, *Papers,* Carton 13, Folder 7.

14. David Gardner interview with Edwin Pauley, April 28, 1965, Gardner, *Papers,* Carton 13, Folder 7.

15. Edward Tolman, "The Oath Controversy at the University of California, Outline of a Speech by E.C.T., 1951," Gardner, *Papers, Carton 11,* Folder 15.

16. Gene Frumkin, editorial, *Daily Bruin,* September 25, 1950, p. 1.

17. David Gardner, interview with Elinor Raas Heller, May 5, 1965, Gardner, *Papers,* Carton 13, Folder 7, p. 29.

18. For Sproul and the regents, see Clark Kerr, Remarks at the 50th Anniversary Symposium on the Loyalty Oath, University of California, Berkeley, October 1999. For the faculty,

see the interview of Howard Bern in *The Loyalty Oath at the University of California, 1949–1952,* conducted by Germaine LaBerge, p. 17, Regional Oral History Office, Bancroft Library, University of California.

19. Ida Wittschen Sproul, *The President's Wife,* p. 290; and Ida W. Sproul, *Duty, Devotion, and Delight in the President's House,* interviews conducted by Edna Tartaul Daniel, 1961, pp. 46ff, Regional Oral History Office, Bancroft Library, University of California. Clark Kerr has written that there were "tragic figures" in the Loyalty Oath: Hildebrand, Neylan, and Sproul. Kerr, *Gold and the Blue,* Vol. 2, pp. 36–37.

20. Norman Mailer, *Advertisements for Myself* (New York: G. P. Putnam, 1959), p. 222.

21. "Loyalty Oath Brings End to Poetry Hours," *Daily Californian,* October 11, 1950, p. 4.

22. Joseph Tussman, *Philosopher and Educational Innovator,* oral history interview conducted by Lisa Rubens, Disk 8, p. 58, Regional Oral History Office, Bancroft Library, University of California, unedited raw transcript in author's possession.

23. Robert Berdahl, opening remarks at the 50th Anniversary Symposium on the Loyalty Oath, University of California, Berkeley, October 1999.

24. Gordon Griffiths, remarks at the 50th Anniversary Symposium on the Loyalty Oath, University of California, Berkeley, October 1999.

EPILOGUE

1. Robert Cohen, personal communication to the author, June 2008. Cohen's criticisms of an earlier draft of this epilogue have been indispensable.

2. For Pauley on Tolman as a traitor, see Clark Kerr, Remarks at 50th Anniversary Symposium on the Loyalty Oath, University of California, Berkeley, October 1999. Pauley was unsuccessful in trying to stop the honorary degree also. Neylan, on the other hand, wrote that he would not have opposed Tolman's L.L.D., but he would have voted against such an honor for Kantorowicz or Stewart. John Francis Neylan to Edwin Pauley, March 23, 1959, in David P. Gardner, *Papers,* 1949–2005, Series 8, Loyalty Oath Controversy, Research Materials, Carton 12, Bancroft Library, University of California.

3. The nub of the problem, according to Free Speech Movement historian Robert Cohen, was that the administration still felt that it had to limit student freedoms "to convince the regents and conservative legislators that it was not 'fostering political radicalism.'" Cohen to author, June 2008.

4. Lehman stated that Kerr and Strong lacked the personal magnetism and the touch of humor that was needed. See Benjamin Lehman, *Recollections and Reminiscences of Life in the Bay Area from 1920 Onward,* interview conducted by Suzanne B. Riess, 1969, p. 271–72, Regional Oral History Office, Bancroft Library, University of California; Agnes Roddy Robb, *Robert Gordon Sproul and the University of California,* interviews conducted by Harriet Nathan, 1996, p. 54, Regional Oral History Office, Bancroft Library, University of California; and Robert Gordon Sproul Jr., in *The Robert Gordon Sproul Oral History Project,* interviews conducted by Suzanne B. Riess, 1984–1985, Vol. 2, Bancroft Library, University of California.

5. In 1964 Sproul was not yet suffering from the dementia that would plague him until his death in 1975.

6. For this insight I am indebted to Robert Cohen. Personal communication, Cohen to the author, April 2008.

7. Cohen distinguishes between the statement that was quoted in the *San Francisco Chronicle* and the words that Kerr said that he had used. See R. Cohen, "The Many Meanings of the FSM," in Robert Cohen and Reginal E. Zelnik (eds.), *The Free Speech Movement: Reflections on Berkeley in the 1960s* (Berkeley and Los Angeles: University of California Press, 2002), pp. 24–25.

8. Because an infuriated crowd demanded his release he was never formally arrested, but instead permitted to speak.

9. Clark Kerr, "Fall of 1964: Confrontation Yields to Reconciliation," in Cohen and Zelnik, *The Free Speech Movement*, p. 374.

10. Charles Muscatine, *The Loyalty Oath, The Free Speech Movement, and Education Reforms at the University of California, Berkeley*, an oral history interview conducted by Germaine LaBerge, 2000, p. 40, Regional Oral History Office, Bancroft Library, University of California.

11. During the Loyalty Oath crisis a *Daily Bruin* editor analyzed the differences between students at Berkeley and UCLA. In addition to the points I've summarized, Hal Watkins noted that Berkeley undergraduates, by living in a student community, were able to shed their family's "long-standing prejudices and narrow-minded attitudes," unlike those in Los Angeles. Hal Watkins, Editorial, *Daily Bruin,* March 23, 1950, p. 8.

12. In a sense they were proved correct, for 1960s radicalism did help elect Reagan governor and Nixon president. But it's not possible to determine precisely how the refugees who resisted the oath divided on the Free Speech Movement, because most of them did not return to Berkeley. It's likely that the culturally conservative Kantorowicz, who had died in 1963, would have agreed with Landauer. But not Erik Erikson, whose highly developed sensitivity to youth and their concerns made him sympathetic to their rebellion. A few years later Erikson even became a qualified supporter of the Black Panthers.

13. In his oral history Tussman is extremely critical of the Free Speech Movement. And yet contemporary accounts (see the various references to his role in Cohen and Zelnik, *The Free Speech Movement*) portray him as a supporter, albeit qualified, of the student movement. Most likely it was not the Free Speech Movement per se, but the movements which followed it that soured him on student activism and led to his Right-wing turn and retrospective negative views of the 1964 crisis. For the coercive methods that disturbed him were much more characteristic of the antiwar activists and the strikes for Black Studies than they were of the Free Speech Movement. It's my hunch that Schachman and other oath veterans who believed that Tussman had betrayed the ideals of their earlier resistance were also conflating the events of the late 1960s and early 1970s with those of 1964. That's why Mary Kent (in *The Loyalty Oath at the University of California,* p. 81) said Tussman became more conservative and also why he was not invited to speak at the 50th anniversary symposium of the oath.

14. The criticism of Muscatine appeared in a news article in the *San Francisco Chronicle,* June 28, 1965, p. 1. A clipping may be found in Joel Hildebrand, *Papers,* Box 1, Folder 2, Bancroft Library, University of California.

15. Article by Hildebrand in *Science,* Sept. 15, 1972. Hildebrand, *Papers,* Box 1, Folder 6 (Writings). And yet there was a glitch in the trajectory of Hildebrand's road to reaction. In 1969 he actually defended Angela Davis, a Communist Party member turned Black Panther,

whom the regents were trying to fire from her job teaching history on the San Diego campus. "The big threat to our society," he wrote, was not posed by the Communist Party, but by "black militants whose patience is exhausted under *white repression,* and by youth, both black and white, who feel outraged at an 'Establishment' which can send them to die in the jungles and swamps of Vietnam in a *futile war.*" Hildebrand, *Papers,* Box 1, Folder 1.

16. Nancy Innis, "Lessons from the Controversy Over the Loyalty Oath at the University of California," *Minerva* 30 (1992): pp. 355–57.

17. Martin Roysher, "Recollections of the Free Speech Movement," in Cohen and Zelnik, *The Free Speech Movement,* p. 141.

18. Cohen, "The Many Meanings," p. 4.

19. Introduction to Stanley A. Weigel, *Litigator and Federal Judge,* interviews conducted by William A. Fletcher, 1990, Regional Oral History Office, Bancroft Library, University of California.

20. Pauley approached his old friend John McCone, the director of the CIA, who in turn enlisted the FBI's Hoover, and this led to that agency providing him with classified information on university personnel. See "Clark Kerr," Wikipedia entry at http://en.wikipedia .org/wiki/Clark_Kerr. The same article reveals that FBI documents released in 2002 indicate that Lyndon Johnson wanted to select Kerr to head Health, Education, and Welfare but withdrew the domination after the agency submitted negative information on him.

21. In plotting to oust Kerr he needed a replacement of stature, so he contacted McGeorge Bundy and John Gardner to ask if they were interested in the job. Neither man was.

22. An appendix to Clark Kerr, *The Gold and the Blue: A Personal Memoir of the University of California, 1949–1967,* Vol. 2 (Berkeley and Los Angeles: University of California Press, 2003) includes selections from his FBI files documenting Pauley's efforts to brand him a subversive.

23. Six years later UC opened a new student cafeteria in the Moffit Undergraduate Library and named it the Free Speech Cafe.

INDEX

Committee, 91, 130, 191, 199;
store committee, 199
Atomic Energy Commission (AEC), 96,
131, 136, 147, 157, 159
Attorney General's List, 6, 42, 194–195
Authoritarian Personality (Frenkel-
Brunswick, *et al.*), 145–146

Bank of America, 9, 111, 173
Barrows, David P., xvi, 18–20, 25–26, 32,
37
Barzun, Jacques, 185
Bechtel, Stephen, 122–123, 127, 148, 179
Bell, Louis, 130
Bendix, Reinhard, 141, 238
Benson, Merritt, 59
Benton, William, 208
Berdahl, Robert, xviii, 230–231
Bern, Howard, 171, 231
Birge, Raymond, 97, 130, 166
Board of Regents: appeals court decision,
204–205; debates firing nonsigners,
174–177, 180–182; enacts Regents'
Special Oath, 65–67; fires Kenneth
May, xvi–xvii, 34–35; history and
composition, 8–11; issues "sign or get
out" ultimatum, 102–110; 1940 "No
Reds" policy, 34–36; rescinds loyalty
oath, 210
Bock, Kenneth, 72
Bohemian Club, 10, 17–18, 30
Boodberg, Peter, 138, 185
Boycott of University of California,
xiv–xv; 166, 179, 188
Brayfield, Arthur (nonsigner), 181, 200
Bridges, Harry, 24–25, 31, 113, 118, 124,
139
Brodeur, Arthur, 93, 126; anti–oath activist,
72, 109, 136–137; communist party
member, 31, 38, 130–131; reasons
for signing, 183–184; speaks at mass
meeting, 120; testifies to P & T,
136–137

Browder, Earl, 40
Brown, Warren (nonsigner), 182–183
Brown v. Board of Education, 218
Broyles Commission (Illinois), 68–69
*Bulletin of the American Association of Uni-
versity Professors,* 47
Bunche, Ralph, 201
Bunzel, Jack, 84, 104–105
Burns, Hugh, 130, 194, 204–207, 213
Butterworth, Joseph, 44–45

Caldwell, James, 47, 87, 137, 170, 175,
201, 209
California Labor School, 140
California Oath Controversy (Gardner), xii,
224
Canaday, William (regent), 176
Canwell Committee (University of Wash-
ington), 44
Carnap, Rudolph, 201
Carnegie Tech, 200
Caughey, John (nonsigner): 15, 95,
108–109, 152–153, 155–156, 184,
200, 219, 231; as anti-oath activist,
88, 116, 175–176, 197, 203; bio,
82–83; critical of UCLA's moderate
leaders, 107, 113–114, 158; returns to
teach, 216; signs Levering Act oath,
195, 216; testifies to P and T, 155
Chambers, Whittaker, 100
Chaney, Ralph, 91, 108–109, 133, 191
Chernin, Milton, 196
Chevalier, Haakon, 31, 33, 38, 40
Chew, Geoffrey, 135–136, 170
Chiang Kai-shek, 57, 85, 101
Chicago, University of, 68–69, 122, 135,
149, 165, 185, 200
Childhood and Society (Erikson), 48, 139
China, Peoples Republic of, 58, 91, 98,
198
Churchill, Winston, 4, 41, 61
Clark, Tom, 6, 36, 42
Coelho, Danny, 105

Fermi, Enrico, 135, 138

Fishbein, Morris, 114

Fisher, Walter (nonsigner), 171, 184

Fishman, Leslie (nonsigner), 84, 120

Fleishacker, Mortimer (regent), 111–112

Fox, Irving David, 96–97, 109–110, 146, 206

Franco, Francisco 32–33, 158

Frederick the Second (Kantorowicz), 75

Free Speech Movement (FSM), xv, xviii, 221–222, 233–242

Friedlander, Isaac (regent), 9–10

Friedman, Lawrence J., 140

From Berlin to Berkeley (Bendix), 141

Fromm, Erich, 2

Frumkin, Gene, 228

Fuchs, Klaus, 100

Fulbright, William, 217, 235

Fundamental Issue (Kantorowicz), 195–196

Gardner, David, xviii–xix, 76, 80, 126, 155, 220, 224, 230–232

Garst, Jim, 87, 98

Genius of Italy (Olschki), 140

Giague, William, 121

Giannini, A. P. (regent), 23, 111

Giannini, Lawrence Mario (regent), 111–112, 115–116, 120, 124–125, 130, 180, 209

Giesey, Ralph (nonsigner), 148

Gleason, Abbott, 4

Gordon, Robert Aaron: 130, 175, 180: on Conference Committee, 95, 99–100, decision to sign oath, 168–169, 186; effect of Korean war on resistance, 166–169, 186; and FSM, 238; infuriates Neylan, 99–100, 186; P & T hearing; speaks at mass meeting, 106

Gordon, Robert J., 167

Graduate Student Association (Berkeley), 9, 104–105, 119

Graduate Student Associatiom (UCLA), 59, 72

Grant, J.A.C. (Cliff), 57, 62, 95–96, 100, 107, 189

"Great Double Cross," 115–117

Grether, Ewald, 168–169

Griffin, Philip, 94

Griffiths, Farnham (regent), 18, 30, 78, 80, 127, 150, 176, 212

Griffiths, Gordon, 33, 74, 76, 80, 240; as anti-oath activist, 72, 93, 230; assesses nonsigners' impact, 224–225, 231; as a communist, 30–31, 37–38, 40–41; relation with father, 30–31

Group for Academic Freedom (GAF), 179–180, 212, 225, 237; fundraising for salaries, 206; goals, 172; hires an attorney, 173–174; nonsigners organize as, 171–172

Grundlach, Ralph, 44–45

Haggerty, Cornelius (regent), 112, 181, 196

Halberstam, David, 212

Hallinan, Vincent, 124, 198

Halprin, Lawrence, 178, 186

Hamby, Alonzo, 4, 41

Hand, Learned, 173–174

Hansen, Victor (regent), 115, 180

Harper, Lawrence, 189

Harris, Robert (nonsigner), 183

Harvard, 16, 118, 146, 196, 200, 205, 216, 237

Hearst, William Randolph, 23, 39

Heller, Edward (regent), 97, 111, 124, 128, 176, 181–182, 226, 228

Heller, Elinor Raas (regent), 228

Hicks, John, 110, 114, 148, 222, 227, 230; bio, 104; as cautious moderate, 117–118, 190, 215, 227; and President Sproul, 118–119; as Senate leader, 104, 115–116, 118, 122–123, 179, 190

Hildebrand, Joel, 57, 67, 93, 95, 131–132, 153, 187, 190, 218–219, 222, 230; amends oath to exclude subversives,